PSI SUCCESSFUL BUSINESS L'

The Rule Book of Business Plans
for Startups

Roger C. Rule

The Oasis Press® / PSI Research
Central Point, Oregon

Published by The Oasis Press®/PSI Research
© 1999 by Roger C. Rule

All rights reserved. No part of this publication may be reproduced or used in any form or by any means, graphic, electronic or mechanical, including photocopying, recording, taping, or information storage and retrieval systems without written permission of the publishers.

This publication is designed to provide accurate and authoritative information in regard to the subject matter covered. It is sold with the understanding that the publisher is not engaged in rendering legal, accounting, or other professional service. If legal advice or other expert assistance is required, the services of a competent professional person should be sought.
 — *from a declaration of principles jointly adopted by a committee of the American Bar Association and a committee of publishers.*

Managing Editor: Constance C. Dickinson
Book Designer: Constance C. Dickinson
Compositor: Jan Olsson
Cover Designer: Steven Burns

Please direct any comments, questions, or suggestions regarding this book to The Oasis Press®/PSI Research:

>   Editorial Department
>   P.O. Box 3727
>   Central Point, OR 97502
>   (541) 479-9464
>   info@psi-research.com *e-mail*

The Oasis Press® is a Registered Trademark of Publishing Services, Inc., an Oregon corporation doing business as PSI Research.

Library of Congress Cataloging-in-Publication Data
Rule, Roger C.
    The rule book of business plans for startups / Roger C. Rule ; edited by Constance C. Dickinson.
        p. cm. — (PSI successful business library)
    Includes bibliographical references and index.
    ISBN 1-55571-519-2 (paper)
    1. Business planning. 2. New business enterprises. I. Dickinson, Constance C. II. Title. III. Series.

HD30.28 .R85 2000
658.1'1—dc21
                                                              00-035619

Printed in the United States of America
First edition 10 9 8 7 6 5 4 3 2 1

 Printed on recycled paper when available.

With love and admiration
To my youngest son,

Ryan Major Rule,

A member of Sigma Pi Sigma Physics Honor Society
Who, concurrently with the first printing of this book,
Reached senior status with 101 credits
At the end of his sophomore year

Contents

Preface ix

Acknowledgments xi

Introduction: Your Business Plan's Preliminaries. 1
          A Professional Presentation   3
          Business Plan Outline for Start-up Companies   5
          A Winning First Impression   8
          The Cover Letter   10
          A Confidentiality and Non-disclosure Agreement   12
          Title Page   14
          Table of Contents   15
          Important Points to Remember   16

Chapter 1.   Executive Summary. 17
          Review Executive Summary   19
          Preview Executive Summary   26
          Important Points to Remember   32

Chapter 2.   Company Description 33
          Name and Business Concept   33
          Ownership and Legal   35
          Leadership and Location   40
          Geographic Sales Area   41
          Current Status and Milestones   41
          Important Points to Remember   44

Chapter 3. Industry Analysis 45
    Sources of Industry Information   46
    Industry Analysis Summary   51
    Industry Description   52
    Industry Size and Maturation   54
    Industry Trends and Impact Factors   57
    Industry Standards   60
    Industry Obstacles   62
    Industry Opportunities   62
    Important Points to Remember   63

Chapter 4. Market and Competition 65
    Market and Competition Summary   66
    Market Description – Segments and Target Markets   67
    Market Size and Trends   76
    Competition Identification   78
    Main Competitors   78
    Competitor Analysis   81
    Market Share   82
    Customer Needs   85
    Market Obstacles   85
    Market Opportunities   86
    Important Points to Remember   87

Chapter 5. Strategies and Goals 89
    Strategies and Goals Summary   90
    Long-range Goals and Strategies   90
    Strategy Implementation   96
    Important Points to Remember   98

Chapter 6. Products or Services 99
    Products or Services Summary   100
    Products or Services Description   100
    Products or Services Positioning   102
    Comparison with the Competition   103
    Technology and Intellectual Protection   104
    Future Products or Services   105
    Important Points to Remember   106

Chapter 7. Marketing and Sales 107
    Marketing and Sales Summary   108
    Marketing Strategy   109

Chapter 7. Marketing and Sales (continued)
Marketing Plan   112
Marketing Budget and Advertising Plan   119
Sales Force and Forecast   121
Important Points to Remember   124

Chapter 8. Management and Organization 125
Management and Organization Summary   126
Management Team   127
Key Personnel Responsibilities and Duties   133
Management Philosophy   135
Key Personnel Incentives   136
Organizational Structure   137
Personnel Plan   139
Important Points to Remember   141

Chapter 9. Operations. 143
Operations Summary   144
Operations Description   145
Human Resources   146
Facility   148
Production   149
Supply and Distribution   154
Fulfillment   156
Customer Service Policy   158
Inventory Control   159
Efficiency Control   161
Cash Flow Control   162
Important Points to Remember   164

Chapter 10. Financial Pro Formas 165
Before You Begin   166
Financial Summary   167
Important Assumptions   168
Opening Balance Sheet   173
Pro Forma Income Statements   177
Break-even Analysis   182
Pro Forma Statement of Cash Flow   184
Pro Forma Balance Sheet   194
Business Ratios   196
Important Points to Remember   202

Chapter 11. Financial Requirement 203
Financial Sources 204
Financial Requirement Summary 205
Start-up Costs 209
Funds Raised and Funds Needed 210
Loan Request Proposal 212
Investment Offering 213
Potential Risks 215
Exit Options 217
Important Points to Remember 218

Chapter 12. Business Plan Exhibits 219
Table of Contents of Exhibits 220
Exhibits 220
The Finishing Touches 223
A Final Comment 223
Important Points to Remember 224

Appendix A. Business Plan Differences for Home Based Businesses: Edwards' Consulting Services 225

Appendix B. Business Plan Differences for Retail and Wholesale Businesses: Eclectic Interiors by Monica 261

Appendix C. Business Plan Differences for Service Businesses: Room Service, Ltd. 283

Appendix D. Business Plan Differences for Restaurant and Combination Businesses: Coffee Museum and Visitor Center 299

Appendix E. Business Plan Differences for Nonprofit Organizations: Newmark Association 302

Appendix F. In-Depth Business Plan Calculations 305
Inventory (for Chapter 10)
Business Ratios (for Chapter 10)
Return on Investment (for Chapter 11)

Appendix G. Financing Sources 313

Index 315

Preface

By failing to prepare, you are preparing to fail.
— BENJAMIN FRANKLIN

A few years ago, only existing big businesses, or startup businesses with big planning, made use of the internal tool known as a business plan. As the concept became better known, its purpose became more general. For many years afterwards, small businesses used the concept of business plan synonymous only with a financial request, a business report used to obtain a loan or investment capital. Most of these business plans were constructed in response to an external request — bankers would require one in evaluating a loan request, investors wanted a business plan in deciding whether to finance the business, or potential buyers and their attorneys demanded one before buying an existing business. Several books were published and business management courses in colleges and universities were generated in response to the need. This began the process of standardization of the concept and content of business plans.

Many times after a business would write its first business plan, the business owner would say, "If I had only had all of that information a few years ago." The truth is that most did, and they should have said, "If I had only looked at and analyzed all of that information a few years ago." With this realization, the purpose of the business plan broadened.

A comprehensive business plan has become a valuable internal management tool as well as document to respond to external requests. But, conceptually, business plans have become an all-purpose vehicle so complex they require more time and resources than can often be justified.

In current usage, business plans:

- Define a new business;
- Set goals, define objectives and programs for achieving them, and identify milestones for monitoring progress;
- Collect and analyze the financial specifics of a business, especially cost of goods, profit margin, cash flow, and break-even requirements;
- Support a loan application or to attract equity investments;
- Provide a vehicle for regular business review — to identify and guide corrective measures and to surmount anticipated obstacles;
- Collect essential industry and marketing data;
- Evaluate a new product, service, or promotion;
- Evaluate expansion — both in size and direction; and
- Assign a value on a business for sale or other legal purposes.

Today, however, business plans with their roots in the 20th Century rarely attempt to serve all these purposes. A comprehensive business plan often requires more than 100 pages. A document that large is too cumbersome for complete review and too expensive to develop. In the new millennium, business plan readers are demanding shorter plans that are more focused on their specific need. In response, business plans are being redefined and redesigned. Most business plans are written for a specific purpose: startup companies pursuing outside capital, expansion companies seeking to increase their capital, or existing companies focusing on specific markets, products, or departments for improved controls and efficiency.

With such diverse and robust purposes, adequately covering all of these subjects would take an encyclopedia of business plan books. Recognizing this, several books will be developed, each volume focusing on a specific business plan purpose and audience. They are presented as a series, *The Rule Book of Business Plans* .... Future volumes will cover how to develop your business plan as a financial package for funding an established business or nonprofit organization and how to use a business plan as an annual planning and development tool for your business or organization.

This volume, *The Rule Book of Business Plans for Startups*, addresses the needs of start-up companies for a business plan they can use for basic planning and development: defining the concept, securing financing, opening, operating, stabilizing, and achieving the ultimate goal, success. To assist you with writing a business plan for your start-up company, a business plan example for a manufacturer accompanies the text, and includes every section and segment necessary to complete a business plan for financing and managing most businesses.

For other types and sizes of businesses that have unique requirements, there are five business plan models in appendices A through E. Each model features differences specific to home based, wholesale/retail, service, restaurant, combination, and nonprofit businesses, avoiding repetition of the text example segments that are handled the same way.

Acknowledgments

The race of mankind would perish did they cease to aid each other.
— Sir Walter Scott

While the materials in this book have taken several years to research, one of the most rewarding experiences has been learning from skilled and knowledgeable professionals, from the hands-on people of start-up companies in various sectors and industries, and from their supporting lenders and investors.

Although it is impossible to thank everyone who has contributed to this effort, I would like to acknowledge several individuals.

Publisher: Emmett Ramey for conceiving a book on business plans for start-up companies and his support of this project; Constance C. Dickinson for championing this series and recruiting me to author it, and her untiring efforts as senior editor and designer in pulling all the materials together into an easy-to-follow format; and Jan Olsson for fine tuning the results in the pre-press process.

Accountants: Steve Akre, eCharge Corporation; Ross Cofer, Burnett, Umphress & Company LLC; Carleton L. Williams, Detor & Williams Certified Public Accountants; and Steven Maslen, CPA.

Attorneys: Kevin McBride, Robert Triantos, Ralph Ogden, and Jack Leebron.

Lenders: Diane Wissing, City Bank; Robert Lawton, Central Pacific Bank; A. Sean Aguilar, Arroyo & Coates; Ken Merport, The Foxboro Group; Mike Federighi, The Prime Source Group; and Nick West, GMAC CM.

Venture Capitalists: Jennifer S. Fonstad, Draper Fisher Jurvetson; and Jim Goldberg, Venture Resources; Evan King, President, Pacific Rim Capital.

Others: Katy Gottschalk, Cornell University; Walter C. Teagle, former Chairman of the Board, Exxon Corporation; Crawford H. Greenewalt, former President of DuPont; and my ever supportive and patient wife, Eileen Lacerte-Rule.

Introduction

Your Business Plan's Preliminaries

When the ancients said a work well begun was half done, they meant to impress the importance of always endeavoring to make a good beginning.
— POLYBIUS

For a start-up business, creating a business plan is like creating a game plan in sports. You need to scout out all the information to create a winning strategy for the game. While business plans for existing companies may have a special focus, such as setting overall goals, reviewing specific operations, evaluating new products, assessing new technology in the industry, or some other specific purpose, the business plan for a start-up company is the blueprint for its formation, its operation, and its success. A business plan exposes a new company's strengths and weaknesses. It reveals ways to capitalize on the strengths and minimize the weaknesses, uncovers every facet of the business that can be developed, and points to the best method for that development. It provides a structure for the company's pursuit of the winner's trophy.

Even though creating a business plan takes time, thought, and effort and may seem like an impediment to getting on with opening or growing your new business, it is imperative in today's competitive business climate for you to have all relative information available and evaluated before opening your doors. With a thoughtfully prepared business plan you will enter the business world prepared, ready to run your business and ready to compete.

Although researching and writing your business plan may seem like a monumental task, these chapters will enable you to proceed step by step as painlessly as possible. As you go through the process, you will develop your knowledge and understanding of your business, improve your chances of success, and diminish your risks of failure as a start-up owner.

Prior to writing your business plan, there are several issues you must resolve. It is beyond the scope of this text to cover all of these in depth; however, a basic checklist with a few recommended reference books is provided, so you can explore some of the subjects more thoroughly. As an entrepreneur of a start-up company:

☐ Are you prepared to operate a business?

☐ Have you already decided upon your product(s) or service(s)?

☐ Have you investigated other types of businesses? Have you explored the broad economic business sectors: manufacturing, wholesale, retail, service, . . . ? Have you considered other industries within the sector of your choice? Have you thought about what types of businesses are strongest for now and in the future?

☐ Have you checked out franchises? To checkout the possibilities and benefits of becoming a franchise outlet owner or franchisor, read Erwin Keup's *Franchise Bible* and this author's books, *No Money Down Financing for Franchising* and *The Franchise Redbook*, all published by The Oasis Press.

☐ Do you have a location in mind? Have you researched the principles of site selection: physical site needs (address, neighborhood, interior lot, corner lot), cost effectiveness, interior space, exterior space, visibility, traffic volume (which side of the street and times of the day), and accessibility? Are you familiar with the advantages and disadvantages of types of sites, such as free-standing buildings, storefronts, regional malls, and many others? Are you familiar with the principles of lease negotiation? See Luigi Salvaneschi's *Location, Location, Location,* published by The Oasis Press.

☐ Have you located the necessary business consultants — accountant, attorney, banker, and others? One resource is *The Small Business Guide to Bankers* by Suzanne Caplan and Thomas M. Nunnally, published by The Oasis Press.

☐ Do you know your financial position, your credit rating, your investment costs? The authors' *No Money Down Financing for Franchising,* covers these topics in detail for any business, not only franchising.

Before going forward, it is assumed you have done the basic homework for each of the elements above, and that you:

- Are ready to go into business
- Have your basic business concept
- Have decided on your basic product(s) or service(s)
- Have your location and facility
- Have a business accountant and attorney
- Understand your financial position and your investment costs

While you may be beyond the basics mentioned, these and other business considerations will be covered in this book. While you develop your business plan, even though you have already explored them, you will be reconsidering and reevaluating the following concepts in detail.

- Vesting
- Business objectives
- Mission statement
- Keys to success
- Industry analysis
- Market analysis
- Competitor analysis
- Strategies
- Marketing plan
- Management
- Organizational structure
- Operations
- Financial pro formas
- Break-even analysis
- Financial requirement

Don't be concerned if you aren't familiar with all of these concepts. Writing a business plan for your new business is a straight forward process that you can move through step by step to completion. The whole process can be accomplished in two to four weeks, depending on your business. To speed up locating much of the material, Internet access can help tremendously, but if it is not readily available to you, other sources are suggested.

Chapters 1–12 cover each section of a start-up business plan and the exhibit section with attention to the composition of each segment. As you progress through these chapters, you can follow a complete business plan of a manufacturing and assembly company, Kona Gold Coffees, which is the most complex type of business. There are also examples in appendices A–E for other types of business — home office, retail and wholesale, service, restaurant, combination, and nonprofit — showing the segments that vary in their presentation or content. Both cash-on-sale and sales-on-credit businesses are considered in the text and represented in the examples. These examples provide a model format for each segment of your start-up business plan.

A Professional Presentation

In surveying many successful business plans, you will find that no *one* format fits them all. Depending upon the nature of the business, certain topics take precedence over others. Often the owners write their business plans since they know the most about their business operation and management, and they have learned what elements to include to make the best impression.

Some typical business plan outlines used by successful businesses over the years are shown in a table on the next page. Currently, the most popular is Plan E or minor variations of it. Plan E is used throughout this book.

Business Plan Outlines

Business Plan A:
- Business summary
- Company history
- Industry analysis
- Manufacturing plan
- Production and personnel plan
- Products or services
- Research and development
- Competition
- Marketing and sales
- Management team
- Financial analysis
- Appendices or exhibits

Business Plan B:
- Executive summary
- Company review
- Products
- Market analysis
- Marketing plan
- Production plan
- Management team
- Financial history and pro forma
- Risks and potential problems

Business Plan C:
- Abstract
- Company overview
- Founders and directors
- Products and services
- Market analysis
- Financial information

Business Plan D:
- Executive summary
- Investment proposal
- Business objectives
- Services or products
- Markets
- Competition
- Company and management
- Financial pro forma
- Advantages to the investor
- Appendices

Business Plan E:
- Executive summary
- Company description
- Industry analysis
- Market and competition
- Strategies and goals
- Products or services
- Marketing and sales
- Management and organization
- Operations
- Financial pro formas
- Financial requirements
- Exhibits

You can see by these outlines, it makes a difference whether your business is a startup or a continuing business, or is in a particular industry, such as automotive, dry cleaning, convenience stores, or quick service restaurants, to name a few. Nevertheless, a common thread runs through them all.

While a business plan can be a way to set the direction and improve the efficiency of a company, usually a primary goal for a start-up company is to obtain financing. Notice Plan D in the table Business Plan Outlines, which has both a section entitled investor proposal and a section devoted entirely to the advantages to the investor. Obviously, this plan is written specifically for finding and acquiring investors. A similar outline could be used for targeting a bank or investment lender.

Your outline determines the organization of your business plan. It is essential for you to consider the purposes for the structure, which are:

1. To organize the business plan in sections in order of their importance to your company;

2. To organize the business plan in sections in order of the importance to the reviewer when the reviewer is defined; and

3. To organize the sections of the business plan in a logical order of development, not for the business plan, but for the logical development of your company.

Although there are several possible approaches, purpose one, above, usually makes the most sense for an existing company. Purpose two has inherent problems in that the writer must second-guess the priority of the targeted reviewer. Usually, advocates of these two structures include a disclaimer, such as, "the sections of business plans are rarely read in order, instead reviewers jump around based on their priorities." And usually, this is true. Often, the reason a reviewer's interest jumps around is because the plan is incorrectly organized or, at least, incorrectly organized from the reviewer's standpoint.

Because one type of business (such as manufacturing) has different priorities than another type (such as a service company), one clear-cut standardized business plan is impossible to achieve. The key to structuring a successful business plan is to keep in mind all three purposes and the several outlines you can use to tell your story.

The third purpose for structuring the business plan is the best approach for a start-up business, whether for manufacturing, assembly, wholesale, retail, service, nonprofit, home based, or whatever business. The best organization for a startup is to walk the reader of your business plan through the sections that represent the logical development of the company.

A plan written in the correct order with reasonable transitions leading from one section to the next, that tells the story of how your company has been designed, and builds up to the final numbers you've derived, doesn't allow the reader's interest to jump around. This is not to say you cannot have different or other specialized categories or sections in addition to the basic ones proposed here, because you can. However, the specialized sections should be correlated with the basic sections in an orderly sequence that describes a logical development of your business.

Business Plan Outline for Start-up Companies

A complete business plan for a start-up company is best organized according to the logical development of the business and is comprised of at least twelve basic components.

1. Executive summary — by definition, to summarize the elements of your business.
2. Company description — for identification, to introduce your readers to your company and your business concept.
3. Industry analysis — to provide a picture of your industry and of the position of your business within the larger framework.

4. Market and competition — to evaluate what you are getting into. While some business plan proponents separate market and competition, it takes an examination of both, together, to come to one very important final conclusion: your market share. Consequently, it is best to examine and present them together.
5. Strategies and goals — to analyze the market and your competition in order to determine how and where your company or products or services fit and to maximize your position with your target market.
6. Products or services — to describe your products or services and how they match your findings of your strategies and goals.
7. Marketing and sales — to market your products or services with the best positioning and to forecast your sales based on the findings of categories four, five, and six, in that order.
8. Management and organization — to present the management and personnel who will run the show. This section can be separated into two sections for more complex companies.
9. Operations — to explain how the business is run.
10. Financial pro formas — to forecast successful financial performance for all activities.
11. Financial requirement — to present the type and amount of financing needed, based on the previous sections, to accomplish the whole plan.
12. Exhibits — by definition, to close the plan, and separate any supporting materials that would otherwise interrupt the flow of the story.

Startup Business Plan Outline

Title Page
Table of Contents

I. Executive Summary

Review Executive Summary

A. Company description
B. Industry analysis
C. Market and competition
D. Strategies and goals
E. Products or services
F. Marketing and sales
G. Management and the organization
H. Operations
I. Financial pro formas
J. Financial requirement

(or)

Preview Executive Summary

A. Business concept
B. Progress status
C. Keys to success
D. Financial overview

II. Company Description

A. Name and business concept
B. Ownership and legal
C. Leadership and location
D. Geographic sales area
E. Current status and milestones

III. Industry Analysis

A. Industry analysis summary
B. Industry description
C. Industry size and maturity
D. Industry trends and impact factors
E. Industry standards

(continued)

Startup Business Plan Outline (continued)

  F. Industry obstacles
  G. Industry opportunities

IV. Market and Competition
  A. Market and competition summary
  B. Market description — segments and target market
  C. Market size and trends
  D. Competition identification
  E. Main competitors
  F. Competitor analysis
  G. Market share
  H. Customer needs
  I. Market obstacles
  J. Market opportunities

V. Strategies and Goals
  A. Strategies and goals summary
  B. Long-range goals and strategies
  C. Strategies implementation

VI. Products or Services
  A. Products or services summary
  B. Products or services description
  C. Products or services positioning
  D. Comparison with the competition
  E. Technology and intellectual protection
  F. Future products or services

VII. Marketing and Sales
  A. Marketing and sales summary
  B. Marketing strategy
  C. Marketing plan
  D. Marketing budget and advertising plan
  E. Sales force and forecast

VIII. Management and Organization
  A. Management and organization summary
  B. Management team
  C. Key personnel responsibilities and duties
  D. Management philosophy
  E. Key personnel incentives
  F. Organizational structure
  G. Personnel plan

IX. Operations
  A. Operations summary
  B. Operations description
  C. Human resources
  D. Facility
  E. Production
  F. Supply and distribution
  G. Fulfillment
  H. Customer service policy
  I. Inventory control
  J. Efficiency control
  K. Cash flow control

X. Financial Pro Formas
  A. Financial summary
  B. Important assumptions
  C. Opening balance sheet
  D. First-year monthly pro forma statement of income
  E. Five-year annual pro forma statement of income
  F. Break-even analysis
  G. First-year monthly pro forma statement of cash flows
  H. First-year quarterly pro forma balance sheet
  I. Five-year annual pro forma balance sheet
  J. Five-year pro forma business ratios

XI. Financial Requirement
  A. Financial requirement summary
  B. Start-up costs
  C. Funds raised and funds needed
  D. Loan request proposal
  E. Investor offering
  F. Potential risks
  G. Exit options

XII. Exhibits
  A. Business plan support documents
  B. Marketing materials
  C. Manufacturing materials
  D. Legal documents
  E. Facility documentation
  F. Insurance coverage
  G. Business references

A professionally written start-up business plan has all twelve of these basic sections presented in the order of the outline. Most of the segments listed will also be reflected in the same order of presentation, although there may be slight variances depending on your type of business. These variances will be discussed and examples given. When your business plan is written to obtain financing, the financial requirement section may be tailored either as a loan request or as an investment offering proposal, then titled accordingly. See Chapter 11, Financial Requirement.

A Winning First Impression

The saying, "There's no second chance to make a good first impression," is highly appropriate when it comes to the opening sections of your business plan and its overall appearance. With current desktop publishing, business plans are looking more professional — prospects are competing for neatness and an impressionable presentation that sets them apart.

Format

As to format, the norm is to bind your business plan in booklet form with high quality materials. Better ones have quality report covers in dark or rich colors and are labeled on the front. The title page serves better than a label if laminated or positioned behind a windowed cover or behind a full clear cover. Most types of binding are available at copy centers: *ibico* and GBC® presentation bindings, Wire Bind™, and Velobinder® are a few of the better ones. Some businesses go the extra step to have printed covers or printed binding strips. Three-ring binders have been used for years and are still acceptable, but you improve your odds for making that favorable first impression by using the latest and most professional-looking, high-tech materials available.

Page Layout

Make sure the layout of each page is balanced and artistically pleasing, with a lot of open or negative space — paragraphs, lines, and characters should not be too closely spaced. With desktop publishing, many types of letter styles (fonts) are available. The text is generally easier to read if the font used has serifs, for example New Courier, New Times Roman, or Charter and the margins justified. For a professional quality, use the sans-serif font, such as Arial, Modern, or Univers, for titles, sideheads, tables, and outlines. Choose one of each and stay consistent throughout the presentation.

Using the latest software printing design tools such as boxes, borders, shadow lines, and enlarged and bold characters, can add a professional look if correctly done without drawing attention to their use and stealing the show from the material itself. Color printing, judiciously placed, is being used more all the time.

Tabs and Titles

Each subject, with titled heading, should have its own section and separated with indexed partitions keyed to the table of contents. Tabbed index partitions make it easier to locate information, especially during a personal presentation. Another feature is to use colored partitions, preferably muted or soft colors that coordinate with the color of the cover and with the colors of any charts or graphs inside. Instead of custom tabs, some plans are assembled with printed tab indices with miniature plastic covers, but if you have access to preprinted laminated tabs, they are preferable. Avery has Index Maker dividers for ink-jet and lazer printers that you can customize with basic desktop software. A recent innovation is hidden tabs that protrude past the pages but not the cover.

Within each section, set off subsections (referred to as segments within this text) with crossheads — such as those used within the chapters of this book — usually set bold in a sans-serif font. When these are justified to the right or left margin, they are referred to as sideheads.

Color and Charts

Charts, graphs, and illustrations are commonly acceptable if appropriate to the text. Color is often better than black and white; however, choose reds and blues, not chartreuses, yellow-oranges, or some other unusual color. In fact, if you are going to use extensive colored charts and graphs, choose a theme of three or four rich colors and use them consistently throughout the work. Reserve photographic prints for the exhibits. Even then, they should be presented in protective sheets and labeled or captioned. If needed in the main body of the business plan, pictures look more professional when converted to color copies with titles and captions in font styles consistent with the rest of your business plan.

Printing

Use laser or ink-jet printers to print on paper of stationery quality. Paper should be the brightest white you can find, laser quality, or one of the muted color résumé stocks in soft gray or ivory. Staying consistent by using the same type of paper for text, graphs, charts, and illustrations yields a quality professional look. Using bits and pieces of different paper gives the impression the plan was thrown together.

Proofreading and Copyediting

Have your figures checked by an accountant and the text proofread by an editor or proofreader. An accurate, easy-to-read, and well-organized text will convey professionalism and credibility. Too often this important step is avoided or forgotten and, despite all the work that has gone into creating an impressive presentation, typos, missing words, poor sentence construction, and figures that don't add up become a significant part of that first impression made on a reviewer.

Business Plan Examples

Examples of the corresponding segments of Kona Gold Coffees' business plan accompany each discussion in the text. These segments are featured in shaded frames as in the first example, Cover Letter. The underlined titles used for the examples throughout the book — Cover Letter, Title Page, Table of Contents, Executive Summary, et cetera — are not meant to be used in your actual documents.

The Cover Letter

Usually a start-up company's purposes for developing a business plan is to obtain financing from lenders or investors or both. Even when you make a personal presentation, which is preferred, the cover letter is necessary because the loan or investment agent may hand your business plan over to another staff director who will read your cover letter later. The purpose of the cover letter is to catch the reviewers' attention and make them want to open the plan and review the executive summary.

Do not use a generic letter for all recipients of your business plan. You should customize your cover letter for each financing source you contact. Call the bank or firm after your initial call to the loan officer and ask an assistant for the loan officer's full name, correct spelling, his or her title, and the correct spelling of the company's name and address. Make sure this information is on your cover letter.

A successful cover letter touches on the main points without totally duplicating the executive summary. It should be written as if the reviewer has no knowledge about you or your business. Describe the business you are in, address why your business will succeed, cover your expected success in terms of sales or dollars, and establish your competitive edge. Also, the cover letter should explain how much money you want and how you plan to use the funds. It should be succinct and cover all the points in no more than one page.

Print the cover letter on quality letterhead stationery, preferably of the business you describe in your plan. This indicates to reviewers that you are progressing and already investing in yourself and your business. Finally, like your business plan, the cover letter should be carefully proofread, copyedited, and corrected.

Cover Letter — Kona Gold Coffees

Kona Gold Coffees
77-6464 Alapa Street
Kailua-Kona, Hawaii 96740
(808) 555-1234
FAX (808) 555-1235
www.KonaGoldCoffees.com

December 2, 20XX

Mr. Stephen J. Clayton
Assistant Branch Manager
Bank of Hawaii
75-5595 Palani Road
Kailua-Kona, Hawaii 96740-9909

Re: Business Plan for Kona Gold Coffees

Dear Mr. Clayton:

Thank you for taking my telephone call. Per our conversation, I am submitting the enclosed copy of our business plan for Kona Gold Coffees LLC located in Kona Industrial Park.

Kona Gold Coffees will manufacture presentational gourmet packages of assorted Kona coffees. While we will have some Internet and direct-mail consumer sales, these packages are to be sold mostly to retailers. Our products are intended to fill a new market niche as a result of a growing awareness of gourmet coffees and of a growing reputation of Kona Coffees. The industry has been growing 9 percent annually both on the mainland and in Hawaii. This new market niche for coffee bars and home consumption is expected to continue for another 15 years. Currently, there is no one answering the need in Hawaii. Our projected sales for the first year are $1,612,000.

To launch our business we have total startup costs of $283,761 of which we have raised $210,000 from two founders. To cover the difference we are seeking a commercial line of credit from your bank for $100,000. We plan to draw a disbursement of $75,000 in January and use the funds to pay off equipment ($46,761) and for additional capital ($25,000) for positive cash flow. Our projections show that we will be able to fully pay this down by the end of the year with a net profit of 12 percent after taxes. We currently have $45,000 on deposit in your bank. Of course, there are many more details supported by diligently compiled analyses in our business plan.

I look forward to our lunch on December 12 and am eager to answer any questions you might have. If you would like to me to clarify anything before then, please feel free to contact me at the number above. Thank you in advance for your consideration and interest.

Very truly yours,

Kona Gold Coffees

David C. Cooper
President

A Confidentiality and Non-disclosure Agreement

A common concern for founders of start-up companies is controlling the confidentiality of their business plan from current and potential competitors who might react to the ideas revealed in the plans if they were to become known. One method to reduce the chances of this happening is to issue a confidentiality agreement or a non-disclosure agreement to the recipients to be executed and returned either before a business plan is sent or concurrently at the presentation. This is standard practice with sophisticated and accredited investors and with most sources of equity financing.

However, it is not standard practice for most debt financing sources. Consequently, since confidentiality agreements are not well-received by conventional lenders, it is recommended to avoid using this form of protection with lenders. Use of the simpler, direct disclaimer — that your plan is confidential — which is printed on the title page (see next segment), is the accepted practice. For extra controls, you can number each plan and record the recipients by number in a log. This usually has a psychological advantage, as it shows the lender you have a serious concern for controlling these documents.

If you choose to use a non-disclosure or confidentiality agreement, it is best to send it ahead of time to allow the recipients and their legal representatives to review it in advance. This will avoid any possible embarrassment for either party if you find yourself in a face-to-face situation, asking them to sign the agreement before sharing your business plan. Refer to the example for a standard format.

Confidentiality Agreement   Kona Gold Coffees

By virtue of our relationship, you will have access to receive, or learn of information, various trade secrets which are of a confidential and proprietary nature to us, including our customers, marketing and promotional plans, pricing, policies and procedures, which is not generally known. If you consent to listening to our presentation or receiving our business plan, we ask that you agree to keep such information confidential and that you agree not to misuse, misappropriate, or disclose any of the trade secrets described herein, directly or indirectly, or use them in any way, except in connection with evaluating your proposed purchase of investment interest from us until such time as we disclose said information to the public in general.

Further, we request that you agree that upon request from us, if you do not so elect to purchase an investment interest, you agree to promptly return to us all such information, including any copies or reproductions thereof, and to make no further use of it.

Any of the information which becomes known to the public through no fault of yours, through disclosure to you without our consent by a third party who does not have an obligation to keep it confidential, or information which you have knowledge of prior to our disclosure, will not be considered confidential.

Agreement is executed by your signature below. Thank you for your cooperation.

By: _____   Date: _____
             (Signature)

Name: _____
            (Printed Name)

Title Page

As the cover is opened, the reviewer should see a professionally laid out title page. Avoid clipart and decorative treatments — these are not well received by lenders or investors. The exception to this would be a replica of your logo, if it has been professionally designed. Indicate your business name and address, the title of the document, Business Plan; the name of the person, title, and company to whom the plan is addressed; the name, title, and telephone number of the person who prepared the business plan; and the date it was prepared. Under the title Business Plan or at the bottom of the page, you can also indicate the plan is confidential.

Title Page

Kona Gold Coffees
Signature Gold
77-6464 Alapa Street
Kailua-Kona, Hawaii 96740
(808) 555-1234 – FAX (808) 555-1111
e-mail: KonaGoldCoffees@aol.com

Business Plan

Confidential Information

Prepared for:
    Mr. Stephen Clayton
    Assistant Branch Manager
    Bank of Hawaii
    75-5595 Palani Road
    Kailua-Kona, Hawaii 96740-9909

Prepared by:
    Terry Jervis
    Office Manager
    (800) 555-1234
    Nov. 17, 20XX

Table of Contents

The table of contents page usually follows the title page. Several professional formats exist; one of the more familiar is shown in the example. Under the heading, Contents, make two columns: one for subjects and one for page numbers or indexed sections. You may head the columns with subject and page number or section, but it is not necessary. Keep it as clean as possible. If you think you need to identify every segment, you might consider an index of segments as the last item in your exhibits.

Table of Contents Page   **Kona Gold Coffees**

Contents

Subject	Section
Executive Summary	A
Company Description	B
Industry Analysis	C
Market and Competition	D
Strategies and Goals	E
Products	F
Marketing and Sales	G
Management and the Organization	H
Operations	I
Financial Pro Formas	J
Loan Request	K
Exhibits	L

Important Points to Remember

- An accurate, easy-to-read, and well-organized business plan conveys professionalism and credibility.
- You improve your odds for making a favorable first impression by using the latest and most professional-looking, high-tech materials available.
- Don't necessarily try to balance the material from section to section, place your emphasis in the proper perspective and accent the features that are most important for your business.
- Always include a cover letter with your business plan because it may get passed on to other staff members who won't know about your venture.

Throughout the next twelve chapters, you will identify the research you need to complete and compile your findings, make logical conclusions, write the segments of each section, summarize each of the sections, then complete the first section of your start-up business plan. The first section, the Executive Summary, is an overview of your entire business plan and is the topic of Chapter 1.

Chapter 1

Executive Summary

The last thing one knows is what to put first.
— BLAISE PASCAL

The executive summary is the doorway to your business plan. It is the single most important section because all business plan reviewers read this section first. If it is written poorly or there are obvious problems or unrealistic expectations in the plan, very few will continue reading the other sections. Even when your executive summary does pass the acid test, those reviewers who continue reading do not always continue on to each section in the order you have laid it out, so the executive summary is the only section that you can count on all of your reviewers to read.

The preferred length for the executive summary is one page, although two or three pages for a plan that is thirty or more pages long can be reasonable — a rule of thumb for a thirty-page plan is one to two pages, and for a forty-page plan, two to three pages.

However, length is not the number one priority. What is important is covering the important details that comprise this section in a concise and convincing manner and presenting an harmonious picture of your start-up company. Nevertheless, the importance of this section should not intimidate you. You do not have to be a great writer, in fact, flowery adjectives and clever prose are discouraged. You want to make it sound interesting and vibrant, but without exaggeration. To establish your credibility with your reviewers, you want to set a mood that indicates you are looking at your business objectively. You will have plenty of space within the body of the business plan to develop enthusiasm for your business concept and your new company, after you have captured the reviewers' interest and placated their skepticism. So for this first summary, it is important to be succinct, to use specific language, and to avoid unsupported adjectives, generalizations, and subjective statements.

Two Formats of Executive Summaries

Start-up companies can choose between two formats for their executive summary. The first and most conventional is referred to as the review format — sometimes called the synopsis style — of executive summary. The second format is the preview executive summary and is usually preferred for start-up companies.

The review format has been described as a little or mini- business plan within the business plan. It covers all of the sections of the business plan, in the order they are presented, briefly paraphrasing each and emphasizing their important features. It is easy to write after you've completed the rest of your business plan. This format is preferred for established businesses, but not necessarily for new start-up businesses, because most of the sections are best based on proven, not projected, business results. Repetitions of "here's what we plan to do" in every section or a summary of several sections that have yet to be tried can put off the reader or lose credibility. However, after you've written your business plan, write your summary in both formats. Writing your first summary in review format will help you create a more effective summary in the preview style. If in the review format your company seems to fall flat or appears to rely too heavily on future outcomes in each section, then the second type, the preview executive summary, may work better for your business.

The preview executive summary is also used by existing businesses that prefer a freer format written in a more narrative style. Even though it is shorter, there is a structure to follow with specific requirements that guarantee a professionally composed executive summary.

Regardless of which format of executive summary you decide to use, the key to writing either is to write the executive summary last, so you can capture the important highlights of each section and to emphasize those that are most essential for your business. However, you can write the executive summary in draft form when you begin, then proceed with the understanding that this section is to be rewritten after you have completed the rest of the work in the section.

Strategically Repeat Important Points

There is one other thing to consider. Repeating some information in a business plan is not only acceptable, it can be crucial. To get especially important elements before reviewers who tend to skip around or who do not like to read business plans from start to finish, it is best to repeat essential conclusions needed to support information presented in other, related discussions. A key conclusion left strategically unsupported can loose a reviewer's confidence in your plan.

Review Executive Summary

The review executive summary is traditionally used by established businesses. Although it is longer, it is the easiest to understand, to explain, and usually to write. This summary should have as many segments as there are sections within the body of your business plan, with each segment presented in the same order as in your plan. When written for a start-up company, this type of executive summary may have fewer segments than the number of business plan sections, because related ones that are less important can be combined. For example, if you have very little information on your industry, you might add what you have as a short statement with your segment on the market, and title the segment, Industry and the Market. However, in the typical review format, you will write ten brief segments fitting the target length for your executive summary. It is your existing business knowledge and that which you will discover through the process of developing your business plan, that will enable you to write these paragraphs succinctly and professionally. The review format includes:

- Company description
- Industry analysis
- Market and competition
- Strategies and goals
- Products or services
- Marketing and sales
- Management and organization
- Operations
- Financial pro formas
- Financing requirement

You may have noticed in the start-up business plan outline in the Introduction that most sections begin with a summary. As with the executive summary, you will develop and write those sections step-by-step, then write their respective summaries to emphasize the important highlights. For your review executive summary, the key is to borrow from each of the section summaries once you have completed them. As to the order of presentation of the segments, they are usually best presented if you place them in their order of importance for your company.

Company Description

Under the heading Company Description, briefly describe the important introductory information from your company description, generated in Chapter 2.

Specific points to include here are:

- Name and business concept — a brief description identifying your business name, industry, business specialty, your market, your primary product or service line, and the purpose of your business.

- Ownership and legal identifies
  - Identity of the owners or major shareholders — those whose identities are relevant, such as those necessary for personal guarantees, for management of operations, or for well-known reputations. If there are owners, other than yourself, that are not keys of your business, then you needn't identify them here, as they will be covered in detail in your company description section. If there are other owners, state your percentage of ownership so that it is clear to the reviewers that you do not have 100 percent ownership.
  - Type of business ownership or vesting and state of formation — sole proprietorship, corporation, S corporation, general partnership, limited partnership, limited liability company, or other.
  - Intellectual Property — any patent, copyright, trademark, trade name, or service mark that your company may own or license.
- Leadership and location — identify the person(s) who operate your business, the business address, and a key feature or two about your location. If your business is location sensitive and you have a strong location, you can emphasize its importance in your executive summary. (The functions of your facility are covered in operations.)
- Geographic sales area — a brief description that best characterizes the geographic sales area your business serves.
- Current status and milestones — a description as to what you have done and where you are in your start-up progress. Mention two key elements — one recently completed and one to be accomplished — that convey to a reviewer the status of your physical progress. Mention any advantages to your timing in the market. If you are halted in your progress because of your current search of funds, state that you are now seeking financing to continue.

Executive Summary – Company Description   Kona Gold Coffees

Kona Gold Coffees is in the roast coffee industry and manufactures presentational packages of fine assortments of Kona coffees. These will be sold both to targeted consumers and to established retailers for resale to our largest markets of end-consumers at opening — gourmet coffee drinkers and tourists. For consumer sales, our market areas are limited only by the Internet and direct mail. For retail customers, our geographic sales areas include six Hawaiian islands and five major West Coast cities on the mainland.

Our president, David Cooper, is CEO and 60 percent owner of our Hawaiian limited liability company. The other 40 percent is owned by Jim Wallace, a member with no active role in the business. The Kona Gold Coffees name is a pending trademark. Our 2,500 square foot location is in the Kona Industrial Park, 77-6464 Alapa Street, Kailua-Kona, centrally located for main supply and distribution channels. Currently we have just completed our leasehold improvements, including fixtures and furniture, and received delivery of our equipment. If we receive our requested funds, we will open January 1.

Industry Analysis

Review your industry summary in Chapter 3 and describe three or four key features from your industry analysis, drawing from your industry description, industry size and maturity, trends and impact factors, industry standards, industry obstacles, and especially, your industry opportunities.

Executive Summary – Industry Analysis   Kona Gold Coffees

Although the manufacturing sector has been stable, the roast coffee industry is expanding moderately fast, at approximately 9 percent both nationally and in the state of Hawaii. Last year, sales in Hawaii totaled $40.3 million from eleven companies.

Although the industry is characterized by two diverse company profiles (either large or small), the overall trend in the industry is to manufacture products of much higher quality than in the past for new markets in gourmet coffee for coffee bars and home consumption. This trend is expected to continue another 15 years. A significant industry standard is an average gross profit margin of 37.6 percent.

Market and Competition

This summary should cover the important highlights of your market and competition from Chapter 4, especially your market analysis including market segmentation, target market, customer and consumer profiles, and geographic sales area. In addition, include your overall market size and trends, key elements of your competition (especially main competitors and your competitor analysis) and your projected market share, customer needs, market obstacles, and market opportunities.

Executive Summary – Market and Competition   Kona Gold Coffees

As a result of a new awareness of gourmet coffees and of a growing reputation of Kona coffees, there is a new specialized market for those seeking an assortment of fine Kona coffees. It is our number one business objective to respond to this need for what we have defined as our three target markets: retailers in Hawaii, retailers on the mainland, and the end-user through direct sales. Because the end-consumer is the common market of all three, we have established our primary consumer profile.

While we have analyzed our competition and our main competitors in detail, currently there are no competitors in Hawaii responding to this market need and capitalizing on the opportunity of this market niche. The general consensus is that our competitors have promoted their own brands for so long they cannot reorganize and consider selling other high-quality brands with their own. Based on competition analyses, we have conservatively estimated our market share at 4 percent with all other Hawaiian companies in our specific industry.

Strategies and Goals

Refer to your Strategies and Goals Summary in Chapter 5 and recap the important highlights here, your long-range goals and strategies, methods of implementing your strategies, and projected long-term milestones. The key for this segment is to include any strategies or features that may show exceptional positioning for your business after an examination of your industry, market, and competition. This lays the foundation for your choice of products or services and marketing strategy in the next two segments. Also, describe one or two of your most important long-range goal(s), overall strategy(ies), and the milestone(s) coordinating with them.

> ### Executive Summary – Strategies and Goals   Kona Gold Coffees
>
> Because of our market specialization and being the first one in it, we expect to become the market leader in this niche market. We will reinforce this with product-driven strategies of quality and specialization and market-driven strategies to develop this new market and position our product line at the apex of this market niche. We anticipate that our market niche is large enough for us to grow, small enough to distract existing competitors, and too expensive for new competition to enter after we've developed it. Our long-range goal is to remain the market leader by increasing market share, improving productivity, and implementing a research and development department.

Products or Services

Provide a general description of the highlights pointed out in your products or services summary, from Chapter 6. You should include the best or unique features of your products or services, their marketplace positioning, any outstanding advantages of yours over your competitors', and any technological advantages. If you are going to have future products or services that will be significant to your business, include a brief description of them, explaining their importance, and the time line for their availability.

> ### Executive Summary – Products   Kona Gold Coffees
>
> Our opening product line consists of three different gourmet presentational packages of seven connoisseur coffees. These each include six Blue Ribbon winners, awarded by the Kona Coffee Forum, and our own trademark Signature Gold. An attractive history of each coffee is included. Because these coffees cannot be purchased anywhere else as a collection, our products are positioned to open a new market which is expected to become a market niche.
>
> Signature Gold will be submitted as a Blue Ribbon candidate this spring. We will continue developing our own proprietary blends every year and we intend to add three new, but similar, presentational packages every two years or sooner if one of our existing products doesn't sell as well as the others.

Marketing and Sales

Your Marketing and Sales Summary in Chapter 7 briefly describes the marketing strategy, marketing plan, marketing budget, advertising plan, sales strategy, sales force, and sales forecast you have developed, or might develop. For this portion of your executive summary, emphasize the features of the most important of these elements for your business. For instance, if your company is marketing driven, there will be much to explain about your marketing strategy and the findings for your marketing plan. On the other hand, if your company is sales driven, you would go into more depth about your sales force and the aggressiveness of your sales program. In other words, it is not necessary to balance the material. Place your emphasis in the proper perspective and accent those features that are more essential to your concept.

Executive Summary – Marketing and Sales   Kona Gold Coffees

Our slogan is "The World's best coffee is Kona coffee — the best Kona coffees in the world are ours." Our message will convey that we have assembled a unique collection that cannot be purchased together anywhere else. KGC trademark will stand for quality.

Our marketing plan includes a first month budget of $16,000 for a powerful send-off. Throughout the year, our reasonable ongoing campaign will cover advertising media matching the demographics of our consumer profile. Promotions involve free taste samplings, press releases, three major cultural events, and others. Advertising includes shopper magazines, tourist activity guides, trade journals, and light television and radio spots. The first year our total marketing budget is $33,600. Our sales program will be executed by owner sales, one salesperson, 209 retailers, direct mail, and Internet sales. Projected sales for the first year are $1,612,000.

Management and Organization

If you are the sole owner and operator of this new business, briefly describe the background, education, or experience that brought you to the decision to open a new business and why you feel it is a sound and timely decision. Keep it short; your complete résumé is inserted in the Management and Organization section, Chapter 8.

If you have managers, briefly introduce the outstanding achievements, experience, and education that qualify them for their key management positions in your operations and add the total years of applicable experience. Also, include highlights of your organization and personnel plan. A complete list, by titles, names, and functions are elaborated later.

If you have a special management philosophy that sets your business apart from others, mention it in your executive summary. Finally, if you plan to add key managers in the first year of business who will affect your operations and improve your ability to make your objectives, briefly include a statement concerning them.

> ### Executive Summary – Management and Organization Kona Gold Coffees
>
> Our president and CEO, David Cooper, a former co-winner of two Blue Ribbon Kona coffee awards, is responsible for overall management and strategic planning. He has 3 years experience as both purchasing and sales manager of a major competitor (reaching $5,000,000 in sales, up from $2,800,000 when Mr. Cooper took over) and over 12 years experience in manufacturing.
>
> Bob Clay heads production and associated operations. Besides having an MBA in production management, he has 6 years experience as PM for our largest competitor, Sandwich Isles Coffees, where he reorganized and modernized their production system. Along with Bob, we have an excellent office manager in Terry Jervis who was controller for Beta Chemical in Los Angeles for 8 years.
>
> Two other key personnel include Larry Fennel, our purchasing agent, who comes to us from Remington Farms where he was purchasing agent for 6 years and learned sophisticated purchasing techniques; and Lisa Orzechowski, our salesperson, who was top producer in sales for Chameleon Waters gifts for 5 years.
>
> Besides these, we have Jean Phillips, our administrative assistant; Linda Lipps, our bookkeeper; and three production operators — a total employee base of ten: six salaried, one on straight commission, and three wage earners under cost of sales. Our total payroll under G & A expenses is $ 290,000, 17.9 percent of sales, which is slightly higher than the industry standard of 16.9 percent.
>
> The overall manufacturing experience of the entire staff is more than 45 years.

Operations

Your operations section covers a complete description of your operations, human resources, facility, production, supply and distribution, fulfillment, customer service policy, inventory control, efficiency control, and cash flow control. For your executive summary, briefly describe your operations and include two or three of the most important results from your operations section, Chapter 9, that stand out for your business.

Although your facility is covered in detail later, any special features about your facility that are extremely important to your operations should be pointed out here in the executive summary.

> ### Executive Summary – Operations Kona Gold Coffees
>
> In our mainstay of operations, production, we buy an average of 850 pounds of coffee each week from 18 suppliers and process and manufacture 188 products a day. Productivity is one unit per 3 workers per 2.3 minutes. Capacity could double or triple by going to shifts and adding more operators. Because we must maintain a 21-day freshness for our product, our operations chief must carefully watch inventory levels of raw materials and finished products. Fulfillment is in-house with wholesale orders shipped by local trucking and retail orders via air freight. Freight on average runs 3.75 percent of sales. For our facilities, we have a ten year lease and mostly new equipment, totaling $48,761.

Financial Pro Formas

Briefly review your financial summary in Chapter 10 then cover your key assumptions here — especially your market share that supports your projected sales and your anticipated annual increases. From your first-year and three- or five-year pro forma income statements, include your cost of sales, operating expenses, your projected sales (both in quantity and dollars) and net profit (both in dollars and as a percentage of sales) for the first-year. Also include your break-even sales and the highlights of your pro forma statements of cash flow and your pro forma balance sheets. Finally, direct the reviewer's attention to one or two of your better business ratios from your pro formas.

Executive Summary – Financial Pro Formas Kona Gold Coffees

For our first year, sales are projected at $1,612,000 for 50,480 products and cost of sales are projected at $713,809 with a gross profit margin of 55.7 percent. All other expenses total $586,167. Sales to break even are $961,512. Our operating profit is $312,024 and net profit is $199,066 or 12.3 percent.

For our five-year pro formas, we have conservatively estimated 8 percent increases in sales (the industry standard is 9 percent) and 4 percent increases in operating costs. This yields a net profit for year five of $345,436 and a sound working capital of $1,511,928. The annual return on equity for the fifth year is 22 percent.

Financial Requirement

Briefly describe your financial requirement and include several highlights from your financial requirement summary — as developed in Chapter 11.

- Total amount of your start-up costs
- Three or four of the major intended uses for the start-up funds and how they will improve your status
- Total amount of funds raised to date and their sources in general, such as company founders, private investors, or a home-equity loan
- Amount of the financial assistance you are seeking
- Return for the investor or the term of payback for a lender
- Your backup plan if this initial plan doesn't work out

As a final component, if your long-range exit strategy is important to your financial source, include your choice of exit options or your exit strategy for the investors, as well.

> ### Executive Summary – Loan Request   Kona Gold Coffees
>
> Our total start-up costs are $283,761. The major costs are leasehold improvements ($60,000), vehicles and equipment ($88,761), fixtures and furniture ($40,000), and working capital ($70,000). To date we have raised $210,000 from our two founders. To cover the difference, we are seeking a commercial line of credit for $100,000. We plan to draw one disbursement of $75,000 in January and use the funds to pay off equipment ($48,761) and launch our business with additional needed capital ($25,000) for positive cash flow. The balance of the credit line will be maintained as a reserve.
>
> For payback, we expect to make ten monthly payments and pay down the balance in full in December. As a backup plan, our founders would seek equity home loans from second mortgages, if necessary.

This completes your executive summary in the review format. The only remaining section in your business plan not represented in this executive summary is the business plan exhibits. References that direct the reviewer to a specific document in your business plan exhibits should be clear and included with the relevant information in the appropriate section within the body of your business plan.

Preview Executive Summary

The format of the preview executive summary allows for much more freedom in its construction than the conventional review format. The four basics to cover are:

- Business concept
- Progress status
- Keys to success
- Financial overview

The four segments of the preview format executive summary are usually presented using these headings. Most of the terms used here are explained in the following chapters. It is advisable to return to this section after you have finished the rest of your business plan before writing the final draft of your executive summary.

Business Concept

The business concept typically introduces the nature of your business to your reviewer. For this segment, state the name of your company, and describe your industry, business specialty, and target market. Make sure your description clearly states the purpose of your business. Explain your major product(s) or service(s) and their important features. Also distinguish your business, or your products or services, from your competitors'. If you are filling a specific market within your market, such as a new market, a niche market, a trend market, or a specific customer focus, specify this or similar strategies that will separate your business or products or services from those of the competition. As a final facet of business concept, include your long-range goal for the business, as described in Chapter 5.

Business concept is one of the more flexible categories and, depending on the type of your start-up business, you may choose one of the alternate approaches: business objectives or mission statement.

Preview Executive Summary – Business Concept   Kona Gold Coffees

Kona Gold Coffees is in the roast coffee industry and manufactures presentational packages of fine assortments of Kona coffees. These will be sold to targeted customers and to established retailers for resale to our largest markets of end-consumers at opening — gourmet coffee drinkers and tourists. Our product line consists of three different gourmet presentational packages of seven connoisseur coffees. These each include six Blue Ribbon winners, awarded by the Kona Coffee Forum, and our own trademark Signature Gold. Signature Gold will be submitted as a Blue Ribbon candidate this spring. With the package, an attractive history of each coffee is included.

We will continue developing our own proprietary blends every year and we intend to add three new, but similar, presentational packages every two years or sooner if one of our existing products doesn't sell as well as the others.

Because these coffees cannot be purchased anywhere else as a collection, our products are positioned to open a new market which is expected to become a market niche. Because of our market specialization and being the first one in it, we expect to become the market leader in this niche market. We will reinforce this with product-driven strategies of quality and specialization and market-driven strategies to develop this new market and position our product line at the apex of this market niche. We anticipate that our market niche is large enough for us to grow, small enough to distract existing competitors, and too expensive for new competition to enter after we've developed it. Our long-range goals are to remain the market leader by increasing market share, improving productivity, and implementing a research and development department.

Business Objectives

Some companies prefer business objectives as an alternate to business concept. These are customized to your business; common ones are market, marketing, sales, management, financial, and profitability objectives. But you may have others. If you use this alternate format, introduce the name of your business, your industry, and business specialty, followed by each objective. These are given their own headings, and the objectives are written as statements which answer the what, why, how, and when questions in the mind of the reviewer. For a specific objective, answer what you plan to achieve (result), why this is your objective (purpose), how you expect to reach the result of this objective (method), and when you plan to reach the result (timing). These objectives should cover the basic introductory material of your product or service lines, their important features, and how your business will meet and beat your competitors. If you use this alternative to business concept, make these objectives specific, measurable, and consistent with the rest of your business plan. The long-range goal for your business should be implicit in one or more of your objectives.

Mission Statement

The mission statement approach is used more often by manufacturing and assembly companies, but this approach can be adapted to any business. It works best for companies with a clear strategy that separates them from their competitors.

In this approach, you first describe the name of your company, your industry, and the products or services that you produce or provide, with the statement of the mission of your business — usually one of the more specific strategies, such as quality-driven, customer-service driven, market-leader driven, or other. See Chapter 5.

Your mission statement should answer three questions: what are you selling, to whom, and why? After you explain your mission, describe the key method(s) you plan to use to execute your mission. Be sure to include important product or service features or other factors that will differentiate your business from your competitors. The long-range goal for your business should be apparent in the mission statement or included as a by-product of it.

Progress Status

The second segment of the preview executive summary includes most of the information necessary for your company description: identification of owners and their involvement, form of ownership (vesting), fictitious business name (dba), state of formation, address, and the focus of the business. Describe your most important objectives and achievements, the milestones you have completed, and the specific items you have left to do, as a start-up business, before opening. Include key dates, especially the date of your projected opening.

This segment frequently establishes the purpose for writing the business plan. For a new start-up business, it is usually financing. If one of your objectives, or milestones, is to seek a line of credit or a loan or to attract equity from investors, this is a good place to introduce it. Describe your total start-up costs and the three or four that are most important to your start-up plan. State the amount of capital you have already raised, the sources of those funds — such as company owner's equity, consumer credit, or loans from relatives — and how the funds have been used. State that you are currently looking for funds and the amount wanted.

You could be writing a business plan to improve marketing, sales, operations or strategies, to correct a problem, or to secure better controls. In any case, state what the current situation is and what you expect to accomplish with this business plan.

In addition to physical progress, it is especially important to explain what market research you've done and when that supports your decision to go into business. Also, list any advanced sales. If you have already opened, give the date and describe the new levels of business activity that you are trying to attain with your projected dates. Present your sales activity to date.

Preview Executive Summary – Progress Status   Kona Gold Coffees

Our president, David Cooper, is CEO and 60 percent owner of our Hawaiian limited liability company. He is responsible for overall management and strategic planning. The other 40 percent is owned by Jim Wallace, a member with no active role in the business. The Kona Gold Coffees name is a pending trademark. Our 2,500 square foot location at 77-6464 Alapa Street is in the Kona Industrial Park in Kailua-Kona, Hawaii centrally located for main supply and distribution channels. Currently, we have just completed our leasehold improvements, including fixtures and furniture, and received delivery of our equipment. We plan to open January 1.

Our total start-up costs are $283,761. The major costs are leasehold improvements ($60,000), vehicles and equipment ($88,761), fixtures and furniture ($40,000), and working capital ($70,000). To date we have raised $210,000 from our two founders. To cover the difference, we are seeking a commercial line of credit for $100,000.

As a result of a new awareness of gourmet coffees and of a growing reputation of Kona coffees, there is a new specialized market for those seeking an assortment of fine Kona coffees. It is our number one business objective to respond to this need for what we have defined as our three target markets: retailers in Hawaii, retailers on the mainland, and the end-user through direct sales. Because the end-consumer is the common market of all three, we have established our primary consumer profile.

Keys to Success

This segment is intended to introduce the reviewer to the primary considerations that make your business different and give it a competitive edge. After you have analyzed your keys to success, describe several of the best ones listed in order of their relative strengths of your business.

As a start-up business, what are your strengths? Introduce this segment with the features you are planning in your company that you believe will make it superior to the competition. What advantages does your business have? If your business is different from others — such as specific geographic or climatic advantages for your business or any other special differences that set it apart from others — describe them here, even if the reasons seem to have a specific place elsewhere in the business plan.

When you have several features you are certain will contribute to the success of your new business — your keys to success — discuss the most convincing ones. For example, one of the keys could be your location; however, emphasize the particular reason why it is an advantage. If specific market opportunities are your major thrust, describe your market strategy and anticipated market share. If you have superior products or services, superior features of products or services, special technology, excellent customer service, competitive prices, a special low-cost advantage, a specific market niche, talented marketing, aggressive sales, or other strategic areas, point them out as mentioned in Chapter 5.

If exceptional managerial talent is guiding your business, give the aggregate number of years in related experience for the combined staff. Also, mention key managers and their experience, education, and achievements, such as appropriate awards in their fields, and state each of their roles in your business.

Preview Executive Summary – Keys to Success — Kona Gold Coffees

Our keys to success come from a current and growing industry trend, our discovery of a niche market not served by our competitors, our marketing plan, and the individual and combined experience of key people.

- The roast coffee industry is expanding moderately fast, at approximately 9 percent both nationally and in the state of Hawaii. Last year sales in Hawaii totaled $40.3 million from eleven companies. The overall trend in the industry is to manufacture products of much higher quality than in the past for new markets in gourmet coffee for coffee bars and home consumption. This trend is expected to continue another 15 years.
- Currently, there are no competitors in Hawaii responding to this market need and capitalizing on the opportunity of this market niche. The general consensus is that our competitors have promoted their own brands for so long that they cannot reorganize and consider selling other high-quality brands with their own. Based on competition analyses, we have conservatively estimated our market share at 4 percent with all other Hawaiian companies in our specific industry.
- Our slogan is "The World's best coffee is Kona coffee — the best Kona coffees in the world are ours." The KGC trademark will stand for quality.
- Our marketing plan includes a budget the first month of $16,000 for a powerful send-off. Throughout the year, our reasonable ongoing campaign will cover advertising media matching the demographics of our consumer profile. Promotions involve free taste samplings, press releases, three major cultural events, and others. Advertising includes shopper magazines, tourist activity guides, trade journals, and light television and radio spots. The first year total marketing budget is $33,600. Our sales program includes 209 retailers, direct mail, and Internet sales.
- Our president is co-winner of two Blue Ribbon Kona coffee awards with 3 years experience as both purchasing and sales manager of a major competitor (reaching $5,000,000 in sales, up from $2,800,000 when he took over) and over 12 years experience in manufacturing.
- Our operations chief holds an MBA in production management and has 6 years experience as PM for our largest competitor, Sandwich Isles Coffees, where he reorganized and modernized their production system.
- Our office manager was controller for Beta Chemical in Los Angeles for 8 years.
- Our salesperson was top producer in sales for Chameleon Waters gifts for 5 years.
- The overall manufacturing experience of the entire staff is more than 45 years.

Financial Overview

This final segment of the preview executive summary combines much of the information in the two sections financial pro formas and financial requirement. The major difference here is that they are reversed, placing the higher priority on the financial requirement for the would-be lender or investor — the funds already raised have been introduced in your progress status.

First, briefly describe your financial requirement and include the highlights from your financial requirement summary as developed in Chapter 11.

- Amount of financial assistance you are seeking
- Uses for funds and how they will improve your status
- Return for investor or term of payback for lender
- Your backup plan if this initial plan doesn't work out

For the second half of this segment, cover the important features emphasized in your financial pro formas summary, as developed in Chapter 10. State your key assumptions — especially your market share, because it supports your projected sales and your annual projected increases. Summarize important features from your first-year pro forma income statements — your cost of sales, operating expenses, and your projected sales (both in quantity and dollars), and net profit (both in dollars and as a percentage of sales) — and highlights of these from your three- or five-year pro formas. Also, include your break-even sales and the key features of your pro forma statements of cash flow and your pro forma balance sheets. Finally, direct the reviewer's attention to one or two of the better business ratios that are projected for the end of your three- or five-year forecasts.

Preview Executive Summary – Financial Overview   Kona Gold Coffees

For the commercial line of credit of $100,000, we plan to draw one disbursement of $75,000 in January and use the funds to pay off equipment ($48,761) and launch our business with additional needed capital ($25,000) for positive cash flow. The balance of the credit line will be maintained as a reserve. For payback, we expect to make ten monthly payments and pay down the balance in full in December. As a backup plan, our founders would seek equity home loans from second mortgages, if necessary.

Our financial pro formas show that for our first year, total sales are projected at $1,612,000 for 50,480 products, and cost of sales are projected at $713,809 with a gross profit margin of 55.7 percent. All other expenses total $586,167. Sales to break even are $961,512. Our operating profit is $312,024 and net profit is $199,066 or 12.3 percent.

For our five-year pro formas, we have conservatively estimated 8 percent increases in sales (the industry standard is 9 percent) and 4 percent increases in operating costs. This yields a net profit for year five of $345,436 and a sound working capital of $1,511,928. The annual return on equity for the fifth year is 22 percent.

Important Points to Remember

- Your executive summary should be the best written section of your business plan because it is the only section that everyone presented with your business plan will read.
- It is essential to write your executive summary after the rest of the business plan is complete in order to capture the highlights of each section.
- Before deciding which format of executive summary to use, first write the easier review executive summary, and borrow key elements from each of the section summaries after you have completed them. Once you have completed it, rearrange the material of the review executive summary and write a preview executive summary. After comparing the two, decide which one best suits your business and your business plan purpose.

If you have attempted a draft of your executive summary before the balance of the business plan is complete, it is essential to return to this section and re-write it emphasizing the prominent findings of the other sections. Even after you have revised it, it is important to compare your final numbers in the executive summary with those in the rest of the business plan to make sure they are all accurate and match exactly.

Now that your reviewers have read your executive summary and opened the door to your business, they are ready to investigate your company in more detail, the subject of Chapter 2.

Chapter 2

Company Description

It is the customer, and the customer alone, who casts the vote that determines how big any company should be ....
— CRAWFORD H. GREENEWALT

After reading your executive summary, reviewers of your business plan are prepared to get a more comprehensive description of your company. For most start-up businesses, this is one of the easiest parts of a business plan to prepare, because there are no calculations involved and hardly any research needed.

The major segments of the Company Description are:
- Name and business concept
- Ownership and legal
- Leadership and location
- Geographic sales area
- Current status and milestones

Name and Business Concept

The opening segment, name and business concept, introduces the reviewer to your company. Use the company name that is the popular name under which your business operates or will operate. Whether or not the popular name is the legal name or a fictitious business name (doing business as, dba), doesn't matter at this point. You will clarify this in the next segment.

The business concept simply identifies the nature of your business in the broadest sense and includes these components:

- Industry
- Business specialty
- Target market
- Major product or service line and important product or service features
- Differentiation from competitors
- At least one long-range business goal

For this segment, write a narrative paragraph introducing your popular business name and describe all of the appropriate details of your business that match the components of the business concept above.

It may be helpful to step back and look at your business and ask: "What business are we in? What do we sell? To whom do we sell?" While later sections will analyze these questions regarding your market and your marketing strategy, focus on your business concept for this section. For example, most restaurants should be selling service and convenience, besides meals. Some sell sizzle instead of steak. Many florists sell love, compassion, congratulations, and celebration, as much as flowers. Does your business have a broader business concept?

Include in this segment a brief and basic description of your product or service lines and their important features in general terms; you have an entire section which covers them in detail later. Also distinguish your business, or your products or services, from your competitors'. Specify whether your market is new, a niche market, a trend market, or a customer focused market and identify strategies that will separate your business or products or services from the competitors'. For assistance, industry classifications are discussed in Chapter 3, target market and competitor differences in Chapter 4, and strategies in Chapter 5. It could be helpful to review these chapters before you finalize your description of this segment.

Name and Business Concept — Kona Gold Coffees

Kona Gold Coffees is part of the industry of manufacturing roasted coffee products. We specialize in bundling premiere Kona coffees in special presentation packages. We have two target markets, the end-user who will use our products, and retailers who will resell our products to the end-user. The end-users comprise three groups that will often overlap: gourmet coffee drinkers, image buyers, and Hawaii tourists with curiosity about the mystique of Kona coffee. Our primary product line consists of sampler packages of Kona coffee consisting of 7 two-ounce selections of the finest Kona coffees.

The most important characteristic of our product line is that the concept is unique in the market for Kona coffees. Our products differ from our competition's in that our competitors offer only individual minimum seven-, eight-, or ten-ounce packages of coffee of their own brand. Our intention is that the company will become the dominant leader in gourmet Kona coffee, promoting our own brand as the best within the assortment.

Ownership and Legal

If you haven't decided on your form of ownership, it is important to be aware of the various types of vesting (ownership). The final decision of vesting depends on the type of financing resources you desire and can obtain. For example, if you are seeking a conventional loan, you may have no need of partners so you could consider sole ownership. Then, there are several types of sole ownership.

If you want more liability protection, you might select a regular corporation; if you want less tax impacts, you might choose a subchapter S corporation. On the other hand, if you want to and are in a position to obtain funds from investors, you may need to select a partnership. Then, your partners may have some influence on the type of partnership vesting — a general or limited partnership or an LLC or LLP.

In any event, it is necessary you understand the types of vesting, so you, and possibly your financing entity, can select the type of ownership that best suits your financial arrangement. The following are the most frequently used types of vesting for small businesses.

Types of Ownership Vesting

While it may seem insignificant at first, it is sound planning to discuss the various types of business ownership with your accountant and attorney. If you and your spouse are going to own 100 percent of the business, you could elect to form a corporation — either a regular or a subchapter S corporation — or a limited liability company.

You could also retain the ownership as a sole proprietorship. If you are going to share ownership with others in addition to your spouse, you could set up a general partnership, a limited partnership, a corporation, or a limited liability company. In terms of your business plan, the main differences lie in the areas of responsibility, liability, control, and tax consequences.

For example, the partners of a general partnership share proportionally in profits and losses, commensurate with their ownership percentages. All partners are equally responsible for debts and are, typically, equally involved in decisions of management. In a limited partnership, however, one partner is the general partner of the partnership and has all the responsibility, while the limited partners have an investor status — no direct involvement in the management and liable only for their investments.

Sole Proprietorship

By far the most common type of ownership for small businesses, the sole proprietorship, is the easiest to set up and the easiest to understand. No special regulations exist; you, as the owner, simply own all the stock and keep all the profit, with earnings taxed personally. The biggest disadvantages are you cannot receive significant insurance and tax benefits and you are personally responsible and liable for every business decision. In the event of retirement or death, there is no business continuation.

Corporation

A regular corporation, sometimes referred to as a C corporation, is often formed as an association of several individuals. Nevertheless, one person can form and own a corporation, which is considered by law as one legal entity similar to one person. Corporations are state regulated.

A corporation affords advantages of protection by limiting personal liability of the owner(s) to the amount invested in the business. A corporation can have the authority to transact business, to buy and sell property, to enter into contracts, and to exercise any other power granted within its charter. Ownership interest can be transferred (sold). While the corporate veil gives some limited protection, you pay taxes first on profits for the corporation and again at the personal level on any personal dividends or salaries. In addition, if your business has the protection of a corporation, most investors and lenders require personal guarantees.

Subchapter S Corporation

An S corporation provides protection similar to a regular corporation, but all profits and losses pass through to the individual shareholders. This cuts out one step in taxation because taxes are assessed the same as for a sole proprietorship. This type of ownership is similar to a general partnership; however, in an S corporation, loss deductions cannot exceed the amount invested by a shareholder. This type of ownership is restricted to a maximum of 50 stockholders, but it is common for one or two individuals to form one. There are some restrictions as to what types of businesses can qualify for S ownership corporations.

General Partnership

A general partnership is a voluntary association of two or more parties to own and manage a business. Sometimes one of the partners may be a corporation rather than an individual. The partners have ownership interests that are agreed-upon percentages, sharing profits or losses according to their percentages of ownership. They also have percentages of control and liability equal to their ownership interests, with a written agreement as the governing document.

Partnerships are much like a marriage; they work well as long as the relationship between the partners is sound, but jealousies and differences of opinion can creep into a partnership and ruin the entire business. For that reason, a clause regarding buying and selling the business should be written into the agreement at the beginning.

Limited Partnership

A limited partnership is comprised of a general partner and one or more limited partners. The general partner operates the business and is legally responsible for it and its indebtedness with unlimited liability. The limited partners, also called limiteds, are investors who are liable only to the extent of their investments, but are not participants in the management of the partnership. In this type of arrangement, you could be the general partner and the investors would be limiteds buying agreed-upon percentages of the business and infusing the capital you need. All profits are divided per the agreement, and earnings are taxed personally.

Limited Liability Companies

This most recently developed type of ownership is a hybrid form of corporation and partnership with the best aspects of both. The limited liability company (LLC) can allow the tax benefits associated with a partnership business while veiling its owners with the limited liability protection of a corporation. It is an unincorporated business but formed under procedures established by state law and controlled by a written agreement.

An LLC is taxed as a partnership for federal income tax purposes, yet the owners are not personally responsible for the debts, obligations or other liabilities of the business entity. The members manage the business, but the control of day-to-day operations can be broad or limited to one manager, by the terms of the agreement. All states and the District of Columbia have passed legislation permitting LLCs. Although many states allow a one-owner LLC, check with your attorney because some gray areas still exist between state laws and the Internal Revenue Service on this issue.

There are two other limited liability entities, an LLP (limited liability partnership) and a FLLC, a family limited liability company. An LLP is similar to an LLC, but its selection is limited to professional groups such as doctors, dentists, lawyers, and accountants who frequently elect this form of ownership when they have two or more working partners who wish to limit their liability from the malpractice of the other partners. An FLLC is a special type of LLC limited to family member ownership and family assets as its core investments. This entity allows periodic transfer of stock with limited tax implications and is particularly desirable for family succession of the business. FLLCs are not yet approved in every state.

After you have made a decision on the form of business ownership, you can complete this segment of your company description. Include the following information as the second segment of your company description either in a table or as a narrative paragraph.

- Legal name.
- Fictitious business name (dba), if applicable.
- Type of vesting (form of business ownership).
- State of record of your vesting entity.
- Municipality — city or county — where you have your business license.
- Identity of the owners or major shareholders by name, title, and percentage of ownership. Include résumés for principal owners who will be personal guarantors of loans. Lenders will require financial statements and the most recent two years of income tax returns for all principal owners, but provide these under separate cover.
- Intellectual property such as trademark, trade name, service mark, patents, or copyrights. List each applicable property noting whether your business owns them or licenses them, and when necessary, explain their purpose. You will repeat this in the Products or Services section.

About Your Location

The oldest axiom in the real estate world is that the three top priorities concerning real estate selection are: location, location, and location, yet the statement remains as appropriate today as it ever was. An advantageous location is still a key to the success of a small business. Even an average-run business can be successful if it has a customer base who frequent it because of the convenience of the location.

A start-up company in an excellent location is out front in the race for profits, and with a properly run business it will stay that way. If you do not already have your location, or are tentatively considering one, you may find the next two topics helpful before making your final selection.

Site Selection

Every business can have a best location, even though it does not play such a vital role for some businesses. If the location matters for your business, it is important to put this in its proper perspective in terms of your business. Retail businesses need to attract customers, manufacturing and assembly companies. Distributors need access to suppliers and transportation for shipping. Professional businesses may need a prestigious address, and most medical firms need approved disposal sources with, usually, other surrounding medical support.

Key elements of site selection to consider are:

- Image of the facility or the address or both
- Market proximity
- Traffic counts (each side of the street and key times of the day)
- Visibility
- Accessibility
- Cost effectiveness — especially in terms of the competition
- Interior space requirements
- Exterior site requirements
- Availability of utilities
- Potential for expansion
- Terms of the purchase or lease

Since your livelihood will depend on your ability to sell your products or services in the area you choose, evaluate the sales potential and the market need in your target area. If there is not enough market for your product or service, no matter how hard you work or how great your products or services are, you will not be successful.

Check sales data of similar or related businesses in your region to get an idea of how a start-up company might do. Seek the help of reputable, local real estate agents and a business accountant. Also, the local chamber of commerce, trade associations, and even general opinion may be helpful.

Here are some questions to answer for choosing the right market area:

- Are there already competitive products or services in the area? Do they do well?

- Are the potential products or services that you are planning better? Are they competitively priced? Would yours offer something new or different to the area?
- Was there ever a business with your products or services in the area?
- Are there already too many companies competing for the same business in the area?
- Are there any ideal locations for your products or services available?
- Is the purchase or lease price of a prospective facility affordable?
- Are there any restrictions imposed by local, state or federal governments? How will you comply?
- Is the population in your area changing; is it expanding or declining?
- Are there any competitive businesses already in the planning looking into this area?

Lease Negotiation

If you are starting from scratch, solicit the assistance of a reputable Realtor. When it is time to negotiate the lease, get the help of an attorney to review the agreement, especially if leases are new to you. Here are some essential elements to consider in a lease negotiation.

- Check to see if the lease conforms to the cost guidelines of your budget.
- Coordinate the period of the lease to be appropriate to the needs of your type of business.
- Avoid a percentage lease in favor of a fixed rental agreement, if at all possible. In a percentage lease, you pay a percentage of your gross sales or net profit to the lessor.
- Look for hidden costs. If the monthly payments are triple net, you will be responsible to pay the agreed rent plus all costs of maintenance and repair, as well as property taxes and insurance.
- Is there a common area maintenance (CAM) charge?
- Attempt to get several months free rent, especially during the downtime before business opening.
- Look for restrictions, such as specific hours of operation or conflicts with planned promotional activities, or restrictions on common area usage.
- Have your attorney draw up or add an addendum to the lease for an equipment waiver to be signed by the lessor. This will allow you protection of your interest in the equipment in case of default on the lease.
- Reserve the right to sublet or assign the lease in the event you want to move or sell your business.
- Make sure the parking is adequate. Try to get a designated number of spaces written into the lease.
- Negotiate for leasehold improvements, such as getting an allowance to be built in with the lease.

> ### Ownership and Legal   Kona Gold Coffees
>
> Kona Gold Coffees is a dba for Kona Gold Coffees, LLC. We are a Hawaiian limited liability company, licensed to do business in California, Hawaii, Oregon, and Washington. The LLC is comprised of two members: David Cooper, 60 percent, and Jim Wallace, 40 percent. Kona Gold Coffee is a pending trademark on the Supplemental Register with the USPTO and can be used with the encircled R at this time for interstate commerce.

Leadership and Location

In this short segment, simply state the name and title of the main operator of your business. If that's you, then list yourself and use either the title, chief executive officer or president. If you have a board of directors or governing membership, describe the entity and the number of directors or members. It is not necessary to state their names — unless their identity enhances your presentation — details will be covered in your management and organization, Chapter 8.

After your statement of leadership, list your business address and any branch addresses, if you have more than one location. Describe the most significant reasons why your location is, or locations are, beneficial to your business. Keep in mind that a complete description of your facility, concerning the operation of your business, will be included in your operations section, Chapter 9.

If your business is location sensitive and you have a strong location, briefly identify the key points that demonstrate your advantage — such as size, exceptional décor for your type of business, customer convenience, or other. Note, for example, whether you are centralized within the area of your target market or have favorable traffic flow, superior access, parking, or proximity to other successful, complementary businesses. State only three or four key advantages about your location that help build the best overall picture of your company.

> ### Leadership and Location   Kona Gold Coffees
>
> Although major financial decisions must be approved by the governing body of the LLC which includes Jim Wallace, the principal operator of Kona Gold Coffees is David Cooper, President. Our business address is 74-6464 Alapa Street, Kailua-Kona, Hawaii 96740. This is a properly zoned area for manufacturing and is known as the Kona Industrial Park. Our small office and production facility is perfectly located for all major supply and distribution channels and only six miles from the Kona Airport for air freight. In addition, we are centrally located for our local retailer customers.

Geographic Sales Area

Very few startups have an exclusive territory. However, if you have made some strategic alliances that give you a definable geographic sales area, or if you have a franchised exclusive territory, or if you have a defined territory through an exclusive distributorship, explain that here and give its physical description.

If you need to define your area in terms of boundaries, proximity to support businesses and to businesses with the same customers, traffic flow, and whatever advantages stand out for your particular area, then include a description of this. If you want to include a map, do so as an exhibit or, if you wish to include it in the body of your business plan, insert it professionally by computer on your business plan stationery. Include a brief description showing your location with boundaries, and key any other points that may be prominent in your description.

If, on the other hand, the description of your sales area can be written with just one sentence, combine this segment with the one above and title it Leadership, Location, and Geographic Sales Area.

Geographic Sales Area   **Kona Gold Coffees**

Our geographic sales area will include all of the six major Hawaiian islands: Kauai, Oahu, Molokai, Lanai, Maui, and the Big Island; and the five major west coast cities on the mainland: Seattle, Portland, San Francisco, Los Angeles, and San Diego; as well as on-line Internet sales and mail order sales throughout the United States and Canada.

Current Status and Milestones

This segment is to give the reviewer a clear understanding of how far you have progressed with your start-up company. Like other segments in your plan, there are two ways to do this: either by writing a couple of paragraphs as a narrative description or by opening the segment with a brief introduction followed by a list of achievements and objectives, known as milestones.

Current Status and Milestones Narrative

As a starting point, state the name of the company's founder and the date founded. To describe your physical progress, give the number of employees that you will have at opening and describe the stage at which your business is at this point in time. Are you still in the planning stage, ready to sign your lease, constructing your tenant improvements, ready to secure your suppliers, ready to purchase your inventory, ready to open, ready to begin production, or ready for sales? If you can answer yes to several of these, choose the one that describes the most advanced stage. Finally, in the description of your physical progress, tell what is left to be done. Do you need to hire employees, purchase final equipment, purchase inventory, or is the only remaining step to acquire additional financing? After you've described three or four steps of your progress, if you aren't open for business yet, include the date you expect to open.

Another item to address in this segment is your current status concerning the market. Have market studies been conducted? Describe why the timing is beneficial for you to step into the market now with your strategy or your products or services. To explain this, you may have to work your way through chapters 4 and 5 and return to this segment after you understand your position in the market considering the competition. Also, include a glimpse of your financial status and investment to date. Explain any capital raised, where it has been spent so far, how much is left, and how much is needed. This should be brief and described in general terms. You will present the details in your financial requirement, Chapter 11. If you are seeking lenders or investors for seed money or additional capital for operations, close with a statement to that affect.

Current Status and Milestones   Kona Gold Coffees

Kona Gold Coffees was founded by David Cooper eighteen months ago. During this time Mr. Cooper has been doing market research, locating the site, obtaining suppliers, setting up retailer distribution, purchasing equipment, and seeking the necessary capital to springboard the company. We will open business with ten employees, including the president, and we stand ready to buy our raw materials and begin production as soon as we acquire the last component of financing. Our target opening date is January 1.

Our market analysis will show (see Market and Competition) that our retail customer base has already arranged for enough orders for six inventory turnovers — approximately three months of sales.

To date, we have raised $210,000 in capital which has mostly been used in start-up costs, leasehold improvements, and equipment. While we have approximately $45,000 in cash on hand, we can see from our cash flow projections that we should establish a commercial line of credit for $100,000 to safely launch our new business.

Current Status and Milestones Chart

Milestones are used to set specific future objectives, to forecast dates to achieve them, and to record the completed achievements for key activities of your business. These are especially important for a start-up company whether you include them in your business plan or not.

Examples of first-year milestones are: articles of incorporation; business plan review; loan submittal; loan approval; first large sales order; three-, six-, nine-month, and annual sales goals; positive cash flow; break-even sales; hiring new employees; loan payoffs; and any number of other specific objectives. Typically, these are presented as tables. Over time, the table is updated to include new objectives, such as moving to a new location, launching a new product or service, or obtaining an agreement of sale from a targeted client.

The format for the table is not formal; you can use whatever works best for you or your business. For instance, if you have a staff, one column might show the departments or the names of the managers who are assigned the responsibility to carry out the objectives of each milestone. Then other columns can be added for the amounts budgeted to achieve the milestones, the actual costs, the variances between budgeted and actual costs (when known), and any other factor that may be appropriate.

However, common to all milestones tables are two columns which show the projected dates to achieve them and the actual dates when they are achieved. Your milestones will change from objectives to achievements and new objectives will be added, as you chart your progress. To make best use of your milestones table, reproduce it as a chart and display it in an office or conference room, so you can actively record changes as they occur.

If you choose to use the milestones approach for this segment, write a brief introduction covering necessary elements discussed in the narrative approach, above, and include a milestones' table similar to the example, tailored to your business and current status.

Milestones Chart

Milestone	Projected Date	Department	Responsibility	Projected Budget	Actual Date	Actual Costs	Variance
Business plan complete	10/30/00	CEO	D.S.	$ 200	In progress		
Loan submittal	11/7/00	CEO	D.S.	0			
Corporation articles	11/15/00	CFO	R.M.	2,000	In progress		
Loan approval	11/22/00	CEO	D.S.	22,500			
Facility complete	12/28/00	DO	J.H.	165,000	In progress		
Grand opening	1/1/01	DO	J.H.	25,000			
Sales $750,000	3/31/01	SM	S.S.	500			
Two export accounts	5/15/01	CFO	R.M.	4,000			
Break-even	6/15/01	CFO	R.M.	0			
Sales $1,500,000	6/30/01	SM	S.S.	500			
Sales $2,500,000	9/30/01	SM	S.S.	500			
Trade show	10/15/01	DO	J.H.	3,200			
Sales $3,400,000	12/31/01	SM	S.S.	500			
Hire marketing director	1/31/02	CEO	D.S.	5,000			
Loan renewal	12/15/02	CFO	R.M.	$ 25,000			

Important Points to Remember

- When writing your business concept, step back and look at your business and ask: What business are we in? You will want to be very clear about your mission. As a florist, you would do well to know the answer to the question: Do we sell compassion, congratulations, and celebration, as well as flowers?
- When you are thinking about the important advantages of your location, also consider the disadvantages and how you can overcome them.
- Use your business plan milestones table as a management tool, setting dates of objectives and recording dates of their achievement.

Now that your reviewers have finished your company description, it is appropriate to show them an overall background of your industry, the subject of your next section and the next chapter.

Chapter 3

Industry Analysis

There is one rule for industrialists and that is: Make the best quality of goods possible at the lowest cost possible, paying the highest wages possible.
— HENRY FORD

A strong industry analysis can seem intimidating to develop and report. Although some established companies downplay the importance of a thorough industry analysis in their business plans, it is considered a necessity for a start-up company, especially if you are in a business that is breaking new ground in its industry or is an industry that is not so popular. Then a detailed review of the industry is vital. Nevertheless, you might be surprised to learn that, armed with the resources presented here, you can gather everything you need for a thorough industry analysis from a well-stocked public library in one day. If you have access to the Internet, your library work could be eliminated or shortened to a few hours.

The elements of an industry analysis are:
- Industry analysis summary
- Industry description
- Industry size and maturation
- Industry trends and impact factors
- Industry standards
- Industry obstacles
- Industry opportunities

Sources of Industry Information

Before you begin, it is helpful to know the numerical code for your business' industry classification. These are assigned by the U.S. Bureau of the Census. Until recently, the standard code was called Standard Industry Classification (SIC). While this is still being used by most companies and lenders in reports, the census bureau changed the system for the 1997 economic census with a new code called the North American Industry Classification System (NAICS). There are 1,170 industry classifications in the United States.

The U.S. Bureau of the Census conducts the economic census every five years (years ending with the digits 2 and 7) and the results are not published until two years later. It wasn't until January, 1999, that the results of the 1992 census and the old SIC numbers were removed from the "U.S. Census Home Page." However, they can still be found on the Internet:

U.S. Census Bureau
1992 Economic Census Results
www.census.gov/epcd/www/92result.html

The census bureau's special report, *Bridge between NAICS and SIC*, is planned for release in the first quarter of the year 2000. For the first few years of the new millennium, it will be important for you to know the numbers of both systems for your business.

The old SIC numbers can be found several ways: through Dun & Bradstreet, Robert Morris Associates, or the U.S. Bureau of the Census, to name three. On the Internet, one of the more convenient sources for locating your industry codes is the SIC Main Page of the University of Houston's Small Business Development Center.

UH Small Business Development Center
smbizsolutions.uh.edu/smbsrsrc/sicmain.htm

You can search the above site one of three ways. If you have no idea of your code, the simplest way is to use the Search Using Query Form and type in the nature of your business in the keyword search. You may discover that you have more than one industry classification. This is not uncommon for many small businesses. If so, scan the list within your group for other descriptions that fit your business and locate each number.

Once you have located your old SIC number or numbers, go to the Census Bureau's Home Page, and under "Business" click on "NAICS." Although there are 29 pages of NAICS, the classification system is well-organized, and you can locate your NAICS number or numbers fairly quickly. The Internet address is:

U.S. Census Bureau
www.census.gov/

Each NAICS number will tell you which sector, subsector, industry group, and industry (and in some cases, U.S. Industry) that your business is in by the position of the digits in your number. Suppose your business is a bed and breakfast inn, and you have identified your number as 721191.

The hierarchic structure of your number would appear as follows:

NAICS level	NAICS code	Description
Economic sector	72	Accommodation and food services
Subsector	721	Accommodation
Industry group	7211	Traveler accommodation
Industry	72119	Other traveler accommodation
U.S. Industry	721191	Bed-and-breakfast inns

The 20 economic sectors are:

NAICS Code	U.S. NAICS Description	NAICS Code	U.S. NAICS Description
11	Agriculture, forestry, fishing and hunting	53	Real estate and rental and leasing
21	Mining	54	Professional, scientific, and technical services
22	Utilities	55	Management of companies and enterprises
23	Construction	56	Administrative and support and waste management and remediation services
31–33	Manufacturing		
42	Wholesale trade	61	Educational services
44–45	Retail trade	62	Health care and social assistance
48–49	Transportation and warehousing	71	Arts, entertainment, and recreation
51	Information	72	Accommodation and food services
52	Finance and insurance	81	Other services (except public administration)
		92	Public administration

Once you establish your codes, you can begin the research necessary for your analysis. Look for total revenues, total units of products or services sold, and total employees for your sector and your industry in all geographic hierarchic levels of your business: national, state, and county or city or both, over a period of time — usually the past three or five years — for trending. Some sources will also give you profits, another topic to follow as closely as you can.

Using the Internet or your local public library or both, start with the U.S. Bureau of the Census. Also look for business and trade publications. Many industries have active trade associations that publish statistics tracking their industry sales, profits, and economic trends. Refer to *The Gale Directory of Publications and Broadcasting Media* listing periodicals or *Information, USA* for association listings. For another index of business magazines and journals, try *Business Periodicals Index*. For two sources on most trade associations, consult the *National Trade and Professional Associations of the United States* and the *Encyclopedia of Business Information Sources*.

In addition to business and trade publications, the government publishes other excellent sources of information. If you have access to a large city or university library, check to see if it is a depository of U.S. government documents. The *American Statistics Index (ASI)*, published annually with monthly supplements by the Congressional Information Service of Bethesda, Maryland, is a reference that provides an index of all statistical publications of the U.S. government. This publication lists the documents of the U.S. Bureau of Labor Statistics and those of the U.S. Bureau of the Census entitled, *Current Industrial Reports (CIR)*. The latter reports comprise a wide range of products with facts on manufacturing, shipping, and inventories. Another volume of the *American Statistics Index* is the *ASI Abstracts*. This large book summarizes the information of the reports indexed in the *ASI*.

Other Census Bureau publications to research are:

- *Bureau of the Census Catalog and Guide*, which describes all reports and data files issued in recent years;
- *Economic Censuses and Related Statistics*, which covers numerous industries and reports actual monthly sales and economic trends by locality, zip code, and type of merchandise; and
- *County Business Patterns*, which reports research on industries on the local market scene.

These and other Census Bureau publications are available through:

CENDATA
(301) 457-4100
waffle.nal.usda.gov/agdb/cendata.html

U.S. Census Bureau
(888) 249-7295
www.census.gov/mp/www/censtore.html

You can access the database edition of *County Business Patterns* at the Census Bureau's web site.

U.S. Census Bureau
www.census.gov/prod/www/titles.html

Current publications are kept as references in libraries and at the 47 district offices of the U.S. Department of Commerce and the 12 regional offices of the U.S. Bureau of the Census listed below.

Regional Offices of the U.S. Bureau of the Census

Atlanta, Georgia (404) 730-3833	Dallas, Texas (214) 767-7105	Los Angeles, California (818) 904-6339
Boston, Massachusetts (617) 424-0510	Denver, Colorado (303) 969-7750	New York, New York (212) 264-4730
Charlotte, North Carolina (704) 344-6144	Detroit, Michigan (313) 259-1875	Philadelphia, Pennsylvania (215) 597-8313
Chicago, Illinois (708) 562-1740	Kansas City, Kansas (913) 551-6711	Seattle, Washington (206) 728-5314

Copies of these publications can be purchased from the U.S. Government Printing Office.

Superintendent of Documents
U.S. Government Printing Office
P.O. Box 371954
Pittsburgh, PA 15250-7954
(202) 512-1800

There are also private sector databases you can subscribe to and use for your research.

Ovid Technologies	**Knowledge Index**
(800) 955-0906	(800) 334-2564
www.ovid.com	
Dow-Jones News Retrieval	**NEXIS EXPRESS**
(800) 522-3567	(800) 843-6476
djinteractive.com	

For analyzing your sector and industry growth rates, you will need to know the growth rate of the gross domestic product (GDP). The Bureau of Economic Analysis uses the GDP rather than the gross national product (GNP) as the primary measure of United States production. International guidelines use the GDP as the standard for economic accounting. You can find the growth rate of the GDP and other growth rates in *U.S. Industry & Trade Outlook*, an annual joint publication by the U.S. Department of Commerce and The McGraw-Hill Companies. It provides data on production for the previous year and forecasts for the current year.

You can also find the GDP and the gross state product (GSP) of every state — by industry — going back the last twenty years on the Internet.

U.S. Bureau of Economic Analysis
www.bea.gov/

You can use the GSPs by comparing the growth rate of your state GSP with the growth rate of your industry in your state. You can also compare the growth rates of your sector and industry in your state with those nationally. Having all the numbers is the first step; analyzing them to see the picture they portray is the basis for your industry analysis.

The sources mentioned above allow you to do all the research yourself; however, you can shortcut much of this if you purchase the results from companies that publish detailed analyses of what is acceptable or normal in your industry. These companies publish financial data and provide averages for nearly every major standard financial entry, such as sales, gross profit, net profit — in terms of dollars and percent of revenue — broken down by SICs and further classified by different sizes of companies based on sales volume categories:

Industry Norms and Key Business Ratios
Dun & Bradstreet (Headquarters)
One Diamond Hill Road
Murray Hill, NJ 07974-1218
(908) 665-5000
(800) 234-3867
FAX: (908) 665-5803
Internet: www.dbisna.com/customer/menu.htm

Annual Statement Studies
Robert Morris Associates
P.O. Box 8500 S-1140
Philadelphia, PA 19178
(800) 677-7621
FAX: (215) 446-4100
e-mail: pubs@rmahq.org

Almanac of Business and Financial Ratios by Leo H. Troy
Prentice Hall Direct
113 Sylvan Avenue
Englewood Cliffs, NJ 07632
(201) 592-3252
(800) 643-5506
FAX: (800) 835-5327
Internet: www.prenhall.com/mischtm/order_fr.html

Economic Sector

In your industry analysis summary, you will be reporting the economic sector that your industry is in as identified by the first two digits in your NAICS number. From the foregoing sources, research your sector on every geographic level — national, state, and county or city — for total revenue, total units of products or services sold, and total employment using annual figures over the last three or five years.

Sector Maturation

You can determine if your sector is growing, and whether growth is slow, moderate, or fast, by comparing the national growth rate of your sector with the growth rate of the GDP. If it is not growing, determine whether it is stable or possibly even declining. To analyze the same economic trends for your sector growth in your state, compare the state growth rate of your sector with the GSP for your state. Businesses are rarely in two economic sectors. If yours is, research both sectors. If one sector is clearly dominant for your business, then research it for your main analysis, and include brief sector information on the less important one.

Also, while you are doing the research, determine if your subsector has any difference in its growth rate from your economic sector. If differences are significant, then you may want to include the information about these differences in your business plan, otherwise omit this category.

Industry

In which industry, or industries, is your business? This is identified by the first five digits of your NAICS number. If your business is in more than one industry, research all the geographic levels (national, state, and local) for sales, units sold, total employees, and profits. Where available, get the annual figures for the past three or five years.

Industry Maturation

Industry maturation is measured using four objective levels: new, if less than ten years; expanding, if the annual change in the total dollars of sales in the industry is increasing faster than the growth rate of the GDP; stable, if the annual change in total sales somewhat matches the growth rate of the GDP; and declining, if the annual change in total sales is less than the growth rate of the GDP.

Total revenue and total units of products or services sold are measures of the size and growth of an industry. For an industry analysis, tabulate the annual figures for three or five previous years with projections for the current and future years. From this, you can calculate the national industry growth rate as a percentage of growth through each of the years you've chosen. Then compare these percentages of growth per year with the percentage rate of growth of the GDP for the same year. Is your industry new, expanding, stable, or declining?

Also compare the state growth rate of your industry with the GSP for your state to determine the same economic growth trends for your sector in your state. These results are usually available from state economic development departments. Record them for your industry and your state to use in your industry analysis below. Once you have gathered all the information and completed the calculations, you are ready to write your industry analysis. The first step is the industry summary.

Industry Analysis Summary

The first segment of your industry analysis is a short narrative summary of the significant points in this section. Like the other opening summaries, write this one after you have finished the section, so you can emphasize the important results of each segment and present them in order.

- Cover the best or unique features of the industry description.
- State your business economic sector.
- Describe your sector's growth level as slow, moderate, or fast.
- Identify your industry and describe its size and rate of growth as compared with the gross domestic product.
- Label your industry's level of maturation, as expanding or stable — supported by the actual growth rate percentage.
- Include trends or factors that affect your industry.
- Explain industry opportunities you consider important to the future of your business.

Remember, this is a summary. You will present the details needed to support your conclusions throughout the rest of this section.

> ### Industry Analysis Summary   Kona Gold Coffees
>
> Kona Gold Coffees is in the coffee roast industry in the manufacturing economic sector. While manufacturing is stable, growing with the population base, the coffee roast industry is expanding moderately fast, currently at about 9 percent+ for the U.S. in the last two years, much faster than the gross domestic product which was at its highest in this decade, 3.9 percent last year. Our local market in Hawaii is similar, increasing at 8.5 percent for the last four years.
>
> In Hawaii, as of last year there were/are eleven companies in the coffee roast industry, with 198 employees, and sales of $40.3 million. While the industry is characterized by two diverse and different company sizes, the overall trend in the industry is to manufacture products of much higher quality for the new markets in gourmet coffee for coffee bars and home consumption. For a typical smaller company such as ours in Hawaii, industry standards are 61 percent of total employees for producing inventory and 39 percent of total employees for non-cost of sales support. These proportions are similar to the ratio of cost of sales to gross profit, 62.4 percent to 37.6 percent. Industry obstacles are high capitalization costs and tough market penetration for both large and small companies; and additionally, developing supply and distribution channels for small companies. The greatest opportunities lie in the market niches and customer specialization in answering the various demands of the new trend in gourmet coffee which is expected to increase for yet another 15 years.

Industry Description

After your industry summary, describe your industry. Identify your NAICS number or numbers. If you have relied on comparative data for their older SIC counterparts, then identify the corresponding SIC numbers. Give the Census Bureau's description of your economic sector based on the first two digits of your NAICS number, and give the other NAICS hierarchic levels' descriptions: subsector, industry group, and industry.

Include your industry's total sales in terms of dollars nationwide for the most recent year. State the range of companies from smallest to largest in terms of dollars in annual sales in your industry and the total number of companies or establishments in your industry in the United States. As to competition within the industry, indicate whether companies in your industry compete around the globe, nationwide, within specific regions, within large cities, on a local level, or a combination of any these.

Describe the dominant company profile in your industry, whether it is composed mostly of a few large companies, small companies, or other grouping. Describe the common elements that best characterize all companies in your industry: size, relative quality, relative pricing, specialization, methods of production, types of products or services, customer profile, market segments, methods of sales, or other. Include these three other characteristics.

- Maturity. State how long most companies have been in business: less than seven years, eight to fifteen years, or over fifteen years.
- Management. State whether most companies in your industry are publicly held, large corporations, subsidiaries of large corporations, professionally managed, or owner-operated.
- Customer loyalty. Describe whether customers of most companies in your industry are loyal to one product or service, loyal to one company, ambivalent to customer loyalty, ambivalent to product or service loyalty, or constantly switching between companies or between products or services.

If companies in your industry are broken down into industry categories, identify them and their relative size in terms of dollars of annual sales in a table (the different industry categories are identified by the number in the sixth position of the NAICS code):

Industry Categories   **Size in Dollars**

1.
2.

As a final topic of your industry description, describe any notable changes occurring in your industry such as undergoing consolidation, a trend toward specialization, an infusion of major corporations or new companies, a shift in power of industry leaders, or an exodus of small companies or recent power players.

Industry Description   Kona Gold Coffees

Specifically, our industry is defined as the roasted coffee industry by the U.S. Census Bureau. Our older SIC number was 2095 until the 1997 system changed. Our new NAICS number is 311920. This identifies our sector, 31, as manufacturing; our subsector, 311, as food manufacturing; our industry group, 3119, as other food manufacturing; and our industry, 31192, as coffee and tea manufacturing.

Last year in the United States, the gross domestic product was $8,110.9 billion. Our sector, manufacturing, represented 17 percent of this, while our industry group represented 8.6 percent of our sector, or $118.5 billion in shipped goods. Shipped sales for our specific industry totaled $3.5 billion from 239 total companies with 45 percent of those having 20 or fewer employees. The total employee base was 15,310 with 64 employees per company on average, showing that 55 percent of the companies dominate our industry. These compete worldwide, especially with many South American companies.

The dominant company profile in this industry is characterized as: 300 employees, annual sales of $58,000,000, in business for more than 15 years, and professionally managed. The secondary profile is quite the opposite: 18 employees, annual sales of $4,580,000, new — averaging less than 8 years in business, and family run. Even with this diversity in companies

(continued)

> **Industry Description** (continued) Kona Gold Coffees
>
> within the industry, the common features are the product in general, coffee; the overall market, coffee-drinkers; processing techniques; and relative pricing of the mainstream products. Generally, among the large establishments, there is an above average consumer loyalty from individuals who favor one brand of coffee, and are consequently, company loyal. For the small companies, customer loyalty exists but falls within a much wider spectrum: both end-users and retailers are loyal for specific offerings of products while retailers alone are loyal for a specific processor service, and there are specific micro-loyalties (loyalties to specific varietals, specific blends, geographic regions, coffees from a specific elevations, and climates). Other industry categories in this industry group are very unrelated — seafoods, potato chips, manufactured ice, macaroni and spaghetti, and food preparations — and are not relevant to this report.
>
> The major change in the industry has been the widespread increase in specialized retail coffee establishments, now numbering 15,000. According to the Specialty Coffee Association of America, SCAA, since 1985 the specialty coffee business has risen from a multi-million dollar industry to a multi-billion dollar industry and is not likely to peak until the year 2015. While these are on the outskirts of the coffee manufacturing industry, they have become new focus customers for manufacturers and because of the increasing trend of their end-users, the overall demand for coffee manufacturing has increased on average 9 percent per year since 1996 and is expected to continue for many years to come.

Industry Size and Maturation

The style of presentation for this segment depends on the complexity of your findings for the size and growth rate of your sector and industry. If possible, use a narrative description limited to one to three paragraphs. On the other hand, if the material is complicated, it might be easier to convey your key points with a short sentence or two introducing a matrix of your findings, followed by a descriptive conclusion.

Size of Economic Sector in the U.S.

For the size of your economic sector, compare your sector's total number of sales, total number of establishments, number of employees, and annual payroll with these averages for all sectors. In your industry analysis, either show these numbers in a table or descriptively label your findings as high, above average, near average, below average, or low. Include the total dollars of sales, the total number of establishments, the number of employees, and the annual payroll in your sector for the most recent year.

Growth Rate of Economic Sector

First, locate the total sales in dollars for your sector for the most recent year and the last three or five years. Calculate the percentages of change. Then compare the percentages of change for your sector with the GDP in the same years. If your sector's sales increased more than the comparable GDP increases, your sector is expanding. If change percentages for your sector are higher than the GDP and getting higher every year, your sector is expanding fast. If they are higher, but the trend is nearly the same, only on a higher plateau, your sector is expanding moderately. If they are slightly above the average GDP every year, your sector is expanding slowly. If they equal the average GDP, your sector is stable. But if the average percent of change for your sector is lower than the average GDP, your sector is declining.

Do this same comparison for your sector in your state with the state's GSP, then draw a conclusion about the growth rate. Is it expanding fast, expanding moderately, expanding slowly, stable, or declining?

Size of Industry

For your industry analysis, show, for the most recent year, the size of your industry on the national level compared to the size of your sector for the topics shown in the table.

	Industry	Sector
Total number of sales		
Total number of establishments		
Total number of employees		
Annual payroll		

You can describe these numbers in a narrative instead of a table if you prefer. Use the same topics to compare the size of your industry in your state with your sector in your state. Finally, if important to your industry, show your city or county figures and compare them to the state or national changes for your industry as a third description of your industry's size.

Growth Rate of Industry

Now locate the total sales in dollars for your industry in the last three or five years. Calculate the percentages of change up to the most recent year. Then compare the percentages of changes of your industry with the GDPs for each of these same years. The results are interpreted the same as in the economic sector growth rates discussion above.

Do this same comparison for your industry in your state with the state's GSP, then draw a conclusion about the growth rate. Is it expanding fast, expanding moderately, expanding slowly, stable, or declining? Finally, if it is important to your industry and you can locate the total number of sales in your city or county for the past three or five years, compare them to the state or national changes for your industry.

From the growth trend of the past three or five years and from estimates of the GDP and GSP for the next year, make projections about the future growth rate of your industry, on national, state, and local levels. This can be stated here or included as part of your discussion of trends below.

Industry Size and Maturation — Kona Gold Coffees

The following table shows a national comparison of the size of our sector to the average:

Last Year in U.S.

Sector comparison	Manufacturing	Average Sector
Sales	$3.5 trillion	$0.7 trillion
Number of companies	444,166	368,317
Employment	21,184,392	5,072,712
Annual payroll	$650.6 billion	$123.7 billion

The growth rate of the manufacturing sector is stable, as shown in the next table, and compares equally with the gross domestic product.

Growth in U.S.	GDP	Manufacturing Sales	Percent
Three years ago	3.5	$3,181 trillion	
Two years ago	2.3	$3,254 trillion	2.29
One year ago	3.5	$3,365 trillion	3.40
Last year	3.5	$3,496 trillion	3.89

The next table shows a comparison of the manufacturing sector with all industries in the state of Hawaii.

Last Year in Hawaii

Sector comparison	Manufacturing	All Industries
Sales	$7.9 billion	$64.8 billion
Number of companies	1,003	31,135
Employment	17,311	440,656
Annual payroll	$0.5 billion	$11.4 billion

In Hawaii, the manufacturing growth has been consistent with the rest of the U.S. — stable — although the GSP for Hawaii has not been.

Growth in Hawaii	GDP	Manufacturing Sales	Percent
Three years ago	1.1	$7.3 billion	
Two years ago	−2.1	$7.1 billion	−2.74
One year ago	−0.1	$7.6 billion	7.04
Last year	2.4	$7.9 billion	3.94

And here's how our industry compares with the sector in both the U.S and Hawaii:

Last Year in U.S.

Sector comparison	Manufacturing	Coffee and Tea
Sales	$3.5 trillion	$3.5 billion
Number of companies	444,166	239
Employment	21,184,392	15,310
Annual payroll	$650.6 billion	$490 million

(continued)

> ### Industry Size and Maturation (continued) Kona Gold Coffees
>
> **Last Year in Hawaii**
>
> | Sector comparison | Manufacturing | Coffee and Tea |
> |---|---|---|
> | Sales | $7.9 billion | $40.3 million |
> | Number of companies | 1,003 | 11 |
> | Employment | 17,311 | 198 |
> | Annual payroll | $0.5 billion | $6.3 million |
>
> However, for our industry, coffee and tea, the growth rate is expanding, as can be seen by the next two tables:
>
> | Growth in U.S. | GDP | Coffee Sales | Percent |
> |---|---|---|---|
> | Three years ago | 3.5 | $2.8 billion | |
> | Two years ago | 2.3 | $2.9 billion | 3.57 |
> | One year ago | 3.5 | $3.2 billion | 10.34 |
> | Last year | 3.5 | $3.5 billion | 9.38 |
>
> | Growth in Hawaii | GDP | Manufacturing Sales | Percent |
> |---|---|---|---|
> | Three years ago | 1.1 | $31.6 million | |
> | Two years ago | −2.1 | $34.5 million | 9.18 |
> | One year ago | −0.1 | $37.5 million | 8.70 |
> | Last year | 2.4 | $40.3 million | 7.47 |
>
> As can be seen by these tables, our industry is expanding faster than the gross domestic product and might be described as expanding moderately fast. The local market for the end-user is more consistent with tourism which will be analyzed in the market analysis. As to speculation about future growth, see the next segment.

Industry Trends and Impact Factors

Nearly every industry has trends that cause sales to go up and down. To successfully deal with these, you need to identify them and recognize their impact on your industry and your business. The most common trends that affect an industry are economic swings and seasonal changes, especially holidays. Other common impact factors are distribution and supply channels, geographic trends and differences, regulatory changes, and technological advancements. Analyze each of these for yourself and decide its effect on your industry.

Is your industry sensitive to economic swings? Often, recessions affect expensive products and services, or big-ticket items, especially those in the luxury categories. The effects are a downturn in sales. However, sales for some industries increase during recessions such as for divorce attorneys, discount stores, and used cars. Some that are virtually unaffected are low-cost items and necessities.

Do seasons and holidays affect your industry? Most retail industries have specific times of the year that are up and down. Most holiday times are the worst for real estate sales and the best for florists, while the Christmas season produces the highest sales of the year for other retailers. Does your industry experience better or worse sales in summer, winter, or for back-to-school days?

High-volume periods for candy sales are Valentine's Day, Easter, and Mother's Day. The wedding industry prepares for June. Sales for outdoor and patio furniture, swimming pools, and boats are stronger in spring and summer than the other half of the year. If seasonal trends influence your industry, adjust your financial pro formas to account for these.

Do distribution and supply channels affect your industry? Is your industry locally dependent upon one main distributor or supplier for your product or service line? If the answer is yes to either or both, then your local industry may get into trouble if your distributor or supplier does. Your costs may be proportionately dependent on these sources and out of your control. If they shut down, your business may have a serious glitch. It is important to check out and even line up alternate suppliers for raw materials and inventory and alternate distributors for your products or product lines.

How does your geographic location influence your industry — a possible overlap of seasonal effects. For example, if you are in a Sun Belt zone, sunglasses and swim gear are a year-round business. Tourism, mountain gear, marine supplies, and snow equipment all enjoy benefits of the correct geographic location.

Can changes in government regulations, whether county, municipal, state, or federal, drastically alter your industry? Regulatory changes have actually been the basis for founding many industries while causing others to falter. For instance, if your industry depends on insurance benefits or Medicare and Medicaid, what changes are you facing?

Finally, how do technological advancements affect your industry? Changes in technology have revamped the entire operations of businesses and often changed the whole face of an industry, such as technological advancements in production and assembly, accounting and administration, access to information, fulfillment, inventory and cash flow control, and marketing. The Internet is one of the more recent technological changes. Could your industry someday be wiped out by online sales or could it be enhanced by them? No one has a crystal ball, but indicators exist that, if read properly, can predict trends and their effects.

For this segment of your industry analysis, write a narrative covering all industry trends and impact factors that affect your business, and explain how you plan to deal with them. If you have accounted for their impacts in your business planning by adjusting your market and marketing plan, advertising plan, sales forecast, financial pro formas, or other areas, mention the adjustments in this segment and direct the reviewer's attention to the later sections of your plan where the actual adjustments are dealt with. There you can repeat brief explanations of why the adjustments are made to account for these industry trends and impact factors.

Industry Trends and Impact Factors   Kona Gold Coffees

Traditionally, the coffee roasting industry has been insensitive to economic swings in the U.S. However, when South American economies have been in trouble, the supply of coffee from those countries decreases and prices go up. Additionally, while the growers of coffee are subjected to many seasonal, climatic, and agricultural impacts, the roasting industry is only affected by these when supply is low or prices are high. Strikes and labor disputes between growers and pickers, growers and transportation, shipping and other distribution channels can all affect supply and pricing. For the coffee roasting industry, these impacts have not caused a significant decrease in sales by consumers. Over the last fifty years, the industry's growth has increased more than the gross national product has, and also, as recently measured, more than the gross domestic product has.

Technologically, there are experiments underway for increasing coffee production, but these have more impact on the agricultural industry. However, if successful, these will mean better supplies of raw materials for the coffee roasters. Because of the latest trend in coffee buying (below), the likelihood of over supply is minimal, and should be of minimal impact to the coffee roasting industry. Other technology in food processing manufacturing has improved productivity and capacity. Kona Gold Coffees is opening with the latest equipment available and will continue to monitor technological advances. We follow trade journals and articles published by the SCAA and their members, and will attend annual trade shows to stay abreast of the latest technology in production, fulfillment, information retrieval, distribution, and sales.

The most exciting change in the industry has been the trend toward gourmet coffees, starting in Seattle in the United States, popular before that in Italy. This has more dramatically affected the retail coffee industry in the form of '90s style coffee bars. As one article from Northwest Imports notes, this "trend that started in Seattle with a mild craving for a good cup of joe [has] filtered down the coast to California [and] is now sweeping eastward like a western prairie fire fueled by fields of fresh roasted espresso beans." Another source, *Glamour* magazine, states that coffee bars are the "in place to meet people in the 1990s."

Supported by this new retail trend, the SCAA predicted retail sales of specialty coffee for home consumption would double between 1989 and 1999 from $1.5 billion to more than $3 billion annually with an additional $1.5 billion from retail and service food sales such as coffeehouses and kiosks. Even in Seattle where it began and would be thought to be reaching a saturation point, the trend has continued. Espresso coffee carts can be found in Nordstrom department stores, the University of Washington, Microsoft corporation, Boeing, the Tacoma airport, in major banks, hospitals, and retail food chains. These have begun to infiltrate other states as well, especially California and Hawaii. They offer a wide variation in location, size, and style of operation — only requiring a minimum of 200 square feet.

Moreover, this trend is international. Last year the SCAA reported that coffee out sold tea in England for the first time in this century. Italy's 60 million people are supported now by 20,000 specialty coffee operations. Comparing this saturation level to that of the United States, one can see that we have a long way to go: 260 million people supported currently by only 15,000 specialty coffee operations.

Industry Standards

In every industry there are financial standards, and you should know all of the industry standards that pertain to your business.

Some of the more common industry standards are:

- Returns and allowances of gross sales
- Credit terms
- Sales commission percentage
- Retail markup
- Distributor markup

Manufacturing and assembly and wholesale companies need to know the industry standard fulfillment costs. Also, manufacturing and assembly companies need to know the industry standard for cost of labor, cost of materials, and cost of overhead items for products. There are also standards for the breakdown of inventory categories: percentages of materials, work in progress, and finished product of your total inventory.

You can order an industry financial report for your new company from Dun & Bradstreet or one of the other private investor service organizations. Such a report will compare your start-up financial statement with others in the same industry and provide you with the numbers for several — usually three — different sized companies based on sales volumes. You can get an idea of standard inventory turnover, standard profit margins, and many, many others. Besides all the financial entries, they also provide most of the popular business ratios which you can use here and later in your pro formas (Chapter 10).

If you have ratios of comparable companies from Dun & Bradstreet or Robert Morris Associates, show the industry information that supports your industry standards in this segment. These industry standards can also be calculated from census bureau reports.

Industry Standards   Kona Gold Coffees

For SIC 2095 and NAICS 311920, the roasted coffee industry, we have the following standards:

In Hawaii:

Average number of employees: 18

Average number of general and administrative employees: 7

Average number of production workers: 11

Average payroll of general and administrative employee: $39,975

Average payroll of production worker: $30,052

Average payroll benefits and taxes: 13%

In U.S.:

Sales: 100%

Industry credit terms: 30 days (both collection and payment)

Cost of Sales: 62.4% as follows:

    Cost of materials, supplies, shipping: 57.3%

    Cost of rent and equipment: 1.8%

    Cost of labor: 2.7%

    Cost of fuel and electricity: 0.6%

Gross profit: 37.6%

Inventory on-hand: 7.8% of sales (100.0%) as follows:

    Finished product: 3.8% of sales (39.1% of inventory)

    Work-in-process: 0.9% of sales (11.6% of inventory)

    Materials, supplies, fuel: 3.1% of sales (49.3% of inventory)

Industry Obstacles

Is your industry too well established for competition to break into easily? This is one of many examples of industry obstacles, sometimes referred to as barriers to entry. Use the research from your industry analysis to identify the major obstacles for entry into your industry.

The most common obstacles are high capitalization costs, complex technological needs, formidable regulatory approvals, expensive promotional costs, cyclical economic extremes, domination by large stabilized companies, market shift to one-stop shopping, industry consolidation where large companies expand by driving small companies out or acquiring them, or dominant firms increase their control.

For this segment, list the most common obstacles for your industry and state how you expect to overcome or offset them.

Industry Obstacles   Kona Gold Coffees

For large companies, the major obstacle for entry into the industry is market penetration of markets that are currently dominated and maintained by large stabilized companies experiencing some industry consolidation. A second major obstacle for large companies is expensive capitalization costs.

For small companies, the major obstacle for entry into the industry is equipment costs. Even for a small processor, used equipment can be expensive. The second major obstacle is distribution. Other obstacles are freshness (shelf life) — storage and inventory turnover, production facilities, proximity to supply and distribution channels, industrial locations, production management, knowledge of the latest technology, and, especially today, knowledge of the product (complicated by the variations of varietals, blends, processing procedures), and reaching the end-consumer markets for these.

Industry Opportunities

For the last segment of your industry analysis, report what you found that affects your industry opportunities. In a paragraph, be as specific as you can and use statistics where applicable. Pay close attention to cause and effect. Look for opportunities within this section to report on, or forecast with, each of your findings.

Opportunities can be found in strategies, see Chapter 5. Look at your industry for the possibility of eventually capturing market share or even dominating it by developing some of the strategies in Chapter 5 for your business: lowest price, best quality, most creative, specialized, most prolific, best customer service, best at solutions, most innovative, most technological, developing a new market, finding a niche market, dominating a market trend, best customer-focus, best marketing, most sales, best management, best at one function, and most professional. Is there an opportunity in your industry for you to excel using any of these strategies? If so, include the opportunities that exist and which of these strategies you believe your company can most readily exploit.

Industry Opportunities   Kona Gold Coffees

A profile of the industry has shown two very distinct types of companies within this industry: the large companies of 300 employees and the smaller ones with 18 employees. The large plants mostly overlap with the agricultural sector and have their own producing farms. Since this industry covers the entire field of coffee roasting, there is a huge overlap between these big companies that cover processing of green coffee to stocking worldwide retail shelves, and the smallest companies that buy brown (preroasted) coffee, grind, package, and distribute to retailers, or sell retail on a very small scale.

While the large companies are usually price-driven, and rarely quality-driven, the small companies prosper because many have found specialized market strategies. This is due to the international and, especially, the national trend toward coffee bars and gourmet coffee for restaurants and home consumption. It has been estimated that this particular demand represents about 27 percent of the overall market and is expanding fast. The larger companies are for the most part answering the needs of the other 73 percent of the market which is stable, growing only as the population does. This condition in the industry allows the smaller companies to be postured for many different specialized markets increasing in market size and in market types.

Important Points to Remember

- Take advantage of the Internet whenever possible for business plan research. It's fast, convenient, and saves time.
- The U.S. Census Bureau has numerous publications available regarding industry and business economic statistics that can be used to develop comparative ratios — much of this is also available to the public through Internet websites.
- Usually the best source for industry information is the key trade organization for your industry — much of your best research data can be obtained from its Internet website.
- The Internet is one of several recent technological changes that impacts greatly the way commerce is transacted. Consider how your industry will someday be changed by online sales. Could it be enhanced, modified, or wiped out by it?
- Use the results of your findings to develop your opportunities.

Having completed your industry analysis, remember to return to your industry summary to emphasize the highlights of your findings in the sequence used within the text of this chapter.

Thus far, your business plan has covered your company and your industry analysis. Now, your business plan reviewers are ready to zoom in on the market and your competition and to see how your company is positioned to capture its market share. The market and the competition are the subjects of the next chapter.

Chapter 4

Market and Competition

... only by supplying what the market wants, and not by your efforts to impose your merchandise, will you get your maximum share of the market's potential.
— WALTER H. LOWY

If you have already decided on your product or service lines, then you already believe in them. But, are they better mousetraps than the competition's? One sure way to build a better mousetrap is to know the mouse. For any business, it is imperative to know who the customers are and to evaluate whether or not the products or services meet their needs. To identify your customers, you must address not only who they are, but also what they want. You can only plan a strategy of marketing and sales once you know the answers to those two questions.

To determine their market, many start-up companies often pay significant fees for private consultants who specialize in these studies while others conduct their own investigations to understand their market. You can research your market for yourself, as well. You can find everything through the same sources as given for your industry analysis in Chapter 3. An excellent book for guiding you through your own market research is David B. Frigstad's *Know Your Market,* published by The Oasis Press.

The segments in this section encompass a detailed report on your market and competition, including:

- Market and competition summary
- Market description – segments and target market
- Market size and trends
- Competition identification

- Main competitors
- Competitor analysis
- Market share
- Customer needs
- Market obstacles
- Market opportunities

Market and Competition Summary

In the opening paragraph of your business plan, summarize the elements of this section. Point out and emphasize the aspects that are important for your business from the findings about your overall market segments, target market, customer profile, market size and trends, growth rate projections, your competition, market share, customer needs, market obstacles, and market opportunities.

Market and Competition Summary — Kona Gold Coffees

As a result of the growing trend in coffee bars, there is a new awareness of gourmet coffees. In part from this and coupled with the growing reputation of Kona coffees as the premier coffees in the world, a new market is emerging for the specialized gourmet coffee drinker in search of fine Kona coffees. These trends have created a tremendous opportunity in the market. It is our goal to respond to this growing market niche.

This specialized consumer market is high-end, quality oriented. Our target market will be both retailers that sell to the end consumer as well as some end consumers through direct sales.

Our customer analysis shows three target markets: retailers in Hawaii, retailers on the mainland, and consumers through Internet and direct mail sales. Since the end user is the most important consideration for all three of these markets, we have established the consumer profile of our primary consumer.

Our competition in general and our main competitors in particular are not responding to this need; instead, selling only their own brands of coffee with no apparent plans to respond to this new market niche. We have conservatively estimated our market share with all other Hawaiian companies in our business at 4 percent of the total of sales based on last year's figures. For our first year we should have sales of $1,612,000.

Market Description — Segments and Target Markets

To write your market description, you will need to develop a market analysis. A market analysis helps you understand:

- Who your customers are,
- Why they use your products or services,
- How many customers are in your market, and
- How you can reach them.

Market Analysis Overview

A market analysis identifies your market by breaking it down in several different ways. The first overall category is called market segmentation, a breakdown of your market into different segments of buyers who will buy the products or services for basicly different reasons. Common ways of separating your market are by geographic segments (for example, 20 percent buyers from the south side, 10 percent buyers from across the river, and 70 percent from downtown) and by type of end-user (for example, 15 percent business offices, 5 percent dental offices, and 80 percent consumers).

In the process of doing your market analysis after your market segments are defined, you can focus on those that are the best match for your products or services. These make up your target market. The process is taken one step further by using a customer analysis to break down your target market into a customer profile. However, this is a little more complicated since you can end up developing as many as seven or more different customer analyses to get to the two objectives: a customer profile and a consumer profile.

Market Segmentation

In developing a market analysis, you start by defining how your market is segmented. Most markets tend to be segmented in different ways, such as by price point, product or service features, product function, specialty, sales method, delivery method, geography, consumer groups, or any combination of these. For example, a popular combination is a market composed of consumers who can be broken down into segments of three financial classes: buyers interested in high quality or brand names (product or service features) who are less concerned with price (price point), buyers who are in the midrange and find a balance between quality and price, and buyers who are most concerned about price. These are basic segments.

Decide how your market is segmented. Then prioritize the segments and assess the two or three most important for your business and use a table to define them as a percentage of your total market, as in the Kona Gold Coffees example.

Target Market

The customer segments that are your customers are your target market. To identify your target market, you must match what you sell at what price and how you sell it with the needs of consumers and customers in your targeted market segments. Customers can be both individual consumers and commercial customers (businesses, professional associations, and institutions). If the end-user of your products or services is not your direct customer, you have two target markets: your direct customer (your distributor, retail business, or other middleperson) and their direct customers (the end-user or end-consumer).

If your direct customers are consumers (individuals), you can identify your target market by focusing closer on your market segments to identify the most precise view of your target market. This is called a consumer profile. To get to this close-up of your consumer profile, you have four tools available to you.

- Customer analysis
- Consumer demographic analysis
- Consumer psychographic analysis
- Consumer geographic analysis

If you have commercial customers in addition to consumers, as your customer analysis will show, then you would want to analyze your commercial customers using these tools.

- Customer demographic analysis
- Customer psychographic analysis
- Customer geographic analysis

Each can be compiled on your type of customer in your target market. For example, if your target market is comprised of consumers, retail businesses, or medical offices, you might want to produce the following analyses to determining your target market.

- Consumer psychographic analysis
- Retail-business psychographic analysis
- Medical-office psychographic analysis

You can get very specific if you want to, but it is seldom necessary for a start-up business. Consider which of these tools are most important for your business and your customer identification. Most start-up businesses will benefit from a combination of consumer analyses, so these will be covered to demonstrate the basics, and business (customer) analyses will be brought into the discussion where applicable.

Customer Analysis

To focus in on your target market from your market segmentation, start with a customer analysis. From your research, obtain an estimate of the percentages of your total market for each of the customer types: individual consumers and various commercial customers.

If your customers are commercial, are they retail businesses, office businesses, governmental agencies, institutions, or professional associations? What is the size of each? For instance, your research may indicate you can expect to have customers similar to those in this customer analysis.

Customer Types

Commercial	
Businesses	12%
Institutions	6%
Consumers	82%
Total	100%

If you have commercial customers, you can further detect the markets within them. For example, your customers might be accounting, engineering, and law offices. If you know the types of businesses that comprise a significant percent of your sales — as shown in the commercial business analysis example below — list those businesses by their industries and include this information in the exhibits. Institutions are usually tracked separately because they are entirely different customers with different buying characteristics such as government offices, schools, or hospitals. They can also be included in your marketing plan in the exhibits as commercial institutions.

Commercial: Businesses		**Commercial: Institutions**	
Accounting offices	4%	Government offices	2%
Engineering offices	5%	Schools	3%
Law offices	3%	Hospitals	1%
Subtotal	12%	Subtotal	6%

Once you move beyond commercial customers to identifying consumer customers, developing consumer profiles is the best method. You can compile the data yourself (see Chapter 3) then use the several types of consumer analyses mentioned above.

Consumer Demographic Analysis

Consumer demographics identify your consumers by further separating them into segments — expressed as percentages — according to certain criteria. Typically, these are: gender, age, marital status, family size, annual household income, occupation, educational level, residential location (urban, suburban, small town, rural), and home ownership. More thorough demographics will include personal interests, such as:

- What magazines the consumers read,
- What television shows they watch,
- Whether or not they access the Internet and the frequency,
- What their favorite hobbies and sports are,
- What their other forms of entertainment are, and
- What their ethnic and political persuasions are.

While you are conducting your own demographic study, you might want to add to the standard profile categories customized to your business. If your major product is a hot tub, for instance, you may want to know some facts about those consumers who already have hot tubs, to target them for supplies or upgrades.

When you assemble two or more of these customer profile analyses, you can make calculations using data from more than one profile to provide more specific determinations. If you want more detail in your customer profile, you can calculate a percentage from the consumer demographics analysis for your customer analysis. For example, if you can show that 37.6 percent of your consumers are males, out of an individual-consumer base of 82 percent, then 30.83 percent of your total customer base are individual male consumers.

37.6% males out of a 82% individual-consumer base equals 30.83% male consumers

$(37.6 \times .82 = 30.83)$

Each of the figures from your demographics can be broken down using a similar calculation to arrive at various consumer category percentages.

Consumer Demographic Analysis

Sex:	Male	37.6%	Income:	Under $40,000	2.4%
	Female	62.4%		$40,000–$59,999	17.9%
Age:	18–24	2.7%		$60,000–$79,999	36.6%
	25–34	16.9%		Over $80,000	43.1%
	35–44	48.8%	Marital status:	Married	52.7%
	45–54	21.7%		Single	47.3%
	55+	9.9%	Education:	Under 12 yrs.	4.2%
				12–14 yrs.	15.1%
				15–16 yrs.	42.3%
				More than 16 yrs.	38.4%

If your target market is comprised largely of business customers, then you will want to develop and include a customer demographic analysis designed for your business customers. For the demographic information, start with the business' economic sector, subsector, industry group, industry, and U.S. industry from the business' NAICS number. Other categories to include are: business age, estimated annual sales revenue, form of vesting, stage of business (new, established, growing), number of employees, employee turnover, number of locations, and size of facility. These are some of the basics, but you can add other categories tailored to your business.

Consumer Psychographic Analysis

A consumer psychographic analysis is less objective but can help you to know and better understand your consumer needs. It attempts to define the psychological reasons your consumers purchase your products or services. The results can show the indirect and intangible benefits your purchaser derives from the product or service or the indirect and intangible need it fulfills. When this analysis is well designed, it can help you understand consumer buying patterns and buying decisions.

Are your consumers price conscious or brand conscious? Are they conservative or liberal? Are they buying to fill an unfulfilled need or a changing need? Are they impulse buyers or deliberate buyers? Are they emotional or rational? Do they need to be given presentations to purchase? Do they need special closing incentives? Can you identify the psychological factors that influence purchases by Dr. Wizard, Ms. Gadget, Miss Glamour, or Mr. Macho?

These factors are very helpful to know when planning your marketing strategy. Objective characteristics to look for are included in the sample Consumer Psychographic Analysis. If your results seem to add significantly to your understanding of your consumers' needs, make a pie chart of the psychographic segments for your business plan.

If your customers include commercial businesses in addition to consumers, assemble a customer psychographic analysis. Are your business customers free-spending or frugal; are they innovative or slow to change; do they have strong management or strong employee input; and are they business or community leaders or slow to make decisions? Are they technologically oriented?

Design your psychographic research to include information as to what publications they subscribe to and advertise in, and what trade associations they are members of. Is their business new, expanding, or entrenched? Are they union or nonunion? What are their relations between management and employees? These characteristics are merely examples. Again, as in the other analyses, you can customize your customer psychographic analysis with characteristics geared to the target market for your products or services.

Consumer Psychographic Analysis

Behavioral	Yes	No	Self-image	Yes	No
Impulse buyer	☐	☒	Trend setter	☐	☒
Deliberate buyer	☒	☐	Family oriented	☒	☐
Socially responsible	☒	☐	Homemaker	☒	☐
Hedonistic	☐	☒	Technologically adept	☒	☐
Cultural					
Conservative	☒	☐			
Liberal	☐	☒			
Environmentally aware	☒	☐			
Brand conscious	☒	☐			

Consumer Geographic Analysis

The most popular form of consumer geographic analysis starts with a description of the area or areas you intend to serve and identifies the density of your customers in those areas. Areas can be national, regional, state, city, county, or neighborhood segments. Parameters can be chosen to fit your business. For example, consumer categories might be broken down into metropolitan, suburban, or rural locations; commercial customers might be categorized by those along the waterfront, downtown, in the financial district, in the regional mall, or located in a new industrial park.

These surveys and analyses might be readily available from your local Chamber of Commerce or obtainable through *County Business Patterns* from the Census Bureau or by other methods discussed in Chapter 3. If you have an exclusive territory, then most of your customers probably reside in that area, but you should locate where they come from within the various interior divisions of it. A certain percentage of people probably come from outside your area, as well.

Consumer Profile

After you have completed the above research and analyzed it, you can use the results to finish your customer or consumer profile (see the example in Kona Gold Coffees). Completing the study is not an exact science. Naturally, the more accurate the research is, the more accurate the complete analysis is, but because most of your information is approximate, quantifying your market is usually a subjective, rather than objective, process.

For this segment, after you've written your market summary and market analysis and have completed your market profiles, write a description of your market segmentation and your target market. Describe how your market is segmented, give the percentages of these segments, and include a customer or consumer profile. Add any of the tables, charts, and graphs you can develop, similar to those displayed in the example, to support the findings that identify your target market. Explain how your products or services meet the needs of this profile.

If your target market includes commercial customers, show a customer profile comprising the business characteristics from your customer demographic, psychographic, and geographic analyses. For your target market businesses, include industry types, their range of annual sales, their locations, and other known data discovered from these tools.

Market Description – Segments and Target Market   Kona Gold Coffees

In a preopening market study conducted by David Cooper over a ten-month period and using information gathered from our trade organization and retailers, we developed the following market data:

The total coffee market is primarily segmented by price point for standard coffees, but specifically by sales channels and target consumer groups for gourmet coffee. Basically, Kona Gold Coffees has two target markets: our retailers who buy from us, and the end-user who buys from our retailers and directly from us via Internet and direct mail sales. For the retailers, we focus on those that can best reach and serve our end user, so it is our end user that commands most of our market focus. The end-user market for coffee can be broken down into three basic segments: the high-end segment for consumers that are more interested in higher quality or specific varietals and are less concerned about price; the mid-range segment for consumers who want to strike a balance between quality and price; and the majority segment of consumers who are mostly concerned about price.

For gourmet coffee, the local (Hawaiian) market is primarily the high-end consumer with some overlap of the mid-range segment. Grouped together as buyers of high-end coffee, these are segmented:

Basic Market Segments	Hawaii Market	Mainland Market	Internet & Mail
1. Gourmet coffee drinkers	45%	45%	75%
2. Tourists	40%	25%	0%
3. Image buyers	15%	30%	25%

The number one segment in size is defined as gourmet coffee drinkers. It comprises approximately 45 percent of the total local high-end market. And it is growing faster than the total market at the pace of about 7 percent per year. The number two segment in size is defined as tourists (although their reasons vary from the curious about Kona coffee to souvenir and gift shoppers). Tourists comprise approximately 40 percent of the state market, a group growing faster than the total market at a pace of about 14 percent per year. The number three segment in size is image buyers, usually called yuppies, making up approximately 15 percent of the state market. This last group is fairly stable, growing equally with the market and like tourists, have many reasons for buying the product, but most of them fall into image categories.

In addition to the types of the end-users, the market can also be segmented by sales channels. The consumer will purchase our products through resort shops, coffee bars, kiosks, super market delis, restaurants, and other non-resort gift shops. These retailers as well as mail-order and Internet consumers represent a complete cross section of our target market of customer types.

Customer Analyses:

Retail:		Consumers:			
Hawaii retailers	32%	Consumer, Internet & mail	25%		
Mainland retailers	43%	Mail-order	5%		
		Internet	20%	Total	100%

(continued)

Market Description – Segments and Target Market (cont.) Kona Gold Coffees

These have been further identified in the following tables.

Hawaii Retailers		Mainland Retailers	
Resorts (26)	28%	Resorts (10)	4%
Coffee bars (10)	26%	Coffee bars (40)	45%
Super market delis (24)	22%	Super market delis (30)	22%
Restaurants (15)	12%	Discount warehouses (9)	16%
Kiosks (5)	7%	Kiosks (10)	10%
Non-resort gift shops (10)	5%	Non-resort gift shops (20)	3%
Total Hawaii retailers	100%	Total Mainland retailer	100%

As a summary, cross multiplying all of these percentages would yield our best market in this order:

1. Mail order and Internet consumers of gourmet coffee drinkers
2. Coffee bars on the mainland for gourmet coffee drinkers
3. Coffee bars on the mainland for image buyers
4. Mail order and Internet consumers for Image buyers
5. Super market delis on the mainland for gourmet coffee drinkers
6. Hawaiian resorts for gourmet coffee drinkers

Our preopening marketing also discovered the following consumer demographics:

Consumer Demographic Analysis

Sex:	Male	46.2%		Income:	Under $40,000	12.1%
	Female	53.8%			$40,000–$59,999	26.8%
					$60,000–$79,999	38.3%
Age:	18–24	4.1%			Over $80,000	22.8%
	25–34	27.5%		Marital status:	Married	63.4%
	35–44	32.0%			Single	36.6%
	45–54	26.3%		Education:	Under 12 yrs.	7.1%
	55+	10.1%			12–14 yrs.	15.3%
					15–16 yrs.	63.2%
					More than 16 yrs.	14.4%

Taken as a group, our end-user might be defined as the elite — enjoying expensive quality who likes to entertain. Common characteristics of products that serve this market are packaged in presentational style and sold in high-end stores or offered via Internet and gourmet mail order. We are well-suited to serve this market because of our creative packaging and high-end distribution plan.

(continued)

Market Description – Segments and Target Market (cont.) Kona Gold Coffees

Consumer Psychographic Analysis

	Yes	No
Behavioral		
Impulse buyer	☒	☐
Deliberate buyer	☒	☐
Socially responsible	☒	☐
Hedonistic	☒	☐
Cultural		
Conservative	☐	☒
Liberal	☒	☐
Environmentally aware	☒	☐
Brand-conscious	☒	☐
Self-image		
Trend-setter	☒	☐
Family-oriented	☐	☒
Homemaker	☒	☐
Technological adept	☒	☐

Consumer Geographic Analysis

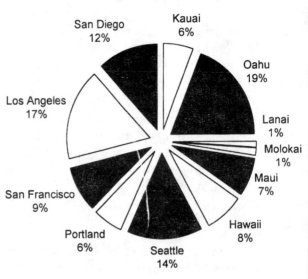

- San Diego 12%
- Kauai 6%
- Oahu 19%
- Lanai 1%
- Molokai 1%
- Maui 7%
- Hawaii 8%
- Seattle 14%
- Portland 6%
- San Francisco 9%
- Los Angeles 17%

Our Primary Consumer Profile

From the market research we can describe our primary consumer profile in terms of the following:

- Gourmet Coffee Drinker
- Female 53.8%
- Age 35–44
- Household income $60,000–$79,999
- Married
- Education 15–16 yrs.
- Both deliberate and impulse buyers
- Socially responsible and hedonistic
- Liberal
- Environmentally aware
- Brand-conscious
- Trend-setter
- Homemaker
- Technologically adept
- Primary purchases from Oahu in Hawaii and Los Angeles on the mainland

(continued)

> ### Market Description – Segments and Target Market (cont.) Kona Gold Coffees
>
> We intend to focus very narrowly on one particular market niche: gourmet coffee lovers of this profile who are not price conscious. Buyers and potential buyers with these needs have not been specifically targeted by any other company, except with one product, not a product mix. While this market niche is small enough not to attract a lot of attention from national corporations, it is large enough for us to realize our growth expectations for the next 5–10 years. It is also a niche that we believe our company will be uniquely qualified to address because of our excellent positioning in the heart of Kona.
>
> Our target consumers tend to be 53.8 percent female, aged 35–44, married, 14–16 years of education, with an annual household income of $60,000–79,999, working full-time or married to a white-collar spouse. Typical occupations include professional people, educators, and personal administrative assistants. They live in suburbs. They tend to read *Entrepreneur* magazine, *Inc.* magazine, *The Wall Street Journal, Gourmet, Architectural Digest,* and *USA Today.* Locally, they tend to listen to KFRC FM and KUMB FM radio stations, they tend to watch A & E, Larry King Live, and David Letterman, as well as premium cable TV movies, and they tend to have e-mail addresses and access the Internet frequently. They often belong to the following community organizations, Outside Circle, Omega Nu, and Toastmasters. They often participate in the following non-business activities, monthly Concerts in the Park, the annual Ironman Triathlon, and the King Kam Parade. Other pertinent characteristics include high-quality dress.
>
> Of particular interest are Hawaiian tourists who, for the most part meet our demographics. Also, because they compose a highly identifiable group with a common question — what is the best Kona coffee — and because they cannot answer this for themselves without purchasing more coffee than they can drink, their specific needs have not been served by any current product line. Ours will.

Market Size and Trends

For your next segment, write a brief description of your market size and trends. Has the research above answered the question: what is the size of your market in terms of customers and consumers? By using your calculations of the market percentages and by doing a little investigation of the population census and the local county or municipal planning departments, you can determine market size and growth rate for your specific geographic sales area.

Do your findings reveal potential for any consumer changes in the future, such as more growth in the target age group, increases in buying habits, more disposable income, or more leisure interests? Is one educational level going to limit an increase of purchases of your products or services? These are only projections, but usually market trends can be anticipated with some basic research.

If your target market includes commercial customers, include the size of your target market and its trends and any projected changes in the market,

such as shifts to smaller companies, home based businesses, or other. After you have completed this review, extract the conclusions you can draw from the calculations about your market size and market trends.

Begin this segment with the current, overall population of your area then describe the percentages of the population that match your consumer and customer profiles. Make comparisons of population, anticipated numbers of customers and overall area in square miles of your sales area or describe it in terms that makes sense for your business, such as by cities, counties, or neighborhoods. Express any trends in your market you can forecast. Can you draw any conclusions about opportunities in the market now and for the future? Here is where to include growth projections of your market size if you can make any.

Market Size and Trends — Kona Gold Coffees

The current population in Hawaii is 1,186,602. However, Hawaii has an enormous tourist traffic per year of another 6,876,140 people. The average stay is 8.38 days. This interpolates to a second annual population base of 157,810 consistently throughout the year, raising the total population to 1,344,412 on average every day of the year. From our best projections, while our primary consumer profile only comprises 5 percent of the Hawaii population, or 59,330; for tourists, this percentage is much higher — 22 percent or 34,718, yielding a total of 94,048 for the primary consumer profile as a major part of our market.

However, when we finished working on our projections, we came back to compare our numbers and from our projections we are conservatively only expecting 1 out of 7 of this market, our primary consumer profile, to buy one product our first year. And, this doesn't include any repeat sales.

For the five mainland cities, the number of consumers with our primary consumer profile is twelve times higher but we have no other research data so it is a more realistic approach to consistently match the expectations of sales with the number, size, and type of retail operations. Doing this we have taken an extremely conservative approach and find that our projections only beg 1.5 percent sales of one sale a year from the large number of consumers that match our primary consumer profile on the mainland in our retailers' cities, not from the whole market.

While the growth in the domestic market for Kona coffee has been increasing in recent years, worldwide interest is now showing promise. The demographic information such as rising income levels, higher education levels, and more familiarity with technology suggests that the overseas markets are ripe for Internet sales. Although sales in overseas markets are currently dwarfed by domestic sales, the firms selling overseas are experiencing very fast growth rates and there is every reason to believe that these will continue for years to come. Eventually, the overseas markets may even be larger than the domestic market.

The most significant development in this marketplace recently has been the baby-boomer and yuppie interest in gourmet everything. It started with connoisseur wines in the 1970s, moved to custom breweries in the 1980s, and has settled in gourmet coffee bars in the 1990s. This trend has now infiltrated home consumption with the implication that packaged coffees in a gourmet presentation will be popular and well-received.

Competition Identification

It is necessary to find as much accurate data as possible about the competition — for your marketing strategy and, if you are seeking financing, for your lenders' or investors' evaluations. Assess all comparable businesses within your sales area, whether they are franchises, chain outlets, or independents. For the next three segments, you will need to conduct a study and compile your own research on the competition. The most common starting point is to check the Yellow Pages for basic information (how many, names, addresses), then make a detailed visual observation with maps.

After this precursory survey, introduce this segment of your market and competition section with a brief summary identifying all of the competitors within your sales area by company name. If you have any specific data that supports a sense of their comparable sizes, such as total number of sales for each or even the number of employees of each, include it with each one to show their relative sizes. A good way to sum up is to take the population of your market area and divide that by the number of competitors in it, including your business, to derive the average number of potential customers for each competitor.

Competition Identification Kona Gold Coffees

From the Census Bureau's County Business Patterns, the SCAA, and a search of the Yellow Pages we have located eleven companies in Hawaii in our industry. Alphabetically these are: Hualalai Slopes Coffee (12 employees), Kauai Mountain Coffee (9 employees), Kealakekua Farms (27 employees), Kona Bayline Coffee (23 employees), Maui Wowy Coffee (4 employees), Mauna Kea Coffee (29 employees), Molokai Coffee (11 employees), Namakua Coffee Processors (15 employees), Ohia Farms (3 employees), Regal Kona Coffee (31 employees), and Sandwich Isles Coffee (34 employees). For these eleven companies, the population of Hawaii, 1,186,602, plus another 157,810 daily tourists, yields a population per capita for each competitor of 122,219 and a factor of .083 of the population per business.

Main Competitors

From the overall list of the competition, identify your main competitors and concentrate on them. There may be as few as one or as many as four or five in your sales area.

Although the procedure is subjective, you can use a tool called a competitor analysis to help you and the reviewer understand how your business compares with the competition. Fill out the form, see the example, using points similar to a grading system. Values are usually one to five with five being the highest appraisal, although sometimes a one-to-ten scale is used.

In assessing each of your competitors, compile a list of factors that would work best for your type of business. Because many considerations are universal, you can make up a worksheet for each competitor using the categories in the Kona Gold Coffees competitor analysis and adding criteria particular to your business. While you will examine many details as you conduct this survey, look for general qualities that assess your competitors' strengths, weaknesses, and keys to success. If you can estimate your competitors' shares of the market, this will help in your calculations.

As you examine your main competitors, prioritize and evaluate their relative business strengths with each other and with your new company. Assign a number as an evaluation of their overall strength. Be as objective as you can for this assessment because you will use this important number later in a calculation to discover your market share.

For other evaluations, compare intangible considerations such as quality of business, image, ambiance, customer service, customer loyalty, employee product knowledge, friendliness, and reputation. Also, compare the more tangible qualities, such as pricing, products or services, years in operation, location, convenience, physical condition, cleanliness, hours of operation, marketing methods, and sales methods.

If the competitors are franchises, compare some of the published franchise data, particularly comparing growth of outlets over the previous three years. What are the corporate strengths of competing franchises in your area? Compare field support services, numbers of corporate employees, growth rates, and numbers of total franchise outlets. This information is readily available in source books such as *The Franchise Redbook*.

If your competitors' ads reveal less competitive prices, particularly poor promotional attempts, or inferior professionalism, use these observations in your evaluation of them.

For this segment, describe your main competitors one at a time by priority of their business strength, addressing these four questions:
- Who are the major competitors?
- What are the keys to their success?
- What are their strengths and weaknesses?
- How do you compare with them?

You will not just report who your main competitors are, but you will describe how they compete. Enter the description here in your business plan, but before you write it, complete and analyze the competitor analysis below. The findings will assist you in material for this description.

As you write this segment and answer the four questions above, include the main focus of each competitor. You will use that information in the main strategy portion of your competitor analysis.

Some examples of main strategy topics are: price, product or service features, quality, expertise, specialization, customer focus, technology, product or service upgrades, distribution, advertising, and sales. Also report whether they are new, growing, stable, or declining.

Main Competitors — Kona Gold Coffees

Competition in Kona coffee companies matches the company profile in our industry across the country, though on a smaller scale. It is divided into two types of companies: larger ones that focus primarily on selling to retailers or wholesalers and are price-driven and the smaller companies that emphasize quality and sell to both retailers and consumers. However, all of these companies have one thing in common that separates them from Kona Gold Coffees. They promote only one brand of coffee, their own, while we will promote several brands with an emphasis on quality.

As the market for Kona coffee continues to mature inside and outside its sphere of influence, buyers have become increasingly discerning and increasingly aware of and interested in the key differences from one competitor's blend to the next. As a result many buyers are placing much added importance on quality coffee and how it tastes and are placing less emphasis on price.

Of the eleven companies in Hawaii, only three promote their own coffee in the type of quality and packaging as ours and target the same retailers to reach our target end-consumer. A detailed competitor analysis is shown below.

Our number one competitor is Kealakekua Farms. With 27 employees and over 10 years in business they are well established in their market. As the competitor analysis shows, they have strong commercial strength, financial resources, a trademark, and their sales do well. This is mainly due to good pricing, updated technology, company friendliness, and strong supply and distribution channels. Their weakness of location, though inconvenient for end-users, has apparently been overcome by time for their supply and distribution systems. However their personnel are underpaid and are poorly motivated. When their retailers' inventory is low, they can provide some delivery. While they do an adequate job of marketing and have a reasonably good customer loyalty, they only offer their own products and will consequently not be competing with Kona Gold Coffees for the same customer specialization and market niche.

Our number two competitor is Maui Wowy Coffee. Their strengths are their location which is excellent for end consumers — their secondary target customer, but not as adequate for their retail market. They have a strong customer loyalty for their product, strong personnel motivation, and a quality product, but they appear overworked with only 4 employees and do not appear to be very friendly and helpful for their walk-in consumers. They have been in business 8 years and appear to be static in the marketplace. Their quality is insured at this point because of strong suppliers, their product knowledge, and their eye-appealing packaging which gives them good perceived value. Their major problem seems to be that they have all the right ingredients to target end consumers if properly managed, but they have tried to focus first on their retail markets, which they are inadequately set up for. Like our number one competitor, Maui Wowy Coffee only offers their own products and will not be competing with Kona Gold Coffees for the same customer specialization and market niche.

Our number three competitor is Kauai Mountain. They have 9 employees and have been in business 5 years. Like the other competitors, they have strong suppliers. They were given a strong grade for commercial strength because of sales volume per employee which is stronger than most small operations and the company appears to be growing. This seems to be in part because of both good pricing and good quality, something hard to achieve. With such a small organization their personnel seem motivated, and friendly, and geared for the primary target customer which is the end user. Although they are located inconveniently for this market, their customer loyalty appears to have offset this in the local Kauai market. While their marketing and packaging is poor, their above average quality affords them extra points in perceived value to the consumer. Like the other two, Kauai Mountain only offers their own products and will not be competing with Kona Gold Coffees for the same customer specialization and market niche.

Competitor Analysis

Once you have completed your survey using your worksheets, create your competitor analysis, a matrix of your findings. At the bottom, total and average the points, and compare the results. You can use these figures and your evaluations to develop the narrative segment, Main Competitors.

Competitor Analysis				Kona Gold Coffees
Item	Kona Gold Coffees	Kauai Mountain	Maui Wowy Coffee	Kealakekua Farms
Commercial strength	2	4	2	5
Years in operation	1	2	3	4
Financial resources	3	2	2	5
Location	5	3	4	1
Production employees	2	3	1	5
Annual sales volume	3	4	2	5
Upgrades, add-ons	5	0	0	0
Main product	5	3	4	3
Pricing	4	4	4	5
Quality	5	4	5	3
Technology	5	3	2	5
Trademarks, patents	5	0	0	0
Perceived value	5	3	4	2
Primary target customer	5	4	4	3
Secondary target customer	5	3	5	2
Main strategy	5	3	3	3
Personnel motivation	5	4	5	1
Friendliness	5	4	2	5
Customer service	5	2	2	3
Customer loyalty	1	4	5	4
Product knowledge	5	3	4	3
Convenience	5	2	4	1
Image or reputation	1	3	4	2
Physical condition	5	2	3	4
Cleanliness	5	2	3	2
Suppliers	5	5	5	5
Distribution	5	3	2	5
Delivery	5	1	1	2
Packaging	5	1	4	3
Marketing	5	1	1	4
Sales competency	5	2	3	3
Total points	132	84	93	98
Average points	4.3	2.7	3.0	3.2

Market Share

Your market share is a percentage estimate of your company's expected share of the total industry sales in your sales area. The easiest but least accurate approach is a per capita estimation. If you were one of ten competitors vying for the market, you would use an objective of 10% of the population. Multiply this by the population and you have your per capita market as an objective. Anyone can see there are some real problems with using this overly simple method. It does not account for differences in competitors, markets already established, and many other factors.

Your market share is a function of the demographics, the quantity and strength of the competitors, the proximity to competitors, and the size of your geographic area. While it is one of the more difficult concepts to objectively quantify, there are several helpful subjective approaches. One of the best is a market share analysis. The objective is to compare your new start-up company with your main competitors.

In column one, list your company, each of your main competitors, and all other competitors grouped together as a single entry. Label your start-up business A. Assume you have three main competitors: B, C, and D. Group all minor competitors as E. Additional columns in the table are for the calculations. Columns two and three use numbers from your competitor analysis.

In column two, list the numbers you have assigned as commercial strengths for your company and for each of your main competitors then an average strength for the others — on a 1 to 5 scale the average is 3.

In column three, list the average points for each of your main competitors and use the average (in this example, 3) for the others.

In column four, list your competitor percentage. If there are ten individual companies in the market (counting those in the group), you would list 10 percent for your company and for each of your main competitors and the balance percentage for the group, so the column totals 100 percent.

Market Share Analysis

Company	Strength Factor		Average Points		One of Ten Competitors		Market Share Calculation
A (your company)	1	×	3.6	×	0.10	=	.36
B (main competitor)	4	×	2.7	×	0.10	=	1.08
C (main competitor)	2	×	3.0	×	0.10	=	.60
D (main competitor)	5	×	3.2	×	0.10	=	1.60
E (group of five)	3	×	3.0	×	0.50	=	4.50
					Total Market Share	=	8.14

Your Market Share is .36 / 8.14 = 4.4%

Finally, the rows are multiplied together and the total of each row is divided by the total of column five to arrive at your market share. In this example, your market share is .36 out of a total of 8.14 or 4.4 percent. This would be one of your expected objectives.

Another method often used is to analyze the census and other trade resources for employee size, payroll, number of establishments, and total sales; and then to calculate their averages and compare them with your start-up company. This will give you an idea of what you can expect for your size of company, all other things being equal. You can make adjustments from there — downward for being a new startup or upward if you feel your strong management, latest equipment, or other reasons will create better results.

After you have developed your market share objective, create a market share distribution. To do this, you need to define your total market in terms of sales (and in some cases, total units), see Industry Size and Maturation, Chapter 3, and Market Size and Trends, earlier in this chapter. For instance, if your market is statewide, it is fairly easy to get the most recent year's total sales from the U.S. Census Bureau. If your market is county wide, you can get these figures from *County Business Patterns,* mentioned in Chapter 3. You may have already assembled the other market totals from other trade resources described in Chapter 3.

In the example, the total sales for these competitors for last year was $45 million. Using the market share percentages above without calculating a possible increase for this year, the market share in dollars as compared to the competitors is shown in the example below.

Market Share Distribution

	Example Business A	Competitor B	Competitor C	Competitor D	All Others E
Sales	$1,980,000	5,985,000	3,330,000	8,820,000	24,885,000
Percent of total	4.4%	13.3%	7.4%	19.6%	55.3%

When you have completed both the market share analysis and the market share distribution, write a final description for your market and competition segment under a heading, Market Share, summarizing the results and emphasizing the important elements of your analysis. If you anticipate increasing your market share because of certain advantages you have over the competition, provide the reasons that support this assumption. This is a good place to use a pie chart to show your market share as compared to your competitors.

Market Share

Kona Gold Coffees

Market Share Analysis

Company	Commercial Strength		Competitor Analysis		Competitor Percentage		Market Share Calculation
Kona Gold Coffees	2	×	4.3	×	8.3% (0.083)	=	.714
Kauai Mountain	4	×	2.7	×	8.3% (0.083)	=	.896
Maui Wowy Coffee	2	×	3.0	×	8.3% (0.083)	=	.498
Kealakekua Farms	5	×	3.2	×	8.3% (0.083)	=	1.328
Others (group of eight)	3	×	3.0	×	66.7% (0.667)	=	6.003
			Total Market Share			=	9.439

Our Market Share: $\dfrac{9.439}{.714} = 0.76 = 7.6\%$

Although it is subjective, based on the numbers assessed for our own commercial strength and competitor analysis, a market share analysis shows that we could have as much as 7.6 percent of the market with these competitors. Using last year's sales of $40.3 million, our share would be $3,062,800.

Using a straight per capita sales basis, our direct percentage 8.3 percent of the total sales would be $3,344,900. But this is a poor figure because we do not have a proven market.

However, dividing sales by the population yields a per capita spending in our industry of $29.97 in sales per person. Multiplying this by the number of people in our primary profile in Hawaii alone sets a forecast of $2,818,618.

Using the ratios from the County Business Patterns from the U.S. Census Bureau for NAICS 311920, we can analytically compare the size of our operation to what we should expect in the way of sales if it were managed properly. Based on the ratios of payroll and inventory to sales in our industry, our total market share (Hawaii, mainland, direct sales) would compute to 4.3 percent of the Hawaiian coffee manufacturers' market using last year's total sales in the ratios. The amount of projected sales would be $1,732,900.

Taking all things into consideration, we believe our market share for the first year to be a reasonably conservative 4 percent of last years sales, which is the projected number that we have included in this business plan and can be seen in comparison with our competitors in the market share distribution below (competitor's numbers based on last year's sales).

Market Share Distribution

	Kona Gold Coffees	Kauai Mountain	Maui Wowy Coffee	Kealakekua Farms	All Others
Total Sales	$1,612,000	$2,015,000	$1,007,500	$5,440,500	$30,225,000
Percent of sales	4.0%	5.0%	2.5%	13.5%	75.0%
Employees	10	9	4	27	148
Payroll	$290,000	$305,190	$135,640	$915,570	$5,018,680

Customer Needs

Now that you have identified your target market and analyzed your competition, review your customer or consumer profiles and the demographics, psychographics, and geographics to assess your buyers' needs. Identify the different benefits your buyer will derive from your products or services. Consider this same question as regards your competition. Consider the tangible and intangible benefits. For example, when a consumer buys a new sports car, the direct benefits are a new mode of transportation, more dependability, possibly more power and more luxury, the protection of warranty, among others benefits. But what about the indirect benefits? These could include happiness, prestige, self-image, and sex appeal, among others.

For this segment, write a brief description of the important customer needs, direct and indirect, that are fulfilled by their buying your products or services. If you find one that surprises you, you may have discovered a customer specialization, a new market, or a market niche. After you have identified the needs, explain how your products or services fulfills them. How are your products or services different from your competitors in addressing these needs? You will need to know the answers to these questions when you formulate your marketing plan in Chapter 7.

Customer Needs   Kona Gold Coffees

The basic need of target customers is to discover the best Kona coffee for themselves. Virtually no competing products address this basic need. Other direct needs that are relatively important include purchasing our products as gifts of assortments. The Kona coffees available do not address these needs as their manufacturers currently only promote their own brands and package them exclusively. However, customers have a need to try several Kona coffees in search of their desire to find their favorite. Retailers who plan to resell our products confirm that this need is not being met by existing alternatives. The average tourist, even as families, are not on holiday long enough to sample more than one or two minimum-sized 7 ounce packages of coffee during their stay. And most do not want to buy seven 7 ounce packages of Blue Ribbon coffee to take home with them even if these were available for the one-stop shopper. For many customers, this need is so prevalent that it is anticipated they will buy our new product simply because it fulfills this need. For indirect benefits, our products fulfill the needs of our customers for improving self-image associated with buying the best.

Market Obstacles

For the next segment of market and competition, include a paragraph or two explaining the obstacles new competition must overcome to enter your market. The obstacles for your specific business and your specific market will have surfaced as you developed your research, analyzed it, and completed your findings. Some examples of possible obstacles for new competition are: substantial startup costs, often the case for manufacturing and assembly companies; increased real estate values; lack of suppliers and distributors; substantial technical expertise, especially for manufacturing and consulting companies; prohibitive governmental regulations; patents; insufficient market; and market saturation, including price wars.

Market Obstacles   Kona Gold Coffees

For large start-up companies, the major obstacle is market penetration of markets currently dominated and maintained by the existing large companies — five of the competitors in Hawaii are in this classification. For these and others, there is also the obstacle of high capitalization costs. For small companies, it takes time to develop their own market for their specific brand. This translates not only into high capitalization costs, but also into a need for more initial working capital to sustain a longer shortfall while spending more money for initial and sustained marketing. For companies to enter our specific niche, they would have to change their entire mission statement and begin promoting brands of other coffee processors, something most will not do as this is viewed as counterproductive to their efforts advanced to date in promoting their own brand above others.

Market Opportunities

For this last segment, write a paragraph reporting your findings that affect your market opportunities. Opportunities are found in strategies. Examine your market research for areas in the market that can be developed by applying some of the market-driven strategies mentioned in Chapter 5.

Is your business capable of being developed as the market-leader — moving quickly to lower prices, increasing advertising, using promotional campaigns, or sacrificing your standard profit margins for short periods of time for some shrewdly timed low-priced offerings? Can you find a new market that is untapped by your competitors to provide a product or service for an unfulfilled need? Can you find a market niche that will set you apart from your competitors, such as better filling their needs? Is there a new trend in the market that you can capitalize on and maximize sales before your competitors do? Are there customers of a specific size, in a specific field, in a specific geographic area, or in a particular stage of development?

Or, are there specific large corporations you could focus on to serve a new, different, or specialized need? Is there a strategic alliance that you could make with a particular company, investor, or association that would allow you to exclusively serve their needs? What other market opportunities can you envision?

> ### Market Opportunities   Kona Gold Coffees
>
> Often, the best opportunities in any market is discovering the market niches or customer specialization that will adequately fill a currently unfulfilled need. Our assessment of the market shows that both retail customers and end consumers have an unfulfilled need for a product such as ours, a presentation package consisting of assorted premium Kona coffees.
>
> Other coffee manufacturers promoting only their own brands, do not want anything to do with this specialization. A company, such as ours, willing to go into the manufacturing business, not just wholesale distribution, can make the numbers work successfully. Since existing manufacturers are reluctant to make this change and given the increasing consumer demand for quality coffee and for sampling premier varieties of coffee, this is a major market opportunity. Add to this the fact that this demand is projected to increase for fifteen years and this opportunity becomes excellent.

Important Points to Remember

- Understand your market findings. If there is not sufficient market for your products or services, no matter how hard you work or how unique or beneficial your products or services are, you will not be successful until there is.
- To identify your customers, you must address not only who they are but also what they want.
- If you cannot write a customer profile, you have not done enough research.
- Developing an accurate forecast of your market share is important, not only because the number will be used to create your sales forecasts and financial pro formas but also because this information is critical for the very success of your business.

After you have completed all the segments in the section, remember to revise your market and competition summary at the beginning, so it includes the important elements discovered in each segment.

Now that your reviewers have learned about your market and the competition, they will want to know how you intend to position your company and your products or services in the market with the competition. You will accomplish this by taking a long range look at your overall company strategies and goals, the subject of the next section in your business plan and the next chapter.

Chapter 5

Strategies and Goals

If you don't know where you're going, you'll end up somewhere else.
— Yogi Berra

After you have finished researching your market and the competition, many business plan authorities steer you directly into marketing. Unlike a franchised outlet where the business operations and products or services are already well defined and strategies set, an independent start-up business has much more to consider. What are your long-range goals? What strategies do you need to employ to compete in the future?

After analyzing your market and the competition, where do your company and your products or services fit in? Do you need to change your products or services or their features to position them better in the marketplace? Or can the products or services that you already have planned remain as they are and be marketed a special way to capture a position in the market that is different from your competition?

Either way, before you open business and before you plan your marketing approach for your planned products or services, you need to set your long-range goals and analyze how various strategies can position your company and your products or services in the marketplace to achieve these goals. Once you have defined your positioning strategy, you will have created the ultimate formula for success. Having a well defined strategy will save you a lot of time, effort, and money in the beginning and keep you from straying off course when the going gets tough.

The purpose of this section is to lay out the long-range goals for your business. These can be set by examining all business strategies and selecting those that define your best positioning in the marketplace considering your competition. Once selected, you need to explore the different methods of implementing your strategies to reach your goals.

This section, like most of the others, begins with a summary for the reviewer. The segments of this section for a start-up company are:
- Strategies and goals summary
- Long-range goals and strategies
- Strategy implementation

Strategies and Goals Summary

Open this section with a summary of the important highlights of each of the segments in this section: your long-range goals, strategies, and methods of implementing the strategies. Remember to return to this opening summary and revise it after you have analyzed all the material, drawn your conclusions, and completed the balance of the segments.

Strategies and Goals Summary   Kona Gold Coffees

After examining our market and reassessing our product line, we are convinced that we have developed a key business strategy of positioning our products in a perfect market niche. We find this market large enough to allow us to grow, small enough to distract existing competitors, and too expensive for others to enter because of the high capitalization costs, which will be especially discouraging after we've captured the lion's share.

Our primary strategies are product-driven, for quality and specialization, and market-driven, for a new market that will become a market niche. Our major long-range goals are to increase market share, improve productivity, and implement a research and development department in year five. We expect to become and remain the market leader in our specialization.

Long-range Goals and Strategies

Beyond your first-year milestones, what lies ahead for your business? Obviously, the major goal of every business is success. How do you define success for your business? Is your company a one-owner business? Are your long-range personal goals in sync with your long-range business goals? Are they conflicting? Your ideas of personal success and business success must come together for the most realistic change to accomplish both. For example, if your idea of success is spending a lot of time with your family and playing golf two or three times a week, this might satisfy your personal goals for success, but it may be unrealistic for your business goals.

Defining your long-range business goals is one area of the business that most start-up companies overlook. If you are seeking investors, this is one area they seriously review. If they are going to invest capital in your business, they are looking for an upside return on their investments. They will want to know the answers to questions like: how big is your company going to get, and what position are you going to hold in the market?

To set your long-range business goals, you need to define your business strategies. Here is an array of the most popular strategies.

1. Price driven. If you are number one in this strategy, you dominate your industry by being the low-price leader with the lowest prices for your products or services. This usually means developing maximum (volume) buying power and streamlining operations for lowest cost of goods and expenses, and sometimes, maintaining a lower profit margin. To capture this goal, a business often has to narrow its product or service line to minimize the number of alternatives and options available to the customer.

2. Products- or services-driven strategies:
   a. Quality driven. If you are known for the best quality in your industry, you provide the most premium products or services of the highest standards to all possible customers. Depending on the nature of your business, this is usually accomplished by operating your business in a top drawer manner.
   b. Creativity driven. To develop a reputation in your industry for having the most innovative products or services, you provide new products or services or new twists to existing products or services that become successful. To maintain this reputation, it is essential to have an active research and development department.
   c. Specialization driven. This is a another strategy for success if you provide products or services that:
      • Are distinctive or unique via design or technology.
      • Are limited in numbers.
      • Are established by a brand name identity.
      • Have particular features that separate yours from your competitors.
   d. Proliferation driven. This strategy works well for larger companies. It allows you to become the top business in your industry by offering the most complete lines of products or services. The company that best implements this strategy is best at responding to the needs of one-stop shoppers.

3. Customer-service-driven strategies:
   a. Highest-standard driven. This is a strategy for success by offering the best customer service in setting a new standard on a higher level for treating customers well, responding to their needs, and offering premium customer services. To reach a

higher standard, you need to develop service policies enabling unequaled attention to your customer needs. Consider all policies that would enhance your type of business, such as lay-aways, access of all credit cards, returns, special orders, follow-up, customer notifications, special deliveries, convenient hours of operation, no-fault damage policies, gift registries, gift wrapping, and, above all, friendly service. This requires a well-trained staff on hand at all times to serve customers in a timely and friendly manner.

b. Most-personalized driven. This strategy is to develop a reputation of catering to customers personally and having them know that this is your most valued goal — to make them feel that they are important to your business. If this is your top objective, employees need to have special training and must be given authority to make instant decisions. Your personalized service should approach the techniques of, and be patterned after, those used by the best vacation resorts.

c. Solutions driven. This strategy for success is to become known as the best for resolving any customer problem, question, request, or desire. To acquire this reputation, your company must develop the most expertise and become the most resourceful. Customers, especially other business customers, will pay an extra premium for this service.

4. Industry-driven strategies:

a. Industry-leader driven. To dominate your industry as its leader, you must be in the forefront in total sales of products or services. This is perhaps the most growth driven of all strategies and takes long-range positioning for your company to reach it. You need to set intermediate goals and to accomplish them in phases, usually by territory (local, state, regional, and even national sales areas).

b. Innovator driven. To develop a reputation as the innovative leader, you will need to adopt innovative and new techniques in all divisions in the operations of your business — purchasing, production, inventory control, marketing, sales, fulfillment, customer service, management, human resources, accounting, and research and development.

c. Technologically driven. A company using this strategy develops success by being the foremost in technology in the industry — on the cutting edge year in and year out. To achieve this, you must have a research and development department that may do nothing other than provide support for this one role. They will need to make technological achievements and foster technological advancements.

5. Market-driven strategies:

a. Market-leader driven. You will need to stay ahead of your competitors by monitoring them closely to develop the reputation as the market leader using only a market-driven strategy. Many times, for short periods, you will have to move quickly to lower prices, increase advertising, use promotional campaigns, and sacrifice your standard profit margins.

    b. New-market driven. You can also use the strategy of focusing on a new market that has been heretofore untapped by your competitors, to become a market leader for your products or services.

    c. Niche-market driven. Another successful strategy for becoming a market leader is to find a market niche for your specific products or services and exploit this specialization with a concentrated effort. In this strategy, although you still have competitors, you are the only one serving this focused market; your competitors are serving a much larger market and will tend to compete poorly in your specialized niche.

    d. One-trend-market driven. To become a market leader, another strategy is to capitalize on and maximize sales of a new trend. This might be a trend in your market or in your geographic sales area or a response to a new consumer demand. Continually being first to adapt your products or service, or their delivery, to the trends can lead to market dominance by the use of this strategy.

    e. Customer-focus driven. Another market leading strategy is:
- To focus on and target companies of a specific size, in a specific industry, in a specific geographic sales area, or in a specific stage of development.
- To provide a specific service for large corporations.
- To limit your customer base to certain criteria to concentrate on their specific needs better than any competitor.

    f. Relationship driven. An often overlooked category as a market strategy is to develop a strategic alliance with a particular company, investor, partner, or distributor, so that you serve each other, creating a market and a win-win situation for both. Licensing and bundling are included in this category. Bundling is the process of selling your products or services to another company who resells them as a part of a larger package.

6. Marketing driven. To rise above the competition, all other things being equal, you can emerge as the leader by focusing on and implementing the best marketing strategy. Find and use the best marketing media and promotional campaigns to best search out your customers and influence their buying decisions. It could be that one method or marketing medium will serve your products or services best, such as the Internet. Another marketing-driven strategy is to develop a name brand for your products or services.

7. Sales driven. To reach number one in sales of your products or services, all other things being equal, an effective direct strategy is to have the most aggressive sales organization. A sales-driven business is usually headed by a sales guru who understands the best motivational and selling techniques including closing, who

hires and trains the best salespeople, and literally, commands that the rest of the operations support the sales division. The sales force is the strength of the company.

8. Management driven. A popular strategy for positioning your company at the top of its field is to hire and place outstanding personnel in key positions. This starts with you. If you know your own limitations, first fill the positions that you are weakest in, to complement your abilities and round out and strengthen the overall management of your company.

9. Operations-driven strategies.
   a. Efficiency driven. Sometimes called numbers-driven, this strategy minimizes overhead, tightening up all the numbers, and efficiently runs all operations to obtain the highest production with the least waste, thus lowering expenses and costs of goods and aiming for specific sales and highest profits. The best run companies operating with this strategy require clear communication between departments and between employees and management.
   b. One-function-excellence driven. This strategy takes one department or one operation and develops it to the maximum potential, surpassing the counterparts of your competitors, to become the key to your success. If this were the sales force, then this strategy would overlap with a sales-driven strategy.
   c. Most-professional driven. While running your company professionally should be a primary strategy for any business, implementing an effective strategy for positioning it at the top of your industry as the most professional depends on your industry. If most of your competitors are non-franchised or small mom-and-pop shops that have never been correctly organized nor efficiently operated, this strategy alone might be enough to give you the top position. Even if your competitors appear to be operating professionally, your business might be able to demonstrate more professionalism to effectively take your place as an industry leader in your marketplace.

While it is impossible to structure all of these strategies in a viable business, it is possible to try to be the best in one category, or several if they overlap, and remain strong in others. A study of large retail businesses in the mid-'90s by Harvard's business school found that of the big three strategies for retail (price, quality, and customer service), businesses that maximized any two of the three and minimized one, were the most successful and had the best chances of longevity. Any retailer that tried to maximize all three didn't survive over the long haul. Examples were given of three active successful business types.

- The large price-discount warehouses that have continued to respect price and quality, but have minimized customer service.
- The successful, large superstore chains that have maintained low prices and top service, but have given less attention to quality.

- The large high-end name-brand department stores that have continued excellent service with top quality products, but have been less conscientious about prices.

Once you have considered your different strategies and long-range goals, decide on which one or two strategies will serve your business the best with your market and competition.

For this segment, write a brief description of your long-range business goals and the strategies you intend to use to reach them for the next three or five years, or longer. State completion dates or the amount of time you anticipate it will take to accomplish them. There will be specific objectives you must achieve in order to accomplish your long-range goals. Set up a three- or five-year, or longer, long-range milestones table and list your objectives using specific numbers for your business plan, as in the example.

Long-range Goals and Strategies — Kona Gold Coffees

Our market research shows that our product line fulfills a need and will hold a strong position in the marketplace. In focusing on this objective, we will be using these strategies:

- Product-driven, with an emphasis on quality and specialization.
- Quality — It is our goal that the quality of our coffee offerings are and remain unsurpassed in the field of premium Kona coffee.
- Specialization — Our product line is unique with particular features that separate us from our competitors. No other manufacturer offers a 14 ounce assortment of seven different brand-named Kona coffees of the finest quality.
- Market-driven, with an emphasis on new market and niche market strategies.
- New-market — We are focusing on a new market that has never been tapped by our competitors and we expect to be the market leader in this field even if others enter it after us.
- Niche-market — From our market and competition analyses, we know that our products fulfill a market niche.

Long-range Milestones

	First Year	Three Years	Five Years
Market share	4%	4.7%	5.4%
Quantity of annual sales	50,480	62,675	73,104
Profit margin	55.7%	55.7%	55.7%
Number of products	3	6	9
Square footage of facility	2,500	2,500	2,500
Number of locations	1	1	1
Number of employees	10	11	12
Salary cap (non cost of sale)	290,000	313,668	339,264
New departments	0	0	R & D

Strategy Implementation

After you have defined your long-range goals and strategies and established your objectives, you must analyze the methods you will use to achieve them. In a survey of businesses, a lengthy list of implementation methods was compiled as a means to accomplish long-range goals and strategies. Decide which of these could apply to the goals and strategies that you have chosen for your business:

- To lower prices
- To narrow focus on (by adding, specializing, or improving):
  - Existing prices or services
  - Distribution
  - Production
  - Marketing, advertising, and sales
  - Engineering
  - Development

- To specialize
- To personalize service
- To develop a dynamic strategy to match a changing market
- To improve compensation for outside contractors, in-house managers, and employees
- To develop market penetration
- To diversify by adding, or expanding your products or service lines
- To expand distribution
- To expand productivity
- To add locations
- To add or improve technology
- To increase profit margin
- To pay off debt

Write a brief statement about the various methods you will use as your strategy implementation plan for the long-range goals you selected in the segment above. List any cost estimates attached to these plans. These costs can be shown on a table for your three- or five-year projections, or longer.

Strategy Implementation   Kona Gold Coffees

To implement the strategies described in the strategies segment, we need only to open business. Our products and our business concept have been designed to incorporate these strategies. To maintain our strategies over the years, we need to stay in tune with the market, the end consumer's attitudes and tastes, and to monitor all trends and changes occurring in the market. This will become a function of our R & D department in year five. Before this, as members of the SCAA, we will attend annual meetings, trade shows, and read updates through various industry trade publications. We will also monitor the SCAA and other web sites and follow Seattle's lead on responsive changes to the sensitivity of the market.

To obtain our market share increases, we will continue our marketing promotions that for most companies, are strongly implemented during the first twelve to eighteen months and then decreased substantially. Our forecasts will show that we intend to continue the same marketing impact on an ongoing basis. Other marketing vigils are covered in the section, Marketing and Sales.

While we have shown a constant profit margin of 56 percent, which means that cost of sales will remain at 44 percent, this has been done to match our financial pro formas in reporting a conservative and viable operation. However, it will be our goal to continually work at improving this by improving our suppliers and costs of raw materials, but not by cutting production payroll — a mistake that our competitors have made and are consequently experiencing unfriendly staffs and poor personnel morale with low or no self-motivation.

Additionally, to maintain all of our strategies, we will stay on top of our market specialty by expanding our product line by adding more products. We expect to increase our numbers of offerings to nine during the fifth year. "Square footage of facility" and "number of locations" will remain the same, as we have planned from the beginning to be able to double our production and capacity from our initial site. The increase in employees will not affect the salary cap, as these are either production operators whose payroll is included in cost of sales or commissioned salespeople. The salary cap shown, accounts only for non-cost of sales payroll and includes a built-in 4 percent per year increase to match the rising gross domestic product. Other incentives and bonuses are discussed in Management and Organization.

As to the last item in the long-range milestones, although our company will still be small by year five, we will add another coffee specialist and label his or her department, Research and Development. This manager's duties will cover much more than may be otherwise implied by this title, see the section, Management and Organization.

As a final goal, we anticipate not only paying off our line of credit once each year to satisfy the banking requirement, but also to maintain it completely paid, as a reserve only from year two forward. We expect to pay a premium for that use, but the benefit to us, of having it available for emergency cash flow and for emergency equipment repair or replacement, more than compensates for its annual use fee, even if we don't use it.

Important Points to Remember

- Before you open for business, you need to set your long-range goals and analyze various strategies to position your company and your products or services in the marketplace to achieve your goals.
- Where do you see your business in three, five, or ten years? What strategies are you going to use to get your company there?
- Defining your long-range business goals is one aspect of business planning that too many start-up companies overlook. If you are seeking investors, this is one area you can be certain will be seriously reviewed.

Once you have completed this section, remember to return to your strategies and goals summary at the beginning and revise it to include anything significant you have discovered and reported as you developed your strategies, long-range goals, and methods of implementation.

Now that your business plan reviewers know about your market, your competition, and your business strategy, they are ready to see how your products or services fit within the overall picture. This is the subject of your next section and the next chapter.

Chapter 6

Products or Services

The first mark of good business is the ability to deliver ... its product or service on time and in the condition which the client was led to expect.
— MICHEL J. T. FERGUSON

The reviewers of your business plan have had introductory glimpses of your products or services in the executive summary and the company description. If they are reading the sections of your plan in order, they have become familiar with your industry, market, competition, and business strategy. They are now ready to see how you will position your products or services in the marketplace. This section provides them with a closer look at your products or services. The segments covered are:

- Products or services summary
- Products or services description
- Products or services positioning
- Comparison with the competition
- Technology and intellectual protection
- Future products or services

While these segments cover the discussion of your products and services, the most important objective of a start-up business plan is to develop the reviewer's interest as much as possible by focusing on the outstanding features of your company. If your products or services are conservative, not unusual and not especially technical, it is best to cover them succinctly. Use only one or two pages to present an adequate visualization of your products or services to the reviewer, so as not to sidetrack their concentration on the more interesting aspects of your plan. On the other hand, if your products or services or their features are unique, special, new, or technical, and are well positioned in the market, devote all the space you need to develop the reviewer's understanding of their special qualities.

Products or Services Summary

As with the other opening summaries, write this one after you have finished the balance of the section so you can cover the highlights of each segment. Write a short narrative summary including the important results of each segment, in the same order as presented in the rest of the section. Include the best or unique features of the products or services description, your positioning in the marketplace, the advantages of your products or services over the competitors' products or services, technological reasons why your products or services are superior, and the intellectual property that your products or services may be protected by. If you have information about future products or services, include this in the summary if it will increase the viability of your business.

Products Summary   Kona Gold Coffees

Our opening product line consists of three different presentational packages, each with six renown Kona coffees and our own Signature Gold. They will be accompanied by a history of each coffee. Because they represent a unique collection already assembled and cannot be purchased anywhere else as such, our products are positioned to open a new market which is expected to become a market niche. Our offerings provide a horizontal selection (across brands) of Kona coffees as opposed to a vertical selection (blends, roasts — same brand) as do our competitors.

Signature Gold is trademarked and will be submitted as a Blue Ribbon candidate in the Kona Coffee Forum this spring. We will continue developing our own proprietary blends every year and we intend to add three new, but similar products every two years.

Products or Services Description

In this segment, introduce the reviewer to an overall description of your products or services and state the basic purpose they serve for buyers. If possible, do this with a narrative description. If your lines of products or services are extensive, there are two ways to handle this:

1. Supplement the description with a table showing each of the lines of your products or services with their prices. This should be a complete mix of all items for sale; or
2. Use a general description of the category or categories of your products or services, with a range of prices or average prices.

The approach you use is determined by the nature of your business and the types of products or services you sell. For example, a restaurant may only describe its menu as specializing in American cuisine, priced moderately for both business lunches and family dinners. A complete menu or sales brochure listing your products or services and their prices may be reproduced as a business plan exhibit. Include in your description the most important features of your products or services. Specifically note the proprietary products or services exclusive to your business.

If you include any reproduced sales brochures or menus in the business plan exhibits, mention their significance here, regarding your product or service line, and direct the reviewer's attention to their location in your exhibits. Their placement within the exhibits should be in the same order as the text about them.

Products Description   Kona Gold Coffees

For our introductory offerings, we feature three basket presentations of premium Kona coffee, each having seven two-ounce packets representing the top 18 brands of Kona coffee that have taken Blue Ribbon prizes at the annual Kona Coffee Forum. This first place ribbon is awarded for three different grades of coffee, and has to date, been awarded for the last 8 years. We feature 18 of the 24 winners representing six of the packets in each presentation basket.

The seventh packet of coffee in each of the three presentations is marketed under Kona Gold Coffees' registered trade mark and is specifically called Signature Gold, a proprietary blend of more than 70 percent Kona coffee, Kona peaberry coffee, and arabica. This is truly a rich and delicious coffee. Although, we think the flavor of Signature Gold is the finest tasting coffee in the world, we do not market it better than the other six within each presentation basket. The consumer is left with the freedom of choice. Early market feedback suggests that most people like Signature Gold as well as, if not better, than the Blue Ribbon accompaniments.

For our send-off year, prices for each basket are the same, $39.95. The baskets are highly attractive with each coffee having a specially designed pouch produced for us by PacBag with a distinctive stylized label, carrying the grower's brand and logo in a stylized format coordinated to harmonize within the assortment. The assortment is arranged in Kona Gold Coffees' black, gold, and cream stylized tissue surrounds within the basket with a small card explaining the award-winning coffees. The entire package is then shrink-wrapped and topped with the distinctive Kona Gold Coffees' ribbon and bow. The presentation, itself, is pleasing to the eye of the gourmet. Because freshness is important and we believe in the rule of 21 days — that no coffee should be ground more than 21 days before brewing — our baskets are dated warning consumers not to buy anything that they can't consume in 21 days from the date the coffee was ground.

(continued)

Finally, under your description provide a revenue break-out by product or service, or product line or service line, depending on your type of business. If you use the table format, prioritize them according to your idea of how well they will sell, as in the example, with number 1 being the best seller. In addition, if you offer options such as upgrades or add-ons, include a schedule describing the most popular ones with their prices.

Products Description (continued) — Kona Gold Coffees

Product Mix

Product	Retail Price	Wholesale Price
Gourmet Basket No. 1	$39.95	$29.95
Gourmet Basket No. 2	$39.95	$29.95
Gourmet Basket No. 3	$39.95	$29.95

Sales Forecast of Product Mix

Product	Wholesale $	Units	Sales $	Retail $	Units	Sales $
Gourmet 1	29.95	13,489	404,000	39.95	3,338	133,333
Gourmet 2	29.95	13,489	404,000	39.95	3,338	133,333
Gourmet 3	29.95	13,489	404,000	39.95	3,338	133,334
Subtotals		40,467	1,212,000		10,014	400,000

Total Wholesale and Retail Units 50,481   Total Wholesale and Retail Sales $1,612,000

Products or Services Positioning

Include a brief statement of how your products or services will be positioned in the marketplace: will they be the lowest priced, best quality, best designed, most advanced, flexible for a broad market response, most innovative, most professional, or most specialized? Will they fill a market niche? Examine your strategies in Chapter 5 and look for the best positioning strategy of your products or services for this segment. If you find that your prices are not the lowest, include a statement about your pricing in terms of your competition: will your prices be low, below average, average, above average, or high?

Products Positioning — Kona Gold Coffees

Our products are positioned to open a new market which will fill a specialized need. Each basket answers this same need: for those customers curious to discover which Kona coffee is the best in their opinion. The primary customers are gourmet coffee drinkers, tourists, and the buyers buying for image, better known in the business world, as yuppies. There are no other products on the market that answer this need, so there is no direct competition; however, if a customer is to compare our pricing, at $2.80 per oz. it is extremely high. On the other hand, if found in one store the same coffees would cost $84.00 on average in regular 7 oz. packets. To date, there is no one-stop shop that offers all of our combinations. With the ability to buy our collector coffees together, in tasting quantities, fresh, and at less than half the price, we have created a perceived value that our price is fair.

Comparison with the Competition

Information about the competitor's products or services is essential to reviewers of your business plan and can assist you in understanding more about your own business and product or service line. From your physical survey and your competitor analysis, describe the important competitive features of your products or services and compare them with those of your competitors. For a start-up company, many lenders recommend that you present a large table — similar to the example, Products Comparative Analysis — comparing your products or services with those of your competitors.

In your description, answer the question of why people will buy your products or services instead of others. Is it because of better features, prices, quality, service, a combination of these, or some other reason?

List your product or service features that differentiate yours from your competitors'. If you have unique or better quality than your competition, describe the various product or service features that you consider as being unique or superior. Do you have other advantages? Compare your products or services with the competition in terms of design, technology, cost, user-friendliness, quality, packaging, and others. If your products or services have several advantages, expand the features category in the table at the end of the Kona Gold Coffees example to include multiple feature remarks.

Comparison with the Competition — Kona Gold Coffees

Although our competitors do not have similar products, we have conducted a survey of their products and show them here as a comparative analysis. Our customers will be buying our products because of the assortment of Kona coffees (a horizontal selection), while our competitors sell by different roasts and flavors manufactured solely under their brand (a vertical selection).

Products Comparative Analysis — Kona Gold Coffees

Item	Kona Gold Coffees	Kauai Mountain	Maui Wowy Coffee	Kealakekua Farms
Product/services #1	GB No. 1	#1	#1	#1a and #1b
Price	$39.95	$7.50	$9.00	$5.50 (#1a, 7 oz.)
Unit sales	16,827	140,000	72,250	164,000
Dollar sales	$537,000	$1,050,000	$650,250	$902,000
Features	7 assortment	Medium Roast	Dark Roast	Medium Roast
Price of #1b				$10.50 (#1b, 16 oz.)
Unit sales of #1b				128,858
Dollar sales of #1b				$1,353,000

(continued)

Products Comparative Analysis (continued)				Kona Gold Coffees
Item	Kona Gold Coffees	Kauai Mountain	Maui Wowy Coffee	Kealakekua Farms
Product/services #2	GB No. 2	#2	#2	#2
Price	$39.95	$8.50	$12.50	$6.50
Unit sales	16,827	82,500	28,580	186,500
Dollar sales	$537,000	$701,250	$357,250	$1,212,250
Features	7 assortment	Dark Roast	Espresso	Flavors
Product/services #3	GB No. 3	#3	None	#3
Price	$39.95	$9.50		$7.50
Unit sales	16,827	27,763		263,100
Dollar sales	$537,000	$263,750		$1,973,250
Features	7 assortment	Flavors		
Competitive strength	2	4	2	5
Target market	Tourists, gourmets, image buyers	Tourists, gourmets	Tourists, gourmets	Local Kona coffee drinkers Mainland, same
Advertising medium	All, see Marketing	Customer newsletters	Resort/airline literature	Newspaper and magazines
Promotions	See Marketing	Unknown	None	Super markets
Methods of sales	Retail/Wholesale	Retail/Wholesale	Retail/Wholesale	Retail/Wholesale
Potential new P & S	3 in 2 years	2 in next year	No plans	1–2 per year
Potential new features	New assortments	Espresso Supremo	N/A	More flavors
Priority of concern	N/A	Low	Low	Moderate

Technology and Intellectual Protection

If your products or services are based on a special technology, include a segment describing this. Use a lay person's language for any technical specifications that you want to be sure the reviewers understand. If your products or services have intellectual protection — trademark, trade name, service mark, patents, copyrights, or special licensing — list it and give a complete explanation as to who owns the intellectual property, how you have rights to it, and what the protection covers. If applicable, include the amount of time remaining before competitors can legally infringe on your advantage or the period of your licensing agreement. Include in the exhibits any significant technical specifications about the products or services. As a caution, it is recommended that you use outside printed materials with discretion and that you only include those items that support your business plan in telling your story.

Technology and Intellectual Protection — Kona Gold Coffees

We have filed an application for trademark registration at the USPTO. At this time, we can use our trademark with a circle R, but are awaiting the required six-month period to file a Statement of Use for final approval of its use as a trademark in interstate commerce. The trademark registration will be effective for ten years and renewable thereafter. The protection of a trademark not only protects our name from being misused, but it insures quality of our products to our customers.

Future Products or Services

The purpose of research and development is to stay on top of your market and adapt your products or services to changes in the market, either with new products or services or with new features such as improvements, upgrades, and add-ons. A business that doesn't adapt is doomed to failure. If your business is large enough to have a research and development division, briefly summarize it here. Explain its significance for your product or service line and refer the reviewers of your plan to your operations section. Include a full description of the operations of your research and development division as a segment in operations under the heading, Research and Development.

Even if you don't have a research and development division, include this segment and state how you address research and development for your products and services in simpler terms. Research and development for a small start-up company can be as simple as subscribing to certain trade publications, attending consumer trade shows, monitoring market trends, checking on new successful products and services offered by competitors, or any combination of these. Describe any trade publications, annual trade shows, or conferences you attend for researching new products or services in your industry.

Finally, describe your long-range strategy for creating, developing, or handling future products or services. If applicable, inform the reviewer of new products or services in the planning, and state your reasons for their need. If comparable to other products or services now on the market, show a comparison with the competition to emphasize the prominent points of yours as opposed theirs. If you have new products or services that are underway, show their status with a schedule like the one in the example.

Future Products
Kona Gold Coffees

Although we plan to add a formal research and development specialist to our company in five years, we will conduct ongoing R & D during our first four years by monitoring our trade publications and other literature, especially those distributed by the SCAA and its body of members. We will monitor other market trends by staying abreast of the competition's products and attending every annual trade show in Seattle.

It is part of our ongoing research and development to attend the annual Kona Coffee Forum's Blue Ribbon trade show and enter a new coffee or new blend in the Blue Ribbon contest every year. Any entry that wins will be added to our product mix and immediately promoted as the winning Blue Ribbon coffee for that year. This year, Signature Gold will be submitted.

We plan to add three new presentation products, similar to our existing ones, every two years, or sooner if one of our existing products does not sell as well as the others.

Schedule of Future Products

Product	Feasibility Review	Research	Planning	Prototype	Near Production	Ready to Release
P #4	Completed	Completed	Completed	Completed	34 months	Beginning Year 3
P #5	Completed	Completed	Completed	Completed	34 months	Beginning Year 3
P #6	Completed	Completed	Completed	Completed	34 months	Beginning Year 3

Important Points to Remember

- If your products or services are unique, special, new, or technical, and are well positioned in the market, devote all the space you need to develop the reviewers' understanding of this.
- Describe how your products or services are positioned in the marketplace, such as lowest-priced, most technical, filling a market niche, or some other way.
- Knowledge about your competitors' products or services is essential to reviewers of your business plan and can assist you in understanding more about your own business and product or service line.

When you have finished this section, remember to return to your products or services summary and revise it to include the main highlights covered, to best summarize this section on your products or services.

Now that your reviewers know what you sell and who you sell to, the next job is to convince your readers that you can reach the customers and get them to buy. This is where marketing and sales come in, the subject of the next section in your business plan and the next chapter.

Chapter 7

Marketing and Sales

People will buy anything that's 'one to a customer.'
— Sinclair Lewis

After you have finished researching your market and the competition, analyzed your strategy, and positioned your company and your products or services, it is time to develop a marketing plan. While the market identifies your customers and their needs, your marketing plan focuses on how you plan to meet those needs. A marketing plan is designed:

- To reach your target market and make potential customers aware of your products or services,
- To convey and reinforce a message that creates customers by motivating them to buy, and
- To generate sales.

To obtain these three results requires two activities, marketing and sales. Marketing is the activity you undertake to reach your target market, to deliver the message, and to reinforce it, thus motivating individuals to become prospective customers. Sales is the activity undertaken to follow-up on a prospective customer and to generate an order.

An important part of marketing is the continual monitoring of customer needs and demand for your products or services. While a sales program concentrates on the salability of products or services, sound marketing determines the level of customer demand for them and actively monitors customers' changing needs. With this information, you can coordinate your business' strengths and weaknesses with the demand for your products or services to maximize your ability to meet your customers' needs. By operating your business using the information you generate, you can deliver your products or services more effectively than your competitors. The segments of a business plan, included in this chapter and in any strong marketing and sales section, are:

- Marketing summary
- Marketing strategy
- Marketing plan
- Marketing budget and advertising plan
- Sales force and forecast

Marketing and Sales Summary

This is another one of those summaries that, while placed as the opening of the section, should really be written last to summarize your analyses, so you can optimize the reviewer's interest in your marketing strategy. Be sure it covers these key elements of your marketing plan and sales program:

- Your message to customers about your products or services;
- Your promotional theme;
- Highlights of your marketing plan;
- Media and advertising used to reach the customer;
- Your promotions, publicity, trade shows, and strategic alliances;
- Your marketing budget or advertising plan (include your opening and first-year budget totals, in terms of dollars); and
- Your sales force and the special training you will provide (include your projected sales for the first year).

Marketing and Sales Summary — Kona Gold Coffees

Our slogan is "The World's best coffee is Kona coffee — the best Kona coffees in the world are ours." Our message will convey that we have assembled a unique collection of the world's finest Kona coffees that cannot be purchased together anywhere else. KGC trademark will stand for quality.

Our marketing plan includes a budget the first month of $16,000 for a relative massive send-off. Throughout the year we will continue a steady ongoing campaign using several advertising media matching the demographics of our consumer profile. These include shopper magazines, tourist activity guides, trade journals, light television and radio spots, direct mail, and an Internet web site. Other promotions will involve free taste samplings, three major cultural events in Hawaii, and press releases. This plan has been specifically allocated by month for our opening send-off, advertising plan, and marketing budget. The first year marketing budget totals $33,600.

Our sales program will be handled through owner sales, one in-house salesperson, 209 retailers, direct mail, and Internet sales. Our projected sales for the first year are $1,612,000.

Marketing Strategy

Simply stated, your marketing strategy is the marketing program you develop for getting customers to buy your products or services. This marketing program should support your overall business strategy and your product or service positioning.

To best influence your target market to purchase your products or services, your marketing program must convey a message. What is the message you want to send to your target market? First, consider the basic information necessary to include in your message. To cover the basics, marketing consultants recommend to start with what they refer to as the 4Ps: product, price, place, and promotion.

Products or Services

The message in your ads or marketing programs should identify what your products or services are. To do this, you must include a description of your products or services or a description of the features of your products or services. This does not mean simply telling the target market what the products or services are, you must include an appeal for your products or services. Professional marketing defines this appeal as: sending a message directly or indirectly that signals to the customer what his or her benefits are when buying the products or services. You will have a better understanding of these benefits after this discussion of the 4Ps.

Price

Part of the message to your potential customers in your ads or marketing programs should be what the prices are for your products or services. In addition to listing the sales price of your product or service, your message should include an appeal for the price by conveying the benefits of the price to your customers.

What are the customer's advantages for paying your price versus paying the price for a similar product or service from your competitors? What special features are your customers getting for the price? Can you include price discounts or new products or services offered with special pricing? Or, if there is no tangible price difference, is there an intangible price advantage that can be conveyed by perceived value?

Place

The message in your ads or marketing programs should tell customers where they can buy your products or services. But here again, the message should include an appeal for the place. This appeal may be a direct or indirect signal of the benefits for the customer to buy from your company. What intangible reasons are there? Is your company associated with quality? Is there a trademark that sends an indirect signal?

If you sell from your facility, what benefits are there from buying at your premises? Do you have a special ambiance or convenience for the customer in terms of ease of access, egress, parking, a drive-through window, or other advantages?

Promotion

The message in your ads or marketing programs should have a promotional value for a customer to buy your products or services. This promotional value should include an additional appeal for making the purchase. It can be direct, like specific promotional incentives projecting extra benefits to the customer if they buy your products or services. Or, it can be more subtle and indirect, sending a signal that the customer will benefit by becoming a better person, achieving greater success, developing more sex appeal, or some other intangible benefit. This part of the message may be in the form of a slogan or delivered via subliminal methods such as an attractive man putting on his new cologne and being rewarded with a kiss from a charming lady or a featured bottle of wine with the camera pulling back to reveal the setting of a plush Romanesque villa on the French Riviera.

The Five Fs of Customer Needs

Common to each of the 4Ps is the recommendation to convey the benefits of your products or services to your customers. Marketing wisdom uses another catchy list, called the five Fs, to ensure customer needs are also addressed. They are: function, finances, freedom, feelings, and future. If you understand how these concepts apply — their context in your marketing messages — they can assist you in conveying the benefits your customers want when buying your products or services.

- Function. Are your customers' needs met as a result of their using your products or services? Does the product or service fill or serve the function for which it was purchased?
- Finances. What is the price advantage or savings to your customers for buying your products or services over alternative choices? How do your prices yield savings to customers in addition to the initial cost?
- Freedom. Does the purchase of your products or services yield a convenience to customers and afford a savings of their time and effort?
- Feelings. Does the purchase of your products or services enhance your customers' self-image or sense of security, provide pleasure, or other?
- Future. By purchasing your products or services now, what benefit is gained in future savings of time, effort, money, or some other benefit?

When you are creating your marketing message using the 4Ps and 5Fs, remember to include an in-direct message for your products or services positioning — best quality, the most technically advanced, most reliable, most personalized, brand name, or other; see Chapter 6. A start-up company cannot afford to simply build up image. Your marketing must lead the customer to action.

Your Promotional Message

After you have developed all the benefits that can be conveyed from examining the 4Ps and 5Fs for your business and marketing, narrow your list to one or two primary considerations that separate your business and your products or services from the competition. Place your focus on these for the central theme of your message. This is the essence of your business promotion. Many businesses develop a slogan to capture and convey it.

For this segment, your marketing strategy, write a description of your marketing message using the 4Ps and the 5Fs to convey the major points and their benefits to the customer. Describe how the major points meet your customers' needs if they buy your products or services.

Define your main theme, such as a slogan, and explain its underlying message. Include how you intend for your message to support your business strategy and the positioning of your products or services in the market. Identify your primary target market, potential customers to whom this will be directed, and any secondary market if appropriate. Explain the important differences between your marketing program and those of your competitors.

Marketing Strategy — Kona Gold Coffees

Our marketing strategy is to promote our products as gourmet assortments of the finest Kona coffees.

Our promotion: "The world's best coffee is Kona coffee — the best Kona coffees in the world are ours," is meant to instill the idea that no other product on the market can provide this message, positioning our products as a unique offering. Each presentation basket will further promote this concept with a small informational card, explaining the Blue Ribbon history of the products. We intend to supplement this with advertising and marketing promotions.

Our message: Our products benefit the customer by being available together, freeing the customer of the effort of researching and collecting them. As a result, the customer is introduced to the best Blue Ribbon Kona coffees available which are satisfying to the palate and to the self-image by having found the finest Kona coffees. The price benefits the customer because the customer would have to otherwise pay nearly two and one-half times as much to buy individual seven-ounce packages to gather the same assortment. For tourists, the alternative usually means a waste of buying more coffee than they can consume. Our brand of coffees benefits the customer by insuring quality by the Kona Gold Coffees trademark and, as a bonus, the customer receives our Kona Gold Coffee Signature Gold coffee only available through our products.

Our target market: Our primary consumers are gourmet coffee drinkers with our consumer profile looking for the best Kona coffees. Our secondary consumers are tourists with our consumer profile, curious to try Kona coffees, and image buyers who seek unique gifts and the best quality coffee for entertaining guests as the focus of a party or a sumptuous end to a fine dinner.

Our competitors' marketing programs: None of our competitors can market their products as an array of the finest Kona coffees available, and instead, promote only their own brands.

Marketing Plan

After you have defined your promotional message, you are ready to focus on your marketing plan. You must first decide how extensive your marketing needs are. How much marketing is needed for your products or services? How can you reach your customers in both your primary and secondary target markets? Can you get by with a guerrilla approach — minimal marketing at lower costs to reach customers by low-cost creative methods? Can you reach your target markets by direct mail, phone calls, faxes, or e-mail using databases? Or will your company need to be advertising focused, with advertising generating most sales and requiring an extensive advertising plan, or sales focused with an aggressive sales effort? See Chapter 5.

Answer these questions before developing your marketing plan. Then look at how much money is available in the budget to implement it. For now, estimate what you will need — your marketing budget will be more exactly determined as you complete the pro formas for your business plan.

You can start by contacting your accountant to get an average of what similar businesses spend for marketing, including advertising. If you have the reports by Dun & Bradstreet or Robert Morris Associates from doing your industry analysis, you can get a close estimate of the norm for this expense for your first-year projection by comparing your SIC or NAICS code with businesses that have the same volume of sales. One way to get a closer idea of how to budget for your advertising plan is to check with your industry association of the American Association of Advertising Agencies.

American Association of Advertising Agencies
www.commercepart.com/AAAA/index.html

For many businesses, two to five percent of sales is common, but this depends on the nature of your business and your competitive environment. For example, the lowest is about 0.8 percent for gasoline service stations and lumber yards, while marketing for time-share sales has been as high as 40 percent of sales.

In the example of Kona Gold Coffees, a monthly two percent of gross sales has been projected for the marketing budget for start-up and the regular first-year budget. For your business, this may or may not be a valid example. Many businesses have a seasonal impact. It may be more accurate for your marketing budget to use three percent of gross sales for some months, one percent for others, and six percent for peak months, with the total of all months averaging to the annual target of four percent. This budget is often adjusted by quarter rather than by month, but monthly adjustments are common due to special holidays and seasonal events with a monthly influence. For start-up companies, there is usually a send-off program causing heavy marketing expenses in the first month or first quarter.

Once you know your budget and have some idea of your marketing needs, you can begin to design your marketing plan and decide where you expect to spend the funds, but there is one other consideration, based on your type of business and your methods of sales.

Sales Methods Considerations

Examine your needs for marketing based on your own sales tactics. What is your primary method of sales? Some examples of these include:

- Owner sales
- Sales force
- Outbound telemarketing
- Inbound telemarketing
- Independent sales reps
- Direct mail
- Distributors or wholesalers
- Selling through retailers
- Internet sales
- Licensing
- Franchising

After you have defined your method of sales, you must decide about how much and what types of marketing support is needed for your method of sales. For your sales, how much of your marketing message do you need to convey to your customers about your products or services, your company, and your location? How frequently does the message need to be reinforced? Which advertising vehicles, promotions, publicity, trade shows, and strategic alliances are best for sending your message to your customers? Allocate which you will use and how often you will use them to complete your marketing plan.

Advertising Vehicles

Because media advertising represents a large portion of most marketing budgets, it is prudent to take a closer look at this. For effective exposure through media advertising, your ads must fit the customer profile, cover several types of media to reach the market, and be repeated. Also, your choices must fit your budget.

Today, marketing consultants advise that it takes from five to nine exposures before a customer notices a product, so repetition becomes essential to assure customer recognition.

Here is a list of the advertising vehicles:

- Ads on bulletin boards
- Advertising gifts, such as caps, notebooks, and calendars with your logo
- Billboards and signs
- Broadcast media advertising, such as television and radio
- Brochures, leaflets, and flyers
- Cultural and special events programs
- Direct mail, including ads on invoices, statements, and envelopes
- Internet web sites
- Print media advertising, including metro, local, and shoppers newspapers; newspaper inserts; regional magazines; business and trade publications; and the Yellow Pages

Even if all of the above apply to your products or services, the target market, the message, your sales methods, and the budget are the four considerations that dictate the priorities of your choices.

Planning an ad to fit your customer profile is a matter of using your market analysis to match up your target markets with a media source that reaches them most effectively. Therefore, you will want to survey which medium serves your customer profile best and, in some cases, at which times. For example, if your consumer demographics reveal your target market is primarily male, age 35 to 44, you might find it desirable to advertise your product or service on local television during baseball or football games. Your research can give you other possibilities. For example, while more men than women read newspapers, women read newspaper ads more often than men. More stay-at-home parents listen to FM radio stations in late morning hours, while more white-collar businesspeople listen to news stations during morning commute hours.

Television and Radio

It's probably no surprise that television and radio are the most costly media. National television and radio ads are usually reserved for promoting or sustaining name recognition for existing big business, chain outlets, or national franchise corporations. These media are not used for targeting specific or local markets; however, local television and radio are another matter.

While still expensive, these local broadcast media can be very strong advertising forums for start-up businesses. Ask to see the demographics of local cable TV and radio stations. Use guaranteed time slots matched to the demographics for the best times for your business. These are a little more expensive than the volume advertising plans that sell a quantity of spots per month in a best-time-available-slots plan. By using guaranteed time slots, you get much better exposure to your consumer demographics and, consequently, a more efficient return.

Magazines

Similar to national television and radio, national magazines serve better for prominent, existing businesses; however, regional magazines are a medium to consider for start-up companies. Reader demographics are available from most magazines, so you can match them with your buyer profiles to find which publications best suit your target market. Magazines are expensive compared to newspapers, but they offer much better print reproduction and much longer exposure life. A disadvantage for most monthly magazines is the long lead-time needed to place an ad before it actually appears in print. It is typically much shorter for weekly magazines.

If you are considering regional magazines in your marketing plan, weigh the demographics of your consumers with those of special interest magazines as well as with those of general interest magazines. You may find a publication that stands out exceptionally well read by a large market segment of your consumers.

Business and Trade Publications

There are, also, several national publications with regional editions, such as *The Wall Street Journal*. Depending on your customer base, business and trade publications are good places to advertise for commercial customers, both businesses and institutions. Magazine advertising is more expensive than newspapers; however, national and regional publications also have relative longer exposure lives. If the journals are of newspaper-type paper quality, there is no reproduction advantage; on the other hand, if they use slick paper with a quality finish, ads can have photographic reproduction as stunning as that which is found in regular magazines. These are considerations to weigh. Again, research the demographics of these publications and match them to your business and institutional customers.

Newspapers
The main advantage of newspaper advertising is their ability to reach specific targeted markets with minimum lead-time. The disadvantages are short-exposure life and poorer quality reproduction. Newspaper advertising can be expensive in a community where one paper dominates circulation.

Direct Mail
Depending on the nature of your products or services, some business and trade publications can supply mailing lists of prospective consumers in your trade area. These can be especially effective for acquiring new customers through direct mail promotions. If your business has a system for recording addresses of previous customers, direct mail is a viable medium for attracting repeat and referral business. Remember that direct mail works better the more personalized it is; the more it resembles form letters or junk mail, the less likely it is to be read.

Yellow Pages
The Yellow Pages of your local telephone book can be one of the best sources of local advertising for the cost, exposure life, and effectiveness, depending on your type of business. One or more copies of the Yellow Pages reach every home and office that has a telephone, and stays there a full year. For the best effect, solicit the help of a good ad designer who will create a visual image that will attract customers. Purchase as large an ad as you can afford if your business is one that stands any chance of customers going to the Yellow Pages to find your products or services or your location.

Cultural and Special Events
Among cultural and special events, one of the most popular for running advertisements is your local movie theater complex, where you can run short video ads. As always, consider your customer demographics. If your consumers are mainly middle-aged and conservative, you don't want to run an ad with the screening of *Return of the Vixen Vampire*, while the true story, *Sarah Winchester, Lady of Mystery*, might be a safer bet.

Watch for special events that might have an audience that fits your customer profile demographics. Look for music, drama, and sporting events at the high school, junior college, college, university, and the semi-pro and professional levels. Also consider municipal events, rodeos, rock concerts, concerts-in-the-park, ice shows, operas, ballets, plays, circuses, special events at the zoo, trade shows, races, and automobile and boat shows. If they reach your consumer, the ads have a strong promotional effect that suggests your business is in the know or in the swing of things.

Billboards and Signs

If billboards are appropriate for your type of business and can reach the target market, they can be very effective. Many Realtors say that all types of signs are their number one advertising media, far outpacing newspapers and publications. Most businesses use a business sign to identify their location for local traffic. If your business has commercial vehicles, an effective use of signage is a business sign or decal on the sides or rear of a vehicle, or both. One vehicle can provide a lot of exposure driving around town during its typical day as a delivery, courier, or shuttle vehicle.

The Internet

For a start-up business, advertising and a site on the Internet can give you an enormous advantage if your business can be served by the web. Some of the more common uses are:

- Products or services sales if you have products that can be purchased by mail order or services that require reservations or provide information,
- Online brochures,
- Products or services information, especially if your products or services are high-tech or new to the mainstream market,
- Interactive catalogs and magazines,
- Questionnaires for developing leads, and
- Other uses such as event schedules, company background, newsletters, bulletin boards, and customer service policies.

If you are considering a web site, consult with a marketing specialist and an experienced web page designer. Ads need to be designed with important power words (adjectives and nouns) used as search engine key words, so your target market will be able to locate your site. And of course, all marketing principles have to be obeyed just like any other advertising medium. You must identify your target market, construct your web site for your demographics and psychographics, customize your message for your market, and place your web site with the correct web directories through Internet service providers or commercial networks or both.

Some current demographics on Internet users are: household income, $70,000; educated; average age, 35; and holder of multiple credit cards. Access is to about 100 million people worldwide. Annual cost of running a home page with a commercial network runs about 20 percent of the cost of a comparable display in the Yellow Pages. Also, do not forget about the benefits of malls, auctions, chat rooms, and e-mail. When formulating your marketing plan, your business might benefit from Internet marketing, so don't overlook this latest media source.

Marketing Promotions

Marketing promotions, sometimes referred to as promotions or incentives, are used primarily to interest new prospects in your products or services or to lure customers away from competitive products or services. Some of the more popular ones are:

- Charity assistance
- Contests
- Coupons
- Discounts
- Exclusive offerings
- Free estimates
- Free products or services
- Free trials
- Frequent buyer cards
- Gifts
- Grand opening
- Guaranteed results
- Mock auctions
- New customer offers
- Point-of-purchase displays
- Rebates
- Rental display cases
- Sales
- Sweepstakes

The use of price-leaders intended to lure new customers with low mark-ups and limited low-price offers has been popular for years. Offering special free gifts with purchases intended to boost low sales periods is another type of promotion that has stood the test of time.

Public Relations

Since publicity is usually free, it does not need to be figured into your marketing budget. However, if you can take the time and effort to focus on the mediums that are the best sources for reaching your target market, your customers are much more likely to respond to publicity around or about your products or services than through regular advertising channels. There are many ways of marketing through public relations, here are some of the more common methods.

- Press packets
- Press releases
- Public speaking
- Video tapes to media
- Telephone calls to media
- Media interviews
- Press conferences
- Product reviews

The publicity channels used for these are: business and trade publications; consumer magazines; metro and local newspapers; national magazines; network, cable, and local television; network and local radio; newsletters; wire services; and the Internet.

Trade Shows

Start-up companies can use trade shows, consumer shows, seminars, and conventions quite effectively to network, develop leads, launch new products or services, demonstrate particular features of products or services, conduct workshops, build relationships with new and existing customers, seek distributors and suppliers, seek new products and services, monitor the competition, and open new accounts. You can attend or participate by having a table, booth, or meeting room. Trade shows and conventions are easy to find on the Internet. You usually can find your choice of industry, location, and date, even if you don't recognize the name of the shows. Here are three excellent sites for learning about upcoming tradeshows.

ExpoGuide
http://www.expoguide.com/shows/shows.htm

CyberExpoSearch
http/www.tsnn.com/bclass/cyberexpo/

Trade Shows & Exhibitions
http://www.world-trading.com/tradeshs.htm

Strategic Alliances

It is in this category you can address special relationships or affiliations with other companies for advertising and promotions or add-on sales. One type of alliance is cooperative advertising where your company and another company share both representation and cost of an ad. A common style is a shopping center that runs an ad for the entire center by featuring some specific stores in the center. Depending upon the amount of copy the stores get, they usually share in the cost. Another type is an ad shared by both a manufacturer and a distributor or wholesaler promoting their common products with shared advertising costs.

When you can afford it, seek professional help from advertising agencies, marketing consultants, graphic artists, copywriters, and public relations advisors. Good ones are well worth the expense. If you choose a professional based on the relevance of their previous successes and are clear in conveying your mission, image, and overall goal and in describing your products or services, they will be able to translate that information into a winning marketing promotion.

For this segment, describe your overall marketing plan for both your business opening and the ongoing advertising and promotions you have planned for the first year. Describe the advertising vehicles and media, marketing promotions, public relations, trade shows, and strategic alliances you expect to include. You can draw from those described in this chapter and from your own resources. Also, note your objectives and the milestones you expect to achieve from each medium. In your description, be specific and make your plan clear to the reviewer.

Marketing Plan   Kona Gold Coffees

To give our new products their send off, we have positioned point-of-purchase displays with many of our retailers, and have arranged for free tasting samples in some of the larger discount-warehouse and department stores. This will be supported by newspaper shopper circulars and special custom display ads in weekly grocery and superstore shopper guides. For the main tourist traffic, we have set up displays in the airports and major resorts and will run ads in all airline shopper magazines and weekly island activity guides. The latter category will include purchase discount coupons. For free publicity, we are sending press packets and press releases to introduce our new products to four radio stations (KZIX, KFAT, KQUF, and KMCC) and two television channels (6 and 9) whose primary listeners and viewers match our consumer demographics statewide. We are currently developing a video tape for media distribution to support our mail order and Internet sales, which is to be ready by the time we open. All of this preopening and opening marketing will be paid out of our start-up costs — $15,000 additionally budgeted for marketing in the first month.

For our annual budget, we have set up another $1,550 per month for ongoing marketing and advertising, a first-year annual budget of $33,600. Our advertising mainstays will be shopper newspapers, Internet web links, direct mail, and some radio and television spots where we plan to piggy-back 30-second coffee bar ads.

During the year, we will continue to distribute press releases for special free tastings at cultural events (King Kam Parade, Ironman Triathlon, and monthly Concerts in the Park) and consumer and trade shows (Kona Coffee Forum's Blue Ribbon and the SCAA annual show, usually held in Seattle). At these shows we will give away baseball caps with the Kona Gold Coffees label and enter our Signature Gold in the taste testing this year.

Throughout the year, we will run ads in business and trade publications to increase our retail penetration. We will continue our slogan: "The world's best coffee is Kona coffee — the best Kona coffees in the world are ours." To support this, we will reach the end consumer by running ads in several consumer magazines whose readers have the demographics of our consumer profile, magazines such as Gourmet, Pacific Rim Traveler, Hotel and all of the resort's concierge booklets.

To capture our own end-user sales, we will use mailing lists that have been acquired from these magazines and other consumer databases and send out direct mail. It is one of our third-year goals to develop and maintain a small company catalog of our six combination products and, hopefully, some individual offerings of popular proprietary Kona Gold Coffees by then. Additionally, for direct sales, we have an interactive on-line web site which is linked to the SCAA and other master trade sites: www.KonaGold@aol.com.

Marketing Budget and Advertising Plan

For the next segment, compile a special budget that schedules and allocates the costs of your marketing plan with respect to advertising media choices, other advertising vehicles, marketing promotions, public relations, and trade show attendance for your first year. This is called a marketing plan budget, or marketing budget. If you have a special allocation for your opening marketing program, show this as a separate budget.

Marketing Budget — Kona Gold Coffees

Our marketing budget consists of a send-off budget allocated from our start-up costs plus our monthly budget. They are represented here by three tables:

Marketing Send-off Costs

Item	Start-up Costs
Point of purchase displays	$ 2,700
Free-tasting samples	5,000
Printed ads and flyers	450
Island magazines and guides	2,000
Video tape	2,500
Broadcast media	2,350
	$15,000

Marketing Budget – First Year

Months	Advertising Agencies	Graphic Design	Printed Materials	Advertising Plan	Direct Mail	Internet	Memberships	Entertainment
January	$1,000	$500	$ 250	$ 1,353	$ 320	$ 50	$ 68	$ 200
February				1,083	320	50		100
March				1,243	320	50		200
April			250	383		50	68	100
May				655	320	50		200
June				658		50		100
July			250	655	320	50	68	200
August				383		50		100
September				655	320	50		200
October			250	1,138	320	50	68	100
November			$1,000	1,353	320	50		200
December				973	320	50		100
Subtotals	$1,000	$500	$1,000	$10,532	$2,880	$600	$272	$1,800

Total: $18,584

(continued)

If a media advertising budget is presented separately in the marketing plan, it is called an advertising plan. Notice the monthly (seasonal) adjustments in some categories in the example.

Advertising Plan (continued) Kona Gold Coffees

Month	Local Television[1]	Fixed Radio[2]	Variable Magazines	Consumer Magazines	News-paper[3]	Yellow Pages	Special Events
January	$ 480	$ 218	$120	$ 260	$ 200	$	$ 75
February	480	218			200	100	75
March	480	108	120	260	200		75
April		108			200		75
May			120	260	200		75
June		108			200		350
July			120	260	200		75
August		108			200		75
September			120	260	200		75
October	480	108			200		350
November	480	218	120	260	200		75
December	480	218			200		75
Subtotals:	$2,880	$1,412	$720	$1,560	$2,400	$110	$1,450

Total: $10,532

[1] Day time cable network   [2] Guaranteed designated spots   [3] Week-end shopper inserts

Sales Force and Forecast

For this segment of your marketing and sales section, describe your primary and other methods of sales you plan to use. Point out at least one or two main features about your sales efforts, and address sales strategies that differ from your competitors. Also, identify the methods of payment you will accept, for example, for cash only: cash, personal checks with proper identification, credit cards, or credit cards with authorization; and for credit: credit after verification of references. Include your terms: pay on delivery, pay in advance, half down and half on delivery, net 30, or other.

You should also have a system for your sales division to track purchasing patterns: where the customer first heard of your products or services, customers' reasons for their first purchase, the amount of purchase, the number of purchases, the frequency of purchases, payment method, and any other information useful to your business. The results of these ongoing surveys can assist you in maximizing the effectiveness of your marketing plan.

If your start-up business requires a sales force, describe the organization and size. Include the name of the manager or director and detail his or her responsibilities. Are sales conducted at your facility with inside salespeople, at homes or offices with outside salespeople, or a combination of these? Do sales take place over the telephone or face-to-face, and if face-to-face, are these by appointment or to walk-in customers? Also describe the staff's compensation. If sales are by commission, indicate the structure with overrides for managers if applicable. As part of the organization, indicate the training, motivational techniques, and sales meeting frequency. Explain how leads are generated, your policy for following up leads, and your process for information storage and retrieval of repeat and referral customers.

Detail the sales promotions you have planned and what you expect to achieve. If frequent, include a schedule with descriptions and objectives and costs of compensation for bonuses, special catering, or party and entertainment. To accompany the description, create a monthly sales forecast for your first year, as in the example.

Sales Force and Forecast   Kona Gold Coffees

Our primary selling methods are through owner sales, one in-house salesperson, retailers, direct mail, and Internet sales. To date we have the following retailer arrangements for wholesale sales:

Retailers in Hawaii (32% of sales):
26 resorts
10 coffee bars
24 super markets
15 restaurants
5 kiosks
10 non-resort gift shops

Retailers on the Mainland (43% of sales):
10 resorts
40 coffee bars
30 super markets
9 discount warehouses
10 kiosks
20 non-resort gift shops

Wholesale sales through these retailers are expected to comprise 75 percent of sales, with the other 25 percent through direct retail channels (mail order, 5 percent; the Internet, 20 percent). For retail sales, we accept all credit cards and have several systems of surveying customers' reasons for their purchase and how they have heard about us (through our mail order forms and Internet feedback). All retail sales are computerized to monitor the frequency of repeat customer orders and to send follow-up cards for future orders. This database will be maintained for catalog orders in the future.

For our wholesale sales, we are using a consignment system with many retailers for the first two months. After sales have been established, all wholesale sales will be credit, net 30 days. We have several point-of-purchase promotions, such as drawings, the chance to win free products, and others, for surveying our consumers through our retailers. We enter the information in our database for follow-up.

While our president, David Cooper, will be continually monitoring sales and striving to increase market penetration, our in-house salesperson, Lisa Orzechowski, is in charge of all retailer accounts and consumer sales. Lisa is paid a 4 percent commission and receives no salary. We are planning to continue this system until the time required to adequately stay on top of sales surpasses six days a week. At that time, we will hire a second salesperson part-time, until the workload becomes full-time. Currently, neither addition is expected until the second year as all of the arrangements for the above retailers have already been made and our first year's sales are based only on these. Our focus this year is improving and increasing sales within these outlets (vertical expansion) rather than adding new ones during the first year (horizontal expansion).

Although additional salespersons may be added, they have not been figured into these projections because their commissions will be included in the overall 4 percent commission base. When added, we'll develop a weekly sales meeting agenda and implement various sales promotion campaigns with extra benefits. These plans are approximately 2 years down the road.

(continued)

Sales Forecast

Kona Gold Coffees

Month	Jan.	Feb.	March	April	May	June	July	Aug.	Sept.	Oct.	Nov.	Dec.
Unit Sales - quantity												
Product #1 retail	156	172	189	208	229	251	277	304	335	368	405	445
Product #1 wholesale	631	694	763	840	924	1,016	1,117	1,229	1,352	1,487	1,636	1,800
Product #2 retail	156	172	189	208	229	251	277	304	335	368	405	445
Product #2 wholesale	631	694	763	840	924	1,016	1,117	1,229	1,352	1,487	1,636	1,800
Product #3 retail	156	172	189	208	229	251	277	304	335	368	405	445
Product #3 wholesale	631	694	763	840	924	1,016	1,117	1,229	1,352	1,487	1,636	1,800
Unit Prices - each												
Product #1 retail	$39.95	$39.95	$39.95	$39.95	$39.95	$39.95	$39.95	$39.95	$39.95	$39.95	$39.95	$39.95
Product #1 wholesale	29.95	29.95	29.95	29.95	29.95	29.95	29.95	29.95	29.95	29.95	29.95	29.95
Product #2 retail	39.95	39.95	39.95	39.95	39.95	39.95	39.95	39.95	39.95	39.95	39.95	39.95
Product #2 wholesale	29.95	29.95	29.95	29.95	29.95	29.95	29.95	29.95	29.95	29.95	29.95	29.95
Product #3 retail	39.95	39.95	39.95	39.95	39.95	39.95	39.95	39.95	39.95	39.95	39.95	39.95
Product #3 wholesale	29.95	29.95	29.95	29.95	29.95	29.95	29.95	29.95	29.95	29.95	29.95	29.95
Total Sales - $												
Product #1 retail	6,235	6,859	7,544	8,299	9,129	10,042	11,046	12,150	13,365	14,702	16,172	17,789
Product #1 wholesale	18,892	20,782	22,860	25,146	27,660	30,426	33,469	36,816	40,497	44,547	49,002	53,902
Product #2 retail	6,235	6,859	7,544	8,299	9,129	10,042	11,046	12,150	13,365	14,702	16,172	17,789
Product #2 wholesale	18,892	20,782	22,860	25,146	27,660	30,426	33,469	36,816	40,497	44,547	49,002	53,902
Product #3 retail	6,235	6,859	7,544	8,299	9,129	10,042	11,046	12,150	13,365	14,702	16,172	17,789
Product #3 wholesale	18,892	20,782	22,860	25,146	27,660	30,426	33,469	36,816	40,497	44,547	49,002	53,902
Total Sales	75,382	82,921	91,213	100,334	110,367	121,404	133,545	146,899	161,589	177,748	195,523	215,075
Unit Costs - each												
Product #1 retail	$14.14	$14.14	$14.14	$14.14	$14.14	$14.14	$14.14	$14.14	$14.14	$14.14	$14.14	$14.14
Product #1 wholesale	14.14	14.14	14.14	14.14	14.14	14.14	14.14	14.14	14.14	14.14	14.14	14.14
Product #2 retail	14.14	14.14	14.14	14.14	14.14	14.14	14.14	14.14	14.14	14.14	14.14	14.14
Product #2 wholesale	14.14	14.14	14.14	14.14	14.14	14.14	14.14	14.14	14.14	14.14	14.14	14.14
Product #3 retail	14.14	14.14	14.14	14.14	14.14	14.14	14.14	14.14	14.14	14.14	14.14	14.14
Product #3 wholesale	14.14	14.14	14.14	14.14	14.14	14.14	14.14	14.14	14.14	14.14	14.14	14.14
Total Cost of Sales - $												
Product #1 retail	2,207	2,428	2,671	2,938	3,232	3,555	3,910	4,301	4,731	5,204	5,725	6,297
Product #1 wholesale	8,919	9,811	10,792	11,872	13,059	14,365	15,801	17,381	19,119	21,031	23,135	25,448
Product #2 retail	2,207	2,428	2,671	2,938	3,232	3,555	3,910	4,301	4,731	5,204	5,725	6,297
Product #2 wholesale	8,919	9,811	10,792	11,872	13,059	14,365	15,801	17,381	19,119	21,031	23,135	25,448
Product #3 retail	2,207	2,428	2,671	2,938	3,232	3,555	3,910	4,301	4,731	5,204	5,725	6,297
Product #3 wholesale	8,919	9,811	10,792	11,872	13,059	14,365	15,801	17,381	19,119	21,031	23,135	25,448
Total Cost of Sales	33,380	36,718	40,389	44,428	48,871	53,758	59,134	65,048	71,552	78,708	86,578	95,236
Total Gross Profit	42,002	46,203	50,823	55,906	61,496	67,646	74,410	81,851	90,037	99,040	108,944	119,839

When preparing your sales programs, if you lack experience in developing sales strategies, there are many references on the market. An outstanding one is *Influence: The New Psychology of Modern Persuasion*, by Dr. Robert Cialdini, on the six principles that compel people to buy. A highly recommended source for designing and establishing effective sales processes and techniques is Hal Slater's *Secrets of High Ticket Selling* published by The Oasis Press.

Important Points to Remember

- The market identifies your customers and their needs and your marketing plan focuses on how you plan to meet those needs.
- An important activity of marketing is the continual monitoring of customer needs and the demand for your products or services.
- Web site ads designed with important power words keyed to search engines will enable your target market to locate your site.
- The best sales methods for your business should be implemented.
- The numbers shown in your sales forecast must match those in your pro forma income statements for sales, so double check to see that that they are, when you've finished your business plan.

Finally, remember to return to your marketing summary and write or rewrite your draft. Highlight the data and essential information you have discovered.

Having read your executive summary, your company description, your industry analysis, your market and competition, your strategies, your products or services, and your marketing plan and sales tactics, your reviewers will want to know whether you are capable of executing all of this with your start-up company. In answer, your next section focuses their attention on your management qualifications and organizational structure. This is covered in the next chapter.

Chapter 8

Management and Organization

The morale of an organization is not built from the bottom up; it filters from the top down.
— PETER B. KYNE

The Management and Organization section is the heart of your business plan. Carefully written, it can instill confidence that your business is well-founded and rock solid with an experienced, capable, and hard working management staff leading the way.

Three general areas need to be addressed: your capabilities for running the business, the relevant experience and skills of your key personnel, and the structure of your organization. Even if you have a home office business and you alone represent your management and organization, this section is still necessary. See Appendix A for more on this section for home businesses.

The management and organization section of your business plan should include these segments.

- Management and organization summary
- Management team
- Manager responsibilities and duties
- Management philosophy
- Key personnel incentives
- Organizational structure
- Personnel plan

Management and Organization Summary

As with most of the previous sections, the management and organization section begins with a summary. Once again, write or rewrite this paragraph after the balance of this section is completed so you can present the analysis of your findings and emphasize the important features.

If you are the sole owner/operator of this new business, open your summary with the fact you are the key employee. Summarize your education, strengths, experience, and successes. Show industry knowledge and emphasize your abilities to plan, manage, and meet and overcome challenges to reach your goals. If your business plan is to be used to obtain financing, this section must convince the reviewers you know what you're doing and that you have what it takes to be successful.

If you have a management team, list your key personnel and their total combined number of years of professional experience. As president or CEO, describe one or two of your key strengths, achievements, or experiences, and your primary responsibilities, such as overall management and strategic planning. If yours is a small company, list only one or two other managers and their supporting roles. If your company has a larger staff of managers, describe only the ones closest to you who have the most importance to the company. If any of them have exceptional, relevant experience, mention it in this summary. Also, mention highlights of your organization and personnel plan.

Finally, if some of your key positions are not filled, explain those you intend to fill in the first year that could affect your operations and improve your ability to reach your objectives.

Management and Organization Summary — Kona Gold Coffees

Our president and CEO, David Cooper, is responsible for overall management and planning strategic direction. He is a co-winner of two Blue Ribbon Kona coffee awards with 3 years experience as both purchasing and sales manager of a major competitor (reaching $5,000,000 in sales, up from $2,800,000 when he took over) and over 12 years experience in manufacturing. Under him are four key employees: operations chief, office manager, salesperson, and purchasing agent.

Our operations chief, Boy Clay, has 6 years experience as production manager for our largest Hawaiian competitor where he reorganized and modernized their production system and was instrumental in developing a Blue Ribbon winner. Our office manager, Terry Jervis, has 8 years experience as controller of a large chemical manufacturing company in California. Our purchasing agent, Larry Fennel, has 6 years experience in purchasing for a larger company in a similar field, where he learned a sophisticated agricultural purchasing system. Our salesperson, Lisa Orzechowski, was top producer in sales for a chain of Hawaiian gift shops for over 5 years. The overall manufacturing experience of the entire staff is more than 45 years.

(continued)

> **Management and Organization Summary** (continued) **Kona Gold Coffees**
>
> As to education, our president holds a bachelor's degree in business, specializing in production; our operations chief has an MBA in business production management, and our office manager has a bachelor's degree in business accounting. Special qualifications and responsibilities are further detailed in this section.
>
> Our organizational structure at opening will be 10 employees: 6 salaried, 1 on straight commission, and 3 wage earners under cost of sales. Our total payroll under general and administrative expenses is $ 290,000, 17.9 percent of sales, which is slightly higher than the industry standard of 16.9 percent.

Management Team

Introduce your managers in a short table of contents by title and name. The order begins with you and continues with each manager in order of importance to your company. If your start-up company has no managers, present your qualifications deftly by marketing your education, experience, achievements, traits, talents, and capabilities to your best advantage. When you are the only manager, it is more appropriate to include your full personal business résumé in this section rather than in the exhibits.

If your business is large enough to include other management staff, all the better. When you present these team members in their designated roles and market their qualifications, you can more confidently show the strength and diversity of your management team. If your management team is small, you can add your team of business consultants — your independent certified public accountant, attorney, and other key advisors — however, accurately depict them as consultants, not employees.

The director or manager roles which most financiers and business plan reviewers expect to see are the chief executive officer (CEO), chief financial officer (CFO), director of operations, and director of sales and marketing. Other key personnel can be added or substituted. In some companies, the director of operations is called chief operations officer and is regarded higher in the chain of command than the chief financial officer. In manufacturing companies, another pivotal manager is the plant manager or production manager. Most large companies have personnel directors. Some startups have specialty positions such as an escrow coordinator, relocation director, research and technical director, or service manager.

Three Alternatives for Two Résumé Formats

For startup companies that have a management team, there are three styles for presenting key managers in this segment. The first style, which follows the brief management introductory table, as in the Kona Gold Coffees example, introduces your management team using summary résumés. You can eliminate the full personal business résumés or append them in the exhibits. Most large companies prefer this style.

In the second style, after an introductory table of contents, introduce your management team by way of full personal business résumés for each manager, starting with yours and continuing with each manager in their order of importance to your company. Many venture capitalists prefer this style.

The third style is simply a combination of these, using the longer personal business résumé for the CEO or president, or possibly one or two other key personnel, and briefer summary résumés for other managers. Also, for those introduced by summary résumés, personal business résumés can be appended in the exhibits. This is the preferred style for home based companies and small companies with few or no managers.

Summary Résumés

If you elect to use the briefer summary résumé rather than the personal business résumé, then under a heading of the manager's title, present the manager's name and one or two paragraphs of background — education and experience — and highlight his or her special awards and achievements. If you use the summary résumé format for yourself, also describe the background, education, or experience that brought you to the decision to start this business, and why you feel it is sound and timely.

Personal Business Résumés

Use the personal business résumé format if you are the only manager; however, be aware the format of a résumé for a business plan is somewhat different from the traditional résumé for obtaining employment. While several good personal business résumé formats exist, one that has broad acceptance introduces categories or topics using descriptions and then uses bullet points to introduce lists. Use whichever form is most appropriate to the individual category.

Use the latest personal computer software programs with desktop publishing options such as borders, boxes, various type sizes and styles, bold face and lines for emphasis or clarity. It is acceptable to use a college-level vocabulary, but avoid flamboyant language in favor of words that are clear and direct. Use objective adjectives when possible, and always avoid first person. Keep the length to no more than two pages; only the principals' and one special manager's résumés are this length. Otherwise, limit those you include to one page.

Chief Executive Officer

Begin the résumé segment with yours, as chief executive officer or president, and continue with each manager in order of their importance to your business. Introduce each résumé with the person's title as a heading. The format for the longer personal business résumé, which you will probably use, is described below. Summary résumés are shown in the example.

Name and Title

Begin with your name and your title: owner, chief executive officer, or president. More than one title is acceptable.

Profile

Under your name and title, introduce your profile with a sidehead or crosshead. Describe your pertinent professional or work experience from the past to the present in three or four sentences; clauses are acceptable.

Qualifications Summary

The next résumé category, the qualifications summary, is one area in which you can embellish your skills and qualifications. While this can be in paragraph form, bulleted lists are considered quicker and easier to read. The more objective your information is, the more believable your qualifications are. Credibility and believeability is also enhanced if the first statement listed in the example can be readily validated.

Education

Except for specialized classes or training that might be directly related to business or the technology of your business, omit your high school years. But do list your undergraduate and graduate education, to the highest grade level you have completed.

In addition to formal education, list all the professional and business-related courses, technical schools, seminars, training programs, computer classes, and other employee training classes or certifications that reflect your educational background, skills, and accomplishments. Arrange the list so your most recent education is listed first, then work your way back chronologically. List the college, university, or private program name, the city and state, followed by the degrees or specific classes in your field, and the years the degrees were issued.

If your educational background is limited, it is acceptable to reach a little into your high school curricula, especially if you had some specialty courses that may be pertinent such as business law or salesmanship. When applicable, apprenticeships should be listed. One company owner who was quite embarrassed that he had never graduated from high school, left education off his résumé entirely. His educational experience wasn't missed with all his business accomplishments filling the page. Another creative entrepreneur with the same problem, boldly typed "On-the-Job Training: 1984 to Present" and listed every project with a terse description of what she had learned. The result was quite impressive.

Experience

The category most often and earnestly reviewed is experience. This part of the résumé is only slightly different from that of job-seeking résumés. Experience, in this case, refers to employment or occupational experience; nevertheless, if you have military experience and feel your training or past duties enhance your ability to orchestrate your current business, then include that background in this category of your résumé. Again, list your experience in reverse chronological order. Under the heading, Experience, list dates in a left column and jobs in a right column. Another popular format gives the name of the company you worked for or owned, your title underneath on the second line, and a short job description under that. Include projects or awards that convey credibility.

First, describe your current position as chief executive officer and owner of your present new start-up business. You may have been told to list every job you've held in a job résumé. However, for your business plan résumé, it is only important to mention the positions that support your viability as the owner or manager of your current business venture. Emphasize those work experiences that are most relevant to your current position.

The strongest picture of your past is one that shows your recent jobs provide a basis for where you are today. This sends a message to the reviewers that you have established momentum, you are moving forward in your career, and you have gained the knowledge and experience necessary for you to succeed in the position of CEO of your start-up company.

References

It is acceptable simply to state that references are available upon request. If you choose to list references, however, mention only those that are professionally relevant or may be strong character testimonies. List the name, title, business, and telephone number of no more than three. While references should be individuals who can verify your honesty, they should also be knowledgeable about relevant areas of your background and abilities. In other words, it is better to have professional than personal references.

Personal Financial Information

Finally, if you are intending to use your business plan to obtain financing, include a statement at the bottom of your résumé that your personal financial statements, including the two most recent years of your personal income tax returns, are included in the exhibits or will be provided under separate cover.

Chief Financial Officer

If you have a CFO who is next in your business' chain of command, present his or her title and résumé next. If you choose to use personal business résumés, follow the same format as above: name and title, profile, qualifications summary, education, experience, and references. Keep the length to one page for this and each succeeding officer. However, the résumé of an outstanding manager whose relevant vitae information requires more space to show all the detail that enhances your business plan can be extended to two pages.

If you choose to use summary résumés, present the vitae information under a heading of the officer's or manager's title in one or two paragraphs that include the individual's name and a brief description of his or her background — relevant education, experience, and special awards and achievements.

If you are using your business plan for financing, and you don't have a chief financial officer, bestow the title of controller, accounting manager, or office manager on an internal bookkeeper and present him or her as your second in-line manager, and present his or her résumé after yours.

Many small start-up companies have no employee for this position and make arrangements with their outside certified public accountant to accept the title of chief financial officer, usually for a small additional fee. Because of the extra liability incurred for corporations, CPAs will usually include the additional stipulation stating they are not to be listed in corporate minutes as treasurer or as a corporate officer.

Director of Operations

If you have a director of operations and he or she is higher in the chain of command than your chief financial officer, include his or her summary résumé immediately after yours. If you don't have this position, but plan to hire someone within the first year, include the title as a heading with an explanation that you intend to fill the position on a target date. Also, mention the qualifications needed in the individual you will seek to fill this position.

Many businesses assign titles to existing managers without fully assigning all the duties associated with the position — this is a questionable practice. If you have no one in this position, no plans to fill the position, or no need of the position in your operations, add the title to your own, or avoid it altogether.

Sales and Marketing Director

Identify your sales and marketing director, if you have one, or designate another employee or yourself. If your business uses an outside sales broker or agent, make arrangements with that person to include him or her as your sales and marketing director, but make it clear that this individual is an outside salesperson, not an employee of your business.

Include other key personnel that may be distinctive to your business, such as, Vice President, Production Manager; Vice President, Human Resources Director; or Director of Research and Development.

Business Consultants

Finally, following your management team, add summary résumés of your business attorney and business accountant. Cover their educational and significant occupational experience.

When you use outside consultants, don't simply photocopy their résumés. Instead, have them reproduced in the same style and format as your business plan's summary résumés, so they will fit seamlessly into your business plan. Your plan will look more professional and will convey the impression these individuals are a part of your team, even though they are not actually employees.

Board of Directors

If your business is incorporated, you are required by law to have a board of directors. If your company is small, the directors of the board are usually the owners and possibly one or two key managers of the business. If, however, you have a board of directors that is different from your management team, indicate key directors by name, possible financial interest in the company, and the area of expertise they bring as advisors on the board.

Management Team   Kona Gold Coffees

Title	Name of Manager
Chief Executive Officer/President	David Cooper
Office Manager	Terry Jervis
Operations Chief	Bob Clay
Salesperson	Lisa Orzechowski
Purchasing Agent	Larry Fennel

While complete résumés for all five of the above key personnel are included in the exhibits (see Exhibits), summary résumés are included here for the reviewer's cursory perusal.

CEO/President

David Cooper has three years of experience in the coffee industry both as purchasing and sales manager at Kealakekua Farms on the Big Island, and more than 12 years experience in the manufacturing business. He was instrumental in formulating two Blue Ribbon winning coffees and received acclaim as co-winner of both awards. For Kealakekua Farms, Mr. Cooper reached a milestone of $5,000,000 in sales and established the co-op of suppliers still used by that manufacturer. Mr. Cooper holds a bachelor's degree in business with a specialty in production from the University of Missouri. He has successfully completed three computer science courses on production software and one seminar by Profit Mentor on financing forecasts and cash flow control. He is married, with two children, and has lived in Kailua-Kona for three years.

Operations Chief

Bob Clay has an MBA in production management from California State University at Stanislaus and has six years experience in production management with our largest competitor in the industry, Sandwich Isles Coffees in Honolulu. While there, he set up a vacuum/flush/nitrogen seal process and modernized their weigh and fill conveyor system. Under his tutelage, Sandwich Isles won one Blue Ribbon award last year. Married with two children, the Clays recently moved to Kailua-Kona, the "coffee king capital," as Bob says.

Office Manager

Terry Jervis comes to us from Beta Chemical's southern Los Angeles headquarters office where she was the office manager for this chemical manufacturing company for the last eight years. Terry is very familiar with all computer accounting for manufacturing and distribution sales. She has a bachelor's in business accounting from California State at Chico and has completed numerous continuing education classes and advanced computer technology software programs for manufacturing. She is married; the Jervis' have recently moved to Kailua-Kona. Her husband is a writer and does not want to relocate again.

(continued)

> **Management Team** (continued)   Kona Gold Coffees
>
> ### Salesperson
>
> **Lisa Orzechowski** has been working part-time with David Cooper for the past six months in advance of opening and is setting up all of our retail outlets. Lisa is 27 and her vibrant and charming personality win retailers and consumers alike. For the past five years, Lisa has been in charge of sales for a small chain of gift shops in Hawaii, Chameleon Waters. She grew up in Kailua-Kona and knows most of the players in the coffee industry. As Bob says, "she even dresses the part," in her sophisticated country style, as she peddles our baskets of gourmet coffee. However, her laid-back style is deceiving because she is extremely competitive and doesn't believe in accepting second place. Already she has shown that she is excellent at follow-up and will work whatever hours the job demands to win customers over. Lisa is single.
>
> ### Purchasing Agent
>
> **Larry Fennel** comes to us from Regal Kona Coffee where he was purchasing agent for the last six years. At Regal, Larry developed a rapport with growers all over Hawaii and especially with Kona coffee growers. Prior to coffee purchasing, Larry was a purchasing agent for Remington Farms, producers of poultry and dairy products, where he had on-the-job-training and learned sophisticated purchasing techniques that he has been able to adapt to the coffee industry. Larry is married and he and his wife have recently moved to Kailua-Kona for this position.
>
> ### Business Attorney
>
> **Ralph Austin** is a specialized business attorney with the firm, Tanaka, Aering, and Cibyll, located in Honolulu, in a branch office at 77-5436 Hualalai Road, Kailua-Kona. TA&C is one of the older firms in Hawaii.
>
> ### Certified Public Accountant
>
> **Ross Lang** is specialized in industrial accounting and is senior partner in the firm of Tower and Lang, located in Honolulu at 737 Bishop Street, Suite 2202.

Key Personnel Responsibilities and Duties

After the segment on your management team, develop a segment headed Key Personnel (or Manager) Responsibilities and Duties. List current and future managerial titles that reflect your staffing plan when you will be operating at peak performance, followed by a paragraph or two describing the responsibilities and duties of each manager in your business. When you are writing these for the first time, two types of problems might surface.

- Gaps. There might be obvious areas of management you have not included or addressed, and
- Overlaps. There might be areas where two managers cross each other's boundaries in managerial responsibilities and duties.

Developing a business plan can identify potential problems early in your business planning phase. Being able to see and correct things before they become problems is one of the undeniable benefits derived from developing a complete business plan. Two things that become apparent are gaps and overlaps in responsibilities and duties because they usually exist when boundaries are not specifically drawn. Lines of responsibility and authority should be well-planned, clearly defined, and communicated to all employees. They should be consistent and logical. For example, are responsibilities allocated according to a master scheme — by function, by territory, by special task, by product?

Common gaps for many new startup businesses involve numerous oversights. For example, who is responsible for training, for hiring, for firing? Who is responsible for conducting sales meetings? Who are the backups for specific responsibilities if someone is absent? Who is responsible for new employee orientation? Common gaps often surface when two managers think a particular responsibility or task is the job of the other. Look for possible gaps in your organization.

Common overlaps might exist between two managers with similar functions. If you have a marketing director and a sales manager, are the lines of separation of their duties and responsibilities clear? Often, an overzealous manager will infringe on the duties or responsibilities of another manager. If responsibilities and activities are examined thoroughly and clearly identified, many problems can be prevented.

Finally, in your list of key personnel responsibilities and duties, label positions that are vacant and describe the qualifications for individuals you are seeking to fill them. Showing you have considered the vacant positions sends a signal to the reviewers of your business plan that you have a total plan and know exactly who you need to complete it.

For a clear idea of how to structure this section, see the Kona Gold Coffees example below.

Key Personnel Responsibilities and Duties — Kona Gold Coffees

President — Responsible for overall management and planning which includes operations, income and expense, buying, production, marketing, sales, after-market satisfaction, personnel, and cash flow control. The president directly supervises the office manager, operations chief, in-house salesperson, and purchasing agent. He is directly responsible for recruiting, hiring, and training of non-production employees. Management of the production staff is the responsibility of the operations chief.

Operations Chief — Supervises all operational matters of manufacturing, production, assembly, inventory control, fulfillment, and equipment maintenance. In addition, he is responsible for productivity, capacity, and cost and quality control and must be prepared for all emergency problems with stand-by programs for variable labor or outside contractors. The operations chief must stay abreast of the latest technology and equipment and manage the work force, in both methods of shop production or production-line, to efficiently perform the production tasks. In our company he is also responsible for personnel matters with respect to production employees and serve as the company safety officer.

(continued)

> ### Key Personnel Responsibilities and Duties (continued) — Kona Gold Coffees
>
> **Office Manager** — Responsible for all accounting reports and related activities: processes payroll and maintains the general ledger and journals via automated software. Her biggest job will be staying on top of accounts receivable, making collections, and the critical timing of paying payables for cash flow control. She is also in charge of insurance and renewal of all governmental fees and licenses.
>
> **Salesperson** — Responsible for all consumer sales via direct mail and the Internet and all wholesale sales to retailers. Paid commissions even on wholesale sales, she is directly involved with setting up and maintaining all retail accounts and processing all orders to production and accounting, as well as following up on all fulfillment and distribution. While marketing programs are directly spear headed by the president, she is instrumental in creating and recommending advertising and promotional campaigns and presides over their execution and success.
>
> **Purchasing Agent** — Directly responsible for supplier rapport, maintaining proper inventories of coffee purchases, cost effectiveness, and works in hand with the operations chief to insure coffee freshness at all times. In this business, it is critical to maintain both minimum and maximum levels of inventory and to be synchronized within 5 percent of sales. To accomplish this, our purchasing agent has developed a system of emergency suppliers, minimum purchases, and expedient deliveries. However, his most challenging role is to purchase freshness and quality at the right price while maintaining our high standards.

Management Philosophy

This section is one of the more valuable for your internal use. It is important for you and your management staff to review and revise this segment of your business plan regularly. It is equally important for business plan reviewers of a financial request to know that you have a planned and well-thought-out management philosophy.

Good management happens when a manager develops these effective management skills:

- Lead by example
- Develop teamwork
- Be fair, consistent, and clear
- Keep good communication
- Recognize achievement
- Reward initiative
- Solicit suggestions and be sensitive to concerns
- Delegate power to be creative

Great management happens when a manager applies these in every situation with everyone in the organization.

Consider these principles and any others that you may have developed for your management style and include a few brief sentences for this segment that reflect the management philosophy that you use or will use for your start-up company.

Management Philosophy — Kona Gold Coffees

While our company is just starting and our management structure is modest, our goal is to establish a strong management policy, not only to implement upon opening but to set the tone for future managers to follow. The keys to good management are fairness and consistency, maintaining clear communication, allowing freedom to subordinates to exercise their creativity, and recognizing and rewarding initiative and achievement. As the company grows, management will continue to be sensitive to personnel problems and solicit suggestions from everyone for improvements. Our major tool for setting good management policy is to model good work ethics and lead by example.

Key Personnel Incentives

Many companies offer monetary incentives in addition to salary to lower personnel turnover, to recognize and reward achievement, and to encourage top performance. Personnel salaries will be listed in the personnel plan later in this section. For this segment, if you offer incentives to your key personnel in addition to their salary, include a statement describing your incentive programs.

Of the many creative incentives that are used, a few examples are:

- Profit sharing — cash distributions given to tenured or eligible employees based on a percentage of pretax annual earnings;
- Stock options — opportunities to purchase stock at a future date, locked-in at current value;
- Stock shares — direct equity in the company; and
- Bonuses — cash based on employee performance or company performance usually offered at the end of the year.

Key Personnel Incentives — Kona Gold Coffees

As a new company we will be very involved with getting off the ground and making our first year goals. The first goal after break-even will be to establish a long-range profit sharing program. For the first year, we will be awarding year-end bonuses based on a percentage of the profits to every employee commensurate with their income. As a motivational technique, all employees will know of this in advance.

Organizational Structure

Your organizational structure is the complete picture of the employees in your business and covers how work is divided between them and their reporting structure. If your organization is small or is a home based business, you might want to avoid this section in your business plan and include any of the applicable material in an appropriate management or key personnel segment.

If you do have an organization, open your description with the number of departments, divisions, or work areas and identify the person in charge, number of staff, and to whom they report. Common company departments are: administration, accounting, manufacturing and production, service, purchasing, shipping and receiving, marketing and sales, research and development, human resources, and customer service, to name a few. For larger companies or companies that have unusual or distinctive division classifications, you may wish to include a brief description of the department responsibilities.

A few generic examples are:

- Administration: Singly guided by the president — responsible for overall company management and for setting and monitoring business strategies.
- Accounting: Managed by the controller, assisted by three employees — responsible for billing, collecting, credit, daily banking, daily cash flow, and preparing monthly financial statements, and government reporting.
- Manufacturing and production: Operated by the production manager, assisted by eight employees — responsible for raw materials re-order levels, manufacturing products, overall inventory control, tools and equipment, fulfillment, and safety.

If your company is small with no clearly defined departmental lines, you can use a narrative paragraph and describe your organization as a small cohesive team that works together toward a common goal and shift your operational focus as issues arise. If you wish to add a table, you can further state, "as a matter of routine the person in charge of the primary functional areas are" — followed by a short table.

Function	Name of Employee
Executive in charge	
Accounting	
Production	
Sales and service	

If you have a department or a functional area that is dependent on outside contractors, provide a brief description, and explain your backup plan if designated outside contractors go on strike, close business, raise prices unreasonably, or disrupt your organization for whatever reason.

Organizational Structure   Kona Gold Coffees

At the start of business, the organization of Kona Gold Coffees consists of the following structure: In administration, at the top is our president and owner, David Cooper. Directly under him are: our office manager, Terry Jervis; our operations chief, Bob Clay; our salesperson, Lisa Orzechowski; and our purchasing agent, Larry Fennel. In the office, we have an administrative assistant/receptionist, Jean Phillips. Jean reports to both Mr. Cooper and Terry Jervis, depending on the task. Also under the office manager, we have a bookkeeper, Linda Lipps. This comprises our general and administrative overhead although our salesperson's income is strictly by commission.

In addition, we have three operators in production under the operations chief whose payrolls are included in cost of sales: Gary Prescott, Tina Davenport, and Barry Barnes. By the end of the first year, depending on horizontal sales expansion, we may hire another employee as an in-house salesperson. For a full roster, see Organizational Chart and Personnel Plan below.

Organizational Chart

In addition to your personnel description, create a diagram called an organizational chart that depicts your management personnel, your consultants, and your employees by function. This shows your operation at peak capacity. This chart defines and displays employees' vertical and horizontal relationships to one another. Even if you have assembled only part of your team at the time you writing your business plan, include positions you expect to fill when you are up and running.

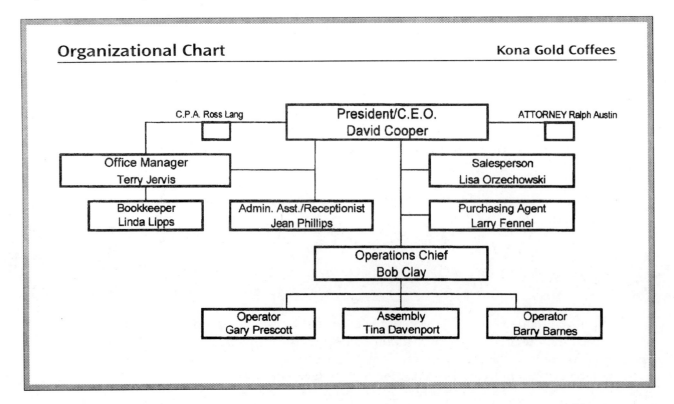

Personnel Plan

Now that you have introduced most of your staff, write a short paragraph specifying the number of employees, both part- and full-time, at the beginning of operations. Also, give the numbers you project to have when you reach peak operational performance. Together with this information, present your personnel plan, which is basically a chart of the departments by employee, function, and salary, as in the example. For salaries, use either gross amounts including benefits or show a total of the payroll taxes and benefits, usually called payroll burden, as a separate line item.

If you are starting from scratch to calculate payroll, ask your accountant who, from experience with other clients, can give you an idea of the prevailing wage rates in your geographic area and these numbers. The payroll burden (employee taxes and benefits) varies from state to state, but your accountant can easily compute it — a rule-of-thumb is to use 13–18 percent of the payroll amount.

Personnel Plan Kona Gold Coffees

Upon opening, we have a total of 10 full-time employees, 6 on general and administrative salaries, 1 on commission, and 3 earning production wages. Our total general and administrative salaries are $290,000 which represent 17.9 percent of sales as compared to the industry average of 16.9 percent of sales. Our production labor with payroll burden represents $2.21 of cost of sales or 6.9 percent of sales. The industry standard for this is only 2.7 percent; however, our product is much more labor intensive due to its different nature from our competition's.

(continued)

To determine your salary, it is helpful to make up a family budget. Realizing the need to keep expenses to a minimum during the start up of a business, personal austerity is going to be your catchphrase for your first year. When compiling your family budget, include such items as:

- Automobile expenses
- Automobile insurance
- Automobile maintenance
- Automobile payments
- Clothing
- Educational expenses
- Food
- Gifts
- Home maintenance
- Homeowner's insurance
- Life insurance
- Medical and dental expenses not covered by insurance
- Medical and dental insurance
- Mortgage payment or rent.
- Property taxes,
- Utilities
- Miscellaneous

Monitor non-itemized expenses closely for three months and reclassify recurring expenses, giving them their own accounts.

Personnel Plan (continued)

Kona Gold Coffees

Division	Employee	Month Jan.	Feb.	March	April	May	June	July	Aug.	Sept.	Oct.	Nov.	Dec.	Year 1
Cost of Sales Payroll														
Production														
Production Operator	Gary Prescott	2,667	2,667	2,667	2,667	2,667	2,667	2,667	2,667	2,667	2,667	2,667	2,667	32,000
Production Assembly	Tina Davenport	2,667	2,667	2,667	2,667	2,667	2,667	2,667	2,667	2,667	2,667	2,667	2,667	32,000
Production Operator	Barry Barnes	2,667	2,667	2,667	2,667	2,667	2,667	2,667	2,667	2,667	2,667	2,667	2,667	32,000
Total Cost of Sale Payroll		8,001	8,001	8,001	8,001	8,001	8,001	8,001	8,001	8,001	8,001	8,001	8,001	96,000
Cost of Sale Payroll Burden		1,280	1,280	1,280	1,280	1,280	1,280	1,280	1,280	1,280	1,280	1,280	1,280	15,360
Non-cost of Sales Payroll														
Marketing & Sales														
Salesperson #1	Lisa Orzechowski	[straight 4% commission]												
General & Administration														
President	David Cooper	5,833	5,833	5,833	5,833	5,833	5,833	5,833	5,833	5,833	5,833	5,833	5,833	70,000
Admin. Assistant	Jean Phillips	2,500	2,500	2,500	2,500	2,500	2,500	2,500	2,500	2,500	2,500	2,500	2,500	30,000
Operations Chief	Bob Clay	5,833	5,833	5,833	5,833	5,833	5,833	5,833	5,833	5,833	5,833	5,833	5,833	70,000
Accounting														
Office Manager	Terry Jervis	3,333	3,333	3,333	3,333	3,333	3,333	3,333	3,333	3,333	3,333	3,333	3,333	40,000
Bookkeeper	Linda Lipps	2,917	2,917	2,917	2,917	2,917	2,917	2,917	2,917	2,917	2,917	2,917	2,917	35,000
Purchasing														
Purchasing Agent	Larry Fennel	3,750	3,750	3,750	3,750	3,750	3,750	3,750	3,750	3,750	3,750	3,750	3,750	45,000
Total Non-cost of Sales Payroll		24,167	24,166	24,166	24,166	24,166	24,166	24,166	24,166	24,166	24,166	24,166	24,166	290,000
Non-cost of Sale Payroll Burden		3,867	3,867	3,867	3,867	3,867	3,867	3,867	3,867	3,867	3,867	3,867	3,867	46,400
Total Personnel		10	10	10	10	10	10	10	10	10	10	10	10	10

Important Points to Remember

- If you intend to use your business plan to obtain financing, your management section must convince the reviewers that you know what you are doing and that you have what it takes to do it.
- Good management comes from developing several management skills; great management comes from managers applying them consistently and fairly.
- While preparing your start-up business plan for lenders or investors, carefully map out your business venture. Then your business plan can be a basic management tool that will ensure the success of your business once you are up and running.
- Make sure the salaries and payroll benefits in your personnel plan match the numbers in your pro forma income statements.

When you complete this section, remember to review your management and organization summary to ensure it covers the highlights discovered while developing this material.

Now you are ready to show reviewers of your business plan how the human resources introduced in this section will work together to carry out the day to day operations of your business, the subject of the next section and the next chapter.

Chapter 9

Operations

To succeed, a business must occupy a field of public usefulness by producing a good article at the lowest price consistent with fair treatment of all those concerned with its production, distribution, and consumption.
— WALTER C. TEAGLE

If the area of management and organization is the heart of the system, operations is the life blood. The operations section of your business plan is where you describe how you and your management team run your business. Defined operations help ensure consistency. Consistency in operations is important to maintain a level of employee efficiency, customer familiarity and contentment, and other stabilizing factors in your business. Achieving production and process consistency can play an important role in increasing profits and lowering costs by improving productivity.

The operations portion of your business plan covers the policies and procedures devoted to making your business run smoothly and to establishing consistency. To attain consistency, you must understand the role of each employee and identify your policies and procedures. Your ongoing task is to seek improvements in your policies and procedures, so you can obtain the ultimate operational goal of reaching maximum efficiency in operations. This is best accomplished by developing and regularly updating an operations manual or a company policy and procedure manual.

Rarely does a start-up company develop policies at the onset, usually they are written on an as-needed basis. However, day-to-day operations should be recorded, so you can develop an operations manual as your company grows. The importance of an operations manual is directly proportional to the number of employees and work processes. Developing an accurate operations manual with consistent policies and procedures that can be refined is key to long-term success of any business operation. A good operations manual begins with a well-structured outline that breaks down primary activities within the organization into chapters on topics such as personnel policies, job descriptions, advertising policies, accounting and financial reports, daily operations, hours and holidays, inventory control, maintenance, product or service specifications, suppliers and subcontractors, distribution and fulfillment, and other topics specific to the nature of your business.

If you haven't developed an operations manual, you don't need to write one for your business plan, but as you work through this section, you may be able to clarify what otherwise could remain undefined policies and procedures. For a business plan, the areas of operations covered are:

- Operation summary
- Operations description
- Human resources
- Facility
- Production
- Supply and distribution
- Fulfillment
- Customer service policy
- Inventory control
- Efficiency control
- Cash flow control

Operations Summary

Your opening paragraph for this section is a summary of the key elements of your operations, policies and procedures. State three or four outstanding features of your operations that are advantageous for your business or that set you apart from the competition. These may include highlights of your operations description, human resources, facility, production, equipment, supply and distribution channels, order fulfillment, customer service policy, or procedures of controls. Like all summaries, it should be written last.

> ### Operations Summary   Kona Gold Coffees
>
> Our operation of production is the motor that drives our system. We buy an average of 850 pounds of coffee each week from 18 suppliers and process and manufacture 188 products a day with three operators under the supervision of our operations chief. Productivity is one unit per 3 workers per 2.3 minutes. Capacity could double or triple by going to shifts and adding more operators. Because we must maintain a 21-day freshness for our product, the operations chief must carefully watch inventory levels of raw materials and finished products. Fulfillment is in-house and wholesale orders are shipped by local trucking and retail orders are shipped via air freight. Freight on average runs 3.75 percent of sales. The operations chief is responsible for shipping, receiving, quality control, and inventory control.
>
> Our 2,500 square foot facility is leased for ten years and we have mostly new equipment costing $48,761; see Production, Schedule of Equipment.

Operations Description

In this segment, describe your business operations. If you have divisions, list them in their order of operations. For instance, starting with sales, show how an order is processed and proceed through your operations to the point where you replenish the inventory, or vice versa, depending on the plan's purpose. If this business plan is for internal planning, you may want to provide greater detail; however, this section is not intended to replace an operations manual, something which you may need to develop later.

If your business plan is being written to secure a loan or investment, describe your operations in as few paragraphs as possible to keep the reviewers' interest. Cover the main issues and avoid the details. You should address the flow of operations important to the success of your business and how you expect to resolve the problems commonly encountered in your type of business.

If your business is a manufacturing, assembly or wholesale company, it is more important for you to convey your complete operational procedures. However, for your business plan, keep your description as terse as possible. If you need more information to complete your operational plans or production designs or to locate specialized equipment, contact your industry's trade associations for consultants in manufacturing design. They should be able to direct you to the resources you need.

It is important to explain your competitive edge, such as the use of new methods of production, improved distribution, or specialized technology. If special technology is a key to your business success, you might want to describe it in a separate segment under a heading, Technology. If it is very technical, yet can be explained understandably, you may want to set up an entire section in your business plan devoted to the subject. In that case, title the section, Technology, and position it between the section Management and Organization and this section, Operations.

> **Operations Description**   Kona Gold Coffees
>
> **Administration.** Our president administers operations, overall management, and strategic planning. He has one administrative assistant who is also the receptionist/secretary.
>
> **Sales.** The activities of operations starts with sales. Our salesperson calls on all retailers monthly (mainland and off-island retailers by telephone; local retailers, in person) and handles all direct mail sales and Internet sales. All orders are entered into the computer which generates a record of sale to accounting and a work order to production.
>
> **Production.** Work orders are processed and fulfilled in production; see special segments on production and fulfillment below.
>
> **Purchasing.** We buy on average 170 pounds of roasted coffee beans per day. Our purchasing agent calls on our suppliers to verify quality and constantly shops for special purchase prices. All purchases are entered into the computer, added to inventory, and a record of purchase is sent to accounting. For more detail, see Supply and Distribution below.
>
> **Accounting.** Our office manager, with the help of one bookkeeper, enters all records of sales and all records of purchases and is responsible for billing, collecting, credit, daily banking, daily cash flow, preparing monthly financial statements, and government reporting. We use double-entry and accrual-basis accounting.

Human Resources

If your company is very small or is a home based business, skip this segment. If you have, or intend to have, several employees you should develop some basic human resources policies. Develop procedures for recruiting, new employee orientation, training, reviewing, salaries and benefits, standardized holidays, incentives, and rewards. Also, identify the person responsible for implementing them. Clear policies, evenly and consistently applied, increase morale and decrease sick leave and the rate of turnover. Once you have defined these policies, include them in your operations manual or create a personnel manual.

Another task of human resources is to monitor the workload of employees. Are any of your employees overloaded? Can any of their tasks be broken down and delegated to others with less to do? What new positions need to be created?

For this segment of your business plan, briefly describe policies and procedures for human resources that are appropriate for your company. In addition to the Kona Gold Coffees example, here are some other samples.

- Hiring procedure: We seek new applicants by running classified ads in the local newspaper and by paying referral bonuses to existing employees. Besides the capabilities needed for their specific position, we look for people who are team players, flexible and willing to work hard.

Our president conducts all personal interviews for managers and evaluates each candidate's past performance and their ability to motivate and direct employees. Other applicants are screened through personal interviews by department supervisors and all references are checked by our human resources officer.

- New employee orientation: Our human resources officer gives to all new employees from out of town a packet of information that explains community activities and lists the locations of medical emergency facilities, churches, schools, the local library and police station, transportation systems, daycare centers, and major shopping facilities. All new employees are given a tour of company departments which includes locations of restrooms and the lunch room. They are given a benefits package, including insurance options, a holiday schedule, a profit sharing guide explaining our program and eligibility and our safety booklet.
- Training: Individual training is done within each department and is the responsibility of the department supervisor. A common element we strive to impart is a sense of teamwork. Throughout the year, outside professionals will be brought in to give short seminars on various levels of company improvement. These include software familiarity, motivational techniques, personal organization, and safety issues.
- Reviewing: All employees are reviewed at regular intervals within each department by departmental supervisors. Whenever possible, we promote from within.
- Salaries and benefits: We try to set our salaries at four to eight percent above the local industry average and give annual raises based on company and personal performance. Our standard benefits include ten paid holidays, paid vacations, two personal leave days, medical and dental insurance, short-term disability insurance, and three company social functions. Managers receive these benefits and a separate incentives program with expense accounts. They have optional group insurance benefits which include long-term disability insurance and several types of life insurance.

As the final element of this segment, describe any new positions to be created and eventually filled that are in addition to those listed in your management and organization section.

Human Resources   Kona Gold Coffees

Although our company is small, our president is responsible for personnel and personnel policies. He handles recruiting, hiring, training, and reviewing of all non-production people and delegates these tasks to the operations chief for production people. The president sets the salaries and benefits and has a standard policy of increasing all salaries every year by the GDP, and offers incentive rewards for those deserving. After the first year, a profit sharing program will be available for those eligible.

(continued)

> **Human Resources** (continued)   **Kona Gold Coffees**
>
> Other benefits include medical and dental insurance and short-term disability insurance. Employees have one week vacation the first year, two weeks each year thereafter until the fifth year, when they begin receiving three weeks. There is no standard policy for personal leave or sick leave; each employee is dealt with individually for these needs with the intention of being as fair and consistent as possible. There are eight paid holidays for everyone.
>
> As we grow, training and reviewing will be handled by the department manager of each department. Standardized reviewing will become a policy, but for the first year we are going to remain informal.

Facility

For this segment of your business plan, describe your facility and location in terms of operational effectiveness.

If you have a home based business, be candid and state that you are operating from your home because you have no need for the expense of an office. In addition to proper zoning and adequate office space, state the advantages of your facility for your specific business. For example, you might always meet at clients' offices, or you might be centrally located for the convenience of your clients and you. Include any other special feature such as having a separate entry for your business or accessible curb side parking.

For site-sensitive retail and service businesses and for manufacturing companies, you will need to develop much more detail. If you have more than one location, describe your main office or headquarters facility and include the important features or purposes of the branches. Define your spatial requirements — the overall square footage of your facility with a breakdown of square footage for the functional layout as planned for the different operational functions: retail and office space, production, order fulfillment, shipping and receiving, service area size, warehousing for raw materials, warehousing for finished products, show rooms, and any other specialized needs that you might have for your business.

Cover the essential site advantages such as suitability to your business, prestigious address, accessibility, visibility, drive-through convenience, number of parking spaces, loading dock, suitability to support services, and proximity to freight transportation (air, rail, and trucking). Briefly explain your facility's advantages over the competition within your market, any cost-savings, and any essentials about your location that a reviewer should recognize and value.

If you have a lease, explain its terms, advantages, and restrictions. Cover the important advantages of your lease — see the lease negotiation materials in Chapter 2. If you have a mortgage, explain the terms and the advantages.

> ### Facility   Kona Gold Coffees
>
> We are located at 74-6464 Alapa Street, Kailua-Kona, Hawaii in the Kona Industrial Park. We have easy access for trucking, both shipping and receiving, and are six miles from the Kona airport for DHL delivery. For our concept, we are better located than our competitors are. Our site has 2,500 square feet: one large bay with loft (1,956 sq. ft. floor area), three offices, a foyer receptionist area, and two restrooms.
>
> The president and the salesperson use the two smaller offices (each 144 sq. ft.) and the office manager, bookkeeper, and purchasing agent share the larger office (240 sq. ft.). Our facilities are served with 220 V 3 phase electrical power for all equipment. Most of the electricity cost for this is included in cost of sales. Since we are not a retail outlet, we have no facilities for walk-in customers; however, we have adequate parking for all employees and four guests.
>
> We have a ten year lease on our premises at the low price of $0.80 per square foot because we took over the shell building and put in all the improvements at our expense, literally restoring the very run-down building which is white and clean today. We keep our production floor sealed and spotless.

Production

Production, as an operation, does not simply apply to manufacturing and assembly companies. Service, retail, and wholesale businesses need to assess this aspect of their operation, as well, to improve their efficiencies and quality and to increase their profit margins.

Examine all your company operations involved to create, produce, buy, or handle your products or services to your specifications and quality standards. Determine if there is anything you could do to improve any of your procedures or processes?

For your production segment write a few paragraphs depicting your production plan. Describe your use of permanent labor, variable labor, and subcontractors and how you cross-train your employees. Indicate whether you utilize the shop method or production-line method. Include information about the number of shifts, the number of workers per shift, and the length of hours of each. State the advantages of your production operation. Explain your average productivity, the output of one unit of product or service per number(s) of workers per period (minutes, hours, or days), and your average capacity, the output of total units per day, week, or month. Also, describe your backup plan for increasing capacity when the need arises. Include a brief description of your specialized equipment and direct the attention of the reviewer to the equipment schedule. If you use any special technology in production, describe it. Finally, state your methods of quality control. If you solicit customer feedback, include a brief description of the process.

Your Work Force

For manufacturing and assembly companies, evaluate how you manage, organize, and deploy your work force. Like a team sport that plays man-to-man or zone defenses, there are two production methods in manufacturing and assembly: the shop or team method and the production-line method.

The shop method allocates one group of workers responsible for the whole job from start to finish. A company using this system will have several shops or teams doing similar jobs. The production-line method sets workers up in a line, each doing one specific task, then relaying a part or a work-in-progress to the next worker in line to do the next successive task. The first worker starts the first task and the last worker completes the final task. In both systems it behooves the employer to change workers' tasks to prevent monotony, boredom, and burn-out, and cross-train workers so that absences will have the least impact on the operations. In the shop method, workers on the same team change tasks within their shop. In the production-line method, workers move to different positions within the line. In both methods, it is important that every worker knows who is responsible for making decisions.

Consider all the information necessary for completely describing your production operation: the number of total permanent workers, both part- and full-time; the number of workers per shift; the number of shifts; the hours of the shifts; the numbers of workers and time per unit of product or service (productivity); the total output of products or services per day, week, or month (capacity).

Supplementing Your Work Force

In addition to a permanent work force, many companies use variable labor and outside subcontractors. Workers hired to do a specialized job for a specific period — for special orders, unusual volume orders, specific off-hours, or seasonal work — are referred to as variable labor. Many of these workers can be classified as part-time employees who will often work for lower wages or will have less impact on the business' benefit package because of their part-time status. It can be advantageous for some businesses to use variable labor to control a lower fixed base of permanent employee salaries, by adding the variable labor only during periods when the increased revenue they generate will compensate them. The disadvantage of variable labor is, typically, they are less trained, less motivated, and less loyal, which can present difficulties in maintaining high standards of quality in both process and product as well as other aspects of consistency and control.

Another way to supplement your permanent work force, yet maintain some control of the base costs in your budget, is to use outside subcontractors for certain production tasks. Since the other companies have a markup, it is typical for unit costs to increase. However, when using outside subcontractors as a supplemental force, the markup is generally offset by the higher efficiency of your permanent work force. This allows you to keep your workforce at maximum capacity, with only the overflow going to subcontractors. By using this approach, you have the advantage of more control over your fixed overhead costs. If you have a manufacturing and assembly company, wholesale, retail, or service business, look into ways of subcontracting some of your tasks, and evaluate the differences in your profit margins after all things are considered.

Equipment

Put together a complete equipment schedule as part of your production segment or append one to your exhibits. Include your manufacturing, assembly, distribution, and shipping equipment; robotics, if any; other specialized equipment; company vehicles; computer equipment; telephone system; office equipment; fixtures; furniture; and all capital equipment that can be depreciated. In a table, show the date of purchase of each piece of major equipment, its purchase price, debt or lease payments, monthly amount of depreciation, useful life (total years of depreciation), and condition or maintenance required. Subtotal the columns that can be added, as in the example. Three other entries that you may want to include are the balance owed, current book value, and the remaining number of years of depreciation, especially if they are not in your accounting reports. For information on locating industrial equipment and associated costs, check the *Thomas Register of American Manufactures*, available in most libraries or on the Internet:

Thomas Register
Internet: www.thomasregister.com/

For sources of information on office equipment, check your local library for the publication *Datapro Office Automation Reports*.

Improving Production with Technology

It should be your inherent mission to improve your operational systems by initially and continually evaluating the latest technology to improve productivity, to decrease costs, and to increase profitability. New technology is constantly being developed for nearly every industry. Consider your production. Can you better utilize computers? Is there better hardware or software or both, than you have, or than you have planned, to assist you in improved production? Are robotics available that can help you cut unit costs after calculating the capital expenditure and depreciation over a period? Can you increase productivity and capacity to gain a competitive edge? Can something be invented to improve your methods of production and other operations?

Are you using technology for information processing, inventory control, supplies and distribution, quality control, or other purposes, in addition to production? You should list and describe in your business plan any such technological improvements, unless they must be safeguarded as a competitive secret. If this is the case, mention them as specifically as you can without allowing them to be duplicated by a competitor who might see an unauthorized copy of your business plan.

Quality Control

Last, but certainly not least, consider your methods of quality control for your production operations. Who is responsible? How are inspections conducted? Do you conduct regular or random testing? What procedures or programs are in place to motivate employees for quality assurance? What training methods and rewards are used? Do you solicit employee suggestions and customer feedback? If so, describe how.

Production   Kona Gold Coffees

Because our operation is small, production is responsible for all receiving, production, inventory control, fulfillment, and the coordination of shipping. These are the responsibility of the operations chief with the help of three operator/assembly persons at the start of business working one eight-hour shift a day.

As sales increase, the numbers for production may have to increase with it. With the same equipment working in shifts, we could double or triple our current production, but we will wait for sales to dictate this since freshness is a key. Because production payroll is a cost of sales, these increases would not adversely affect our pro formas; on the contrary, our profit margins would increase in theory because our rent per unit would go down.

When coffee is brought in, the lots are verified by computer then received by the operations chief. In the weekly routine, incoming coffee beans are sorted, weighed, and conveyed to storage bins awaiting grinding. Daily, coffee beans are transferred from bins to three operating grinders that grind the beans and convey the dry product to weigh and fill machines that dispense precisely 2 ounces in each bag and seal the tops. To control the separation of the types of coffee, grinder 1 grinds coffees A & B, grinder 2 grinds coffees C & D, and grinder 3 grinds coffees E & F; A, C, and E in one 160-minute period; B, D, and F in another. In between grinding periods, grinders are cleaned so that new coffee types do not take on the characteristics of the coffee from the previous job. With seven coffees instead of six, our operations chief has a unique scheduling system for this process.

Our production department grinds, bags, and labels approximately 165 pounds of completed product each day. These are then assembled, packaged, shrink-wrapped, and dated. Average daily production with one shift is about 188 packages at optimum — not capacity.

Before all products go out, orders are verified by computer, then transferred for fulfillment and shipment (see fulfillment below). This is the heart of the daily production operation.

Obviously much more goes on behind the scenes to keep this operation flowing smoothly. Coffee is kept cool, not refrigerated, and ground no more than two days before shipping. The product remains fresh for 21 days after bagging. Although we use the latest equipment, the best production techniques, and efficient inventory and waste management, we have no competitive edge in production, other than efficiency, as opposed to those competitors who are not efficient. Our competitive edge lies in the product itself.

At start up, our operations chief will be using a production-line method for the three-person team. Each one will change jobs every 110 minutes during loading, grinding, and packaging procedures. A period is set aside every day for clean-up, maintenance, safety meetings, training, or miscellaneous scheduled production techniques or some combination of these. Each member

(continued)

Production (continued)   **Kona Gold Coffees**

of the three-person team will become familiar with every job and cross-trained to cover an absence. Our average productivity is 1 unit per 3 workers per 2.3 minutes, or $2.21 per unit labor; and our average capacity is 188 units per day.

Our special production equipment is the latest in technology and includes overall: one used delivery van for special deliveries, three Ditting KR1403 stainless steel grinders, one Pacific Bag Weigh & Fill Conveyor, three Pacific Bag Weigh & Fill Dispensers, one Vacuum/Flush/Sealer, and two Bussel industrial shrink-wrappers, 20 feet of Advanced Dispensing Systems plastic bins, and one Twist tie peel & stick label applicator.

For daily emergencies, we will use temporary human resources, several in Kona, and for longer — seasonal or special holiday runs — we will use variable labor. In a pinch, we have lined up one outside contractor who is capable of producing 60 percent of our daily workload with about a 10 percent efficiency drop at a price equal to 80 percent of our costs.

In addition to the shipping and receiving quality control methods already described, our operations chief, the person responsible for quality control, conducts a random sampling several times per day. Our assembly operator checks five finished products at the end of every run. If no problem is found, testing is stopped. If a problem emerges, she continues more thorough testing, even a whole batch run, if required. We solicit employee suggestions and customer feedback for quality control via point of purchase displays and our Internet web site.

Schedule of Equipment

Equipment Description	Manufacturer Name	Model	Serial Number	Date of Purchase	Purchase Price	Monthly Payment	Depreciation Schedule	Useful Life	Maintenance Required
Delivery van	Ford	XL Van	999-23x	11/28/XX	$ 9,500	$600	$263.89	3	Used
SS grinders	Ditting	KR1403	1434	11/29/XX	2,795	0	23.29	10	
SS grinders	Ditting	KR1403	2871	11/29/XX	2,795	0	23.29	10	
SS grinders	Ditting	KR1403	9935	11/29/XX	2,795	0	23.29	10	
Weigh and fill conveyor	Royce	R-23	34-56	12/03/XX	2,317	0	19.31	10	
Weigh and fill dispensers	Royce	R-31	34-888	12/03/XX	6,595	0	54.96	10	
Weigh and fill dispensers	Royce	R-31	34-892	12/03/XX	6,595	0	54.96	10	
Weigh and fill dispensers	Royce	R-31	34-793	12/03/XX	6,595	0	54.96	10	
Vacuum/flush/sealer	Royce	R-420	7601	12/03/XX	4,424	0	73.73	5	
Shrink-wrapper	Bussel	MR-678	n2y34	12/14/XX	450	0	18.75	2	
Shrink-wrapper	Bussel	MR-678	n3s45	12/14/XX	450	0	18.75	2	
20 ft. plastic bins	APS	N/A	N/A	12/15/XX	2,800	0	233.33	1	
TTP/SL applicator	Moses	JN301	N/A	12/15/XX	650	0	18.06	3	
Appropriate totals					$48,761	$600	$880.57		

Supply and Distribution

For this segment of your operations, supply represents your incoming raw materials for a manufacturer, incoming parts for an assembly company, or incoming wholesale products for wholesale and retail companies, while distribution is the operation for your outgoing finished products or services. Your suppliers and distributors are essential support companies for the success of your business. If you have yet to find this support for your company, consult your trade association or check the *Thomas Register of American Manufacturers* for suppliers and distributors.

Although it is important to your business to develop strong relationships with these companies, on occasion nearly every business operation experiences problems with main suppliers and key distributors. For this reason, do not rely totally on one supplier for one type of incoming goods or one distributor for your outgoing products or services. Suppose one of your key suppliers or distributors goes on strike, or it experiences problems out of its control with its sources or deliveries. Locate alternate suppliers and distributors that you can conscript as backups if emergencies arise or your relationship deteriorates with your primary supplier and distributor.

When choosing your suppliers, it is very tempting to consider price alone to keep your cost of goods as low as possible; however, in the long run it is more important to assess other qualities in addition to price. Choose quality suppliers who are consistent in service and deliveries and who will work within your parameters of cash flow and credit terms. Then, for the health of your business, develop a strong relationship with them so they can maintain familiarity with your changing needs. It is also important to choose suppliers who are capable of delivering goods to your specifications and standards and with whom you can establish a good working relationship. If it is necessary to your business, make sure your suppliers can respond quickly to your needs providing goods or materials via overnight delivery. Also consider whether or not your suppliers will contract for no-minimum orders, minimum orders, volume orders, or any combination of these and whether or not the levels or amounts and the cost of these orders severely impacts your costs of goods.

If the nature of your business dictates you can use only one distributor and your sales activity depends on it, the selection of this distributor may be the most important business decision you make. Again, develop a strong relationship and be loyal and responsive to their needs. Plan your operations to synchronize with theirs. When choosing your distributor, check out its reputation with retailers or customers and determine its reliability, integrity, and length of time in business. Find out if it serves your competitors and whether it provides fair and equal service to all of its client companies. Find out the distributor's payment methods. Will you pay a fixed fee or percentages or commissions, or does the distributor purchase from you and resell? In the case of the latter, find out the distributor's payment procedure and reputation of payment. If the nature of your business permits you to use more than one distributor, do so for the health and strength of your business.

Break this segment of your operations section into two parts. First describe your supply operations. State the name and title of the person responsible for purchasing. List the materials required, their sources, average cost per unit, credit terms, and backup sources with average costs and credit terms. Specify the extra costs incurred for minimum orders and for fast-response orders. Describe any competitive edge you may have by using these suppliers. In addition, explain your procedure for receiving and who is responsible by title or name.

In the second part, describe how your products or services are distributed to your customers. If you use a distributor, give its name and mention whether or not it is your exclusive distributor. If you have just one distributor, describe its reputation and the advantages you have for using it. If you have more than one, include each and explain how each one best serves you. Explain whether they pay you or you pay them and whether their fee is fixed or is a percentage or a commission. List the backup distributor(s) you will use for emergencies and additional pertinent information about them.

Supply and Distribution   Kona Gold Coffees

For incoming coffee beans, we have 18 suppliers of famous Blue Ribbon coffees. For proprietary reasons we do not want to disclose the actual names of these companies, but they are all located on the Big Island. Generally, every week Larry Fennel, our purchasing agent, buys 850 pounds of beans, which we receive via the suppliers and ship directly to our location on Tuesdays and Wednesdays. Beans are sorted and temporarily stored in separate labeled bins to await grinding. Labels and package materials are purchased from two suppliers in Seattle and shipped by sea freight to keep costs down. These same materials can be transported via overnight air if necessary.

Because all of our main suppliers are local, we can use our own delivery van and pick up minimum or no-minimum orders from most of them any day of the week so the response time is usually less than one day. Receiving is the ultimate responsibility of the operations chief who cross checks all incoming purchases by computer. If any problem exists, these are verified by the purchasing agent. Once accepted, all receipts of incoming materials are entered into the computer database by the operations chief.

For each product, our unit costs run the same:

Unit Cost:

Coffee	$ 8.40
Packaging	2.81
Rent & Equipment	0.54
Labor	2.21
Energy	0.18
Total	$14.14 each

(continued)

> ### Supply and Distribution (continued)   Kona Gold Coffees
>
>   For distribution, we do not use a distributor per se. Wholesale packages are picked up daily by Klemmet's trucking which distributes the packages to local retailers and to Kawaihae Harbor which is then barged to the other islands by Young Bros., received by Klemmet's at the other major island harbors and transported to their final destinations. For mainland deliveries, we use air freight once a week transported to the Keahole Point, Kona airport (6 miles) by Klemmet's and received in the five major cities (Seattle, Portland, San Francisco, Los Angeles, and San Diego) by five different trucking companies that distribute the product by route delivery. For shipping costs, see Fulfillment below. Although the first two months have been set up for some consignment shipments, at the end of that period we will be invoicing those retailers, like the others at opening, for shipments ordered; terms are net 30 days.
>
>   Mail orders and Internet orders (approximately 38 units per day) are picked up by DHL at our location and shipped daily to their destinations by air freight. All consumer purchases are cash via credit card or check, and not shipped until payment is verified. Shipping is the responsibility of the operations chief. Orders are first cross-checked by computer and verified by the in-house salesperson if any complication is discovered.

Fulfillment

If you will have an internal order fulfillment operation, a start-up company needs to closely evaluate the process of preparing products for shipping and delivery to customers. Will you have an order processing department? If so, examine the communications procedures amongst order reception and processing, inventory maintenance, and shipping. Is it computerized? Does the paperwork flow smoothly? Are there appropriate forms and logs for these operations to keep track of the status of an order? Are there unnecessary forms and logs that bog down the efficiency and expedience of fulfillment? Have you found the best computer software for your business to process and track all the operations of fulfillment?

    If your products are fragile, you need a system to control breakage. If your products have a short shelf-life or can spoil, you will need to take extra measures during fulfillment to safeguard their freshness and insure their speedy delivery to the customer. Do you have a system for rush orders? How are your products packaged and shipped? Does your procedure insure that orders are filled promptly and accurately?

    Many companies use outside contractors called fulfillment houses to take over this process: storage of product inventory, maintenance of inventory levels, responsibility and insurance for inventory loss and breakage, processing of orders received, receipt of payment, packaging, shipping, tracking, customer returns, and restocking. A fulfillment house will give you a per-unit price for all of this which yields much greater fixed cost control. Oftentimes, this alone can make it worth the cost, even though they are making a profit. Have you checked out fulfillment houses? Obviously, these work best if they are near your business and close enough to keep your shipping costs low for getting your products to them.

You can check these and others on the Internet:

National Fulfillment Services	**Fulfillment Systems International**	**Rush Order, Inc.**
100 Pine Avenue	908 Niagara Falls Boulevard	6600 Silacci Way
Holmes, PA 19018	North Tonawanda, NY 14120-2060	Gilroy, CA 95020
(800) NFS-1306	(716) 692-2855	(408) 848-3525
FAX: (610) 586-3233	FAX: (716) 692-2856	(800) 522-5939
Internet: www.nfsrv.com	Internet: www.fsisameday.com/	Internet: www.rushorder.com/
e-mail: tkrueger@nfsrv.com		

For this segment, describe your fulfillment operation from sales through delivery to your customer. Include your procedures for receiving orders and processing them, and the communications involved for getting orders through to fulfillment. Include advantages that give you a competitive edge through the use of technology, expedient procedures, and outside contractors. Cover your methods for rush orders, breakage control, safeguards for freshness, ensuring accuracy, tracking, packaging, and shipping. Identify all of the types of shipping you use and the average cost per unit shipped. Also, state your cost per unit for fulfillment, your percentage of returns, and the cost of returns.

Fulfillment   Kona Gold Coffees

We do our own in-house fulfillment. Sales are filled by production and sold finished products are transferred to our designated shipping area. There, orders are processed and products are packed for shipment with computer generated labels. At that point, a computer entry is made that the order is ready but not shipped. Ready to ship orders are then divided by carrier awaiting pick-up. This is part of the daily routine of production. When a sold order is picked up (every morning), the computer is updated that the order has been shipped. This daily routine avoids spoilage and ensures freshness. Any finished product not sold is used first to fill new orders received. Freshness in our business is directly tied to Inventory Control, see below.

Rush orders in our business are usually not a demand; however, we have a delivery van that can deliver rush orders to local retailers if the need arises. Our salesperson stands ready to do this by policy. All consumer orders — direct mail, telephone, facsimile, or Internet — can be fulfilled by overnight service for an extra charge.

Our shipping costs to retailers runs a whopping 5 percent because of the interisland and destination trucking. After careful consideration and because of our contacts, this is still much less expensive than going through distributors. For consumers, a shipping and handling charge is added to the price of the product as is customary, and consequently is not an expense. Since we anticipate approximately 25 percent of sales to be consumer sales, our overall freight costs assumption reduces to 3.75 percent. Other costs of fulfillment are included in cost of sales.

Customer Service Policy

Every business needs a customer service policy. Once you have developed one, you must ensure its implementation through employee training and constant monitoring. The most common method of monitoring is through customer complaints; however, this is definitely not the best procedure. Many customers may have a complaint that is never reported — these customers are usually lost. Whenever possible, it is best to anticipate complaints.

The best insurance against customer dissatisfaction is proper training and employee consistency in following the customer service policy. Another helpful policy for dealing successfully with complaints, thus keeping customers happy and coming back, is to train and authorize employees to make decisions about accepting returns. Other methods to reduce problems include implementing customer feedback programs. There are several ways you can solicit customer suggestions and feedback on a regular basis. One is to give away free samples or promotional items through drawings to customers who provide answers and opinions on questionnaires.

Your customer service should not stop with the sale. Make sure your customer service policy addresses after-sale issues: warranty, repair, returns, and refunds. Good customer service can be a valuable marketing tool for developing repeat and referral customers.

For this segment, describe your overall customer service policy. Include the methods you use to train your employees, for monitoring consistency, and for surveying customer opinion and attitudes. Describe your after-sale policies on warranties, repairs, returns, and refunds. Include any service and repair programs you offer and give the percentage of your orders that require repairs and plans to improve that figure.

Customer Service PolicyKona Gold Coffees

Our customer service policy is designed to monitor customer feedback. Our salesperson will call on all retailers at least monthly and request their feedback or any feedback from their consumers. To support this, each month for the first three months then quarterly thereafter for the first year, we are placing point-of-purchase drawings for free products using a questionnaire entry form that will address several marketing and quality concerns and allow space for consumer remarks. Our Internet site has e-mail feedback that requires certain questions to be answered as a prerequisite to submitting the e-mail transmission. Any requests for product returns and refunds are promptly accepted without question, although we will politely try to discover the reason to improve our quality. All customer calls are directed to our administrative assistant/receptionist or to our in-house salesperson. Both employees are informed of our customer service policy.

For additional after-market responses, a small SASPC is included with each product to allow customers to express their opinions regarding our product. We politely requested this be returned to help us improve our product.

Inventory Control

It is the purpose and function of inventory control to insure that a balance of materials in and finished product out is maintained without too much of either on hand. If there is too much of either or both on hand, assets that could be better used for other purposes are tied up. If materials are too low, finished product cannot keep up with orders. If finished product is too low, orders can't keep up with sales.

All of these problems can be avoided with proper inventory management. Mismanagement or lack of control of your inventory can materially affect your profit margins. Inventory management is a process of monitoring sales and, on an ongoing basis, keeping both purchasing (for materials) and production (for product manufacture or assembly) appraised of the current status of sales. To consistently maintain the best balance in inventory control, it is important to have suppliers that allow the smallest possible orders of materials and can get them to you quickly.

At minimum, your inventory control policy should include the person who is responsible for inventory control, a fixed minimum level of materials to be constantly maintained, the assured amount of time required to get materials from suppliers, an established shortest period of time to produce the finished product, and safeguards against inventory theft.

There are several inventory management systems for the purchasing cycle. Two techniques used before computers became commonplace, EOQ and ABC, are still popular. EOQ (economic order quantities) calculates the optimum lot sizes for purchasing items. ABC is a classification system for many small parts and works well for hardware stores. The first production and inventory control method developed for use with computers was Materials Resource Planning (MRP). For details on these systems, see Robert J. Low's book, *Bottom Line Basics*, published by The Oasis Press.

Today, the two most common types of inventory control are an "as needed" system and the Management Information System (MIS). In the as-needed inventory control system, just enough materials are ordered to produce finished products for current orders as needed. While this system depends on clear and near perfect communication, it also relies on a strong relationship between the company and the suppliers. Since few start-up companies have established relationships with their suppliers, the trust required for this system to work is probably yet to be developed.

However, a Management Information System is highly recommended for your start-up company. This system is computerized for communication of information regarding sales, orders, product inventory, materiel stock levels, and reorder status. Sales can be tracked easily and historical data is compiled for management review. The reliability of the system is dependent upon up-to-the-minute and accurate input of any changes in all functions and departments. For your particular business needs, consult an MIS computer program specialist who is familiar with your industry to help you locate and install the correct hardware and software. If possible, choose a consultant who will train you and your employees how to put the system you choose to optimum advantage in your company.

Your inventory control policy for inventory in stock should also include methods for accurate record keeping and assigning values. There are several systems: actual cost (for big-ticket items that are easy to track), standard cost (setting a standard throughout the period reported), weighted average, and the two most common valuing systems:

- FIFO, which stands for first in, first out, and
- LIFO, which stands for last in, first out.

FIFO provides more accurate current costs for your balance sheet and is usually a better way to approximate how goods actually flow. But, it also reports higher income (with higher taxes) during inflationary times. LIFO, on the other hand, brings your income statement more in line with current costs (with lower taxes) when prices are climbing. Whichever you use, consult with your accountant before you make a final decision, because the tax differences that exist in these two valuation systems should be considered.

For this segment, describe your inventory control policy. Identify the person responsible, your minimum level of materials on hand at all times, the amount of time required to get materials from suppliers, the minimum amount of time necessary to produce your finished product, and your safeguards against inventory theft. Explain the system of inventory management you use. If you use the as-needed system, identify your key suppliers. If you use an MIS system, identify your computer program. Also state which inventory valuation system you will use.

Inventory Control   Kona Gold Coffees

All sales are monitored on an ongoing basis. Sales received are sent to purchasing for managing replenishment of inventory and sent to production where work orders are generated to begin manufacture. Our operations chief is responsible for inventory control. Our minimum level is 3 days inventory, and our maximum level is 15 days; but when sales are strong, 15 days is the target. We use the Management Information System and a management software program that has been specifically designed for our operation. Inventory valuation is set by the FIFO method of record keeping. The standard amount of time needed to obtain coffee from suppliers is one week, but we can use our own delivery van and make emergency runs in one day. Some suppliers provide one day delivery for an extra charge if we need it. Packaging materials are readily available and can be shipped overnight if necessary. Finally, our product manufacturing time is so short that the only main concern is set up time. A minimum run can be set up and completed in one hour. One product can be manufactured and assembled by hand in less than 8 minutes.

Theft is not a high risk in our industry, although all materials and supplies are kept in the production bay which is locked and unlocked by the operations chief. There are only two entrances, one through the office and one through a large exterior door to docking for shipping and receiving. The president has the only other key. Our outside premises are fenced with chain link and barbed wire top strands and the only gate is locked after hours.

Efficiency Control

In order to develop efficiency while running a start-up company, you and your managers must approach operational decisions with the detachment that comes from looking at the bigger picture. To avoid the pitfalls of crisis management and to develop operational procedures for handling processes not part of the daily routine, this must be done regularity.

Annual Business Planning

All companies should have a policy for annual development of their business plan. Your start-up company should begin work on your update about three months ahead of the time you need it for the next calendar year. A detailed look at what goes into an annual plan is the subject of another book; however, here are some guidelines for the purpose of this segment.

- Involve everyone in the company in the process.
- Remain focused on the direction of the company and the role each employee has in its support.
- Update only those sections that are obviously in need of change.
- Have key personnel develop their own area budgets that will later be adjusted within the company's budget.
- Allow department heads to change, subject to final approval, the budgeted line items in the plan without changing the subtotal for their departments to derive more useful middle-management input.
- Entertain alternatives to the business plan suggested by others.
- Consider new initiatives.
- Reassess current operations for any improvements or efficiencies.
- Gear the objectives of the annual plan to improving performance.

Pay Attention to the Larger Issues

Often while planning, managers become too focused on their own agendas and many good ideas are lost in debates over unimportant issues. As CEO, you must remove yourself from your daily routine at periodic intervals and brainstorm alone or with your managers for improvements to various aspects of your operations. Focus on the larger issues, such as:

- Can we increase prices of our major products or services?
- Should we seek a new market?
- Should the percentage of sales for marketing be adjusted?
- Can we trim the ship by eliminating an unnecessary job?
- Are expenses remaining proportional to sales?

Most well-managed companies watch closely the last item on this list when sales are low; however, a common oversight for start-up companies is to minimize the value of expense control when sales are increasing and exuberance is high.

The Often Unassigned Operations

Procedures involving insurance, governmental regulations, and safety is an aspect of business startups often overlook when defining their operations. An oversight in these areas can result in unnecessary emergencies or financial losses. The rule is, don't assume, assign.

Designate an office manager or accountant to be in charge of investigating all insurance needs. Insurance requirements and coverage should be reviewed annually and the need for new policies should be explored.

Also, assign a manager or accountant the role of monitoring governmental regulatory compliances, such as the renewal of your business licenses and permits, any bonding requirements, and any other legal renewals needed that may not be sent to you as a routine matter of course.

Designate a safety officer. If you have a manufacturing and assembly business, this is a must. The job should be delegated to the production manager or a manager with related responsibilities. Make sure he or she maintains all the safety codes, displays safety posters, distributes safety literature, conducts regular safety meetings, and secures employee signatures for safety meeting logs. Have an accident policy for emergency procedures as part of your operations, and post a large step-by-step summary of the policy in your main production area in case of emergency. Your safety officer should also be in charge of the maintenance of first-aid kits, fire extinguishers, and any other safety equipment necessary for your operations.

For this segment, describe your efficiency controls. State whether or not you will do annual planning and, if so, what your areas of focus will be. Mention some of larger issues that are appropriate to your business and the attention you give them. Also, identify your special operations and the persons who have responsibility for insurance, government regulations, safety, and any other area that may have a specialized need in your business, unless they are included in other segments of your business plan.

Efficiency Control Kona Gold Coffees

We will complete an annual business plan every year and start the process three months before the end of our first year. Everyone in the company will be involved or interviewed in that process. We will be considering possible price adjustments, possible new markets, adjustments in marketing, new promotions, and a close review of all operational expenses.

Cash Flow Control

Paying too little attention to money handling can lead to an unnecessary turmoil in cash flow. Don't simply rely on monthly reports, update your cash flow pro formas frequently. Most CFOs watch this daily. Two reasons why businesses run into cash flow problems are: slowing down receivables by not sending out timely invoices and losing discounts or incurring unnecessary charges because suppliers aren't paid timely.

Create systems that can be monitored to ensure promptness. Streamline the procedures as much as possible and use the latest accounting and data retrieval systems software. Develop a strong system for follow up of delinquent accounts receivable (see Cash Flow, Chapter 10). For expedient collections, you must be prepared to send out timely overdue letters, make collection calls, and stop selling to customers who fall outside your collection limit. You should also know what your percentage of bad debt from bad checks is so you can monitor and improve it. Also, your accounts payable should be readily accessible and closely monitored for payment. As CEO, you should receive daily information on sales and expenses.

Skimming can be another problem. Coordinate with your accountant to create safeguards against embezzling and theft in financial operations. If your particular business is at high risk in this category, consult with a computer specialist to develop checks and balance systems in your financial operations programs.

For this final segment of your operations, describe your cash flow control policy and explain your money handling procedures. Include who is responsible for financial operations, who handles invoicing and collections, what your average collection time is per order, how delinquent accounts are processed, your percentage of bad debt from checks, who is responsible for paying bills, and what systems are used for financial operations. If skimming is a common problem in your type of business, explain your safeguards against it.

Cash Flow Control   Kona Gold Coffees

While all cash flow procedures are computerized, daily cash flow statements are generated by accounting and reviewed by our president. The president also reviews daily reports on sales and expenses. As a team, the president and office manager create monthly cash flow pro formas. Our first year cash flow pro forma has been set up to pay all suppliers within the credit terms, to forego any credit charges and to maintain supplier discounts. Our office manager will notify the president, as timely as possible, if any deviation in this is expected. At that point, the president can decide whether or not to initiate a draw from our credit line or infuse more capital.

Invoices to retailers will go out daily concurrently with shipments (after the initial consignment group) and terms are net 30 days. For collections, we anticipate an average collection days of 45. Accounting will send out timely overdue letters and our office manager will make personal collection calls. All accounts over 60 days will be given a stop order for no further products and will receive a call by our president. Our percentage for bad debt on personal checks is anticipated to be 0.2 percent, or one out of 500, an industry standard.

To guard against embezzlement, password protection has been added to our computer software, and the password is known only by the president who changes it monthly.

Important Points to Remember

- Look for gaps and overlaps in managerial responsibilities and duties. One of the purposes of the business plan is to find problems and correct them in your business planning phase.
- Be candid if yours is a home based businesses. State that you operate from your home because you have no need for the expense of an outside office.
- Be sure to address operational procedures involving insurance, governmental regulations, safety, and others specific to your business. Many new businesses neglect to cover these matters.
- Double-check to ensure the numbers in your equipment lists match those in your opening balance sheet and your pro forma financial statements.

When you finish this section, remember to return to your operations summary to make sure it covers the key highlights discovered in each segment throughout this section

For the next section, your reviewers are ready to see how all the numbers come together in the financial pro formas of your start-up company, the subject of Chapter 10.

Chapter 10

Financial Pro Formas

It is better to have a hen tomorrow than an egg today.
— Thomas Fuller

From a reviewer's perspective, this section of your business plan is the most critical for assessing just how much dollars and sense your business makes. As a start-up company, the financial material you include in this section deals only with your starting position and predictions about your expectations for the future of the business you are preparing to launch. In accounting, the Latin term pro forma identifies a financial projection presenting forecast, rather than current or past, data.

Even though these financials are forecasts, the numbers are determined by logical and real assumptions. The three pro formas, though comprised of several financial statements, are:

- Pro forma income statements
- Pro forma statements of cash flow
- Pro forma balance sheets

Unless your company sells on credit or maintains an inventory or both, these financial pro formas are fairly simple to develop, and you can probably construct them yourself by following this text. The pro forma section can vary significantly, both in content and terminology, between different types of businesses, but most entries are the same for all businesses. Many of the significant variables are discussed and examples presented. Even so, if you choose to create the pro formas yourself, it is still a good idea to have your accountant check them for completeness and accuracy.

Before You Begin

Before you can develop your pro formas, you must identify the important assumptions you will use as the basis of your projections and create an assumptions chart and an opening balance sheet to support the hypotheses of your pro formas.

Start-Up Costs

One of the first things you must do is to verify the total start-up costs for your business to open. If you have not developed numbers for some of these, this chapter will help you forecast them. Before you've finished, make sure you have considered all of the costs that pertain to your business.

- Purchase or initial lease or rent
- Lease or rent deposit
- Utility deposits
- License and permit fees
- Leasehold improvements
- Insurance
- Equipment
- Fixtures and furniture
- Freight and installation
- Sales taxes
- Opening inventory
- Supplies
- Signage
- Marketing printed materials
- Advertising
- Accounting and legal fees
- Hiring expenses
- Training expenses
- Grand Opening
- Working capital requirement

Probably the least understood of all the costs listed here is the working capital requirement, so it will be explained in more detail in the discussion of pro forma statement of cash flow below. The owner's draws and personal budget should be included in the owner's salary which is listed in the personnel plan as a part of the expenses in the pro forma income statement.

All start-up costs should be included in your financial pro forma statements in this section. You will provide a separate list of them in your financial requirement section, also. Items in this list included in your first month's operating expenses are entered in their corresponding categories in the first month of the pro forma income statement. The same expenses will be covered in your pro forma statement of cash flow, along with the proceeds from any loan or investment capital — to cover your working capital requirement — and any ongoing payments. Cash, funds paid, and funds still owed will show up in the opening balance sheet as current assets, long-term assets, current liabilities, long-term liabilities, or equity.

Accounting Method and Bookkeeping System

In addition to verifying your start-up costs, you must decide on your accounting method. There are two accounting methods used in recording business transactions: the cash method and the accrual method. In the cash method, income and expenses are reported when money is actually received and when bills are actually paid. In the accrual method, income and expenses are reported when they are committed — an order sold in January is recorded as income in January, even though it might not be paid until February. If the money cannot be collected, accounting adjustments are made to reverse the sale and write off the loss.

Because the cash method gives a truer picture of your cash position and your ability to meet obligations, the cash method is usually recommended for most small businesses, especially service businesses and cash and carry retailers. It is not ideal for companies that maintain an inventory. The accrual method of accounting gives a truer picture of income and expenses for a reporting period and, consequently, is favored by larger companies and companies that deal in inventory and credit sales.

There are also two bookkeeping systems: single-entry and double entry. Single entry bookkeeping tracks the flow of income and expense and is considered a partial system generating a profit and loss statement without a balance sheet. It is sufficient for some home based businesses and companies that have no employees.

Double entry bookkeeping is more conventional, and transactions are recorded in journals and ledgers that can be used to show activities in a profit and loss statement as well as a balance sheet. It assures greater accuracy and control. Business software programs, such as Quicken, allow small businesses to make entries similar to a single-entry system and yet receive most of the benefits of a double-entry system.

This section of your business plan, like others, begins with a summary for the reviewer. The segments are:

- Financial summary
- Important assumptions
- Opening balance sheet
- Pro forma income statement for one year and three or five years
- Break-even analysis
- Pro forma statement of cash flows
- Pro forma balance sheets for one year and three or five years
- Business ratios (as conclusions drawn from the financial pro formas)

Financial Summary

The first segment of the financial section should begin with a brief summary of your financial plan. Just two or three paragraphs will suffice and should briefly cover the important findings from:

- Your key assumptions
- Your break-even point
- How well you expect to do overall in the first year
- How fast you expect to grow after you reach peak performance

- Your peak performance for
  - Sales
  - Cost of sales
  - Non-cost of sales operating expenses
  - Profit
- How well you expect to do, predicted for three or five years

As with the other summaries, you can more effectively point out the highlights if you compile and analyze all your research, first, before you begin to write your summary.

Financial Summary   Kona Gold Coffees

In developing our financial pro formas, we have used our market share of 4 percent. Based on our anticipated mix of wholesale and retail sales, our sales on credit works out to 75.2 percent and cost of sales, to 44.3 percent. This is in sync with our sales forecast.

In examining our cash flow pro forma prior to loan proceeds, we would have $65,947 negative beginning-cash the third month from our opening balance sheet without adjusting our cash flow pro forma. However, our pro formas have been adjusted for short-term loan proceeds of $75,000 in January. Sales for the first year are projected at $1,612,000 and cost of sales at $713,809, with a gross profit margin of 55.7 percent. All other expenses total $586,167. Our total sales to break even during the first year are $ 961,512. Our operating profit is $312,024 and our net profit is $199,066.

For our five-year pro formas, we have conservatively estimated 8 percent increases in sales (the industry standard is 9 percent) and 4 percent increases in operating costs, which is commensurate with the GDP. This yields a net profit for year five of $345,436 and a sound working capital of $1,511,928. While all business ratios are strong, the annual return on equity for the fifth year is 22 percent.

Important Assumptions

While assembling your financial forecasts, you or your accountant can make basic assumptions to estimate the predicted sales, cost of sales, general and administrative expenses, tax rates, amounts of credit sales versus cash sales, days credit, time lapses for accounts payable, days of inventory on hand, interest rates, and others. These estimates are all necessary to plan and run your business and to support the financial pro formas of this section of your business plan. To obtain your financial requirement, the numbers must be realistic for your investors or lenders to believe in the viability of your business. However, don't lose sight of the fact that these assumptions and the forecasts they support are only predicted financial outcomes and do not become known factors until your business is up and running. That is why they are called assumptions instead of actuals.

For this section on the financial pro formas, you need to develop your financial material for one year and expand it to include three- or five-year projections. This means creating your assumptions using information based on the research that you have discovered concerning your facility, your industry, your market, your products or service, your marketing plan, your personnel plan, and your sales forecast. You have already compiled much of this research, and those remaining such as cost of sales and accounts payable are covered in this chapter.

The table below provides a quick view of the assumptions necessary to address for most businesses.

Important Assumptions by Type of Business

Market share	All businesses
Average monthly sales	All businesses
Cash sales	All businesses
Sales on credit	Most businesses except those S & R with cash only sales
Collection days	Most businesses except those S & R with cash only sales
Cost of sales	All businesses
	S: direct cost
	R: cost of goods sold
	W: cost of goods sold
	M: includes direct costs labor, materials, and overhead
	Restaurant: cost of food and beverages
Average monthly cost of sales	All businesses
Cost of sales accounts payable	Only businesses that maintain inventories
Cost of sales payment days	Only businesses that maintain inventories
Commissions	Only businesses with commissioned sales
Freight	All businesses except service businesses
Payroll taxes and benefits	All businesses
General accounts payable	All businesses: non-inventory items
General payment days	All businesses: non-inventory items
Inventory on-hand	Only businesses that maintain inventories
Interest rate (short-term)	All businesses
Interest rate (long-term)	All businesses
Income tax rate	All businesses, except non-profit

Legend: S = Service; R = Retail; W = Wholesale; M = Manufacturing and Assembly

The following example of important assumptions for financial statements covers most of the generic assumptions you will need to consider. Many of them are used in the calculations for financial pro formas. You can ignore the ones that do not apply to your start-up business.

Present your important assumptions as a table introduced by an explanation of those assumptions critical to your forecasts and those not easily portrayed in the table. When you have finished this section, be sure all of the important assumptions you present here match those you end up using in your forecasts in the next segments.

Important Assumptions Kona Gold Coffees

In developing our financial statements, we have used the assumptions shown in the table below. Cash sales stands for the percentage of sales that we project to have in cash — our consumer sales through mail order and the Internet. Sales on credit represent wholesale sales. Cost of sales accounts payable shows that we are buying our inventory on 30 day credit. While our freight runs 5 percent, we have used the average of 3.75 percent to offset retail consumer sales that will pay freight in addition to the price of the products.

Five-year Assumptions for Financial Statements Kona Gold Coffees

	Year				
	1	2	3	4	5
Market share	4%	Increase 8% annually every year			
Average monthly sales	$134,333	$145,080	$156,686	$169,221	$182,759
Cash sales	24.8%	24.8%	24.8%	24.8%	24.8%
Sales on credit	75.2%	75.2%	75.2%	75.2%	75.2%
Collection days	45 days	45 days	45 days	45 days	45 days
Cost of sales	44.28%	44.28%	44.28%	44.28%	44.28%
Average monthly cost of sales	$59,484	$64,243	$69,382	$74,933	$80,928
Cost of sales accounts payable	100%	100%	100%	100%	100%
Cost of sales payment days	30 days	30 days	30 days	30 days	30 days
Commissions	4%	4%	4%	4%	4%
Freight	3.75%	3.75%	3.75%	3.75%	3.75%
Payroll taxes and benefits	16%	16%	16%	16%	16%
General accounts payable	100%	100%	100%	100%	100%
General payment days	30 days	30 days	30 days	30 days	30 days
Inventory on-hand	15 days	15 days	15 days	15 days	15 days
Interest rate (short-term)	9%	9%	9%	9%	9%
Interest rate (long-term)	10%	10%	10%	10%	10%
Income tax rate	35%	35%	35%	35%	35%

Important Assumptions Explained Step-by-Step

Market share. This is the market share percentage from your research in Chapter 4.

Average monthly sales. This is the average monthly sales in dollars projected from your research in Chapter 7.

Cash sales. This is the percentage of sales that will be paid for at the time of the transaction. Most retailers will use 100 percent for this assumption. This percentage and the one for sales on credit (below) must total 100 percent.

Sales on credit. This is the percentage of sales that will be made on credit. Many non-retail businesses will use 100 percent for this assumption. This percentage and the one for cash sales (above) must total 100 percent.

Collection days or credit days, days credit, or days of sale. This is the average number of days that your credit customers take to pay you. Include only sales on credit in this average, because cash sales from customers who pay you instantly are calculated separately. For a start-up business, if you and your accountant assume that about half of your customers will pay in 30 days and the other half in 60 days, use the average of 45 days. You may want to revisit this assumption more closely when you are completing the other financial documents, because the calculations can get complicated when not figured on full months (for accounting purposes, all months are 30 days). If your business does cash only sales, enter zero or delete this assumption from your list.

Cost of sales. This is a percentage of the cost of sales to your total sales. Cost of sales are all direct costs of the products or services you have sold.

> For a service company, cost of sales is usually called direct costs and consists mostly of the cost of labor (of personnel providing the service) and any other incidental costs directly related to providing the service or producing the sale.
>
> For a retailer or wholesaler, cost of sales, usually called cost of goods sold, is the cost for the products that you have sold, not for those still remaining in inventory or merchandise.
>
> For a restaurant, cost of sales is usually figured as your purchase cost of food and beverages.
>
> For manufacturing and assembly companies, cost of sales includes only the direct costs of the finished product or service, which are direct labor (payroll, payroll taxes, and benefits), raw materials, fulfillment (except freight), and factory overhead (pro rata rent, utilities, and insurance). Direct labor costs do not include other payroll, payroll taxes, and benefits included in your non-cost of sale expenses or marketing and general and administrative expenses. When the finished product is completed on the warehouse floor, there are no more assigned costs for costs of sales. Marketing, commissions, and freight costs are variable expenses that are a function of sales but not costs of sales. Other non-costs-of-sales items are considered fixed expenses, also not part of costs of sales, such as other payroll, other rent, other utilities, and other insurance. If yours is a manufacturing company, don't make the common mistake of including a worker's payroll twice: in the cost of sale, and again in your general and administrative expenses.

Average monthly cost of sales. This is the monthly average of your costs of sale.

Cost of sales accounts payable. This is a percentage of the total expenses for the cost of sales that will be paid on credit. If you purchase 40 percent of your inventory and other cost of sales expenses on credit, then your assumption here would be 40 percent. Generally, service businesses do not have purchases on credit for costs of sales, so enter zero here or delete this item from your list.

Cost of sales payment days or days cost of sale. This is the average number of days you take to pay your expenses on credit for cost of sales. Do not include any expenses you pay with cash in this average, because cash purchases are calculated separately. Also do not include expenses on credit for non-cost of sales items in this category. Generally, service businesses do not have purchases on credit for costs of sales.

Commissions. This is the percentage of sales you pay for commissions. If you don't pay commissions in your business, eliminate this assumption.

(continued)

Important Assumptions Explained Step-by-Step (continued)

Freight. For retail and wholesale, this is the cost of shipping your sold orders. For manufacturing and assembly companies, freight is usually separated from cost of sales, similar to commissions and marketing expenses. Service businesses seldom have this account and can eliminate this expense.

Payroll taxes and benefits. This is the percentage of gross payroll you pay for your share of payroll taxes including other employee benefits. The employer's share of your employees' income taxes is subject to many variables, such as the level of your employees' pay and your unemployment rating. A typical estimate for this is 13 percent. Determine what is required in your state for other employee benefits. Typically this category includes unemployment insurance and worker's compensation and disability benefits. If you pay wages, you are obligated to pay federal and state unemployment insurance. It is common to add 3 percent for other benefits, bringing the total for this category to 16 percent of payroll, but get your accountant's best estimate of this percentage in your state for your company.

General accounts payable. This is the percentage of non-cost of-sales items or services that you will buy on credit. If you purchase 60 percent of non-cost-of-sales and non-payroll-related items on credit, then this assumption is 60 percent. This category does not include payroll expenses, depreciation, or income taxes.

General payment days or days general accounts payable. This is the average number of days that you will take to pay for non-cost of sale items or services that you purchase on credit. Do not include what you pay for in cash, because cash purchases are calculated separately.

Inventory on-hand. This is the average number of days of sales it would take to use up your inventory if you were not replenishing it. If you continued business without restocking and you would be completely sold out of inventory in 90 days, your number is 90. As you will see when doing the financial statements, the accounting for this category can get quite complex. Although it can be very straight forward and easy to manage if your business is small, and you can use and expense your inventory as you buy it. In that case, your inventory is never an asset. Service businesses can delete this assumption.

Interest rate (short-term debt). This is the estimate of your annual interest rate for short-term debt, commonly about 2 percent over the current prime rate.

Interest rate (long-term debt). This is the estimate of your annual interest rate for long-term debt. If you haven't acquired a business loan yet, but need to include debt service in your projections, you can use 3 percent over the current prime rate for this assumption.

Income tax rate. This is the percentage of net income you will pay for all income taxes. Check with your accountant to accurately gauge this for your business in your location for your anticipated income level — 36 percent is a **rule of thumb for a start-up business.**

Opening Balance Sheet

As an integral part of your business plan, your investors or lenders are looking to see how much equity you and other existing equity partners have in your business. They look for this information on a financial statement called a balance sheet, which is divided into two parts: a top half that is balanced to a bottom half. The top half shows the assets of the company, so reviewers can see what they are and their value. On the bottom half, under liabilities and equity, reviewers can see who owns them. The top half is balanced to the bottom half; the totals of both must be equal.

An easy way to understand a balance sheet is to consider how your home, if you have purchased one, would be reflected on your personal balance sheet. The upper half (your assets) would show the value of your home, say $200,000. Balanced to this in the lower half would be your home mortgage, say $140,000 (your liability and the lender's ownership), and the difference of $60,000 (your equity, your ownership).

Since a business' financial status is dynamic and changes daily, a balance sheet is like a snapshot affixing the changing image of the business' financial status and bringing it into focus for that one day in time — the date of the balance sheet. For your financial pro formas, you need to have a balance sheet with a starting date that the other forecasts are tied to.

Periodic balance sheets are important tools used for locating hidden cash. When you examine your balance sheet, you might notice excessive inventory that can be used up or sold to generate more cash. You might notice that too much money is tied up in accounts receivable that could be collected, or factored by selling them to a factor company who will pay you a discounted cash value for them. A closer examination of fixed assets might reveal underutilized assets you could sell for cash, or assets you could get loans against. You might even be able to free up cash by selling your utilized assets to a leaseback company then leasing them back.

Your company's opening balance sheet is presented after your important assumptions segment. It should have a date that corresponds to the start of the business plan, and all assumptions and findings should be founded on the information contained in the balance sheet.

For this segment, present your company's opening balance sheet. Make sure that your total assets equal your total liabilities plus equity, and be sure the date corresponds with the start of the business plan.

Opening Balance Sheet

Kona Gold Coffees

Assets   November 17, 20XX

Current Assets:	
Cash	$ 45,000
Marketable securities	—
Accounts receivable	—
Inventory	31,864
Other current assets	25,000
Total current assets	101,864
Long-term Assets	
Depreciable assets	188,761
Accumulated depreciation	—
Net depreciable assets	188,761
Non-depreciable assets	—
Total Long-term Assets	188,761
Total Assets	**$290,625**

Liabilities and Equity

Current Liabilities:	
Cost of sales accounts payable	$ 31,864
Non-cost of sales accounts payable	48,761
Taxes payable	—
Short-term notes payable	—
Total current liabilities	80,625
Long-term Liabilities	—
Total Liabilities	80,625
Equity	
Shareholders equity	210,000
Retained earnings	—
Total Equity	210,000
Total Liabilities and Equity	**$290,625**

Balance Sheet Explained Step-by-Step

Date. The date on your opening balance sheet must match the date of your business plan. The opening balance sheet shows all the assets, liabilities, and equity (net worth) of your company as of the date of the document.

Assets. This is a title entry of everything the company owns.

Current Assets. This is a subtitle entry for all assets that can be converted into cash, or liquidated, within one year. Major current assets include cash, marketable securities, accounts receivable, and inventory.

    Cash (on hand and in banks). This includes currency, savings accounts, money market accounts, and checking accounts.

    Marketable securities. These include publicly traded stocks, U.S. Treasury bills, maturing bonds, and any securities that can be converted to cash within one year.

    Accounts receivable. This is money owed to you, usually from sales on credit, due to regular business transactions.

    Inventory. This includes raw materials to be used for finished products, work in process, and finished goods for sale (not sold), also called merchandise by wholesalers and retailers. If any part is not yet paid for, there will be an offsetting accounting entry of liabilities owed against them.

    Other current assets. These are all other assets that can be liquidated within one year. Examples of these are cash value of insurance and prepaids, such as utility deposits, lease deposits, prepaid rent, prepaid insurance, and prepaid taxes.

    Total current assets. This is the sum of all current assets.

Long-term assets. This is a subtitle entry for all assets that cannot be easily converted into cash within one year. While often called fixed assets on many forms, the label "fixed" is not applicable to all the assets in this category which include land, buildings, leasehold improvements, fixtures, furniture, equipment, and vehicles. Certain assets in this category — such as particular kinds of equipment and vehicles which can usually be liquidated within one year — are customarily included in long-term assets, not in current assets.

    Depreciable assets. Certain long-term assets that depreciate over time that include buildings, leasehold improvements, fixtures, furniture, equipment, and vehicles. This category does not include land. Depreciation is an accounting calculation that tracks the diminishing value of these assets. It is assumed that a specific percentage of value is lost every year for each of these assets. While there are different methods of depreciation, the most conservative is called straight-line depreciation. There are specific straight-line depreciation schedules governed by tax laws for different types of long-term assets. These schedules are: for buildings, depreciation is amortized over 40 years; for leasehold improvements, over the life of the lease; for fixtures (treated as leasehold improvements if attached to the building and as furniture if not attached); for furniture, over 10 years; for equipment, the schedules are type specific, such as for computers, over 5 years and for motor vehicles, over 3 years. **Regardless of the depreciated value, when listing your depreciable assets, their value is based on their purchase prices, not by their depreciated or current fair market value.**

    Accumulated depreciation. This category includes all of the depreciation accumulated to date on all of the assets listed above as depreciable assets. Under straight-line depreciation, if you've owned your building for 13 months, the value is depreciated 13/(40 yr. $\times$ 12 mo.) or 13/480 of the purchase price. A 17-month-old computer is depreciated 17/(5 yr. $\times$ 12 mo.) or 17/60 of the purchase price.

    Net depreciable assets or net fixed assets. This is a subtotal calculated by subtracting the total accumulated depreciation from the total depreciable assets for a depreciated value of the total depreciable assets.

    Non-depreciable assets. These include all long-term assets that cannot be depreciated — usually only land falls in this category.

    Total long-term assets. The sum of your net depreciable assets (depreciable assets after they have been depreciated) and non-depreciable assets.

(continued)

Balance Sheet Explained Step-by-Step (continued)

Total Assets. The sum of your total current and total long-term assets. This is your total for the top half of the balance sheet. It will balance with the total at the bottom of the sheet when the document is complete.

Liabilities and equity. This is a title entry. Liabilities are what the company owes. Equity is the difference between what the company owns and what it owes. On your Balance Sheet, your liabilities and equity must equal your assets.

Current liabilities. This is a subtitle entry for all the debts that the company must pay within one year and includes accounts payable (both cost of sales and non-cost of sales accounts payable), taxes payable, and short-term notes payable.

> **Accounts payable.** These are amounts owed that are not secured by notes, usually owed to vendors on credit, through regular business transactions. This item is usually omitted from the Balance Sheet or shown only as a heading when it is broken down into cost of sales accounts payable and non-cost of sales accounts payable.
>
>> **Cost of sales accounts payable.** A subset of accounts payable, these are amounts owed to vendors exclusively for cost of sales items — mostly inventory.
>>
>> **Non-cost of sales accounts payable or operating accounts payable.** This is another subset of accounts payable. It is the amount owed to vendors exclusively for non-cost of sales items and includes all taxes except income taxes.
>
> **Taxes payable or income taxes due.** This account is for all income taxes that the business owes. Other taxes, such as inventory tax or sales tax should be included with non-cost of sales accounts payable items.
>
> **Short-term notes payable or short-term debt.** This is funds or notes owed, such as bank credit lines and notes that must be paid within one year.

Total current liabilities. This is the sum of all current liabilities.

Long-term liabilities or long-term debt. These are amounts owed, usually secured, and due in more than one year.

Total liabilities. The total amount you owe: the sum of current liabilities and long-term liabilities.

Equity. This is a subtitle entry for the difference between the company's assets and its liabilities which is its net worth or equity, usually itemized as shareholders' equity and retained earnings.

Shareholders' equity. This is paid-in capital, owner's stock, minority interest, preferred stock, common stock, and treasury stock. Sometimes, rather than totaled, this item is broken down into specified equities.

> For a sole proprietorship, it is usually recommended to enter a zero or eliminate this account and use the retained earnings account to reflect the net worth of the owner.
>
> For a partnership or corporation, this is the total investment made from outside sources into the company: money invested in the business including start-up capital plus any additional capital infusions that did not come from internal funds within the company.

Retained earnings. This is the amount of profit after tax — or net income after tax — that has been kept in the company. This figure is the sum of the prior period's retained earnings and this period's net profit after tax. Since a startup business has no prior period, you can calculate this figure in two steps from this Balance Sheet.

> Step 1. Add up all your assets and subtract all your liabilities. The result is your net worth or total equity (below).
>
> Step 2. Now subtract any shareholder stock from your total equity to determine your retained earnings.

Total equity. This is the sum of shareholders stock and retained earnings, or it is the difference between the total assets and the total liabilities. For later balance sheets, if you calculate total equity both ways, the answers should check, or equal each other.

Total liability and equity. This is the sum of total liabilities and total equity. This sum must equal (balance with) total assets, hence the name balance sheet.

Pro Forma Income Statements

One of three main financial statements, the income statement is often the only one used by small businesses — not a sound accounting practice, but it illustrates the perceived importance of this document. An income statement — formally called a statement of income and informally called a profit and loss or an income and expense statement — is a measure of a company's profitability during the period of the statement's dates. It shows a breakdown of sales and expenses and what is left over — net profit. The expenses are broken down into two categories regardless of the type of your business. The first category is most frequently called "cost of sales" or "cost of revenue earned" — universal terms for all businesses, although it has been called costs of goods sold, direct costs, cost of food and beverages, and others. It includes the expenses that are the direct costs of producing your sold products or services. For a detailed explanation of what this group of expenses comprises, see cost of sales in the table, Assumptions Explained Step-by-Step, above. The second category of expenses includes those not classified as cost of sales, and is usually called "marketing and general and administrative expenses" and sometimes "non-cost of sales expenses."

As a startup company, you will not be introducing a regular income statement in this segment, but instead, a forecast of your first year's income on a first-year pro forma income statement. A pro forma income statement depicts all the projections for your operations over a specified planning period. It pulls together all of your budget figures into one document and shows whether your business will make a profit. Net profit is the customary bottom line after you pay income taxes.

First-year Pro Forma Income Statement

For this segment of your financial pro formas, enter your detailed month to month first-year pro forma income statement. While working out the numbers, keep in mind your strategies. You cannot expect to tell your reviewers that you are going to be a sales-driven company and then not show some coordinated numbers in commissions, advertising, or other marketing expenses to support this claim. When you have made up this statement, you may have to come back and revise your interest entries for your final pro forma income statement after you have completed the next pro forma, your pro forma statement of cash flow, for reasons explained below.

As you complete your pro formas, you will have a better idea of which entries are the most speculated and which are more accurate. Inevitably, at the end of the first year, start-up business owners look back with hind-sight and say that they knew they were really shooting from the hip on a couple of numbers and they should have investigated them in more detail for their pro formas. You may feel the same way. For any numbers which still cause you concern, consider making one more attempt at getting better comps by checking your NAICS numbers or finding an accountant/consultant with experience in your field. These numbers are usually routine for most accountants, given personal input from you.

First-year Pro Forma Income Statement

Kona Gold Coffees

	Month Jan.	Feb.	March	April	May	June	July	Aug.	Sept.	Oct.	Nov.	Dec.	Year 1
Sales	75,382	82,921	91,213	100,334	110,367	121,404	133,545	146,899	161,589	177,748	195,523	215,075	1,612,000
Costs													
Cost of Sales													
Labor (payroll and payroll burden)	5,208	5,728	6,301	6,931	7,624	8,387	9,226	10,148	11,163	12,279	13,507	14,858	111,360
Materials (coffee and packaging)	26,462	29,109	32,020	35,222	38,744	42,618	46,880	51,568	56,725	62,397	68,637	75,501	565,883
Overhead (rent, equipment, utilities)	1,710	1,881	2,069	2,276	2,504	2,754	3,029	3,332	3,665	4,032	4,435	4,879	36,566
Total Cost of Sales (1)	33,380	36,718	40,390	44,429	48,872	53,759	59,135	65,048	71,553	78,709	86,579	95,237	713,809
Gross profit	42,002	46,203	50,823	55,905	61,496	67,645	74,410	81,851	90,036	99,039	108,943	119,838	898,191
Marketing and Sales													
Commissions	3,015	3,317	3,649	4,013	4,415	4,856	5,342	5,876	6,464	7,110	7,821	8,603	64,480
Advertising	1,353	1,083	1,243	383	655	658	655	383	655	1,138	1,353	973	10,532
Other marketing *	17,388	470	570	468	570	150	888	150	570	788	570	470	23,052
Total Marketing and Sales (2)	21,756	4,870	5,462	4,864	5,640	5,664	6,885	6,409	7,689	9,036	9,744	10,046	98,064
General and Administrative Expense													
Freight	2,827	3,110	3,420	3,763	4,139	4,553	5,008	5,509	6,060	6,666	7,332	8,065	60,450
Payroll	24,167	24,167	24,167	24,167	24,167	24,167	24,167	24,167	24,167	24,167	24,167	24,167	290,004
Payroll taxes, benefits	3,867	3,867	3,867	3,867	3,867	3,867	3,867	3,867	3,867	3,867	3,867	3,867	46,401
Rent	2,000	2,000	2,000	2,000	2,000	2,000	2,000	2,000	2,000	2,000	2,000	2,000	24,000
Utilities	130	130	130	130	130	130	130	130	130	130	130	130	1,560
Telephone	250	250	250	250	250	250	250	250	250	250	250	250	3,000
Equipment	600	600	600	600	600	600	600	600	600	600	600	600	7,200
Depreciation	2,824	2,824	2,824	2,824	2,824	2,824	2,824	2,824	2,824	2,824	2,824	2,824	33,888
Maintenance and repairs	200	200	200	200	200	200	200	200	200	200	200	200	2,400
Insurance	300	300	300	300	300	300	300	300	300	300	300	300	3,600
Supplies and postage	450	450	450	450	450	450	450	450	450	450	450	450	5,400
Auto, travel, and entertainment *	250	250	250	250	250	250	250	250	250	250	250	250	3,000
Legal and accounting	160	160	160	160	160	160	160	160	160	160	160	160	1,920
Other outside services	200	200	200	200	200	200	200	200	200	200	200	200	2,400
Non-income taxes and fees	40	40	40	40	40	40	40	40	40	40	40	40	480
Other G & A expenses	200	200	200	200	200	200	200	200	200	200	200	200	2,400
Total G & A Expense (3)	38,465	38,747	39,058	39,400	39,776	40,190	40,646	41,146	41,697	42,303	42,970	43,703	488,103
Total Operating Costs (total rows 1 + 2 + 3)	93,601	80,335	84,910	88,694	94,288	99,614	106,665	112,604	120,939	130,048	139,293	148,986	1,299,976
Operating Profit	(18,218)	2,586	6,303	11,641	16,079	21,791	26,879	34,295	40,650	47,700	56,230	66,089	312,024
Interest Expense	563	555	547	540	532	524	517	509	501	494	486	0	5,768
Profit Before Income Taxes	(18,781)	2,031	5,756	11,101	15,547	21,267	26,362	33,786	40,149	47,206	55,744	66,089	306,256
Income Taxes	(6,573)	711	2,015	3,885	5,442	7,443	9,227	11,825	14,052	16,522	19,510	23,131	107,190
Net Profit	(12,208)	1,320	3,741	7,215	10,106	13,823	17,135	21,961	26,097	30,684	36,233	42,958	199,066

Income Statement Explained Step-by-Step

Sales/Total Sales. This is the total sales anticipated to be made after discounts, adjustments, or returns are figured in. These monthly entries should match the sales projections shown on your Sales Forecast in Chapter 7. Your study of the industry and market undoubtedly revealed yearly increases that will help you develop your longer range, three- or five-year, forecast of gross sales. If you are making assumptions about seasonal impacts or trends and how they affect your monthly or yearly figures, different entries should reflect this. Notice also, in the example, that sales gradually increase through the year for most start-up businesses.

Cost of sales. This is a title (not an entry) of your product's cost of sales figures.

Total cost of sales. This is a total of all the direct costs of your products or services that you have sold. Cost of sales does not include costs that are not directly associated with the finished product or service. While cases can be argued about what costs should be included, as a standard accounting practice, cost of sales does not include fulfillment (except for manufacturers), commission, marketing, advertising, and general and administrative expenses (such as other payroll, rent, utilities, and insurance). Don't make the common mistake of including a worker's payroll twice: in the cost of sale and again in your general and administrative expenses.

> For a service company, cost of sales is usually called direct costs and consists mostly of the cost of labor (of personnel providing the service) and any other incidental costs directly related to providing the service or producing the sale.
>
> For a retailer or wholesaler, cost of sales — usually called cost of goods sold — is the cost for the products that you have sold, not for those still remaining in inventory or merchandise.
>
> For a restaurant, cost of sales is usually figured as your purchase cost of food and beverages.
>
> For manufacturing and assembly companies, cost of sales are direct labor (payroll, payroll taxes, and benefits) and direct costs (raw materials, fulfillment, and factory overhead) of products sold. For these companies, this one line item is often broken down to show the items noted in the parentheses. When direct labor is included in cost of sales, only payroll, payroll taxes, and benefits of those personnel directly providing the labor is included, not other payroll, payroll taxes, or benefits that are included in your general and administrative expenses.

Gross profit. This is a subtotal calculated by subtracting total cost of sales from sales.

Marketing and sales. This is a title (not an entry) of the division of accounts used to isolate marketing and sales expenses not customarily considered costs of sales. As a rule of thumb, cost of sales are only those costs incurred to produce the finished product; it does not include those incurred to sell it.

> **Commissions.** If commission salespeople sell your products or services, compute their commission as a percentage of the net sales. Be sure you use the same commission percentage you use in your Assumptions. If you do not have commissioned salespeople you can drop this expense from your Pro Forma Income Statement.
>
> **Advertising.** If you developed a separate advertising plan in addition to your marketing budget in Chapter 7, subtract the monthly totals of the advertising plan from the monthly totals of your marketing budget and use the monthly advertising totals for these monthly entries. Enter the remainders from your marketing budget in the next category, other marketing. If you did not separate advertising, delete this expense or insert zeros.
>
> **Other marketing.** If you have not and do not plan to develop a separate advertising plan, use the monthly entries from your marketing budget in this expense category. See advertising above.

Total marketing and sales. This is the sum of commissions, advertising, and other marketing.

General and administrative expense. This is a title (not an entry) of a division of accounts used to separate all non-cost of sale expenses from marketing and sales expenses.

> **Freight.** Use the percentage from your Assumptions and multiply it by the sales for this entry. For service businesses, this is usually not an account, so eliminate this expense. For retail and wholesale, this is the cost of

(continued)

Income Statement Explained Step-by-Step (continued)

shipping your sold orders. For manufacturing and assembly businesses, freight is usually separated from cost of sales, similar to commissions and marketing expenses.

Payroll. This is your gross payroll of wages, salaries, bonuses, and incentives. This category does not include the employer portion of employee income taxes and employee benefits, and it does not include any payroll that should already be included as direct costs under cost of sales. To arrive at these entries, start with your monthly total payroll expenses from your personnel plan in Chapter 8 then add any adjustments for bonuses or incentives that do not show and for any special part-time or variable labor that will not be included in cost of sales.

Payroll taxes and benefits. If the payroll in your personnel plan is complete, you can use those monthly payroll taxes and benefits figures for this pro forma item. If you had to make any adjustments to the line item above (Payroll), multiply your new month-to-month payroll entries above by your payroll and benefits assumptions percentage (Important Assumptions) to complete these entries.

Rent. If you haven't selected your site yet, you will need to develop a number for this budget item, then you can revise it when you know your actual lease or mortgage payment. To estimate it, start with some basic statistics from businesses in the same industry in your area. Often, your business accountant can assemble some realistic estimates of rent and related expenses for your line of business. From here, you can begin your own research. Contact a real estate agent or check the classified section of your newspaper for sites similar to what you need in size, zoning, and site location. Once you have your lease, the monthly entries should stay the same each month, and if your lease has an annual increase clause, use the percentage to adjust your three- or five-year pro forma.

Utilities. If the facility is not new, you can contact the local utility companies and determine the previous average monthly utility bills. If it is new, your accountant probably has a good idea of what it will be if the site is local or within proximity to his or her other clients.

Telephone. The amount of this expense depends on the nature of your business, the number of telephones, and the types of services you need, as well as the long-distance calls you make. Your accountant can probably give you some idea of what you can expect. A small start-up company with limited telephone use can count on spending at least double the basic rate charged by the local telephone company. If you foresee using several of the new communications tools and services offered by telephone and cell-phone companies, contact one of their local representatives for an estimate based on your planned usage.

Equipment. Review your equipment schedule in the Operations section, Chapter 9, under Production. Enter the total of the monthly payments for your equipment, furniture, and fixtures.

Depreciation. This is your monthly portion of the depreciation on your building, leasehold improvements, capital equipment, and vehicles. Refer to depreciable assets and opening balance sheet under Balance Sheet Explained Step-by-Step, above, for the explanation of how to calculate this number using your Schedule of Equipment from Chapter 9.

Maintenance and repairs. For your facility maintenance, obtain a history of maintenance from the proprietor or previous tenants. With the help of your accountant, add in an allowance for maintenance and repair of your equipment. Equipment on service contracts should have the contract set up as part of the equipment cost, or tracked through outside services below. For outside services, such as landscaping and cleaning, see outside services below.

Insurance. Consult with your business accountant to confirm the types of insurance and amount of coverage you should carry. Typically, you need business liability, comprehensive fire and damage, and workers' compensation insurance. For certain businesses you will need specialized insurance such as equipment insurance, non-owner vehicle insurance, errors and omissions, malpractice, product liability, and others, but your state my have some additional requirements. Contact your insurance agent to get the exact premiums to budget the payments in the appropriate month. Not included here is any insurance intended for your employee benefit package.

(continued)

Income Statement Explained Step-by-Step (continued)

Supplies and postage. The more sales you have, the more supplies you use. A typical small business can use as much as two percent of gross sales for business supplies and postage. For large direct mailing promotions, include the postage in marketing instead of this category. Again, your accountant can give you an estimate from his or her experience with other clients.

Auto, travel, and entertainment. This account is for local transportation that you may provide to employees including mileage reimbursements. If you provide any vehicles, their lease or purchase payments should be included here along with additional expenses for gasoline. However, maintenance, insurance, and licensing should be in their own separate categories. In addition, if you use your own car separate from the business, the expenses should be included as a salary expense under Management and Organization (Chapter 8). This category also covers overnight travel and entertainment (T&E) expenses. However, large promotions for the company should be figured into your marketing budget and included in marketing expenses.

Legal and accounting. You probably will not have ongoing attorney fees, but it is necessary to budget a figure anyway. A common plan is to budget the equivalent of three or four appointments a year. Ask your attorney for a typical appointment charge and set it up for the first month of each quarter. Your business accountant also should give you a fixed monthly fee for specified services, possibly with an extra charge for the month taxes are prepared. You can set up a monthly fee and add the tax preparation charge to the month it is due. Any in-house legal or accounting people should be dealt with in payroll.

Other outside services. In addition to outside services for ongoing facility maintenance, such as landscaping and cleaning, this category includes all other contracts that require regular monthly fees. Also, this is the category where all other consultants and temporary human resource services are included.

Non-income taxes and fees. This account is for all taxes and any governmental fees that are not income taxes, such as inventory taxes, property taxes, licenses, and permits.

Other general and administrative expenses. This is similar to a miscellaneous account and includes all other operating costs except cost of sales expenses. Although every expense imaginable should be predicted, each month there always seems to be some expense that creeps into the accounts to be paid, as in your personal budget. Most businesses set up a flat-rate amount to cover this, say $200 or so. If it becomes obvious that some expense continually shows up in this category, make it a regular line item both here and in your monthly chart of accounts.

Total general and administrative expenses. This is the sum of all general and administrative expenses.

Total operating costs. This is the sum of total cost of sales, total marketing and sales, and total general and administrative expenses.

Operating profit. Subtract the total operating costs from total sales.

Interest expense. For this category, multiply your short-term interest rate and your long-term interest rate (both listed in your Important Assumptions) by your short-term liabilities and long-term liabilities (given on your Opening Balance Sheet) respectively; then add the two results and spread the total over the twelve months of this pro forma. All of these figures will need to be adjusted after your financial requirement is met.

Profit before income taxes. Subtract your interest expense from your operating profit.

Income taxes. Multiply your profit before income taxes by the income tax rate from your Important Assumptions. When your profit before income taxes is negative, the result will be negative, but you want to track this anyway because negative income taxes carry forward monthly and offset positive income taxes.

Net profit. This is the result of subtracting your income taxes from your profit before income taxes.

Five-year Pro Forma Income Statement

Nearly all business plans include a three- or five-year pro forma income statement with totals given for each year. Your industry and market growth findings (chapters 3 and 4) should give you an idea of your percentage of increases for this forecast. How do the percentages of growth of your industry or market compare with the gross domestic product (GDP)? Do you think you will gain on your competitors at these percentages, or do you think you will lag behind them in growth for a period of time? These are some of the considerations to weigh when making your choices of percentages of increase for future sales. Also, remember that expenses may go up. A rule of thumb is to use the projected GDP percentages for determining those expenses that are not defined in contracts. A good software program you can use for figuring these long range forecasts is *Profit Mentor*™ available through Management Advisory Services.

Management Advisory Services, Moss Adams LLP
1001 4th Avenue, 27th Floor
Seattle, WA 98154-1199
(206) 442-2600
FAX (206) 233-9214

Break-even Analysis

After you have developed your pro forma income statements, it is a relatively easy task to construct your break-even analysis. For your break-even analysis, you are looking for that magic number of sales, the minimum it takes every year to cover all your expenses — the point at which you begin to make a profit. This is more important for internal planning than it is to a lender or investor, but you should identify the number of sales you need to reach break even.

It is not simply a matter of adding up all your fixed expenses to arrive at your costs, because there are some variable expenses included in your non-cost of sales expenses that make this somewhat of a sliding scale. You can use the formula below to calculate the number of sales it takes to break even (to cover all of your non-costs of sales expenses for the year) in your first year. The numbers you need to work with come from both your First-year Pro Forma Income Statement and your Important Assumptions. The formula is presented, then the process is described in six steps.

$$\text{Break-even sales} = \frac{\text{Operating Expenses} - (\text{Cost of Sales} + \text{Commissions} + \text{Freight})}{1 - (\% \text{ of Cost of sales} + \% \text{ of Commissions} + \% \text{ of Freight})}$$

Step 1. Add: Total costs of sales of year one + total commissions of year one + total freight for year one.

Step 2. Subtract the result of Step 1 from the total operating expenses of year one.

Step 3. Locate your percent of costs of sales and your percent of commissions and your percent of freight in your Important Assumptions. Change all three of these percentages to decimals.

Five-year Pro Forma Income Statement

Kona Gold Coffees

	Year 1	2	3	4	5
Sales	1,612,000	1,740,960	1,880,237	2,030,656	2,193,108
Costs					
Cost of Sales					
Labor (payroll and payroll burden)	111,360	120,269	129,891	140,282	151,504
Materials (coffee and packaging)	565,883	611,154	660,046	712,850	769,877
Overhead (rent, equipment, utilities)	36,566	39,491	42,651	46,063	49,748
Total Cost of Sales (1)	713,809	770,914	832,588	899,195	971,130
Gross profit	898,191	970,046	1,047,649	1,131,461	1,221,978
Marketing and Sales					
Commissions	64,480	69,638	75,209	81,226	87,724
Advertising	10,532	11,375	12,285	13,267	14,329
Other marketing *	23,052	24,896	26,888	29,039	31,362
Total Marketing and Sales (2)	98,064	105,909	114,382	123,532	133,415
General and Administrative Expense					
Freight	60,450	65,286	70,509	76,150	82,242
Payroll	290,004	301,604	313,668	326,215	339,264
Payroll taxes, benefits	46,401	48,257	50,187	52,194	54,282
Rent	24,000	24,000	24,000	24,000	24,000
Utilities	1,560	1,622	1,687	1,755	1,825
Telephone	3,000	3,120	3,245	3,375	3,510
Equipment	7,200	7,200	7,200	7,200	7,200
Depreciation	33,888	33,888	33,888	20,556	20,556
Maintenance and repairs	2,400	2,400	2,400	2,400	2,400
Insurance	3,600	3,744	3,894	4,050	4,211
Supplies and postage	5,400	5,616	5,841	6,074	6,317
Auto, travel, and entertainment *	3,000	3,120	3,245	3,375	3,510
Legal and accounting	1,920	1,997	2,077	2,160	2,246
Other outside services	2,400	2,400	2,520	2,520	2,640
Non-income taxes and fees	480	480	500	500	520
Other G & A expenses	2,400	2,400	2,400	2,400	2,400
Total G & A Expense (3)	488,103	507,134	527,260	534,923	557,122
Total Operating Costs (total rows 1 + 2 + 3)	1,299,976	1,383,958	1,474,230	1,557,650	1,661,668
Operating Profit	312,024	357,002	406,007	473,006	531,441
Interest Expense	5,768	0	0	0	0
Profit Before Income Taxes	306,256	357,002	406,007	473,006	531,441
Income Taxes	107,190	124,951	142,103	165,552	186,004
Net Profit	199,066	232,052	263,905	307,454	345,436

* Some travel and entertainment in other marketing

Step 4. Add together all three decimals from Step 3.

Step 5. Subtract the result of Step 4 from 1.00.

Step 6. Divide the result of Step 2 by the result of Step 5. The answer is the total number of sales needed to cover all of your non-cost of sales expenses, called your break-even sales, for year one.

Now that you know how much you must sell before you begin making a profit for the first year, you can repeat this exercise for years two through five. Show your break-even sales results under a heading, Break-even Analysis, using numbers from your Three- or Five-year Pro Forma Income Statement. Also, write a brief explanation identifying the first month you will reach your total sales to break-even and its percentage of total sales, as in the example.

Break-even Analysis   Kona Gold Coffees

	Years				
	1	2	3	4	5
Total sales	1,612,000	1,740,960	1,880.237	2,030,656	2,193,108
Break-even sales	961,512	996,704	1,033,820	1,044,568	1,085,202

For the first year, we will reach break-even sales sometime after the eighth month ($862,065) during the ninth month ($1,023,654) when sales hit $962,512, which is 59.7 percent of total sales for the year ($1,612,000).

Pro Forma Statement of Cash Flow

This financial projection, the Pro Forma Statement of Cash Flow, is used to demonstrate your actual cash position in any given month, to determine whether your company has enough cash to pay the bills. It is possible for even a profitable business to close its doors due to the lack of cash to pay its bills. A monthly cash flow statement is not essential for cash and carry businesses because the cash can easily be seen; however, a pro forma statement of cash flow is still necessary for determining the capital requirements at the start of business. For start-up businesses that sell on credit, monthly cash flow statements and pro forma cash flows are critically important financial tools for monitoring your changing cash position.

The simple method used to develop a pro forma statement of cash flow for cash-and-carry businesses provides a good example because it is similar to the running total of the monthly profit or loss. On your Pro Forma Income Statement, review the third line from the bottom called profit before income taxes. If you were to add another line below it for running totals or the cumulative profit before income taxes from one month to the next, the results would be an operating cash flow for a cash-and-carry business. Use parentheses to represent negative numbers.

	Month					
	1	2	3	4	5	6
Profit Before Income Taxes	(2,243)	(1,182)	(321)	568	1,984	2,856
Cash Flow — a cumulative total	(2,243)	(3,425)	(3,746)	(3,178)	(1,194)	1,662

It is typical for all new businesses to have a negative cash flow for the first few months of business. In the example above, cash flow is negative every month until the sixth month when this small business has $1,662 in positive cash flow available. The worst month of cash flow in this case is the third month, negative $3,746. This is called the *shortfall*. If this business had $3,746 more cash in the first month, it would look like this:

	Month					
	1	2	3	4	5	6
Profit Before Income Taxes	1,503	(1,182)	(321)	568	1,984	2,856
Cash Flow — a cumulative total	1,503	321	0	568	2,552	5,408

Notice the zero in the third month. If months 7 through 12 continue to climb or stabilize, this business could pay back a loan of $3,746 in the sixth month, or begin making payments even in the fourth month.

Being able to see this is one of the more important functions of a cash flow pro forma. It is a tool you can use to arrive at the amount of additional capital you may need to cover the bills before it is too late. Nevertheless, in the case of the small business above, it would be cutting it dangerously close to borrow just the shortfall of $3,746, because the business would still have no cash at the end of month three. In addition, if funds are borrowed, an allowance for the repayment and costs of borrowing money are not included in this example. They would ordinarily start with a payment in the second month and by the third month, even with the adjustment of adding another $3,746, the business could not make the third monthly payment which would have then become negative because of the second month's payment. In order to insure enough cash in the third month the amount borrowed needs to be increased by an amount that includes the cost of the money, the repayment schedule, and some available cash for the third month. The cash flow pro forma can then be reworked, something like this:

	Month					
	1	2	3	4	5	6
Profit Before Income Taxes	(2,243)	(1,182)	(321)	568	1,984	2,856
Add loan proceeds	4,000					
Repayment of loan		(38)	(38)	(38)	(38)	(4,050)
Cash Flow — a cumulative total	1,757	537	178	708	2,654	1,460

There is a rule of thumb for assessing the working capital for small cash and carry businesses. The amount should be 150 percent of the shortfall. So for the small business in this example, the amount of additional needed capital would be $3,746 times 150 percent, which equals $5,619 or $5,600 rounded to the nearest $100. This affords a margin of safety because your cash flow pro forma is only a pro forma, and many things can change.

A pro forma cash flow statement that involves cash needs, including loan repayment, allows for two important conclusions to be drawn.

- The worst case cash scenario. In the example above, the worst case shows that this business needs a minimum of $3,746 working capital in the third month to handle its negative cash requirements (without loan costs and interest charges); and,
- A loan repayment window. In the example above, this occurs as the cash flow turns positive in the sixth month. If lender funds are used, the sixth month is the earliest a payment can be made unless the borrower increases the working-capital requirement to allow the cash flow to handle earlier payments including the costs of borrowing.

For businesses that sell on credit, the pro forma cash flow becomes a much more important management tool. Cash flow statements, by themselves, only allow you to watch the cash. To be effective, you need to examine the statements and take appropriate actions. For a start-up company these activities include:

- Collecting payments from customers as expeditiously as possible,
- Holding off paying vendors as long as you can without jeopardizing your credit, and
- Watching your cash in inventory management by
  - Controlling the balance of inventory to sales and
  - Avoiding big discount deals that could save a few bucks in your cost of sales but drain cash that you could put to better use.

Here's another simple example of how the cash flow works:

	Month		
	1	2	3
Starting cash	$14,510	$ 8,010	$11,510
Sources of cash	16,000	14,000	15,000
Uses of cash	(22,500)	(10,500)	(24,000)
Net change in cash	(6,500)	3,500	(9,000)
Ending cash	$ 8,010	$11,510	$ 2,510

In this example, the cash flow calculation starts from the amount of cash at the beginning of the month, then all the cash coming in (sources of cash) is added and all the cash going out (uses of cash) is subtracted. The remainder is the ending cash position. The net change just shows what the monthly change is (the difference between the sources of cash and the uses of cash within the month), independent of your starting and ending cash.

The starting cash for the second month is the same as the ending cash from the first month, and so on.

When your company has several sources of cash coming in and several uses of cash going out, the calculation is the same using the subtotal of sources of cash and the subtotal of uses of cash, only the statement itself gets longer due to the itemization of your sources and uses. It is standard accounting practice to track all the monthly sources and uses and itemize them on the cash flow statement. For businesses with an inventory that constantly changes with sales and those that buy inventory on credit, the statement gets longer yet. The Statement of Cash Flow Explained Step-by-Step describes the adjustments needed for businesses that deal with inventories and sales and purchases on credit. For these and many seasonal businesses, a monthly cash flow pro forma is crucial for maintaining control.

A monthly pro forma statement of cash flow for operations is basically a forecast of the cash receipts (sources of cash coming in) and cash disbursements (uses of cash going out) showing the starting and the ending balances of cash each month. The document's detail of these sources and uses can help you understand what you need to know to make management decisions and achieve desired outcomes.

Statement of Cash Flow Explained Step-by-Step

Starting cash position. The starting cash entry will be the same as the ending cash position entry of the previous month. However, for a start-up company that has no ending cash position in a previous month, your starting cash for the first month is the same number as the cash position on your Opening Balance Sheet (see Opening Balance Sheet, Current assets, Cash).

Cash receipts (sources of cash). This is a title entry that introduces the sources from which your business will receive cash.

    Cash sales. Multiply your monthly sales by your percentage of cash sales (from your Important Assumptions) for these figures. Do this for every month of your first-year pro forma cash flow.

    Sales on credit. Few service businesses or retail businesses sell on credit and can enter zeros or delete this line. For businesses that sell on credit, the first number you need is the number of your collection days — the average number of days that it takes you to collect cash for sales on credit — from your Important Assumptions.

        For example, if your average number of days is 30 and the current month is March, you will collect 100 percent of the cash from sales on credit made in February. To calculate using this example, multiply the total sales in February by the percentage of sales on credit (also from your Important Assumptions). The result would go in the March entry for your cash flow pro forma (cash received in March from sales on credit).

        If your collection days are 60, then you would make the same calculation but use the total sales in January instead of the total sales in February. For 90, it's the same calculation but substitute the total sales in December for the total sales in February.

        If your collection days are 45 or anything other than a 30-day increment, get an experienced accountant to develop the number for this entry.

        For your first-year pro forma cash flow, use zero for each monthly entry until you reach the month you can make this calculation. For the example of 30, you would have only one zero, in the first month of business.

(continued)

Statement of Cash Flow Explained Step-by-Step (continued)

Short-term loan proceeds. Enter the total proceeds (money coming in) from short-term loan sources in the month(s) they were received. See under Cash Disbursements, below, for how to deal with the corresponding entries: Interest and Short-term liabilities payments.

Long-term loan proceeds. Enter in the month(s) received the total proceeds (money coming in) of all long-term loans for each month. See under Cash Disbursements, below, for how to deal with the corresponding entries: Interest and **Long-term** liabilities payments.

Equity capital proceeds. Enter the total proceeds of any new equity contributions for each month. If in August you or a partner will infuse more outside capital — say $10,000 from you and $30,000 from a partner — enter $40,000 in the entry under August.

Total cash receipts (sources). This is the sum of all cash receipts entered for each month.

Cash disbursements (uses of cash). This is a title entry that identifies the uses for which your business will pay cash.

Cost of Sales – Inventory. For service businesses and businesses that do not have inventory, enter zeros or delete the entry from your pro forma cash flow. If your business has ongoing inventory, get your accountant's assistance to compile these entries. For the ambitious among you who want to tackle this yourself, refer to Inventory, Appendix F.

Payroll. Here you use the monthly payroll expenses from your Pro Forma Income Statement.

Payroll taxes and benefits. Here you use the monthly payroll taxes and benefits expenses from your Pro Forma Income Statement.

Non-payroll expenses. The figures you insert here are calculated using numbers from your Important Assumptions and Pro Forma Income Statement. The first number you need to know is the number of your general payment days (from your Important Assumptions) because it will determine which month's figures you will use to make your calculations.

> For example, assume that the average number of days you take to pay cash for your expenses on credit for your general accounts payable (also called general and administrative expenses) is 30. Assume also that the current month is March. For March you will pay for 100 percent of the general and administrative expenses on the credit debt you incurred in February (30 days prior to the current month).
>
> The second number you will use is your general accounts payable percentage (from your Important Assumptions).
>
> The third number you need is the non-payroll expenses in February (the previous month). To get this number: (1) add together your payroll expense plus payroll and employee benefits expense and your depreciation expense for February (from your Pro Forma Income Statement); then (2) subtract that total from your total general and administrative expenses for February (from your Pro Forma Income Statement); the result is your third number, your non-payroll expenses for February.
>
> To arrive at your non-payroll expenses for March, multiply your general accounts payable percentage by your third number, your non-payroll expenses in February.
>
> If your first number is 60 days, you would perform the calculations based on your expenses for the month of January (60 days prior) to arrive at your third number. For your non-payroll expenses for March, multiply the second number by your non-payroll expenses for January.
>
> If your first number is 90 days, your third number is calculated from December's expenses (90 days prior). Multiply your second number by your third number to arrive at your non-payroll expenses for March.
>
> If your first number is 45 days or any other number than a 30-day increment, the process for determining your third number requires using portions of months, so you may want to solicit the help of your accountant.

(continued)

Statement of Cash Flow Explained Step-by-Step (continued)

Depreciable asset purchases. Here is where you enter the full purchase cost of proposed purchases of depreciable assets (including buildings, leasehold improvements, capital equipment, and vehicles) in the months that the purchases will be made. If you have any corresponding debt, it will be accounted for in either short- or long-term proceeds from the lender(s).

Non-depreciable asset purchases. Here is where you enter the full purchase cost of non-depreciable assets, such as land, in the months that the purchases will be made. If you have any corresponding debt, it will be accounted for in either short- or long-term proceeds from the lender(s).

Interest. These monthly entries will be exactly the same numbers as your interest expense from your Pro Forma Income Statement, so simply transfer them month for month. It is assumed that interest is paid on a cash basis. If you end up changing your short- or long-term liabilities during the process of developing your financial pro formas, remember your interest calculations will need to be adjusted accordingly. Once you know your correct interest, make sure you transfer this interest expense from here to your Pro Forma Income Statement. Also remember to include the payment(s) for any short-term or long-term loans in your cash disbursements (uses of cash) under the short-term or long-term liability payments if they will be paid within your forecast period.

Short-term liabilities payments. Here is where you enter payments toward principal of short-term liabilities in the months the payments will be made. Interest has been covered above.

Long-term liabilities payments. Here is where you enter payments toward principal of long-term liabilities in the months the payments will be made. Interest has been covered above.

Dividends or owner's draw. Here is where you enter any dividends or payments to be made to owners in the appropriate month the dividends or payments will be made.

Total cash disbursements before taxes. This is the sum of all your cash disbursements without income taxes.

Income taxes. Enter the monthly entries of your income tax estimates from your Pro Forma Income Statement in the months they will become due. While these are usually paid quarterly for state and Federal, check with your accountant to refine these entries.

Total cash disbursements after taxes. This is the sum of the two lines above, your total cash disbursements before taxes plus your income taxes.

Net change in cash. Subtract your total cash disbursements from your total cash receipts. The results show the future net change in your cash position for each month, without considering your starting cash or ending cash position.

Ending cash position. Add your net change in cash to your starting cash position. This shows you the amount of cash you will have on hand at the end of each month (or period, if you use pro forma cash flow for quarterly or annual periods). The most important step remaining is to transfer the number of your ending cash position to the starting cash position of the following period, even if this means moving it from December of one year (at the end of an annual pro forma cash flow), to January of the next year's annual pro forma cash flow.

Another Use for a Pro Forma Statement of Cash Flow

One of the functions of a pro forma statement of cash flow, especially useful for start-up companies, is to determine whether or not your company is undercapitalized. Now that you have developed your opening balance sheet and your pro forma income statement, you can create your pro forma statement of cash flow. If, when you have completed it, you find that you end up with negative numbers in the starting and ending cash positions, you are undercapitalized. You need money.

Look at the example of Kona Gold Coffees' "Draft" First-year Pro Forma Statement of Cash Flow. Notice that the short-term proceeds and long-term proceeds are all zeros. Notice also that interest, short-term liabilities payments, and long-term liabilities payments are zeros. This tells you that the cash flow was created without a loan or investment capital. It is strictly tied to the opening balance sheet and your draft pro forma income statement.

Next, take note of the starting and ending cash position entries. Their worst case is the ending cash position for February — negative $65,947 — which is the starting cash position for March. Like the example for the small business in the opening of this cash flow discussion, if Kona Gold Coffees plugged in $65,947 additional dollars (with no cost of loan or interest), Kona Gold Coffees' ending cash position for March would be zero. However, in order to have a safety margin they actually need to seek 150 percent of this amount.

Getting funds costs money. In this case Kona Gold Coffees is requesting a $100,000 line of credit. More than they actually need, their plan is to draw down $75,000 the first month, and make interest payments for ten months, paying off the balance at the end of the year, which is traditional for lines of credit.

Examine the actual First-year Pro Forma Statement of Cash Flow used by Kona Gold Coffees in their business plan. Notice the changes: first the most impressive is that the negative numbers for starting and ending cash positions have gone away. Under short-term loan proceeds, $75,000 is shown as being disbursed in January. There are now monthly interest payments and ten payments, entered as principal-only, in short-term liabilities with a final paydown in December. Kona Gold Coffees is not using the 150 percent margin of safety in their draw of proceeds, but they are requesting approximately that in the amount of their commercial line of credit, $100,000.

Use the same two step exercise to develop your cash flow pro forma for this segment. Create a draft to discover whether or not you are undercapitalized, then if you are, look to see which month's ending cash position is the worst. Multiply that by 150 percent to find your safety margin. Then revise your final first-year pro forma of cash flow with the adjusted figures.

At this point, you will need to decide how you are going to attempt to acquire the needed funds. If by debt financing, enter the funds in either short- or long-term proceeds and the principal payments in either short- or long-term liabilities payments and interest. Also, in this case, don't forget to go back to your first-round pro forma income statement and adjust its interest to match, which will complete that document. If, however, you are seeking equity financing, enter the funds in the month you expect to get them in equity capital proceeds and enter the corresponding agreed-to payments in either short- or long-term liabilities or as dividends to owners, depending on the structure of the equity financing arrangement you are seeking.

For this segment of your business plan, include your adjusted First-year Pro Forma Statement of Cash Flow. Make sure the starting cash position matches to the cash position in your Opening Balance Sheet and that the monthly entries, especially interest, are coordinated with your First-year Pro Forma Income Statement.

First-year Pro Forma Statement of Cash Flow – Draft

Kona Gold Coffees

Month	Jan.	Feb.	March	April	May	June	July	Aug.	Sept.	Oct.	Nov.	Dec.
Starting Cash Position	45,000	(38,437)	(65,947)	(65,167)	(62,779)	(56,874)	(48,824)	(37,166)	(23,368)	(4,769)	17,287	42,936
Cash Receipts (sources of cash)												
Cash sales	18,846	20,730	22,803	25,084	27,592	30,351	33,386	36,725	40,397	44,437	48,881	53,769
Sales on credit	0	28,268	59,364	65,300	71,830	79,013	86,914	95,606	105,166	115,683	127,251	139,976
Short-term loan proceeds	0	0	0	0	0	0	0	0	0	0	0	0
Long-term loan proceeds	0	0	0	0	0	0	0	0	0	0	0	0
Equity capital proceeds	0	0	0	0	0	0	0	0	0	0	0	0
Total Cash Receipts	18,846	48,998	82,167	90,384	99,422	109,364	120,300	132,331	145,563	160,120	176,132	193,745
Cash Disbursements (uses of cash)												
Cost of sales - inventory	31,864	18,206	38,387	42,226	46,449	51,094	56,203	61,823	68,005	74,806	82,287	90,514
Payroll	24,167	24,167	24,167	24,167	24,167	24,167	24,167	24,167	24,167	24,167	24,167	24,167
Payroll taxes and benefits	3,867	3,867	3,867	3,867	3,867	3,867	3,867	3,867	3,867	3,867	3,867	3,867
Non-payroll expenses	48,761	29,363	12,760	13,662	13,407	14,559	14,997	16,673	16,698	18,529	20,482	21,856
Depreciable asset purchases	0	0	0	0	0	0	0	0	0	0	0	0
Non-depreciable asset purchases	0	0	0	0	0	0	0	0	0	0	0	0
Interest	0	0	0	0	0	0	0	0	0	0	0	0
Short-term liabilities payments	0	0	0	0	0	0	0	0	0	0	0	0
Long-term liabilites payments	0	0	0	0	0	0	0	0	0	0	0	0
Dividends or owners draw	0	0	0	0	0	0	0	0	0	0	0	0
Total Cash Disbursements	108,659	75,603	79,181	83,922	87,890	93,687	99,234	106,530	112,737	121,369	130,803	140,404
Income taxes	(6,378)	905	2,206	4,074	5,627	7,627	9,408	12,003	14,227	16,695	19,680	23,131
Total Cash Disbursements After Taxes	102,283	76,508	81,387	87,996	93,517	101,314	108,642	118,533	126,964	138,064	150,483	163,535
Net Change In Cash	(83,437)	(27,510)	780	2,388	5,905	8,050	11,658	13,798	18,599	22,056	25,649	30,210
Ending Cash Position	(38,437)	(65,947)	(65,167)	(62,779)	(56,874)	(48,824)	(37,166)	(23,368)	(4,769)	17,287	42,936	73,146

First-year Pro Forma Statement of Cash Flow for Loan Request

Kona Gold Coffees

Month	Jan.	Feb.	March	April	May	June	July	Aug.	Sept.	Oct.	Nov.	Dec.
Starting Cash Position	45,000	36,197	7,305	6,708	7,723	12,260	18,948	29,248	41,693	58,944	79,657	103,968
Cash Receipts (sources of cash)												
Cash sales	18,846	20,730	22,803	25,084	27,592	30,351	33,386	36,725	40,397	44,437	48,881	53,769
Sales on credit	0	28,268	59,364	65,300	71,830	79,013	86,914	95,606	105,166	115,683	127,251	139,976
Short-term loan proceeds	75,000	0	0	0	0	0	0	0	0	0	0	0
Long-term loan proceeds	0	0	0	0	0	0	0	0	0	0	0	0
Equity capital proceeds	0	0	0	0	0	0	0	0	0	0	0	0
Total Cash Receipts	93,846	48,998	82,167	90,384	99,422	109,364	120,300	132,331	145,563	160,120	176,132	193,745
Cash Disbursements (uses of cash)												
Cost of sales - inventory	31,864	18,206	38,387	42,226	46,449	51,094	56,203	61,823	68,005	74,806	82,287	90,514
Payroll	24,167	24,167	24,167	24,167	24,167	24,167	24,167	24,167	24,167	24,167	24,167	24,167
Payroll taxes and benefits	3,867	3,867	3,867	3,867	3,867	3,867	3,867	3,867	3,867	3,867	3,867	3,867
Non-payroll expenses	48,761	29,363	12,760	13,662	13,407	14,559	14,997	16,673	16,698	18,529	20,482	21,856
Depreciable asset purchases	0	0	0	0	0	0	0	0	0	0	0	0
Non-depreciable asset purchases	0	0	0	0	0	0	0	0	0	0	0	0
Interest	563	555	547	540	532	524	517	509	501	494	486	0
Short-term liabilities payments	0	1,022	1,022	1,022	1,022	1,022	1,022	1,022	1,022	1,022	1,022	64,780
Long-term liabilities payments	0	0	0	0	0	0	0	0	0	0	0	0
Dividends or owner's draw	0	0	0	0	0	0	0	0	0	0	0	0
Total Cash Disbursements	109,222	77,180	80,750	85,484	89,444	95,233	100,773	108,061	114,260	122,885	132,311	205,184
Income taxes	(6,573)	710	2,014	3,885	5,441	7,443	9,227	11,825	14,052	16,522	19,510	23,131
Total Cash Disbursements After Taxes	102,649	77,890	82,764	89,369	94,885	102,676	110,000	119,886	128,312	139,407	151,821	228,315
Net Change In Cash	(8,803)	(28,892)	(597)	1,015	4,537	6,688	10,300	12,445	17,251	20,713	24,311	(34,570)
Ending Cash Position	36,197	7,305	6,708	7,723	12,260	18,948	29,248	41,693	58,944	79,657	103,968	69,398

First- and Five-year Pro Forma Statement of Cash Flow for Investor Offering

Kona Gold Coffees

	Month Jan.	Feb.	March	April	May	June	July	Aug.	Sept.	Oct.	Nov.	Year 1	2	3	4	5
Starting Cash Position	45,000	61,563	34,053	34,833	37,221	43,126	51,176	62,834	76,632	95,231	117,287	142,936	127,208	386,106	615,229	862,275
Cash Receipts (sources of cash)																
Cash sales	18,846	20,730	22,803	25,084	27,592	30,351	33,386	36,725	40,397	44,437	48,881	53,769	435,240	470,059	507,664	548,277
Sales on credit	0	28,268	59,364	65,300	71,830	79,013	86,914	95,606	105,166	115,683	127,251	139,976	1,377,132	1,397,120	1,508,890	1,629,601
Short-term loan proceeds	0	0	0	0	0	0	0	0	0	0	0	0	0	0	0	0
Long-term loan proceeds	0	0	0	0	0	0	0	0	0	0	0	0	0	0	0	0
Equity capital proceeds	100,000	0	0	0	0	0	0	0	0	0	0	0	0	0	0	0
Total Cash Receipts	118,846	48,998	82,167	90,384	99,422	109,364	120,300	132,331	145,563	160,120	176,132	193,745	1,812,372	1,867,179	2,016,554	2,177,878
Cash Disbursements (uses of cash)																
Cost of sales - inventory	31,864	18,206	38,387	42,226	46,449	51,094	56,203	61,823	68,005	74,806	82,287	90,514	792,032	828,513	896,403	968,114
Payroll	24,167	24,167	24,167	24,167	24,167	24,167	24,167	24,167	24,167	24,167	24,167	24,167	301,604	313,668	326,215	339,264
Payroll taxes and benefits	3,867	3,867	3,867	3,867	3,867	3,867	3,867	3,867	3,867	3,867	3,867	3,867	48,260	50,191	52,198	54,286
Non-payroll expenses	48,761	29,363	12,760	13,862	13,407	14,559	14,997	16,673	16,698	18,529	20,482	21,856	233,077	242,681	258,190	275,023
Depreciable asset purchases	0	0	0	0	0	0	0	0	0	0	0	0	0	0	0	0
Non-depreciable asset purchases	0	0	0	0	0	0	0	0	0	0	0	0	0	0	0	0
Interest	0	0	0	0	0	0	0	0	0	0	0	0	0	0	0	0
Short-term liabilities payments	0	0	0	0	0	0	0	0	0	0	0	0	0	0	0	0
Long-term liabilites payments	0	0	0	0	0	0	0	0	0	0	0	0	0	0	0	0
Investor dividends or owner's draw	0	0	0	0	0	0	0	0	0	0	0	45,938	63,550	60,901	70,950	179,716
Total Cash Disbursements	108,659	75,603	79,181	83,922	87,890	93,687	99,234	106,530	112,737	121,369	130,803	186,342	1,428,523	1,495,954	1,603,956	1,816,403
Income taxes	(6,376)	905	2,206	4,074	5,627	7,627	9,408	12,003	14,227	16,695	19,680	23,131	124,951	142,102	165,552	186,004
Total Cash Disbursements After Taxes	102,283	76,508	81,387	87,996	93,517	101,314	108,642	118,533	126,964	138,064	150,483	209,473	1,553,474	1,638,056	1,769,508	2,002,407
Net Change In Cash	16,563	(27,510)	780	2,388	5,905	8,050	11,658	13,798	18,599	22,056	25,649	(15,728)	258,898	229,123	247,046	175,471
Ending Cash Position	51,563	34,053	34,833	37,221	43,126	51,176	62,834	76,632	95,231	117,287	142,936	127,208	386,106	615,229	862,275	1,037,746

Short-term loan proceeds, interest, and short-term liabilities payments are entered as zeros to show differences from the First-year Pro Forma Statement of Cash Flow for Loan Request. Note the $100,000 equity capital proceeds received in January and the investor-dividends payback in years 1–5. (Also, see Kona Gold Coffees' Investment Offering Summary in Chapter 11.)

If your lenders or investors require a long-range pro forma statement of cash flow, you can include one for the second- or third-year using quarterly periods. Long-range pro forma cash flows are rarely expected or requested in a business plan for start-up companies because most reviewers believe long-range pro forma cash flows stand too much of a chance of being inaccurate. Since planning is so important for success, undertake these pro formas for your business anyway, but omit them from your first business plan if they are not requested for review.

Pro Forma Balance Sheet

The pro forma balance sheet is an estimate of future assets and liabilities predicting equity, or net worth, at a given point in time. There is no difference in the format from your opening balance sheet, covered earlier in this chapter. The only difference is the points of time or dates of the balance sheets and of course the entries tailored to their respective dates. Remember, a balance sheet is like a snapshot, a picture of your assets, liabilities, and equity frozen in time on the date of the document. Its numbers are accurate as of that one day.

Your opening balance sheet has been designed to reflect your assets, liabilities, and equity as of the date your business plan was begun. In your financial plan, your reviewers want to see how your balance sheet will look at the end of each quarter during your first year. They also want to see a longer-range forecast of your balance sheet commensurate with your three- or five-year pro forma income statement. These projected balance sheets are called pro forma balance sheets.

For this segment, include two documents:

- Your first-year pro forma balance sheet showing your equity at the end of each quarter and
- Your three- or five-year pro forma balance sheet using year-end annual numbers.

Refer to the chart Balance Sheet Explained Step-by-Step for what to include in each category. For your cash position on the first quarter of your First-year Pro Forma Balance Sheet, use your ending cash position of the third month from your Pro Forma Statement of Cash Flows, and likewise, for each quarter thereafter tie the quarters to their respective ending months. It is standard practice to round off cents to the dollar, so some of your entries from document to document will be off by one dollar.

First-year and Five-year Pro Forma Balance Sheets

Kona Gold Coffees

	Quarter				Year				
	1	2	3	4	1	2	3	4	5
Assets									
Current Assets									
Cash	6,709	18,950	58,948	69,403	381,855	671,883	989,883	1,345,074	
Marketable securities	0	0	0	0	0	0	0	0	
Accounts receivable	99,505	132,441	176,279	234,627	163,215	176,272	190,374	205,604	
Inventory	20,195	26,880	35,777	47,619	32,121	34,691	37,466	40,464	
Other current assets	25,000	25,000	25,000	25,000	25,000	25,000	25,000	25,000	
Total Current Assets	151,409	203,271	296,004	376,649	602,191	907,846	1,242,723	1,616,142	
Long-term Assets									
Depreciable assets	188,761	188,761	188,761	188,761	188,761	188,761	188,761	188,761	
Accumulated depreciation	8,472	16,944	25,416	33,888	67,776	101,664	122,220	142,776	
Net depreciable assets	180,289	171,817	163,345	154,873	120,985	87,097	66,541	45,985	
Non-depreciable assets	0	0	0	0	0	0	0	0	
Total Long-term Assets	180,289	171,817	163,345	154,873	120,985	87,097	66,541	45,985	
Total Assets	331,698	375,088	459,349	568,061	773,177	1,060,490	1,382,593	1,744,211	
Liabilities and Equity									
Current Liabilities									
Cost of sales accounts payable	42,226	56,203	74,806	99,566	62,951	69,596	75,164	81,177	
Non-cost of sales accounts payable	13,662	14,997	18,529	22,891	19,108	20,325	21,624	23,036	
Taxes payable	0	0	0	0	0	0	0	0	
Short-term notes payable	72,956	69,890	66,824	0	0	0	0	0	
Total Current Liabilities	128,844	141,090	160,159	122,457	82,059	89,921	96,788	104,213	
Long-term Liabilities	0	0	0	0	0	0	0	0	
Total Liabilities	128,844	141,090	160,159	122,457	82,059	89,921	96,788	104,213	
Equity									
Shareholders equity	210,000	210,000	210,000	210,000	210,000	210,000	210,000	210,000	
Retained earnings	(7,146)	23,998	89,190	199,065	431,117	695,022	1,002,476	1,347,913	
Total Equity	202,854	233,998	299,190	409,065	641,117	905,022	1,212,476	1,557,914	
Total Liabilities and Equity	331,698	375,088	459,349	531,522	723,176	994,943	1,309,264	1,662,127	

Business Ratios

Once your pro forma financial statements are complete, many interesting assessments can be made. Known as business or accounting ratios, these assessments compare specific figures in the statement of income and the balance sheet to arrive at a useful ratio — expressed as a decimal or percentage. While business ratios are valuable tools for financiers and lenders in measuring a business' solvency, liquidity, efficiency, and profitability, they are also valuable to you as management aids for determining the health of various aspects of your business. Because a start-up business typically has poor ratios the first year, reviewers tend to put more emphasis on capital requirements, the break-even point, and the calculation of business ratios on projections for future years. For ongoing businesses, ratios are analyzed on past, current, and pro forma financial statements.

If you choose to report the results of some of the important business ratios, either list them at the bottom of the pro forma statement of income or prepare a separate chart, as in the example below.

Using computer software, you can easily graph these ratios to visually enhance your business plan. Some of the more popular graphed ratios are included for Kona Gold Coffees' business plan after this discussion.

Key Business Ratios — Kona Gold Coffees

	Year 1	Year 2	Year 3	Year 4	Year 5
Quick ratio	2.69	6.95	9.71	12.45	15.12
Current ratio	3.08	7.34	10.10	12.84	15.51
Debt to assets	0.23	0.11	0.09	0.07	0.06
Debt to equity	0.47	0.22	0.16	0.13	0.10
Collection days	53.1	34.2	34.2	34.2	34.2
Sales to assets	2.84	2.25	1.77	1.47	1.26
Working capital	$254,192	$520,132	$817,925	$1,145,935	$1,511,928
Accounts receivable turnover	6.87	10.67	10.67	10.67	10.67
Gross profit margin	55.7%	55.7%	55.7%	55.7%	55.7%
Net profit margin	12.3%	13.3%	14.0%	15.1%	15.8%
Return on assets	37%	32%	27%	23%	21%
Return on equity	49%	36%	29%	25%	22%
Inventory turnover days	10.8	6.7	6.7	6.7	6.7
Inventory turnover	33.9	54.2	54.2	54.2	54.2

Most-used Business Ratios

It is unnecessary for you to calculate all of the ratios. They are presented here for you to choose from if you want to use any in your business plan or in case a lender requests a particular one. Some of the ratios presented have other names; those given are the most universally used.

Several organizations such as Robert Morris Associates (RMA) or Dun & Bradstreet furnish comparative data using many of these ratios, so you can evaluate how your business stacks up against others. These consulting organizations assign your business one or more SIC (standard industrial classification) numbers, depending on your specialties. For the new NAICS (North American Industry Classification System), you may have to make the conversions (see Chapter 3). Once your particular SIC or NAICS number is identified, the consultant will narrow down the field by matching your business to those with similar earnings. They can provide comparisons of your standard ratios with ratios of businesses in the same categories of your SIC or NAICS and range of earnings. It is not necessary to include the RMA (Robert Morris Associates) ratios in your business plan because banks and lenders have their own access to RMA ratios. However, RMA or Dun & Bradstreet ratios can provide an important management tool for tracking your company with your peers as a measure of control. To help you understand how to use these ratios, 14 of the more popular business ratios are explained below.

Quick Ratio

A liquidity ratio, the quick ratio equals quick assets divided by current liabilities (from the balance sheet). Quick assets are those assets that can be converted to cash quickly or are equivalent to cash, such as cash, accounts receivable, and marketable securities. A low ratio means you could have difficulty in meeting your current credit responsibilities. A high ratio indicates you could have excess in cash, securities, or both, or it suggests you could have poor collection of your accounts receivable. A ratio of 1.40 demonstrates that, for every $1.00 you have of current liabilities, you have $1.40 in cash, securities, or accounts receivable to pay off those obligations.

Current Ratio

Another liquidity ratio, the current ratio equals current assets divided by current liabilities (from the balance sheet). Current assets are defined as those assets that can be converted to cash within one year. Likewise, current liabilities are those obligations that must be paid within one year.

A low ratio signifies the company may have problems in meeting its short-term obligations as they become due. A high ratio may represent an excessive investment in current assets or a low utilization of short-term credit. A ratio of 2.75 means that for every $1.00 of current liabilities, you have $2.75 in current assets to meet them. Working capital is negative when the current ratio is below 1.00; conversely, when the current ratio is above 1.00, working capital is positive. Current assets minus current liabilities equals working capital.

Debt to Equity

A safety ratio, debt to equity equals total liabilities divided by total equity (from the balance sheet). This is a measure of the business' financial commitment. A low ratio is better than a high ratio, but a low ratio can imply the company may be underutilizing its leveraging ability. A high ratio sends signals that the business is more risky than average. A ratio of 1.40 reveals that for every $1.00 you have invested in the business, creditors have $1.40 invested in it with you. This is regarded as one of the more important safety ratios to be read as a measure of the business' ability to weather a slow period in sales and profits.

Working Capital

Called an operating ratio and sometimes a liquidity ratio, this is really a mathematical difference rather than a ratio. Working capital equals current assets less current liabilities (from the balance sheet). This is similar to the current ratio, but it is a measure in terms of dollars and is the requirement to pay short-term obligations. A low figure can indicate you have difficulty making payroll or payments to suppliers. When the current ratio is below 1.00, working capital is negative; in the same way, when the current ratio is above 1.00, working capital is positive.

Gross Profit Margin

Also called the gross profit ratio, this profitability ratio is expressed as a percentage. It is arrived at by dividing your gross profit margin by your sales (from the Income Statement). It shows what percentage of each dollar is left after paying all costs of goods or direct expenses. The gross profit ratio is used to examine the effectiveness of your pricing policies and the efficiency in providing your products or services. For example, a 39 percent gross profit margin means that for every $1.00 of sales generated, a gross profit of $0.39 is earned.

EBIT-to-Interest

EBIT is an acronym for "earnings before interest and taxes." It is another safety ratio you can use if you have any interest expense (from the income statement). Determining the ratio is a three-step calculation. First, you need to figure the gross profit ratio (above). Then you figure the EBIT which is the gross profit ratio minus the non-cost of sales expense. To get the EBIT-to-interest ratio, divide the EBIT amount by your total interest expense.

    Step 1. Gross profit ratio = Gross profit/Sales
    Step 2. EBIT = Gross profit ratio − Non-cost of sales expense
    Step 3. EBIT to interest = EBIT/Interest expense

Lenders will review your financial statement for this ratio as a measure of your business' ability to generate sufficient profit to pay interest payments.

Collection Days

For cash-and-carry businesses this is an irrelevant statistic. For others, it is an efficiency ratio. Collection days, sometimes called average collection, or simply, collection, equals accounts receivable divided by sales (from the income statement), and that result is multiplied by 365 — Dun & Bradstreet uses 360. This is the estimated average number of days for collecting payment of bills. This assumes the accounts receivable ending balance used is typical for the period.

Sales to Assets

An operating ratio, sales to assets is equal to sales (from the income statement) divided by total assets (from the balance sheet). A low ratio can suggest you are investing too much in assets compared to your level of sales. A high ratio could indicate you might not be spending enough, suggesting you may need to upgrade equipment or other assets. A ratio of 9.64 indicates that for every $1.00 invested in assets, you have $9.64 in sales.

Inventory Turnover

Another operating ratio, inventory turnover equals cost of sales (from the income statement) divided by inventory (from the balance sheet). The ratio points out the number of times you turn over inventory in a year. A low number may imply over-stocking, could suggest a surplus of out-of-date inventory, or could represent a planned surplus. A high number may reveal a shortage of needed inventory or a more successful marketing effort than anticipated.

Inventory Turnover Days

The inventory turnover in days is calculated by dividing 365 by the inventory turnover ratio (above). For example, if your inventory turnover ratio is 21.38, then 365 days divided by the ratio (21.38) equals 17 days, or an inventory turnover of 17 days.

Inventory turnover days: 365/21.38 = 17 days

Accounts Receivable Turnover

Accounts receivable turnover is an operating ratio that is equal to sales divided by accounts receivable (from the income statement). This ratio is a measure of the number of times accounts receivable were collected during the period. Again, this assumes the ending balance for accounts receivable is typical for the period used.

Accounts Payable Turnover

This is another operating ratio, sometimes referred to as an activity ratio. Accounts payable turnover equals cost of sales divided by accounts payable (from the income statement). This yields the number of times accounts payable were paid off during the period, assuming the ending balance for accounts payable is typical for the period used.

Return on Assets

Return on assets, a profitability ratio also known as an operating ratio, equals net profit (from the income statement) divided by total assets (from the balance sheet) and is expressed as a percentage. It is an indicator of the efficiency of your assets in generating a return. If your return on assets is 35 percent, it means your business produced a return of $0.35 for every $1.00 used for assets.

Return on Equity

Another profitability ratio, return on equity equals net profit (from the income statement) divided by total equity (from the balance sheet) and is expressed as a percentage. Because total equity is your investment in the business, this ratio is a measure of the return your business is generating on your investment in the company. If the return on equity is 12 percent, this signifies that for every $1.00 you invest in the business, the business produces a return of $0.12, or 12 percent. As an investment tool, owners watch this one closely. However, you cannot simply compare this to a return on other investments because, in addition to the return, your business is paying the bills and developing other hidden equities, such as an increasing business value and possibly real estate equity.

For further discussion and the equations for many of the more popular ratios, see Appendix F.

For additional information on the use of these and other analytical tools, see The Oasis Press' publication, *Business Owner's Guide to Accounting and Bookkeeping*, by José Placencia, Bruce Welge, and Don Oliver.

Key Five-year Ratios
Kona Gold Coffees

Quick Ratio
- Year 1 2.69
- Year 2 6.95
- Year 3 9.71
- Year 4 12.45
- Year 5 15.12

Current Ratio
- Year 1 3.08
- Year 2 7.34
- Year 3 10.1
- Year 4 12.84
- Year 5 15.51

Net Profit Margin
(Bar chart, Years 1–5, ranging from ~12% to ~16%)

Debt to Assets
(Bar chart, Total Assets vs. Total Liabilities, Years 1–5)

Debt to Equity
(Bar chart, Total Equity vs. Total Liabilities, Years 1–5)

Working Capital
(Line chart, Years 1–5, rising from ~$200,000 to ~$1,500,000)

Important Points to Remember

- You will have to make some basic assumptions to arrive at the numbers for your financial pro formas. Keep a record of them both for your own reference as you work through your business plan and for fine-tuning the Important Assumptions section of your finished plan.
- Use the same date for your opening balance sheet as the date of your business plan.
- Develop a *draft* pro forma statement of cash flow before using adjustments created from loan proceeds — to see a picture of how things are *as-is* without any funds from a loan. Use this draft to assist you in accurately calculating your working capital requirement.
- Include a pro forma income statement month-to-month, a pro forma statement of cash flow month-to-month, and a pro forma balance sheet by quarters for the first year.
- Develop a *draft* pro forma statement of cash flow before using adjustments created from loan proceeds — to see a picture of how things are *as-is*, without any funds from a loan. Use this draft to assist you in accurately calculating your working capital requirement.
- Include the longer range forecasts of a year-to-year three- or five-year pro forma income statement and a year-to-year three- or five-year pro forma balance sheet.
- Include only those business ratios that make your company look its best or show a vast improvement in your three- or five-year forecast over your first-year pro forma.
- Make sure all the numbers in these pro forma financial statements are consistent with all the numbers in your projections in other sections.

After you have assembled all the financial information, analyze it for the most important points. Return to your financial summary and rewrite it to emphasize your significant findings about the financial aspects of your business.

Once your reviewers have seen all the operating numbers, you will want to show them your start-up costs and your working capital requirement and to present your loan request or investment offering. These are the subjects of the next chapter.

Chapter 11

Financial Requirement

The best we can do is size up the chances, calculate the risks involved, estimate our ability to deal with them and then make our plans with confidence.
— HENRY FORD II

This final section of the body of your business plan is reserved for your financial request. It expands the financial requirement you introduced in your executive summary and details the amount and type of financial assistance you want to obtain. You can title this section, Financial Requirement, or you can title it specifically as a Loan Request or Investment Offering.

Typically, as a new start-up company, your sources are more limited than those for an existing business. Regardless, the sources really depend on the type of your business, the amount of funds you need, and the amount of cash or liquid assets, if any, you have invested in your new business venture. This chapter summarizes potential financial sources and the financial requirement segments of your business plan, which are:

- Financial requirement summary
- Start-up costs
- Funds raised and funds needed
- Loan request proposal
- Investment offering proposal
- Potential risks
- Exit options

Once you have verified your total start-up costs for opening your business, compared it to your assets, and developed your financial pro formas, you will know the amount of capital you need to springboard your new business. If you don't have all of the funds, you will need to raise the difference from a source of equity or debt financing.

Financial Sources

Basically there are two methods of financing, debt and equity. You are probably most familiar with debt financing where you acquire a loan, then make principal and interest payments to the lender until it is paid. It is not difficult to raise funds through conventional lenders for many hard costs, such as a real estate loan or an equipment lease. Loans for soft costs, such as marketing, salaries, and operations overhead, however, are usually more difficult to find. Since personal loans are easier to acquire than business loans, the first option of choice for most new business owners is to tap into their personal resources, including home equity loans, consumer credit, equipment leases, personally-guaranteed sale and leaseback programs, cash value of life insurance, other liquid assets, and family and friends.

Sources for business loans to cover soft costs are commercial lenders, the Small Business Administration (SBA), SBA-backed lenders, commercial finance companies, investment clubs, insurance companies, Small Business Investment Companies (SBICs), and others; however, these lenders seldom make loans to start-up companies. SBICs are entities licensed by the Small Business Administration (SBA) to provide either equity or long-term debt financing to qualified small businesses. Much of the financing made available by SBICs is borrowed from the SBA at attractive rates.

Equity financing is a method of raising capital by selling a portion of your business to investors. Major sources are venture capitalists, some Small Business Investment Companies (SBICs), and individual investors (angels). See Appendix G.

Venture capital financing is a specialty area of finance that is characteristically high risk — created for businesses that have the potential to yield high returns to offset the risks. They assist in second- and third-round financing for existing companies, more often than for startups. Usually start-up companies, especially small and low-tech businesses, do not fit within venture capital criteria unless they have a real possibility of growing large enough within about five years to go public (major public offering) or to be purchased by a takeover company. They also look for a manager on board that is a proven winner, and a personal referral is typically needed.

When individual investors provide capital to a start-up business, they typically want ownership and involvement in the operation, either directly in management, or indirectly, as a member of your board of directors.

Other equity sources, such as private placement offerings of stock with accredited and sophisticated investors, are usually beyond the scope of most start-up businesses. However, if your start-up business intends to start on a large scale, the culture of your new business is innovative and nearly unique, or it is based on special technology, these sources are possibilities.

If you prefer to use equity financing and want to sell interest in your company, discuss with your attorney which is the best form of agreement for you and your investors (vesting types). Also, depending on your type of agreement, cover the differences in shareholder interests, such as classes and preferences of stock, common or preferred stock, or convertible debt.

Financial Requirement Summary

Once you complete the segments in this section, write an opening summary entitled Loan Request Summary or Investment Offering Summary. This targets the type of lender or investor arrangements you are going after, including capital from a limited or general partner or from an investor or member of a limited liability company. To cover all the bases, you may wish to write both versions and submit the proper plan to the appropriate financiers.

Loan Request Summary

For this summary, write a narrative beginning with your total start-up costs, the amount of funds you have already invested, and the amount of funds you have available. Describe your loan request and desired terms. While writing your summary, it is important to remember that every money source usually requires the answers to five essential questions.

- How much money do you need?
- What do you plan to use it for?
- How can the money improve your business?
- How are you going to pay it back?
- If your plan for the above doesn't work, what is your backup plan?

Respond to these questions in your loan request summary even if the answers are repeated elsewhere in your business plan.

Loan Request Summary   **Kona Gold Coffees**

Our total start-up costs are $283,761. The major costs are leasehold improvements ($60,000), vehicles and equipment ($88,761), fixtures and furniture ($40,000), and working capital ($70,000). To date we have raised $210,000 from our two founders which includes $45,000 cash on hand. The difference between our start-up costs and what we have raised is $73,761. To cover this we are seeking a commercial line of credit for $100,000. We are willing to pay two points and 9 percent interest and would like the monthly payments to be amortized over 5 years, to be fully paid during one full 30-day period each year, and subject to renewal. We plan to draw one disbursement of $75,000 in January and use the funds to pay off equipment ($48,761) and launch our business with additional needed start-up capital ($25,000) for positive cash flow. We expect to maintain the balance of the line as a reserve.

(continued)

> **Loan Request Summary** (continued)   **Kona Gold Coffees**
>
> As our cash flow pro forma shows, we anticipate making ten monthly payments of $1,599 (approximately $1,000 in principal) for ten months and pay down the line in full in December with a balance payment of $64,780. We believe this is a safe course of action as we should still have $69,403 in cash after paying income taxes at that point. However, as a backup plan our founders would seek equity home loans from second mortgages, if necessary. Their personal financial statements are included in the exhibits showing relative values for this contingency.

Investment Offering Summary

Instead of a loan request, or as an alternate plan, this summary may also serve as an offering to investors for limited partners, general partners, or members of an LLC. Begin as you would for a loan request with your total start-up costs, the amount of funds you have already invested, and the amount of funds you have available.

Describe your equity offering and the structure for the investors' involvement. This descriptive summary should also answer the five essential questions which every money source is looking for, as mentioned above. Unique to the investment offering is the exit option. For the investors' possible exit, you can propose several options. The owner or founding partners will eventually:

- Purchase the investor's interest at a certain point,
- Replace their interest with a bank loan at a specified point,
- Sell shares via a second round private offering or to a larger company
- Go public; or
- Use other exit options, as discussed later in this chapter.

Remember to include a backup plan, usually presented in the form of a second exit option.

Investment Offering Summary — Kona Gold Coffees

Our total start-up costs are $283,761. The major costs are leasehold improvements ($60,000), vehicles and equipment ($88,761), fixtures and furniture ($40,000), and working capital ($70,000). To date we have raised $210,000 from our two founders which includes $45,000 cash on hand. The difference between our start-up costs and what we have raised is $73,761.

To cover this we seeking an investor to invest the outside capital needed of $100,000 in exchange for 15 percent preferred ownership stock in our limited liability company for five years. The exact use of the funds as shown on our request detail $48,761 to pay off equipment; $25,000 to launch our business with the additional start-up capital needed for positive cash flow; and $26,239 as a cash deposit in our company interest-accruing checking account to be held as a contingency reserve.

With this type of ownership, the investor as a preferred return member will be paid dividends of 15 percent per year for five years, at which time the company founders will buy out the investor's 15 percent portion for the original amount invested of $100,000.

From our pro formas the investor would receive 15 percent dividends each year based on the profit before income taxes which would be:

Kona Gold Coffees	Year 1	2	3	4	5
Profit Before Income Taxes	$306,256	$357,002	$406,007	$473,006	$531,441
15% to Investor	$ 45,938	$ 53,550	$ 60,901	$ 70,950	$ 79,716

By the end of the fifth year, the investor will have received $311,055 plus his or her buy-out of $100,000, or $411,055. This is a total of 411 percent return over 5 years, or an average annual return of 82 percent.

As a backup plan, should the initial plan fail, our founders will personally guarantee to return the investor's original investment at the end of two years together with 12 percent annual interest by securing equity home loans through second mortgages on their personal homes. Their personal financial statements are included in the exhibits showing relative values for this contingency.

Our cash flow pro forma on the next page shows equity capital proceeds entered as $100,000 and investor dividends at the end of years one through five. Notice also that the fifth dividend includes the investor's buy-out.

The exact details and terms of preferred stock are specified in the Agreement of Formation of the limited liability company, see Exhibits.

First- and Five-year Pro Forma Statement of Cash Flow for Investor Offering

Kona Gold Coffees

	Month												Year				
	Jan.	Feb.	March	April	May	June	July	Aug.	Sept.	Oct.	Nov.		1	2	3	4	5
Starting Cash Position	45,000	61,563	34,053	34,833	37,221	43,126	51,176	62,834	76,632	95,231	117,287	142,936		127,208	386,106	615,229	862,275
Cash Receipts (sources of cash)																	
Cash sales	18,846	20,730	22,803	25,084	27,592	30,351	33,386	36,725	40,397	44,437	48,881	53,769		435,240	470,059	507,664	548,277
Sales on credit	0	28,268	59,364	65,300	71,830	79,013	86,914	95,606	105,166	115,683	127,251	139,976		1,377,132	1,397,120	1,508,890	1,629,601
Short-term loan proceeds	0	0	0	0	0	0	0	0	0	0	0	0		0	0	0	0
Long-term loan proceeds	0	0	0	0	0	0	0	0	0	0	0	0		0	0	0	0
Equity capital proceeds	100,000	0	0	0	0	0	0	0	0	0	0	0		0	0	0	0
Total Cash Receipts	118,846	48,998	82,167	90,384	99,422	109,364	120,300	132,331	145,563	160,120	176,132	193,745		1,812,372	1,867,179	2,016,554	2,177,878
Cash Disbursements (uses of cash)																	
Cost of sales - inventory	31,864	18,206	38,387	42,226	46,449	51,094	56,203	61,823	68,005	74,806	82,287	90,514		792,032	828,513	896,403	968,114
Payroll	24,167	24,167	24,167	24,167	24,167	24,167	24,167	24,167	24,167	24,167	24,167	24,167		301,604	313,668	326,215	339,264
Payroll taxes and benefits	3,867	3,867	3,867	3,867	3,867	3,867	3,867	3,867	3,867	3,867	3,867	3,867		48,260	50,191	52,198	54,286
Non-payroll expenses	48,761	29,363	12,760	13,662	13,407	14,559	14,997	16,873	16,698	18,529	20,482	21,856		233,077	242,681	258,190	275,023
Depreciable asset purchases	0	0	0	0	0	0	0	0	0	0	0	0		0	0	0	0
Non-depreciable asset purchases	0	0	0	0	0	0	0	0	0	0	0	0		0	0	0	0
Interest	0	0	0	0	0	0	0	0	0	0	0	0		0	0	0	0
Short-term liabilities payments	0	0	0	0	0	0	0	0	0	0	0	0		0	0	0	0
Long-term liabilites payments	0	0	0	0	0	0	0	0	0	0	0	0		0	0	0	0
Investor dividends or owners draw	0	0	0	0	0	0	0	0	0	0	0	45,938		45,938	53,550	60,901	70,950	179,716
Total Cash Disbursements	108,659	75,603	79,181	83,922	87,890	93,687	99,234	106,530	112,737	121,369	130,803	186,342		1,428,523	1,495,954	1,603,956	1,816,403
Income taxes	(6,376)	905	2,206	4,074	5,827	7,827	9,408	12,003	14,227	16,695	19,680	23,131		124,951	142,102	165,552	186,004
Total Cash Disbursements After Taxes	102,283	76,508	81,387	87,996	93,517	101,314	108,642	118,533	126,964	138,064	150,483	209,473		1,553,474	1,638,056	1,769,508	2,002,407
Net Change In Cash	16,563	(27,510)	780	2,388	5,905	8,050	11,658	13,798	18,599	22,056	25,649	(15,728)		258,898	229,123	247,046	175,471
Ending Cash Position	61,563	34,053	34,833	37,221	43,126	51,176	62,834	76,632	95,231	117,287	142,936	127,208		386,106	615,229	862,275	1,037,746

Start-up Costs

In a brief paragraph, describe your total start-up costs explaining major items or anything that is not easily identifiable in the item descriptions in your schedule of start-up costs. Describe necessary detail for expenses that need justification. State your shortfall amount from your cash flow pro forma, and show you've increased it, as a planning standard, with a margin of safety for your working-capital requirement. Include with your paragraph of explanation a schedule, or table, detailing all of your start-up costs. Use columns for the items' descriptions, the estimated amount of each expense, actual costs and dates paid or completed for items that have been paid, and the balance to be paid with the dates they will be paid.

For your internal planning you might want to develop a spreadsheet detailing your start-up costs on a monthly basis for your first year.

Loan Request Start-up Costs   Kona Gold Coffees

Our start-up costs are $283,761. This includes our owner's vehicle that was purchased several months ago and has been contributed as part of his capital basis. It also includes leasehold improvements and fixtures and furniture, which have been paid. The bulk of our equipment has been purchased and is awaiting payment of $48,761 for delivery. The amount of our additional working capital requirement established from our cash flow pro forma is actually $65,947 after the equipment for which we are seeking this line of credit is paid.

In the examples above and below for Kona Gold Coffees, the first four sentences are the same in each. The only difference lies in the last clause of the last sentence in each. In the top example, Kona Gold Coffees is seeking a line of credit. In the bottom one, Kona Gold Coffees is seeking investment funds. In both cases, the line of credit and the investment funds, the $100,000 which is sought includes the recommended safety margin for required working capital.

Investment Proposal Start-up Costs   Kona Gold Coffees

Our start-up costs are $283,761. This includes our owner's vehicle that was purchased several months ago and has been contributed as part of his capital basis. It also includes leasehold improvements and fixtures and furniture, which have been paid. The bulk of our equipment has been purchased and is awaiting payment of $48,761 for delivery. The amount of our additional working capital requirement established from our cash flow pro forma is actually $65,947 after the equipment is paid, for which we are seeking investment funds with a working capital safety margin.

Start-up Costs

Kona Gold Coffees

Start-up Cost Description	Total Estimated	Actual Paid	Date Paid	Balance to Pay	Date Needed
Initial lease/purchase	$ 2,000	$ 2,000	8/7/XX	$ 0	
Lease deposit	2,000	2,000	8/7/XX	0	
Utilities deposit	200	200	8/10/XX	0	
Licenses and fees	140	140	8/15/XX	0	
Leasehold improvements	60,000	60,000	11/30/XX	0	
Insurance	1,000	1,000	11/30/XX	0	
Other prepaids	11,967	11,967	12/15/XX	0	
Equipment	48,761	0		48,761	01/30/XY
Vehicle	40,000	40,000	12/15/XX	0	
Fixtures and furniture	40,000	40,000	12/15/XX	0	
Freight and installation	included	included	12/15/XX	0	
Sales taxes	included	included	12/15/XX	0	
Opening inventory	in first month			0	1/30/XY
Supplies	2,500	2,500	12/15/XX	0	
Signage	120	120	12/15/XX	0	
Marketing materials	in first month			0	1/15/XY
Advertising	in first month			0	
Accounting	2,673	2,673	12/05/XX	0	
Legal	2,400	2,400	12/10/XX	0	
Hiring expenses	0	0		0	
Training expenses	0	0		0	
Grand opening	in marketing			0	
Working capital	70,000	45,000	12/15/XX	25,000	1/15/XY
Appropriate totals	$283,761	$210,000		$73,761	

Funds Raised and Funds Needed

The schedule of start-up costs shows every cost, which ones that have been paid to date and which are left to be paid. However, it does not show the sources of the funds used for those costs that are paid, nor does it show whether you have the funds in-house to pay the balance of what you owe. If you are seeking a loan or investor funds specifically to cover the start-up costs you still need, apart from those that you may have already paid, a statement of funds raised and funds needed will complete the information about your start-up costs lenders or investors need.

Points to include are:

- Total start-up costs (from your Start-up Costs segment above);
- Total amount raised so far, with a breakdown of individual amounts from different sources, identifying the sources in general terms; and
- Total amount needed, which should be the difference between the total start-up costs and the total amount raised, listing the anticipated source and payback.

Loan Request Funds Raised and Funds Needed Kona Gold Coffees

As can be seen by the start-up schedule, our projected start-up costs are $283,761. Of this, we have already raised $210,000 — $126,000 from David Cooper and $84,000 from Jim Wallace. Except for cash on hand of $45,000, the balance has been used as shown on the start-up costs table. This table also shows that we are using a working capital requirement of $70,000 and have an equipment payable of $48,761. Netting this against our cash, we still need to raise an additional $73,761. We are now seeking a business line of credit for $100,000 from Bank of Hawaii. We have projected drawing proceeds of $75,000 in January, making monthly payments and paying it down fully by the end of the year. We expect to maintain the balance of the line only as a reserve. The one-time $75,000 draw will be used to pay off our equipment and to launch our business with additional start-up capital for positive cash flow.

In the examples above and below for Kona Gold Coffees, notice the first five sentences explaining the funds raised and funds needed are the same. The difference lies in the last part of these statements. In the first example, funds are being sought through debt financing from a line of credit. In the second example, funds are being sought through equity financing from investors. Both mention a ceiling of $100,000, which has been set high enough to include a safety margin for the working capital needed.

Investment Proposal Funds Raised and Funds Needed Kona Gold Coffees

As can be seen by the start-up schedule, our projected start-up costs are $283,761. Of this, we have already raised $210,000 — $126,000 from David Cooper and $84,000 from Jim Wallace. Except for cash on hand of $45,000, the balance has been used as shown on the start-up costs table. This table also shows that we are using a working capital requirement of $70,000 and have an equipment payable of $48,761. Netting this against our cash, we still need to raise an additional $73,761. We are now seeking to raise $100,000 in outside investor funds to pay off our equipment and to launch our business with additional start-up capital for positive cash flow and a reasonable contingency reserve.

If you are seeking a loan from lenders, use the title, Loan Request Proposal for the next segment. If you are anticipating generating capital through investor programs, use the title, Investment Offering.

Loan Request Proposal

Because a picture speaks louder than words, the schedule in this segment lays out your loan request proposal in terms and a form that most lenders are familiar with. They can easily see your start-up costs broken down into hard costs and soft costs and seven areas of focus specifically labeled: hard costs, soft costs, total start-up costs, loan amount needed, loan requested, remarks, and collateral.

In a typical proposal, as shown here, all start-up costs are added to obtain a total of the funds you need to open, then your cash investment is

Loan Request Proposal — Kona Gold Coffees

Hard Costs		Soft Costs	
Facility/site	Leased	Deposits	16,167.00
Leasehold improvements	60,000.00	Licenses and fees	140.00
Equipment	48,761.00	Insurance	1,000.00
Vehicles	40,000.00	Inventory*	Credit purchase*
Furniture	8,000.00	Supplies	2,500.00
Fixtures	32,000.00	Other pre-opening costs	5,073.00
Signage	120.00	Working capital	70,000.00
Total Hard Costs	**$188,881.00**	**Total Soft Costs**	**$94,880.00**

* Included in Cost of Sales

Total Start-up Funds	$283,761.00
Less our cash investment	210,000.00
Loan Amount Needed	**$ 73,761.00**

Loan Requested: Commercial Line of Credit for $100,000.00 for the year 20XX, 2 points fee, 9 percent interest, payments amortized over 5 years, to be fully paid down during one 30-day period within the first year, with the possibility of renewal.

Remarks: We request that net proceeds of $75,000.00 be disbursed in the form of a first draw in January. Although a prepayment penalty is not customary for a line of credit, we would like to formally request a waiver of any prepayment penalty for early loan payoff.

Collateral: For hard collateral we anticipate and pre-approve your institution to lien our equipment and operation with a full encumbrance for this loan.

subtracted to arrive at the minimum amount you will need. To arrive at your requested loan amount, remember to increase your working-capital requirement to include a margin of safety, as discussed in Chapter 10.

After presenting these financial calculations, describe the terms you are requesting and the types of collateral you are proposing. Most lenders want tangible collateral such as a second-mortgage on your home or other real estate, securities, heavy equipment, or certain types of inventory. Some will consider intangible collateral such as a life insurance policy, a special assignment or lien, a personal guarantee, or a combination of these. Even though you may have specific ideas about the terms you want, investigate the programs of various lender's, so you can coordinate your request with a program your lender already offers.

Be sure to recheck the numbers on your loan request. It is imperative they be consistent with the pro forma financial data in the rest of your business plan.

Investment Offering

If you are designing your financial request as an investment offering, in this segment enclose a schedule listing your financial needs in terms of hard costs and soft costs, total start-up costs, and investment needed. Instead of setting loan terms, as in the Loan Request, include in your offering the involvement you propose for the partners or investors.

- The type of vesting entity
- The return of the investors' funds
- The return-on-investment to the investors
- Their exit options

The previous segments — investment offering summary, start-up costs, funds raised and funds needed — and this proposal, do not finalize or complete an investment offering. What you have covered thus far is a simple proposal, similar to a letter of intent. Once your investors show strong interest, you will need to provide additional information that are defined by the securities and disclosure requirements in your state and a complete agreement that encompasses the legal issues that vary from state to state. Your business attorney will be able to assist you with these.

When you have completed your loan request or investment offering proposal, review them for clarity and accuracy. And, because states have different laws involving investment offerings, it is a good idea to have your attorney as well as your accountant review your final business plan draft. In particular, have your attorney review your business plan if it is prepared as an investment offering before you present it to prospective investors.

Investment Offering
Kona Gold Coffees

Hard Costs		**Soft Costs**	
Facility/site	Leased	Deposits	$16,167.00
Leasehold improvements	$ 60,000.00	Licenses and fees	140.00
Equipment	48,761.00	Insurance	1,000.00
Vehicles	40,000.00	Inventory*	Credit purchase*
Furniture	8,000.00	Supplies	2,500.00
Fixtures	32,000.00	Other pre-opening costs	5,073.00
Signage	120.00	Working capital	70,000.00
Total Hard Costs	$188,881.00	Total Soft Costs	$94,880.00

* Included in Cost of Sales

Total Start-up Funds	$283,761.00
Less our cash investment	210,000.00
Difference	$ 73,761.00
Investor Reserve	$ 26,239.00
Investor Requirement	$100,000.00

Offering Proposal: A Limited Liability Company
Investor's capital: $100,000
Ownership of investor: 15%

For his or her investment, the investor member of the LLC will receive dividends based on 15 percent of the profit before income taxes in each December for the first five years. Upon payment of the fifth dividend, the original founders will buy out the investor member's interest for the original investment of $100,000 together with the face amount of the fifth dividend and the investor member will have no further ownership or claims upon Kona Gold Coffees.

Potential Risks

If you are using your business plan to sell a lender or investor on your company, it is only natural to want to embellish the facts about your business and to avoid disclosing any possible negatives. However, both lenders and investors will be assessing the possible risks of loaning you money or investing in your business, regardless of whether you point out those factors. For both lenders and investors, it is better to address your business risks in the beginning because it will increase the lenders' and investors' confidence that you have weighed and mitigated the downside as well as the upside potential of your business. But, more important, there is less opportunity for investors to sue for something that goes wrong when it is disclosed up front as a possible risk. There are such serious legal ramifications concerning this issue, you should check with your attorney to be sure you cover everything necessary before you make a presentation to an investor.

In preparation for writing this segment, examine every section of your business plan and analyze them for possible risks: company description, industry, market and competition, strategies, products or services, marketing and sales, management and organization, operations, financial pro formas — especially costs, and financial requirement. The most common risks are:

- Company — as a startup, the risk of uncertainty.
- Industry — the risk of changing trends.
- Market and competition — the risk of market changes; the risk that market acceptance may take longer than planned; the risk of competing with better, well-established competitors; the risk of new competition; and the risk of existing competitors responding to your entry into the market with counter moves, especially when there are only a few competitors.
- Strategies — the risk that a new strategy may not receive the expected buyer response.
- Products or services — the risk that buyers do not accept your products or services, and the risk competitors will make changes to their products or services or add or improve features making your products or services inferior or obsolete.
- Marketing and sales — the risk that your marketing plan is not effective and the risk that sales do not meet your market share.
- Management and organization — the risk that your management and personnel cannot meet the challenges of your business plan.
- Operations — the risk of losing suppliers or distributors, the risk of competitors developing new technology or production techniques, the risk of poor inventory control or cash flow control, and many others.
- Financial pro formas — the risk that projections cannot match reality.
- Financial requirement — the risk that the funds you seek cannot be obtained and the risk that the funds requested are insufficient for success of the venture.

These are only a few of the risks that potentially could be drawn from examining your research and your business plan. Consider, also, those external risks that can occur outside your industry, such as a worldwide or national economic downturn or regulatory impacts from government agencies and changing legislation.

When you have assessed the risks, consider the advantages you have listed, or should list, throughout your business plan to offset them. You can minimize a risk with statements designed for them based on these advantages, such as:

- Competition will be slow to react because our product positioning is aimed at a relatively small market share.
- We will be using a specialized promotion to counteract this risk.
- If our competition lower prices, we can match them because of our strong profit margin.
- There is a significant demand because our products or services will better fulfill customer needs.

In addition, you can offset many risks by adding specialized insurance coverage: business disruption, loss of receivable information, employee liability, and others.

For this segment, use a table or narrative summary and describe three or four major risks that you can foresee for your business and present a plausible solution for how you should be able to overcome or offset it. Refer to the example to see how Kona Gold Coffees intend to counteract their risks.

This segment is written the same for both a loan request and an investment offering.

Potential Risks   Kona Gold Coffees

As a new start-up company, there is always the accompanying risk of uncertainty. We believe that the combined experience of the president, operations chief, and other key employees will prove this to be an unnecessary concern.

Since our product is totally new to the market, there is risk of market acceptance. This is both a product risk and a market risk. We believe that our preopening market surveys have mitigated this and show that we should, in fact, have 4 percent of the market share or higher, as was pointed out at length in our market analysis.

In manufacturing, there is always the risk of losing key suppliers. However, because of our pre-arranged relationships and the fact we have so many suppliers, we believe this risk has been minimized for our company.

Another risk would be missing our gross profit margin of 55.7 percent. Since the industry standard is 40 percent, we believe we have a built-in safety net with this number.

Exit Options

As the last segment in this section and in your business plan, it is most appropriate to make a brief statement that covers your exit options. Many businesses, particularly start-up businesses, overlook this because it is the one area that is the last thing on the mind of an entrepreneur planning a new business.

If one of the reasons you are writing your business plan is to obtain financing, and your plan is to obtain debt financing with a loan, your lender will not much care about your exit options as long as you remain in business long enough to pay the loan back. However, if you are looking for capital from equity financing, an exit strategy is something your investors will be looking at closely. Investors want to know what their options are for getting out of a business at some future point. Even though you may have included one idea of an exit plan for investors in your offering request proposal, they might reject it yet still want to invest in your business. They could be looking at alternate exit possibilities. It is equally as important for you to look at all your exit options, for long range planning, so include this as a final segment even though you may not be using the business plan for financing purposes.

Examine all the possibilities, including:

- A hand down — turning the company over to your heirs
- A buyout — selling your shares to other stockholders
- A sale — selling your business to individuals
- An acquisition — selling your business to another existing company
- An IPO (initial public offering) — selling shares in the company to the public

In most of these cases, except turning the company over to heirs, you will receive cash for your investment. Although the securities laws in the United States have made it less expensive and easier to do a small public offering, IPOs are generally beyond the scope of small businesses. Unless your company grows significantly and you are prepared to accept the risk of future legal entanglements and the challenges that go with them, this exit option should be omitted.

There are two additional options for changing the structure of you company. They are franchising (licensing or leasing your business format through franchise agreements) and merging (joining an existing company). Usually, these are not considered exit options, but they could be. Franchising would require that you retain your ownership as a parent company. The parent company, to be effective, usually becomes larger with strong growth potential and typically expands rather than winds down. However, once franchised, if the organization is set up correctly, your ability to sell the company through an acquisition is usually enhanced. In a merger you might receive some cash, but usually in the form of stock. You could also still be in for the long haul as part of management with the new merger company, depending on the merger agreement.

If you are planning to show a best scenario to investors, profit projections substantial enough to allow you to buy them out from internal funds or large enough to support a loan to buy them out with debt financing is usually the best received. This projection should be shown to occur within the period of your long-range forecast.

If you are seeking cash from venture capitalists, they will usually dictate an exit option after reviewing your proposal if they are not comfortable with the one you suggest. If you accept their suggestion, you will need to revise your exit options to align your exit plan with theirs.

For this final segment, briefly describe the exit plan for your company in a few sentences and make sure it is commensurate with your proposals. This segment can be the same for both requests and offerings.

Exit Options Kona Gold Coffees

While it is early to plan exit options, our LLC will be considering our overall trend of growth. If we continue growing the second five years as fast as we forecast to grow the first five, we will more than likely seek an acquisition from a major competitor, perhaps even one on the mainland.

Important Points to Remember

- Develop a *draft* pro forma statement of cash flow before using adjustments created from loan proceeds or investment cash infusions — to see a picture of how things are *as-is*, without any funds from a loan or investment. Use this draft to assist you in accurately calculating your financial requirement.
- Always remember to cover the answers to the five essential questions of every lender or investor: How much money do you need? What do you plan to use it for? How can the money improve your business? How are you going to pay it back? What's your back-up plan?
- Make sure the numbers in this section are consistent with those in the previous sections of your business plan.
- Consider your exit option from your business plan reviewers' point of view as well as your own.

Finally, when you have finished this section, return to your financial requirement summary and revise it to emphasize the important findings throughout this section.

The next section of your business plan is the final one, the business plan exhibits, and the subject of the last chapter.

Chapter 12

Business Plan Exhibits

In everything one must consider the end.
— Jean de La Fontaine

While the most relevant supporting information and schedules should be included in their respective sections, many documents are either too cumbersome or have no particular place in the body of your business plan. Since support documentation of this type is still needed by the reviewer, it is grouped together as exhibits at the end of the business plan.

It is important to limit the size of this section. The days of the 100-page business plan are gone. The rule of thumb now is that the group of exhibits should be no longer than the main body of the business plan and, preferably, much shorter.

If you elect to use the long-form personal résumé rather than the shorter summary résumé introduced in Chapter 8 for the principals and managers of your start-up business, it is best to locate them in the exhibits section. Due to their length, inserting them into the Management and Organization section can disrupt the reviewer's concentration. However, if you are the only manager in your new business, it is best to place your own long-form personal résumé in that section.

It is important to prepare your exhibits so they are easy for the reviewer to find, such as using index tabs on each exhibit or to begin each group of exhibits. This chapter discusses the elements of the exhibits section.

- Table of contents
- Exhibits

Table of Contents of Exhibits

Introduce your exhibits with a table of contents identifying each of the items included by page number or letter. This page should be entitled, "Contents of Exhibits," "Exhibits," or "Business Plan Exhibits" and be in the same format you used for your business plan table of contents.

Contents of Exhibits　　　　　　　　　　　　　　　　　Kona Gold Coffees

1. Industry Research
2. Résumés
3. Personal financial statements
4. Limited Liability Company Agreement of Formation
5. Application for trademark registration
6. List of Supplier Agreements
7. List of Letters of Intent from Retailers

Exhibits

Although the exhibits suggested below relate to many businesses, you are the best person to judge those exhibits most important to support your business plan and those necessary to customize your plan for the reviewer you are targeting. To control the size of your plan, it is best to present only those items that support your text. Do not introduce new material in the exhibits. If you have new material that is significant, it is best to rewrite the appropriate section; but if time does not permit, present the new material as a separate addendum to your business plan with a different cover.

Once you have gathered your exhibits, if you feel your total business plan presentation may be too large because of numerous or awkward-sized documents, take out the least supportive and most inconvenient items and list them on an Addendum Directory page. This page then goes into your business plan exhibits with a note that these additional items are available under separate cover. Package these secondary items together in a separate binder with the title, Addendum to the Business Plan, and provide a table of contents for it. Keep it on file for anyone who requests it.

A comprehensive list of materials that can be included in various business plans is included here for your consideration within the context of your business plan. Identify and use only those that are essential for yours.

Business Plan Support Documents
- Research findings on your industry, market, and competitors that is too cumbersome to enclose in the appropriate sections of your business plan
- Résumés, personal financial statements, and credit reports
- Equipment, fixtures, furniture, and signage lists, including costs
- Your start-up inventory, including costs

Marketing Materials
- Sales brochures
- Flyers
- Menus
- Technological reports or product descriptions intended for customers

Manufacturing Materials
- Technological reports
- Specifications
- Engineering drawings
- Equipment descriptions

Legal Documents
- A copy of your business license
- Other pertinent licenses such as real estate broker, general contractor, license to manufacture, health permit, or certificate of need
- A copy of any fictitious business name statements
- A copy of the certificate of incorporation, articles of corporation, and your state Status of Good Standing Certificate if your business is a corporation or partnership
- If your business is a general partnership, a limited partnership or limited liability company, a copy of the statement of partnership or agreement of formation

Facility Documentation
- If you lease your facility, a copy of the lease or a summary that gives all the major recitals. Include address; whether your facility is free-standing, in a regional mall, or at a strip center; the square footage; monthly rent; cost per square foot; period of lease; amount of deposit; and specified increases.
- If you are buying your facility, a preliminary title report and a copy of your contract or signed escrow instructions
- If you have already purchased your facility, a copy of the deed, escrow closing statement, or some evidence of purchase
- A layout or floor plan of your facility and the site layout, especially showing parking and the locations for entering and exiting
- A copy of a real estate appraisal of your facility, if available. Lenders must obtain their own appraisal since federal regulations have become

tighter, but if you have one available include it, especially if the appraisal is necessary to your business plan and the numbers are strong
- Strategic photographs of your facility

Insurance Coverage

Provide a list of your business insurance. Here are examples of the typical coverage needed.

- Worker's compensation insurance, generally required by state law, to cover employee losses due to job related injuries
- Liability insurance, which covers your liability if anyone is injured or suffers damage to their property at your location
- Life insurance on you, as owner, and any other principals
- Fire, burglary, and business-interruption insurance, the latter of which provides you with an income, typically up to a specific amount for a specific period of time, if your business is stopped due to fire or other circumstance beyond your control
- Inventory insurance, if the nature of your business dictates the need.
- Product liability insurance, to protect against customer lawsuits for injury caused by items you produce and sell
- Errors and omissions insurance, if your business is involved in contracts or agreements

Business References

- Trade references, the company name, trade relationship, name of contact person, address, and telephone number
- Lender references, with the same detail as above
- Previous or current partner and business references
- Endorsements from sources or customers
- Purchase agreements or letters of intent from existing or future customers
- Photographs of your operation, if it is open for business

Remember, you can include anything else you deem necessary as supporting documents for the text of your business plan, but weigh the significance of each document with the importance of brevity.

Other Financial Documentation – under separate cover

- Your personal tax returns for two years
- Co-investors tax returns for two years

As mentioned before, tax returns are usually too bulky to be included in the exhibits. They are best presented under separate cover.

The Finishing Touches

Before you make copies of your business plan to distribute, have your figures checked by an accountant or bookkeeper and the text proofread by an editor or proofreader. Then make the corrections, reprint the pages, and check that your changes were done accurately.

An accurate, easy-to-read, and well-organized text conveys professionalism and credibility. Too often, the important step of checking the accuracy of the entire business plan is avoided or forgotten and, despite all your work, a few typos, missing words, poor sentence construction, or inaccurate figures can spoil an otherwise good presentation. Until you do these things, your business plan is not really a finished product.

A Final Comment

Starting and owning your own business is personally rewarding and can lead to financial independence. Once you have selected your industry and business specialty, researched your business concept, and narrowed the field to the best market for your chosen location, usually the biggest hurdle to opening your new business is attracting the required capital. This is true for most entrepreneurs.

By examining your financial picture and understanding your capital requirements, types of vesting, and financial options, you can see your position as lenders and investors will and can establish a realistic, achievable goal. While preparing your business plan for acceptance by lenders or investors, carefully map out your business venture with realistic objectives and forecasts. This activity provides the basis of a management plan that will assure the successful operation of your business once it is opened as well as the basis for a reviewer to recommend your business for funding.

After you have completed your business plan, be sure to have it reviewed by your proofreader, attorney, and accountant before you present it for review, so you will have the benefit of their expertise in creating the most successful presentation possible. Even after your plan is completed, you will probably receive additional information — such as, during your interviews with lenders and investors — you can use to further fine tune it.

Now you are prepared to tenaciously search out financing, through as many sources as it takes, that will afford you the opportunity of reaching out and grabbing hold of the new American dream — owning, opening, and operating your own business. To achieve it, be guided by the slogan:

The one who gets the most nos also gets the most yeses.

Effort is rewarded.

Important Points to Remember

- In your exhibits, only include appropriate documents that enhance the rest of the plan.
- Once you have completed your start-up business plan, have your accountant or bookkeeper and a professional proofreader or editor review it for accuracy, typos, punctuation, and grammar.
- Remember the need for an aesthetically pleasing layout. Is there anyone you know who is more qualified than you who can assist in improving the look of your business plan?

Appendix A

Business Plan Differences for Home Based Businesses

This abridged business plan is for Edwards' Consulting Services (ECS), a one-person consulting service operating from a home office. Although the Industry Analysis and Market and Competition have been omitted (as explained in the Preface), their summaries have been fully constructed so that you can easily follow the overall plan. All other sections are complete.

The Executive Summary is another example of the preview format. It covers all the elements of a service business, a one-person operation, and a home office. Notice that the writer, the CEO of the business, follows the rule to avoid first person and uses the company's name or pronouns where possible, rather than overusing his own name. This develops a more professional image for both the business plan and the company.

The Company Description again shows how each segment can be written and adapted for a one-person service business with a home office. In the leadership and location segment, notice the straight-forward honesty. First it states that the business is home based, then it gives the advantages that enhance the fact.

The Strategies and Goals section purposely directs the reviewer's attention to *the company* and to ECS, rather than to the owner as the sole employee. An important point is made in the strategy implementation segment: A key to the implementation of these strategies is keeping costs low for this type of one-employee operation by using a home based office.

The Services section offers an example of how to set up this segment for services specifically for a consulting business. However, in the service description, note that the services for ECS are based on both a "per job" basis and a "per month" basis, depending upon the service type. In the last three segments, services positioning, comparison with the competition, and future services, the format follows similarly to the example in the text for Kona Gold Coffees.

The Marketing and Sales section for a service business is similar to one written for products. The single, primary difference can be seen in the format of the sales forecast. For ECS, it is extensive. Note the upper half of the forecast is for sales, itemized by type of service and by month, whereas the lower half is for costs of sales — called direct costs for a service business — by type of service and by month. The totals in this form are used in the first-year pro forma income statement in Section 10.

The next section, Management, takes on a very different approach for a one-person operation. Here, Stan Edwards' résumé becomes the center of focus. Since there are no other employees, the conventional title, Management and Organization, becomes Management. For "management team," the company's consulting attorney and accountant have been included to enhance the overall image. If they weren't included, this segment would simply be titled, Management. The other conventional segments of this section have all been reduced to one segment, owners salary.

In the Operations section, the segments of a larger manufacturing business — human resources, supply and distribution, fulfillment, and inventory control — have all been excluded. In the operations description, ECS has broken down the one-person operation into five functions. Since it is home based, ECS has taken the opportunity to detail the financial impact of the owner's home on the business, which explains many of the numbers in Section 10. Production, even for a one-person service company, is applicable in the business plan, as are the final segments — customer service policy, efficiency control, and cash flow control.

In Section 10, Financial Pro Formas, the only real difference is in the balance sheets (opening and pro formas) and the pro forma income statements, where "cost of sales" is shown as "direct costs" for a service business. The emphasis on business ratios for this business model are collection days and accounts receivable turnover.

Finally, Section 11 shows another structure for a loan request. Compare this request with the first-year pro forma statement of cash flow in Section 10. Note that there is $20,000 to be received in January (cash receipts, short-term loan proceeds), and that the $400 principal payments (cash disbursements, short-term liabilities) are set up February to December of Year One, with an annual total principal payment of $15,600 — the pay-off — for Year Two. The balance of $15,600 consists of eleven monthly principal payments of $400 together with a balloon principal payment of $11,200 during that year (interest is tracked in the account, cash disbursements, interest).

Edwards' Consulting Services
Kailua-Kona, Hawaii

Business Plan

Confidential Information

Prepared for:
Mr. Stephen Clayton
Assistant Branch Manager
Bank of Hawaii
75-5595 Palani Road
Kailua-Kona, Hawaii 96740-9909

Prepared by:
Stan Edwards
(800) 555-5678
e-mail: EdwardsECS@aol.com

November 17 – December 15, 20XX

Contents

Executive Summary

Company Description

Industry Analysis

Market and Competition

Strategies and Goals

Services

Marketing and Sales

Management

Operations

Financial Pro Formas

Loan Request

Exhibits

Executive Summary — Edwards' Consulting Services

Business Concept

Edwards' Consulting Services, ECS, is in the land development industry and provides consulting services for those requiring planning, government approvals, and developer services. The primary customers are land developers and secondary customers are civil engineers who will hire ECS as an outside contractor for their clients, also land developers.

ECS's opening service line consists of 14 services. Services consist of three categories: planning services, government and community approvals, and developer services. These are further defined by specific type of service and type of regulatory body necessary for approval. Because of the owner's background and expertise and the growing economic market in land development, ECS's services are well positioned in this market for the Big Island at this time and should prove to be for the next five years.

Since the company's pricing is approximately 15 percent to 20 percent below the main competitors, ECS's services are also well positioned to be used as outside contractor services until they become fully in demand by the end-consumer through direct sales.

To accomplish this, ECS must concentrate on the quality, pricing, scheduling, and professionalism of its services. The major thrust will be to develop a reputation of winning cases, performing tasks in less time than has been required in the past, and costing the clients less than they anticipate. Once achieved, the services of ECS will be positioned at the top of its field by popular demand, and will be increasingly in demand by new as well as repeat clients.

Because the demand for development management and planning services is expected to increase steadily over the next five years, the timing is perfect for a new entrant in this field. It is ECS's long term goal to be the best provider of these services — first on the Big Island in the next five years and eventually throughout the state within ten years.

Progress Status

ECS is a one-employee sole proprietorship owned by its president, Stan Edwards. Because most of the daily business of the owner is in the field, a home based office was chosen although the office, at 77-6452 Alii Drive, Kailua-Kona, Hawaii, has an outside entrance and is set up professionally to conduct client business when necessary. Most of ECS's market will come from three major developing areas on the Big Island: Hilo, Waikoloa, and Kailua-Kona. Currently ECS has just completed its office improvements, has several signed contracts, and is ready to begin business officially January 1.

The total start-up costs are $117,320. To date, ECS has raised owner capital totaling $97,320, which includes $17,600 pro rata home equity, $42,400 from two pre-existing loans, and $37,320 in cash ($10,000 still on hand). The difference between the start-up costs and the capital raised is $20,000.

As a result of the new upswing in land development in Hawaii, there are many development companies planning new projects to be developed over the next five years. This will mean a large influx of various county and state planning applications and most of those will continue to become jobs in progress requiring various forms of development management. It is the goal of ECS to respond to this growing market by providing services on both levels.

While civil engineers and some agrarian land owners have need of ECS services, the primary consumers are land developers. On the Big Island, the profile is: male, age 32–58, married with families, household incomes of $180,000 plus, 14 or more years of education, not afraid of risks,

(continued)

Executive Summary (continued) — Edwards' Consulting Services

but methodical in business planning. In Hawaii, there are 54 companies in land development. Of these, 22 are on the Big Island. ECS has already secured six project contracts and eight letters of intent which represent over two thirds of the needed business to meet forecasts for the first year.

Keys to Success

ECS's success can be foreseen and attributed to specific keys:

- Currently on the Big Island, land development is enjoying an economic upswing that is expected to continue for another five years at a growth rate of 12 percent, much faster than the current GDP at 3.9 percent.
- New competition is unlikely because of the rare combination of expertise and talent needed to enter this market: expertise in land use planning, expertise in land development, and an established report with the existing county and state planning and administrative officials.
- ECS's competition charge high rates, do little marketing, and are not focused on the market's specific needs because they provide these services as supplemental services to their primary service lines which are separate from this market specialization.
- ECS is planning a relatively strong and well-rounded marketing plan aimed at the target market that will surpass any marketing efforts of the competition. The ECS plan includes a budget the first month of $1,267, an average monthly spending of $280, and an overall budget of $3,342 for the first year.
- The owner/president of ECS has a degree in construction management, other formal education in business and land planning, and eight years of experience in development management and land use planning both in county administration and in the private sector.
- From his roles as county Assistant Planning Director for three years and project manager for private developers of many development projects, the owner/president understands the needs of government planning officials, the needs of the public, the needs of developers, and has been able to coordinate these into win-win-win solutions to perfection for the past three years.
- Because ECS services are time sensitive, the company will use a combination of two software programs to develop project schedules and a master schedule to plan workloads consisting of project management, research and writing of reports, public hearing addresses, and meetings with clients and potential clients.
- Pricing of ECS services are lower than the competition because of a lower overhead, in part from a one-man operation and in part from operating from a home based office.

Financial Overview

To cover the working capital needs, ECS is seeking to increase the consumer credit limit of the president's personal Bankoh Visa Gold Card from $5,000 to $25,000 at 12 percent. ECS plans to draw one disbursement of $20,000 in January to use as supplemental working capital to launch the new business. For payback, ECS will make twelve minimum payments and pay off the balance in one year. After that, Mr. Edwards plans to keep this limit open and to use it only for unforeseen emergencies as a reserve option.

The cash flow pro forma shows this is viable financial planning as ECS should still have $8,234 in cash after the paying the card completely down. As a backup plan, Mr. Edwards would seek an equity home loan in the form of a second mortgage, if necessary, as the current first trust deed is only 60 percent loan to value. His personal financial statement and recent two years tax returns are included in the exhibits.

Executive Summary (continued) — Edwards' Consulting Services

The ECS market share of 20 percent was used in developing the financial pro formas which is consistent with the quality and quantity of early signed contracts and letters of intent.

The cash flow pro forma prior to loan proceeds discloses a need of $20,000 of additional working capital in January created by the conservative pro formas based on an accounts receivable collection of 90 days. With this adjustment, sales for the first year are projected at $173,400 and direct costs at $5,808, with a gross profit margin of 96.7 percent. All other expenses total $29,740. The total sales to break even during the first year are $33,194. The operating profit is $135,510 and the net profit is $74,021.

For the five-year pro formas, ECS has conservatively estimated 7 percent increases in sales (the industry is expected to grow 12 percent) and 4 percent increases in operating costs, which is commensurate with last year's GDP. This yields a net profit for year five of $112,234 and a high working capital of $316,098. While all business ratios are healthy, the annual return on equity for the fifth year is a strong 33 percent.

Company Description — Edwards' Consulting Services

Name and Business Concept

Edwards' Consulting Services is part of the industry of development management and planning services. The business specializes in consultant management of development projects from the earliest conceptual stage through completion of land improvements. This may include a few specific tasks or the overall management of an entire job. ECS has two target markets: real estate developers, the primary market; and engineering firms, the secondary market. At start, ECS has identified fourteen distinct services, although there is some overlap from one to the other. These include project management and special reports for specific tasks for projects in progress and the acquisition of regulatory approvals both at county and state levels. Fees are set by the complexity and time required to perform the service. The most important features of ECS services will be the owner's personal experience and professional standing with the decision-makers in the community in the approval processes. ECS's services will differ from the competitors' chiefly because ECS has established this background through Mr. Edwards' previous employment and because ECS will set fixed fees and will charge consistently from one customer to the next and from one job to the next. Clients will develop confidence that ECS pricing is fair and the service thorough and timely. It is ECS's objective for the company to become the industry leader as a consulting firm in land development management and land and planning consulting services in Hawaii.

Ownership and Legal

Edwards' Consulting Services (ECS) is a dba for Stan Edwards' Consulting Services, a sole proprietorship, owned by Stan Edwards. The company is licensed to do business in both the state and county of Hawaii. The owner is a licensed A-1 general engineering contractor in the state of Hawaii since 1992.

(continued)

Company Description (continued) — Edwards' Consulting Services

Leadership and Location

The principal operator of Edwards' Consulting Services is Stan Edwards, President. The home based business address is 77-6452 Alii Drive, Kailua-Kona, Hawaii 96740. This is a properly zoned area for residential with home commercial uses. Although most of ECS's client interaction will take place at client locations, the ECS office is perfectly adequate and centrally and conveniently located for the few clients that choose to come to ECS. The site is an oceanfront property with a serene ambiance conducive to pleasant working conditions.

Geographic Service Area

The geographic service area will cover the three major developing centers of the Big Island during the first year. These are the city of Hilo, the north community of Waikoloa, and the surrounding areas of the town of Kailua-Kona where the company is based. Very little development activity is underway in the southern half of the island, largely because of the active volcano. As the company grows, or as the clients dictate, the service area will branch out to the neighboring islands. For state approvals, many trips to Honolulu will be required.

Current Status and Milestones

ECS was brainstormed a year ago. During this time Mr. Edwards has been conducting outside consulting work via part-time employment status with several companies while retaining his primary assignment as assistant planner in Subdivisions and Industrial Division, County of Hawaii. After deciding on a home based business with no employees, Mr. Edwards' private residence was modified with minor improvements and the office's equipment and furniture were installed during December. For accounting purposes, the company will officially begin doing business January 1. Because it is a standard in the industry that developers are slow paying, the company has been planned to sustain a 90-day accounts receivable. A small financing window is required to accommodate this which is the next step to accomplish before opening.

As to the market, fourteen of the twenty projects targeted for this year have either signed contracts (six) or executed letters of intent (eight). The others are planned with existing clientele and will be signed before the end of the second quarter. According to County Business Patterns published by the U.S. Census Bureau; records of the Hawaii County Planning Department; and statistics of all nineteen Hawaii chambers of commerce (see market), the real estate market for development activity has been growing slowly and steadily for the last two years. History has shown these to be seven-year cycles (see industry), so the timing appears perfect for land planning of the right projects over the next five years.

To date, ECS has raised $117,320 in capital used mostly for start-up costs: leasehold improvements (including 20 percent equity of the house for the office), office equipment, and one new truck. While there is $10,000 cash on hand, cash flow projections based on the 90-day credit accounts show that $20,000 is needed the first month to sustain a positive cash flow. ECS is therefore seeking a solution by requesting an increase in the owner's consumer credit limit to cover an additional $20,000 for cash withdrawals to safeguard the launching of this new business.

Company Description (continued) — Edwards' Consulting Services

The chart below shows the activity of ECS's current milestones.

Current Milestones

Milestone	Projected Date	Budget	Actual Date	Costs	Variance
Graphic design	30 Oct.	$750	15 Nov.	$750	$0
Jobs 100–104 signed	1 Nov.	N/A	1 Nov.	N/A	N/A
Job 105 signed	3 Nov.	N/A	3 Nov.	N/A	N/A
Job 106 signed	5 Nov.	N/A	5 Nov.	N/A	N/A
Jobs 107, 108 signed	24 Nov.	N/A	LOI	N/A	N/A
Leasehold improvements	1 Dec.	$3,500	1 Dec.	$3,700	$200
Jobs 109, 110 signed	3 Dec.	N/A	LOI	N/A	N/A
Printing of brochures	9 Dec.	250	9 Dec.	$185	$0
Jobs 111, 112 signed	10 Dec.	N/A	LOI	N/A	N/A
Job 113 signed	12 Dec.	N/A	14 Dec.	N/A	N/A
Business plan complete	15 Dec.	$80	15 Dec.	$80	$0
Credit limit submittal	15 Dec.	$0	15 Dec.	$0	$0
Trade journal ad	15 Dec.	$120	15 Dec.	$120	$0
Yellow pages ad	15 Dec.	$110	15 Dec.	$110	$0
Newspaper ad	29 Dec.	$35			
Credit limit approval	2 Jan.	$0			
Use of funds	15 Jan.	$0			
Job 103 completion	30 Jan.	$60			
Job 104 completion	30 Jan.	$60			
Job 102 completion	30 Mar.	$320			
Sales breakeven	15 Apr.	N/A		N/A	N/A

Industry Analysis

Edwards' Consulting Services

Industry Analysis Summary

While ECS is technically in the industry of management consulting services, the company is more closely tied to the land development industry by the types of consulting services it provides. Real estate in general is an up and down industry that goes through sporadic economic swings. For the last 200 years, the land development industry has been going through three-year down cycles and seven-year up cycles. Currently on the Big Island, land development completed a down cycle about two years ago and has since just completed its second year of an upswing that is expected to last another five years. The rate of growth during this period is projected to be 12 percent annually, which is much faster than the GDP during recent years (3.9 percent last year).

There are serious obstacles for new companies to get into this specialized field. These come in the form of three keys that are needed and are rarely found together: expertise in land use planning, expertise in land development, and an established report with the existing county and state planning and administrative officials. If any one of these is lacking, a new business in this field cannot do well. ECS has all three.

Industry Description

Industry Size and Maturation

Industry Trends and Impact Factors

Industry Standards

Industry Obstacles

Industry Opportunities

Market and Competition — Edwards' Consulting Services

Market and Competition Summary

As a result of the new upswing in land development in Hawaii, there are many development companies planning new projects to be developed over the next five years. This will mean a large influx of various county and state planning applications and most of those that are successful will continue to become jobs in progress requiring various forms of development management. It is the goal of ECS to respond to this growing market by providing services on both levels.

While civil engineers and some agrarian land owners have need of ECS services, the primary consumers are land developers. On the Big Island, the profile is: male, age 32–58, married with families, household incomes of $180,000 plus, 14 or more years of education, not afraid of risks, but methodical in business planning. In Hawaii, there are 54 companies in land development. Of these, 22 are on the Big Island.

ECS's three major competitors for this consumer have exercised little marketing, charge high rates, and have not focused on the market's specific needs of land use planning, regulatory approvals, and development management. ECS estimates its market share for the first year will be 20 percent. With six signed contracts and eight letters of intent, ECS already holds the key to two-thirds of this market share for the first year.

The greatest opportunities lie in the specialization itself. So specialized is this field that very few companies explore it, yet there are strong needs for these services by every developer in various stages of every project. These needs increase dramatically during an economic upswing.

Market Description – Segments and Target Markets

Market Size and Trends

Competition Identification

Main Competitors

Competitor Analysis

Market Share

Customer Needs

Market Obstacles

Market Opportunities

Strategies and Goals

Edwards' Consulting Services

Strategies and Goals Summary

After examining the industry and market, the demand for development management and planning services is expected to increase steadily over the next five years. Because of this, the timing is perfect for a new entrant in this field providing the correct specialized services in obtaining governmental approvals and project management that are so needed and valued by developers and civil engineers. It is ECS's long-term goal to be the best provider of these services — first on the Big Island over the next five years and eventually throughout the state within ten years.

To accomplish this ECS must concentrate on the quality, pricing, scheduling, and professionalism of its services. The emphasis will be to develop a reputation of winning cases and performing tasks in less time than has been required in the past, and costing the clients less than they anticipate. Once this is achieved, ECS will be positioned at the top of its field by popular demand and will be increasingly in demand by new and repeat clients.

Long-range Goals and Strategies

The need for the services of ECS is going to be strong over the next five years. It is a company goal to challenge this specialized market with superior service by never losing a case in the approval process and by always completing each assigned management task a few days earlier than initially scheduled for a few dollars under budget. The overall goal is to position ECS as the leader in this specialized field. To execute this goal, ECS will be:

- Services driven — specializing in services that separate the company from competitors with superior quality;
- Customer-service driven — providing the highest-standards in service to ECS clients;
- Niche-market driven — offering development management as an outside contractor in the specialized area of government approvals; and
- Operations driven — executing these services in the most professional manner.

Long-range Milestones

	At end of:			
	First Year	Three Years	Five Years	Ten Years
Specialization leader:				
On the Big Island			X	
Statewide				X
Market share	20%	23%	26%	
Annual sales	$173,400	$198,526	$227,292	
Profit margin	96.7%	96.6%	96.7%	
Number of services	14	18	22	
Office	home based	home based	home based	
Number of locations	1	1	1	
Number of employees	1	1	1	
Net profit after owners draw	$74,021	$89,822	$112,234	

Strategies and Goals (continued)   Edwards' Consulting Services

Strategy Implementation

To implement these strategies, ECS will market the special services offered by personally calling on developers and civil engineers. It will penetrate the market with personalized service at reasonable and consistent prices and a proven record of successful client representation in government approvals. Once established, ECS anticipates many repeat and referral clients by word of mouth based on this reputation and bolstered by newspaper publicity and consistent institutional marketing through several trade publications.

To carry out the business plan, ECS is showing conservative increases of market share because this is a market of specialized services that require the exclusive attention and expertise of the owner and must be performed personally because of his unique talent and background. It is anticipated that some business will have to be turned away until such time when Mr. Edwards can find other associates with these specialized skills. A key to the implementation of these strategies is keeping costs low for this type of one-employee operation by using a home based office.

The cash flow projections show that ECS will not have to borrow more than $20,000, and then only in the first year. The debt is to be repaid within twelve months to save the increased limit requested as a reserve for added protection throughout the first five years.

Services   Edwards' Consulting Services

Services Summary

ECS's opening service line consists of 14 services provided directly to land developers and to civil engineers seeking these same services for their clients. The services consist of three general categories: planning services, government and community approvals, and developer services. These are further defined by individual type of service and the type of regulatory body necessary for approval. Because of the owner's background and expertise and the growing economic market in land development, ECS's services are well positioned for the Big Island at this time and should prove to be for the next five years.

Since the company's pricing is approximately 15 percent to 20 percent below the main competitors, ECS's services are also well positioned to be used by competitors as outside contractor services until they become fully in demand by the end-consumer through direct sales.

Although it is premature to say that ECS services are better than the competitors, it is the company's intention to offer more personalized service and to provide the company services more expediently without failures or denials of approval. Since the owner has a winning record of pre-company successes in this field, this experience will be marketed to set the tone for this quality of performance.

(continued)

Services (continued) — Edwards' Consulting Services

Services Description

At opening, ECS provides 14 services directly to real estate and land developers and indirectly to this same market through civil engineers. These are best listed with price ranges as each service depends upon the complexity of the project and extent of the required task.

Service	Fee
1. Project Management	$1,000 to $3,500 per month, 1–24 months
2. Zoning Change	$6,000 to $10,000 per job
3. Subdivision Approval	$2,000 to $5,000 per job
4. Use Permit	$6,000 to $8,000 per job
5. Variances to the Standards	$1,500 to $6,000 per job
6. Due Diligence Studies	$1,000 to $2,000 per month, 1–4 months
7. Project Feasibility Reports	$4,000 to $8,000 per job
8. Pro Forma Analysis	$2,000 to $3,000 per job
9. Project Analysis	$3,000 to $4,500 per job
10. Well-drilling and Pump-installation Permits	$5,000 to $8,000 per job
11. Boundary Line Adjustments	$750 to $1,400 per job
12. Other County Approvals	Depends on tasks, $2,000 per month
13. State Special Permits	$6,000 to $8,000 per job
14. State Easement Acquisitions	$1,000 to $2,000 per month

Fees for ECS have been established at approximately 15 percent to 20 percent less than standard fees imposed by engineering and attorney firms that must include an overhead allocation in their direct costs. Currently, the direct costs for ECS are calculated exactly as a function of costs of supplies, cell phone usage, a portion of auto expenses, and an allowance for equipment deterioration without assessing the owner's time which must be allotted through gross profit for sole proprietorships. This results in a minimal direct cost average of 3.35 percent of sales.

Services Positioning

ECS's services are positioned to fill a specialized need that can only be filled by companies with expertise in this field and a strong report with county and state officials. The few businesses that meet both requirements have large offices with high overhead. By charging 15–20 percent less than these firms, ECS is positioned to sell its services to these firms during the first year allowing them to adequately build in their markup. As real estate and land developers become more aware of ECS's services and pricing, the markets will change with more direct end-users and fewer civil engineers hiring out this work through ECS.

Comparison with the Competition

At the start of business, ECS's pricing is based on a comparison of fees of major civil engineers and real estate attorneys that provide these services. There are only three main competitors on

Services (continued) — Edwards' Consulting Services

the Big Island. The comparative analysis of services below presents a view of ECS's fees with these three competitors for six of the more frequently used services:

Services Comparative Analysis

	ECS	J.M. Toll Engineering	Seth-Pell Engineering	Levine, Collins Attorneys at Law
Service #1	Project Management	X	X	
Price	$1–3.5K per month	15% higher	20% higher	N/A
Dollar sales	$93,000	$124,000	$285,417	
Service #2	Zoning changes	X	X	X
Price	$6–10K per job	15% higher	20% higher	25% higher
Dollar sales	$24,000	$30,360	$34,560	$51,000
Service #4	Use permits	X	X	X
Price	$6–8K per job	15% higher	20% higher	22% higher
Dollar sales	$15,500	$49,000	$34,800	$31,250
Service #14	State special permits	X	X	X
Price	$6–10K per job	15% higher	20% higher	15% higher
Dollar sales	$8,000	$22,960	$13,920	$12,500
Service #5	Variances	X	X	X
Price	$1.5–6K per job	15% higher	20% higher	10% higher
Dollar sales	$5,500	$6,578	$7,656	$6,875
Service #3	Subdivision approvals	X	X	X
Price	$2–5K per job	15% higher	20% higher	18% higher
Dollar sales	$4,000	$25,300	$28,800	$40,120
Competitive strength*	2	5	4	4
Marketing*	3	3	2	1
Methods of sales	Owner	Staff engineers	Staff engineers	Staff attorneys
Priority of concern	N/A	Moderate	Low	Low

* Grading scale used: 1 (low) to 5 (high)

Future Services

It is ECS's plan to add two services each year through year five. Based on the heavy outcome of project management contracts for the first year, early indications are that additions of more developer services in land improvements will be needed next year. Two services that have already been requested are creating development plan financial pro formas and assistance in creating development schedules with construction interest analyses. After the two new ECS services are narrowed down and defined, client solicitation will begin in November to begin offering them as part of the regular program of ECS services to all of the client base. These will then be added to the ECS brochure in December.

Marketing and Sales   Edwards' Consulting Services

Marketing and Sales Summary

The ECS slogan is "If ECS takes the job, it's a done deal." The company's main message is that ECS services will not be contracted unless ECS believes there will be a successful outcome. ECS will market assurance, pricing, and timing.

Although ECS's services are in an industry represented by low-key marketing, the marketing plan includes a budget the first month of $1,267, an average monthly spending of $280 and an overall budget of $3,342 for the first year.

As a home based business, all sales are owner-sales by telephone or personal appointment. Leads are generated through the marketing plan which includes an ad in the Yellow Pages, weekly ads in the major newspaper, bimonthly ads in the major trade journal, and an Internet web site. Other leads will be cultivated by close contact with developers and civil engineers through a Builder's Industry Association (BIA) membership. All prospects will be followed up with telephone calls, an initial direct mailing of the ECS brochure, repeat mailing with an ongoing newsletters every two months, and personal appointments with four lunches planned every month just for new prospects. Projected sales for the first year are $173,400.

Marketing Strategy

The company's marketing strategy is to promote each ECS service as an efficiency service for development management and as a sure thing for government approvals. The message is: ECS's services assist developers with planning approval and efficiency management benefiting them by providing an assurance of expertise and freeing them from performing these services in-house or hiring other outside services that do not provide the same level of personal service. ECS prices are standardized and are set 15–20 percent below the competition. This benefits the client by cost savings, including time not wasted, because ECS can accomplish the approval process in less time than the competition. Before a case is accepted, ECS will do its own feasibility of the outcome at its own cost, and ECS will become known as the place that will only take on the job when confident of a successful outcome, benefiting the customer with an assurance of approval.

The promotion: "If ECS takes the job, it's a done deal," is meant to instill the idea that ECS service can provide the confidence of a successful outcome. ECS competitors take on any job and cannot provide this assurance, and in fact, drill home that there are no guarantees. This slogan will be featured in every ad and on all business cards, estimates, contracts, and stationery.

The target market: ECS's primary consumers are real estate and land developers on the Big Island. The secondary market the first year will be civil engineers and attorneys that will bundle ECS services with theirs to the same end-consumer. ECS's consumer profile: real estate developers on the Big Island, male, ages 32–58, married with families, household incomes of $180,000 plus, with 14 years or more of education, who are not afraid of risks, but are methodical in business planning.

The competitors marketing programs: ECS competitors practice very little marketing beyond running institutional ads in monthly trade journals and even then place emphasis only on their mainstream services. For engineering companies, this is design and field surveys; for attorney firms, this is general legal assistance for developers.

Marketing Plan

ECS is a professional service competing with others in a low-key marketing format. Since the doors will open with six signed contracts and eight letters of intent for nearly two-thirds of

Marketing and Sales (continued) — Edwards' Consulting Services

the service projections for the first year, ECS's marketing plan appears on the surface to be nearly overkill.

The plan starts with a four-color brochure, total cost $935: $750 for design and $185 for additional printing set up in the first month budget. For professional organizations, the owner has joined the BIA and obtained a mailing list of all land developers on the Big Island, ECS's target market. Direct mail will be sent out every other month to each developer, first with a brochure introducing ECS's services and price list, and as ongoing newsletters with copies of newspaper clippings of successful ECS approvals, other industry updates, and pending approvals and appeals. To reach developers personally, the budget is structured for the owner to sponsor four developer lunches every month, separate from the lunch plans and budget set up for existing clients of four client lunches every month. For published ads, ECS has a small Yellow Page ad for regulatory approvals under developer services, continuous week-end professional ads in the Big Island newspaper, and bimonthly ads in the BIA professional trade journal.

For free publicity, the owner is sending press releases to introduce ECS services to the local metro newspaper, West Hawaii Today, and to three radio stations (KZIX, KFAT, and KMCC) whose primary listeners include ECS consumer demographics statewide. As a final component, ECS has an interactive on-line web site, www.EdwardsECS.com, which is linked to the BIA home page, www.BIA.BigIsland.com.

The annual advertising budget is $890 and the total marketing budget is $3,342 as distributed in the two tables below (these do not include direct costs and other general and administrative expenses, see Pro Forma Income Statement, Financial Pro Formas section).

Marketing Budget

The marketing budget is represented by two tables, Marketing Budget and Advertising Plan. A prepaid of $1,000 has been entered in the Opening Balance Sheet as a current asset and does not show in the pro forma income statement as a January expense.

Month	Graphic Design	Printed Materials	Advertising Plan	Direct Mail	Memberships	Entertainment
January	$750	$185	$ 95	$ 62	$75	$ 100
February			145			100
March			95	36		100
April			35			100
May			95	36		100
June			35			100
July			95	36		100
August			35			100
September			95	36		100
October			35			100
November			95	36		100
December			35			100
Subtotals	$750	$185	$890	$242	$75	$1,200

Total: $3,342

Marketing and Sales (continued) — Edwards' Consulting Services

Advertising Plan

Month	Trade Magazines	News-Papers	Yellow Page
January	$ 60	$ 35	$
February		35	110
March	60	35	
April		35	
May	60	35	
June		35	
July	60	35	
August		35	
September	60	35	
October		35	
November	60	35	
December		35	
Subtotals	$360	$420	$110

Total: $890

Sales Force and Forecast

As a home based office, ECS's sales are exclusively handled by the owner. Sales are typically face to face or by telephone, and will often be closed during lunch. While some leads are expected to be generated through the various vehicles of the marketing plan, most leads in this business are received by word-of-mouth. All leads will be added to our database and followed up by telephone and direct mail.

In the typical process, when a prospect defines his or her needs, the owner evaluates the viability of the objective by checking the general plan and the appropriate and applicable codes and by making several calls to specific planning or public works officials to arrive at findings. If the project is feasible, the owner will write an estimate for the service and arrange an appointment to present the estimate in person and to describe the service, timeline, pricing structure, and explain the preliminary findings of the feasibility for this project. Most appointments will be held at the client's office or at a restaurant appropriate for a business lunch. If the client is apprehensive about signing the contract, ECS will offer to reserve an allocation of time for the project if the client wishes to sign a letter of intent for services.

Potential clients who have signed letters of intent will be followed up every two weeks or more frequently if the project is close to its timetable, and all letters of intent will be followed up with actual contracts before work is scheduled or started.

To date, ECS has six signed contracts and eight letters of intent for approximately two thirds of the first years' sales. The eight letters of intent are strong and represent projects that are in the early stages of planning. For details of each, see Exhibits.

Sales Forecast

Edwards' Consulting Services

Net Sales - $

			Month												Year
	Description		Jan.	Feb.	March	April	May	June	July	Aug.	Sept.	Oct.	Nov.	Dec.	1
Service #1	Project Management	Job #100	2,000	2,000	2,000	2,000	2,000	2,000	2,000	2,000	2,000	2,000	2,000	2,000	24,000
		Job #101	3,500	3,500	3,500	3,500	3,500	3,500	3,500	3,500	3,500	3,500	2,500	2,500	35,000
		Job #109					2,500	2,500	2,500	2,500	2,500	2,500			20,000
		Job #111							3,500	3,500	3,500	3,500			14,000
Service #2	Zoning Change	Job #102	2,000	2,000	2,000										6,000
		Job #110					2,500	2,500	2,500	2,500					10,000
		Job #114												2,000	8,000
Service #3	Subdivision Approval	Job #106												2,000	4,000
Service #4	Use Permit	Job #105		2,000	2,000	800	800	800	800						8,000
		Job #112				2,000	2,000								7,500
Service #5	Variances	Job #103	1,500								1,500		1,500		1,500
		Job #116												2,500	1,500
		Job #118											1,000		2,500
Service #6	Due Diligence	Job #113								1,000	1,000	1,000			4,000
Service #7	Project Feasibility	Job #107				4,500									4,500
Service #8	Pro Forma Analysis	Job #119												2,500	2,500
Service #9	Project Analysis	Job #120												3,000	3,000
Service #10	Well drilling permit	Job #115										5,000			5,000
Service #11	Boundary Line Adj.	Job #104	1,400												1,400
Service #12	Other County														0
Service #13	State Spec. Permit	Job #117					1,000	1,000	3,000				4,000	4,000	8,000
Service #14	State Easement	Job #108					1,000								3,000
Total Net Sales			10,400	9,500	10,300	13,800	14,300	12,300	17,800	18,000	16,000	19,500	13,000	18,500	173,400

Direct Costs

			Jan.	Feb.	March	April	May	June	July	Aug.	Sept.	Oct.	Nov.	Dec.	Year 1
Service #1	Project Management	Job #100	65	65	65	70	70	65	65	65	70	70	65	68	803
		Job #101	75	75	75	75	75	75	75	75	75	75	50	50	750
		Job #109					50	50	50	50	50	50			400
		Job #111							100	80	75	75			330
Service #2	Zoning Change	Job #102	200	60	60										320
		Job #110					200	60	60	60	200	50	50	50	380
		Job #114												50	350
Service #3	Subdivision Approval	Job #106		150											150
		Job #105			30	30	30	30	30						375
Service #4	Use Permit	Job #112			75	75	75				40				295
Service #5	Variances	Job #103	60						180	75					60
		Job #116											60		60
		Job #118												90	90
Service #6	Due Diligence	Job #113								85	85	85	85		340
Service #7	Project Feasibility	Job #107				300									300
Service #8	Pro Forma Analysis	Job #119												100	100
Service #9	Project Analysis	Job #120												75	75
Service #10	Well drilling permit	Job #115										150			150
Service #11	Boundary Line Adj.	Job #104	60												60
Service #12	Other County														0
Service #13	State Spec. Permit	Job #117						60					180	60	240
Service #14	State Easement	Job #108				50	60								180

Management   Edwards' Consulting Services

Management Summary

As a home based office business, ECS's only employee is Stan Edwards, company founder and owner. Officially the president of ECS, Mr. Edwards has worked in the industry since 1993 with eight years of experience in development management and land use planning both in county administration and in the private sector. Mr. Edwards has a degree in construction management and additional formal training in business and land use planning. He served as county Assistant Planning Director for three years and managed many projects for developers. His strong suits are project management, land use planning, and understanding the approval processes — the needs of government planning officials, the needs of the public, the needs of developers, and being able to coordinate these into win-win-win solutions for everyone. He has been performing this role to perfection for the last three years. His complete résumé follows.

Management

Owner/President: Stan Edwards

Profile — Over seven years as Planner and three years as Assistant Planning Director in Subdivisions and Industrial Division, County of Hawaii. During this stint, Mr. Edwards wrote and submitted county staff recommendations for approval or denial for all subdivisions and land development issues to the County Planning Commission and the County Council. As AP Director, he won notoriety for having all his recommendations approved. In the last two years, Stan has worked with many developers in an advisory capacity, and coordinated successful efforts between developers and county leader wishes in every case.

Qualifications Summary

- Has successfully written over one thousand reports on land use, boundary line adjustments, change of zone, subdivision approvals, cultural plans, and a variety of state special permits in the last three years.
- Is an excellent organizer, combining creativity with tenacity and strong verbal, written and presentation skills.
- Has expertise in the latest computer software and specialized programs such as Microsoft Project, CADD, and Quicken.

Education

- University of California at San Francisco
  Continuing education courses in land use – 1998
  Continuing education courses in planning – 1996

- University of the Pacific, Stockton, California
  Post-graduate courses in business – 1993

- University of Missouri, Columbia, Missouri
  Bachelor of Construction Management – 1992

Certificates and Licenses
  Hawaii General Contractors License A-1 for General Engineering.

Experience

- 1998–date Lincoln-Hayes Development

    Development Manager. Responsible for subdivision improvements and golf course development for five subdivisions and two golf courses.

    Sales: $17,000,000 three years

- 1994–1999 Subdivisions & Industrial Division, County of Hawaii

    Assistant Planning Director. Responsible for feasibility studies and recommendations on land use and all permit processes for staff to County Planning and Council.

    Awards:
    - Received Hawaii County Council Award for Best Civil Servant, 1997
    - Planner of the Year, State of Hawaii, 1999

References: Available upon request

Business Attorney

Gunner Burley is a specialized real estate attorney with the firm, Lamont and Bryant, located in Honolulu, with a branch office at 77-5436 Hualalai Road, Kailua-Kona. Mr. Burley is a graduate from the University of Colorado law school and his firm is renown for land use and development issues.

Certified Public Accountant

Shirley Wright is specialized in construction accounting and is a partner in the firm of Lyons, Wright, & Wong, located in Honolulu at 753 Bishop Street, Suite 151. Their construction and development software is Timberline.

Owners Salary

Because a sole proprietorship cannot set up a salary nor conventional payroll taxes and benefits, Mr. Edwards' personal compensation must basically come from the bottom line, net profit. For this new business, he has restructured his financial obligations and will be able to manage his personal budget with an income of $3,000 per month for the first quarter, set up as an owner's draw. For the second and successive quarters, the basic draw will be maintained but supplemented from profits: a monthly total of $5,000. For subsequent years, this will be increased commensurate with the increase in sales percentage.

Operations   Edwards' Consulting Services

Operations Summary

In the development industry, all of the services provided are very time sensitive; consequently, the key to the operations of ECS is scheduling. To design and monitor the project schedules, ECS will use a combination of two software programs. The workload schedules include management of projects, timely research and writing of reports, addressing public hearings, and meeting with clients and potential clients.

(continued)

Operations (continued)   Edwards' Consulting Services

    Because most of this daily business is conducted out of the office, a home based office was chosen for overhead efficiency. One of the major industry problems is that developers are slow paying. Invoices are sent out at the end of every month net 30 days, and a good collection system has been established as another control measure. But as an added precaution, all pro formas have been set up with payment of accounts receivable in 90 days.

Operations Description

Administration: It is the president's plan to review strategic planning continuously; however, he has scheduled dates of the last business day of every month to set aside actual time for this. As to other administrative business, Mr. Edwards is adept at Microsoft Office in addition to the specialized software programs mentioned in his résumé and handles most of the paperwork by computer. Most of the correspondence is handled through WinFax Pro.

Sales: The president follows up on all leads (see marketing and sales) and calls on new clients personally. This is supported by telephone calls and special personal follow-ups to present estimates and secure letters of intent and final contracts. Every other month a newsletter will be sent to all land developers and civil engineers. Mr. Edwards also follows trade publications and attends BIA meetings regularly where most new leads are generated. New signed contracts are entered into the computer and schedules of the services are developed for each project in Microsoft Project and then transferred and collated into a master schedule designed by Mr. Edwards in Excel.

Field Operations: Field work is divided into four categories: public relations with existing clients, public relations with prospective clients, field research for existing contracts, and supervision and field management for existing contracts. All four of these categories are scheduled daily for each upcoming month. The last two are scheduled in the master schedule and project schedules by task for the duration of the job.

Office Operations: Office work is divided into several categories on a routine basis: computer accounting to include invoicing and payment of bills; collections; research for existing projects; coordination of project management jobs; filing; compiling, writing, printing, and binding reports; and following up leads.

Accounting: Accounting is handled by the president in Quicken's QuickBooksPro99. Year-end taxes are verified and filed by the company's outside CPA.

Facility

ECS is located at 77-6452 Alii Drive, Kailua-Kona, Hawaii, the oceanfront home of Stan Edwards. A home based office was chosen because most of the daily business of the owner is conducted in the field, researching data for reports; addressing public hearings, planning commissions, and county councils; managing projects; and meeting clients and prospective clients at their premises. This is a huge savings of unnecessary external office rent. As a sole proprietor, Mr. Edwards is not allowed to pay himself rent; however, a pro rata portion (20 percent) of the house is used for office and has been taken as an asset, $44,000, with a 39-year straight-line depreciation ($94) as set by the IRS for commercial home based offices. This is offset by its share of the mortgage, $26,400 ($212 pro rata principal payment), and a pro rata interest expense at 9 percent. The office has been modestly but professionally decorated and is centrally located with convenient access for the few clients that wish to meet and appointments that must be made at ECS. The office has been remodeled with a separate exterior entrance from the main entrance of the house. Street-side parking is adequate. During the day callers can reach the answering machine to leave recorded messages or reach Mr. Edwards personally by cell phone. Recorded messages are monitored remotely three or four times per day.

Operations (continued) — Edwards' Consulting Services

Production

Sales are booked when contracts are signed, not letters of intent. Once a contract is signed, the project is scheduled in Microsoft Project with moderate allowances for error and any possible unforeseen problems. After the project schedule is finalized, it is coordinated into the custom-designed Excel master schedule which continuously shows twelve-months as a sliding forecast schedule forward from the current month as month one. Previous months move to a historic schedule which can be accessed to help refine new schedules. Mr. Edwards uses the schedule as a target, but does not make the schedule public because it has been determined that sometimes a circulated published schedule can slow down a project's progress and jeopardize previous gains.

For project management, all field inspections are conducted in the afternoons, recorded, and lists prepared for project coordination. Telephone calls are returned based on preference to those who wish to be reached in the evening and those who prefer morning calls.

For county and state approval processes, all key dates for notices, applications, and agendas are logged into the computer and synchronized with the project schedule. Key dates with built-in preparation times are then logged into the master schedule which identifies them throughout the months, in the worst case one month in advance. As a backup plan, the key dates and their preparation time are also simultaneously (by software) logged into a master memo program that is checked at the end of each day; this assures accurate scheduling which is one measure of quality control for ECS.

Equipment Schedule

Equipment Description	Manufacturer Name	Model	Serial Number	Date of Purchase	Purchase Price	Monthly Payment	Depreciation Schedule	Useful Life	Maintenance Required
Automobile	Ford	Ranger		15 Dec.	$19,000	$509	$528	3	Used
Computer	HP	Pavilion		8 Dec.	3,900	0	65	5	
Printer	HP	1170Cxi		8 Dec.	650	0	11	5	
Copier	Xerox	5388		8 Dec.	6,500	0	108	5	
Fax	Canon	B640		8 Dec.	180	0	3	5	
Lateral file, steel	Hon	400		8 Dec.	180	0	2	10	
Lateral file, furnature	Miller			8 Dec.	420	0	4	10	
Desk	Miller	Dbl. Ped.		8 Dec.	650	0	5	10	
Executive chair	Office Max			8 Dec.	400	0	3	10	
Client chairs	Office Max			8 Dec.	280	0	2	10	
Credenza	Miller	4-drawer		8 Dec.	570	0	5	10	
Other furnature				8 Dec.	400	0	3	10	
Appropriate totals					$33,130	$509	$739		
Memo note for Depreciation:									
Leasehold improvements					3,700		31	10	
Portion of Home (20%) @ $220,000*					44,000		94	39	
Total monthly depreciation							$864		
Depreciable asstes					$80,830				

* Home loan $132,000   Home loan portion (20%) $26,400

Operations (continued)   Edwards' Consulting Services

Research is conducted and reports are compiled on an as-needed basis from mid-morning to mid-afternoon.

As an additional aid to quality control, all reports are edited, proofread, printed, and bound in-house. The only outside work involves reducing large color formats to $8 1/2$ by 11 inches or laser printing a transparency, both of which are processed at one of three available copy centers. Everything else is completed in-house because copy centers historically will not provide the same attention to detail as the high standards set by ECS for report reproduction and binding. Final reports are submitted in person to the principal for whom they are directed (client, county, or state office), and copies are circulated by direct mail or, in the case of a few pages, by fax.

Because scheduling and the professionalism of finished reports are such integral parts of the business of ECS, Mr. Edwards monitors new software programs and stays abreast of the latest in technology through trade journals and office supply catalogs. Most supplies are purchased through Office Max in Hilo on a business account that allows a 30-day credit.

Customer Service Policy

ECS monitors customer service through one-on-one relationships between the president and each of the clients. This is an advantage of an owner-direct business that larger organizations attempt to emulate using junior personnel.

If a refund for services is ever requested, the president is prepared to offer a full refund in exchange for the reason for dissatisfaction to avoid the same problem in the future, to preserve the good will of the client, and to maximize the reputation of ECS.

For other outside input, ECS offers e-mail interaction through the ECS web site which includes an e-mail feedback hyper link. Requests for information about the company or ECS services are answered within 24 hours. Client calls that are recorded via the answering machine are returned within 24 hours, including calls monitored from remote locations.

Efficiency Control

ECS will execute an annual business plan every year and begin the process three months before the end of the first year. In the process, the president will consider the competition's adjustments to ECS's positioning in the marketplace, possible new services, price adjustments, client feedback throughout the year, marketing adjustments, and all operational expenses.

Cash Flow Control

Cash flow procedures are computerized and daily cash flow statements can be generated through in-house software programs. These will be monitored closely the first three months during the critical phases shown by the cash flow pro forma (next section). In addition to these, cash flow pro formas will also be developed every month.

All payables will be paid within the 30-day credit period.

Invoices to clients will go out at the end of each month, and terms are net 30 days. Although ECS has this 30-day credit policy for accounts receivable, it is common practice in the industry for developers to pay 60 to 90 days late. Because of this, ECS has planned all financial pro formas as if every client will pay 90 days late. This is a conservative measure, but it may be realistic in a worst case scenario. Timely collection letters will be sent out and the president will set aside one day per month to follow-up each with a personal call. Accounts over 60 days will receive

Operations (continued)   Edwards' Consulting Services

a second letter, and the president will call on the client in person. For accounts over 90 days, a third collection letter will go out, and the president will contact those clients and notify them that all work on their projects will cease until payments are made. At this point, each situation will be evaluated and a negotiation for at least partial payment with scheduled timely progressive payments may be accepted in cases waiting for funding. Mitigating conditions will be verified to the president's satisfaction if negotiation is accepted. If not, the client will be notified that a mechanics lien will be filed, and the problem will be turned over to ECS's attorney, Gunner Burley.

Financial Pro Formas   Edwards' Consulting Services

Financial Summary

The ECS market share of 20 percent has been used to develop the financial pro formas and is consistent with the quality and quantity of early signed contracts and letters of intent.

In examining the cash flow pro forma prior to loan proceeds, the beginning cash for June would be a negative $17,500 based on ECS's opening balance sheet. However, the pro formas have been adjusted for short-term loan proceeds of $20,000 in January with appropriate interest increases. Sales for the first year are projected at $173,400 and direct costs at $5,808, with a gross profit margin of 96.7 percent. All other expenses total $29,740. The total sales to break even during the first year must be $33,194. The operating profit is $135,510 and net profit is $74,021.

For the five-year pro formas, ECS has conservatively estimated 7 percent increases in sales (the industry is expected to grow 12 percent) and 4 percent increases in operating costs, which is commensurate with last year's GDP. This yields a net profit for year five of $112,234 and a high working capital of $316,098. While all business ratios are healthy, the annual return on equity for the fifth year is a strong 33 percent.

Important Assumptions

The assumptions used in the table below were used in developing the financial pro formas in this section. Notice all sales are on credit, and collection is 90 days, which was explained in Cash Flow Control, Operations. Direct costs and average monthly direct costs are actually calculated from the Sales Forecast shown in Marketing and Sales. Direct costs accounts payable are shown at 50 percent and general accounts payable at 20 percent because most purchases such as local supplies, gasoline, and lunches are by credit card. Because Mr. Edwards is self-employed and a sole proprietorship, FICA is paid with income tax.

(continued)

Financial Pro Formas (continued) — Edwards' Consulting Services

Five-year Assumptions for Financial Statements — Edwards' Consulting Services

	Year 1	Year 2	Year 3	Year 4	Year 5
Market share	20%	Increases 7% annually every year			
Average monthly sales	$14,450	$15,462	$16,544	$17,702	$18,941
Cash sales	0%	0%	0%	0%	0%
Sales on credit	100%	100%	100%	100%	100%
Collection days	90 days	90 days	90 days	90 days	90 days
Direct costs	3.35%	3.35%	3.35%	3.35%	3.35%
Average monthly direct costs	$484	$518	$554	$593	$635
Direct costs accounts payable	50%	50%	50%	50%	50%
Direct costs payment days	30 days	30 days	30 days	30 days	30 days
General accounts payable	20%	20%	20%	20%	20%
General payment days	30 days	30 days	30 days	30 days	30 days
Interest rate (short-term)	12%	12%	12%	12%	12%
Interest rate (long-term)	9%	9%	9%	9%	9%
Income tax rate and FICA	43%	43%	43%	43%	43%

Financial Pro Formas (continued) — Edwards' Consulting Services

Opening Balance Sheet — ECS

Assets	November 17, 20XX
Current Assets:	
Cash	$10,000
Marketable securities	—
Accounts receivable	—
Other current assets	6,490
Total current assets	16,490
Long-term Assets	
Depreciable assets	80,830
Accumulated depreciation	—
Net depreciable assets	80,830
Non-depreciable assets	—
Total Long-term Assets	80,830
Total Assets	**$97,320**

Liabilities and Equity	
Current Liabilities:	
Cost of sales accounts payable	$ 0
Non-cost of sales accounts payable	0
Taxes payable	0
Short-term notes payable	0
Total current liabilities	0
Long-term Liabilities	42,400
Ford Ranger (3 years) $16,000	
20% of house loan $26,400	
Total Liabilities	42,400
Equity	
Shareholders equity	54,920
Retained earnings	—
Total Equity	54,920
Total Liabilities and Equity	**$97,320**

First-year Pro Forma Income Statement

Edwards' Consulting Services

Month	Jan.	Feb.	March	April	May	June	July	Aug.	Sept.	Oct.	Nov.	Dec.	Year 1
Sales	10,400	9,500	10,300	13,800	14,300	12,300	17,800	18,000	16,000	19,500	13,000	18,500	173,400
Costs													
Direct Costs (1)	460	350	305	610	560	340	560	490	595	555	490	493	5,808
Gross profit	9,940	9,150	9,995	13,190	13,740	11,960	17,240	17,510	15,405	18,945	12,510	18,007	167,592
Marketing and Sales													
Advertising	95	145	95	35	95	35	95	35	95	35	95	35	890
Other marketing	172	100	136	100	136	100	136	100	136	100	136	100	1,452
Total Marketing and Sales (2)	267	245	231	135	231	135	231	135	231	135	231	135	2,342
General and Administrative Expense													
Portion of house payment	212	212	212	212	212	212	212	212	212	212	212	212	2,544
Utilities and telephone	120	120	120	120	120	120	120	120	120	120	120	120	1,440
Auto	509	509	509	509	509	509	509	509	509	509	509	509	6,108
Depreciation	864	864	864	864	864	864	864	864	864	864	864	864	10,368
Maintenance and repairs	25	25	25	25	25	25	25	25	25	25	25	25	300
Insurance	280	280	280	280	280	280	280	280	280	280	280	280	3,360
Supplies and postage	120	120	120	120	120	120	120	120	120	120	120	120	1,440
Travel and entertainment	220	220	220	220	220	220	220	220	220	220	220	220	2,640
Legal and accounting	0	0	50	0	0	50	0	0	50	0	0	650	800
Other outside services	0	0	0	0	0	0	0	0	0	0	0	0	0
Non-income taxes and fees	0	0	0	0	0	0	0	0	0	0	0	140	140
Other operating expenses	50	50	50	50	50	50	50	50	50	50	50	50	600
Total G & A Expense (3)	2,400	2,400	2,450	2,400	2,400	2,450	2,400	2,400	2,450	2,400	2,400	3,190	29,740
Total Operating Costs (total rows 1 + 2 + 3)	3,127	2,995	2,986	3,145	3,191	2,925	3,191	3,025	3,276	3,090	3,121	3,818	37,890
Operating Profit	7,273	6,505	7,314	10,655	11,109	9,375	14,609	14,975	12,724	16,410	9,879	14,682	135,510
Interest Expense	514	506	498	490	483	475	467	459	451	443	435	427	5,648
Profit Before Income Taxes	6,759	5,999	6,816	10,165	10,626	8,900	14,142	14,516	12,273	15,967	9,444	14,255	129,862
Income Taxes and Owners FICA	2,906	2,580	2,931	4,371	4,569	3,827	6,081	6,242	5,277	6,866	4,061	6,130	55,841
Net Profit	3,853	3,419	3,885	5,794	6,057	5,073	8,061	8,274	6,996	9,101	5,383	8,125	74,021

Financial Pro Formas (continued) — Edwards' Consulting Services

Five-year Pro Forma Income Statement — Edwards' Consulting Services

	Year 1	Year 2	Year 3	Year 4	Year 5
Sales	173,400	185,538	198,526	212,422	227,292
Costs					
Direct Costs (1)	5,808	6,216	6,651	7,116	7,614
Gross profit	167,592	179,322	191,875	205,306	219,678
Marketing and Sales					
Advertising	890	926	963	1,001	1,041
Other marketing	1,452	1,510	1,570	1,633	1,699
Total Marketing and Sales (2)	2,342	2,436	2,533	2,634	2,740
General and Administrative Expense					
Portion of house payment	2,544	2,544	2,544	2,544	2,544
Utilities and telephone	1,440	1,498	1,558	1,620	1,685
Auto	6,108	6,108	6,108	0	0
Depreciation	10,368	10,368	9,240	2,904	2,904
Maintenance and repairs	300	312	324	337	351
Insurance	3,360	3,494	3,634	3,780	3,931
Supplies and postage	1,440	1,498	1,558	1,620	1,685
Travel and entertainment	2,640	2,746	2,855	2,970	3,088
Legal and accounting	800	832	865	900	936
Other outside services	0	0	0	0	0
Non-income taxes and fees	140	140	175	175	175
Other operating expenses	600	600	600	600	600
Total G & A Expense (3)	29,740	30,140	29,461	17,450	17,899
Total Operating Costs (total rows 1 + 2 + 3)	37,890	38,792	38,645	27,200	28,253
Operating Profit	135,510	146,746	159,881	185,222	199,039
Interest Expense	5,648	2,777	2,297	2,218	2,139
Profit Before Income Taxes	129,862	143,969	157,584	183,004	196,900
Income Taxes and Owners FICA	55,841	61,907	67,761	78,692	84,667
Net Profit	74,021	82,063	89,823	104,312	112,233

Break-even Analysis — Edwards' Consulting Services

	Year 1	Year 2	Year 3	Year 4	Year 5
Total Sales	173,400	185,538	198,526	212,422	227,292
Break-even Sales	33,194	33,704	33,103	20,780	21,353

First-year Pro Forma Statement of Cash Flow

Edwards' Consulting Services

	Month												Year
	Jan.	Feb.	March	April	May	June	July	Aug.	Sept.	Oct.	Nov.	Dec.	2
Starting Cash Position	10,000	21,391	12,199	2,715	2,179	377	278	1,405	2,872	3,196	7,495	14,811	17,524
Cash Receipts (sources of cash)													
Cash sales	0	0	0	0	0	0	0	0	0	0	0	0	0
Sales on credit	0	0	0	0	0	0	0	0	0	0	0	0	0
Short-term loan proceeds	0	0	0	10,400	9,500	10,300	13,800	14,300	12,300	17,800	18,000	16,000	190,154
Long-term loan proceeds	20,000	0	0	0	0	0	0	0	0	0	0	0	0
Equity capital proceeds	0	0	0	0	0	0	0	0	0	0	0	0	0
Total Cash Receipts	20,000	0	0	10,400	9,500	10,300	13,800	14,300	12,300	17,800	18,000	16,000	190,154
Cash Disbursements (uses of cash)													
Direct costs	230	405	328	458	585	450	450	525	543	575	523	492	6,204
Non-payroll expenses	1,442	1,785	1,810	1,700	1,748	1,730	1,758	1,690	1,788	1,700	1,748	2,322	22,329
Depreciable asset purchases	0	0	0	0	0	0	0	0	0	0	0	0	0
Non-depreciable asset purchases	0	0	0	0	0	0	0	0	0	0	0	0	0
Interest	514	506	498	490	483	475	467	459	451	443	435	427	2,777
Owner's draw	3,000	3,000	3,000	3,000	3,000	3,000	3,000	3,000	3,000	3,000	3,000	3,000	36,000
Short-term liabilities payments *	0	400	400	400	400	400	400	400	400	400	400	400	15,600
Long-term liabilites payments	517	517	517	517	517	517	517	517	517	517	517	517	5,336
Total Cash Disbursements	5,703	6,613	6,553	6,565	6,733	6,572	6,592	6,591	6,699	6,635	6,623	7,158	88,246
Income taxes	2,906	2,579	2,931	4,371	4,569	3,827	6,081	6,242	5,277	6,866	4,061	6,129	61,907
Total Cash Disbursements After Taxes	8,609	9,192	9,484	10,936	11,302	10,399	12,673	12,833	11,976	13,501	10,684	13,287	150,153
Net Change In Cash	11,391	(9,192)	(9,484)	(536)	(1,802)	(99)	1,127	1,467	324	4,299	7,316	2,713	40,001
Ending Cash Position	21,391	12,199	2,715	2,179	377	278	1,405	2,872	3,196	7,495	14,811	17,524	57,525

* Total loan pay-off is shown in 2nd year

First-year and Five-year Pro Forma Balance Sheets

Edwards' Consulting Services

	Quarter				Year				
	1	2	3	1	2	3	4	5	
Assets									
Current Assets									
Cash	2,714	278	3,196	17,524	57,525	112,031	178,824	253,398	
Marketable securities	0	0	0	0	0	0	0	0	
Accounts receivable	30,200	40,400	51,800	51,000	46,385	49,631	53,106	56,823	
Other current assets	6,490	6,490	6,490	6,490	6,490	6,490	6,490	6,490	
Total Current Assets	39,404	47,168	61,486	75,014	110,400	168,152	238,420	316,711	
Long-term Assets									
Depreciable assets	80,830	80,830	80,830	80,830	80,830	80,830	80,830	80,830	
Accumulated depreciation	2,592	5,184	7,776	10,368	20,736	29,976	32,880	35,784	
Net depreciable assets	78,238	75,646	73,054	70,462	60,094	50,854	47,950	45,046	
Non-depreciable assets	0	0	0	0	0	0	0	0	
Total Long-term Assets	78,238	75,646	73,054	70,462	60,094	50,854	47,950	45,046	
Total Assets	117,642	122,814	134,540	145,476	170,494	219,006	286,370	361,757	
Liabilities and Equity									
Current Liabilities									
Cost of sales accounts payable	153	170	298	247	259	277	297	317	
Non-cost of sales accounts payable	363	344	363	492	370	379	286	296	
Taxes payable	0	0	0	0	0	0	0	0	
Short-term notes payable	19,200	18,000	16,800	15,600	0	0	0	0	
Total Current Liabilities	19,716	18,514	17,461	16,339	629	656	583	613	
Long-term Liabilities	40,849	39,298	37,747	36,196	30,860	25,524	24,648	23,772	
Total Liabilities	60,565	57,812	55,208	52,535	31,489	26,180	25,231	24,385	
Equity									
Retained earnings	57,077	65,002	79,332	92,941	139,005	192,826	261,139	337,372	
Total Equity	57,077	65,002	79,332	92,941	139,005	192,826	261,139	337,372	
Total Liabilities and Equity	117,642	122,814	134,540	145,476	170,494	219,006	286,370	361,757	

Financial Pro Formas – Business Ratios   Edwards' Consulting Services

Key Business Ratios	Year 1	2	3	4	5
Quick ratio	4.59	175.48	256.19	409.07	516.81
Current ratio	4.59	175.48	256.19	409.07	516.81
Debt to assets	0.36	0.18	0.12	0.09	0.00
Debt to equity	0.57	0.23	0.14	0.10	0.07
Collection days	128.0	99.3	82.7	67.7	57.3
Sales to assets	1.19	1.09	0.91	0.74	0.63
Working capital	$58,675	$109,770	$167,496	$237,837	$316,098
Accounts receivable turnover	3.4	4.0	4.0	4.0	4.0
Gross profit margin	96.7%	96.6%	96.6%	96.7%	96.7%
Net profit margin	42.7%	44.2%	45.2%	49.1%	49.4%
Sales breakeven	$961,538	$996,725	$1,033,842	$1,044,589	$1,085,224
Return on assets	51%	48%	41%	36%	31%
Return on equity	80%	59%	47%	40%	33%

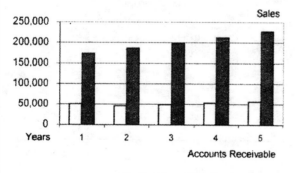

Accounts Receivable Turnover

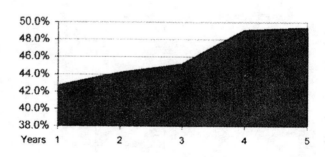

Net Profit Margin

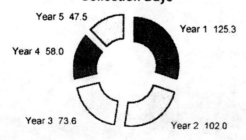

Collection Days

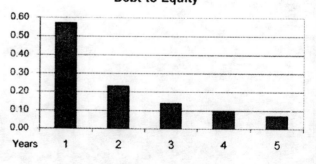

Debt to Equity

Loan Request   Edwards' Consulting Services

Loan Request Summary

The total start-up costs are $117,320. To date, ECS has raised owner capital totaling $97,320 which includes: $17,600 pro rata home equity, $42,400 from two pre-existing loans and $37,320 in cash ($10,000 still on hand). The difference between the start-up costs and the capital raised is $20,000.

To cover this, ECS is seeking to increase the owner's consumer credit limit on the president's personal Bankoh Visa Gold Card from the current limit of $5,000 to $25,000 at 12 percent. ECS has planned to draw one disbursement of $20,000 in January to make up the difference in working capital needed to launch the new business. For payback, ECS will make twelve minimum payments and pay off the remaining balance in one year. After that, it is Mr. Edwards' plan to keep this limit open and only use the card for unforeseen emergencies as a reserve option.

The cash flow pro forma shows that this is viable financial planning as ECS should still have $8,234 in cash after the paying the card completely down. As a backup plan, Mr. Edwards would seek an equity home loan in the form of a second mortgage, if necessary, as the current first trust deed is only 60 percent loan to value. His personal financial statement with the most recent two years tax returns provided under separate cover.

Start-up Costs

Description	Total Estimated	Actual Paid	Date Paid	Balance to Pay	Date Needed
Initial lease/purchase	$ 44,000	$17,600	N/A	$26,400	Existing loan
Lease deposit	N/A	N/A	N/A		
Utilities deposit	100	100	1 Dec.		
Licenses and fees	140	140	2 Dec.		
Leasehold improvements	3,700	3,700	1 Dec.		
Insurance	1,000	1,000	4 Dec.		
Other prepaids*	1,200	1,200	8 Dec.		
Equipment	14,130	14,130	8 Dec.		
Vehicle	19,000	3,000	15 Dec.	16,000	Existing loan
Fixtures and furniture	In equipment				
Freight and installation	Included	Included			
Sales taxes	Included	Included			
Supplies	650	650	9 Dec.		
Signage	—	—			
Marketing materials	1,000	1,000	9 Dec.		
Advertising	—	—			
Accounting	—	—			
Legal	2,400	2,400	10 Dec.		
Working capital	30,000	10,000	N/A	20,000	15 Jan.
Totals	$117,320	$54,920		$62,400	

* Includes cell phone, $100; software, $500; decor items, $600

(continued)

Loan Request (continued) — Edwards' Consulting Services

Start-up Costs

The total start-up costs are $117,320 including a $44,000 asset contributed as a pro rata home asset for Mr. Edwards' home office and a $19,000 asset for the company vehicle. Both of these assets have existing loans: $26,400 and $16,000 respectively. Other major costs include equipment and furniture, $14,130 (see equipment list, Operations); and home remodeling for the office, $3,700. A breakdown of this work can be provided with paid receipts. The $1,000 prepaid marketing was primarily for the brochure design and printing and is reflected in the marketing budget and shown in the opening balance sheet as a current asset, but it is not set up as a January expense in the pro forma income statement.

As seen in the start-up schedule, all of these costs have been paid either by cash or existing loans with the exception of the full amount of the working capital required to open business. This amount of working capital was ascertained by creating a pro forma statement of cash flow which conservatively estimated that clients, on average, will be stalling accounts receivable payments for 90 days. The total working capital of $30,000 has enough room for safety because some clients will be paying their invoices on time.

Funds Raised and Funds Needed

ECS is using a total home value of $220,000 and the pro rata share for the office is 20 percent. The existing 60 percent mortgage is $132,000 and the pro rata share of the mortgage is $26,400.

From this basis, the total funds raised by Mr. Edwards are $97,320. This is represented by $17,600 in pro rata home equity of the home based office, $3,000 in equity of the company vehicle, $26,400 in pro rata home mortgage, $16,000 in auto loan, cash prepaids of $24,320 for the other prepaid items, and $10,000 in cash on hand to use for working capital.

Since the total start-up costs are $117,320 as shown in the schedule, this yields a funds-needed amount of $20,000 to complete the start-up costs including working capital and to begin doing business from a healthy financial position upon opening.

Loan Request (continued) — Edwards' Consulting Services

Loan Request Proposal

Hard Costs		Soft Costs	
Facility/site	$44,000.00	Deposits	$ 100.00
Leasehold improvements	3,700.00	Other prepaids	1,200.00
Equipment and furniture	48,761.00	Licenses and fees	140.00
Vehicles	40,000.00	Insurance	1,000.00
Total Hard Costs	**$80,830.00**	Supplies	650.00
		Marketing	1,000.00
		Legal	2,400.00
		Working capital	30,000.00
		Total Soft Costs	**$36,490.00**

Total Start-up Funds	$117,320.00
Less our cash investment	97,320.00
Loan Amount Needed	$ 20,000.00

Loan Requested: Increase of credit limit for cash withdrawal of $25,000.00 to Mr. Edwards' Bankoh Visa Gold Card at the adjusted rate of 12 percent interest.

Remarks: ECS will be using net proceeds of the first draw of $20,000 in January, 20XY, and making minimum payments of 3 percent of the outstanding balance, calculated at $400 principal reductions until the final payment is made in full, scheduled internally to be February, 20XZ, our second year of business.

Collateral: For hard collateral we anticipate and pre-approve your institution to lien our equipment and operation with a full encumbrance for this loan.

Potential Risks

Risk is inherent in any new start-up company. ECS has attempted to mitigate its risk as much as possible by contracting clients for fixed fees using strong contracts and solid clientele that have been in business for many years. Additionally, ECS will take on only new clients that have a reputation for paying for their work or that have new project loans already in place.

The biggest risk for any one-man company is that the performance of the business relies on the health of the business operator. Although Mr. Edwards is in excellent health and maintains his physical condition by working out three times a week at Gold's gym where he is a member, he has also taken a preventative precaution for this concern. Mr. Edwards has made a strategic arrangement with David White, master builder and owner of White Development for 15 years: each will cover the responsibilities of the other in supervising their jobs in project management should one of them become incapacitated. While this arrangement calls for compensation to be paid to the working person by the non-working person, fees from contracts (sales) would continue from all project management jobs in progress. The pro forma income statements would only be altered slightly and business shouldn't be seriously disrupted unless the period of time exceeds three months. Business disruption insurance is also available, although it is expensive.

(continued)

Loan Request (continued) — Edwards' Consulting Services

The second biggest risk in this industry is collection days. While the accounts receivable policy is net 30 days, ECS has mitigated this risk by implementing the conservative approach of building in a collection period of 90 days for all clients.

Exit Options

Although it is early to plan exit options, Mr. Edwards believes that once ECS's business is established with a strong database of repeat and referral clientele, the business will be an attractive buyout consideration by any of the mainstream and established civil engineers in Hawaii who have existing planning divisions. This could become a reality as early as three years, but would more than likely be a product of seven to ten years.

Exhibits — Edwards' Consulting Services

A. Market Research

B. Personal financial statements

C. List of Development Agreements

D. List of Letters of Intent

Appendix B

Business Plan Differences for Retail and Wholesale Businesses

This model business plan is for Eclectic Interiors by Monica, abridged from the previous two models presented: Kona Gold Coffees (shown throughout the text) and Edwards' Consulting Services (Appendix A).

Eclectic Interiors by Monica is a small retail business. The differences detailed in this business plan cover businesses of both retail and wholesale products. For the first six sections of your business plan (Executive Summary, Company Description, Industry Analysis, Market and Competition, Strategies and Goals, and Products) and Section 9 (Operations), follow the Kona Gold Coffees examples. For most of Section 7, Marketing and Sales, the same is true; however, a difference occurs in the format of the sales forecast which is the first detailed table shown in this business plan. Likewise, Section 8, Management and Organization follows the example of Kona Gold Coffees, with the exception of one table, the personnel plan, shown here for a small retail business with fewer employees and fewer departments than shown for Kona Gold Coffees.

Sections 10 and 11 have been fully constructed for this model. In Section 10, Financial Pro Formas, the major differences lie in the balance sheets (both opening and pro formas), the first- and five-year pro forma income statements, and the first-year pro forma statement of cash flow. On the balance sheets, note that cash is usually separated into "cash in register" and "cash in bank." Sometimes, an accountant will simply use cash-on-hand to include that which is in the register. Also, inventory is termed merchandise for retail and wholesale companies. On both balance sheets and income statements, "cost of sales" is called "costs of goods sold."

Section 11, Loan Request, has been structured as an example of a start-up business applying for a Small Business Administration (SBA) loan. In this case, Eclectic Interiors by Monica is applying for an SBA loan for a minority start-up company which qualifies because its owner is a woman in business. Her merchandise is to be used as hard collateral along with 100 percent of the business assets. As a backup plan, the owner will pledge marketable securities, if necessary, in a larger amount than the face value of the loan. Notice how the structure of the funds to be received and the payments to be made match the first-year pro forma statement of cash flow in Section 10. The funds generated by the loan, $40,000, are shown to be received in January (cash receipts, long-term loan proceeds). The monthly principal payments of $505 for this loan have been added to the monthly vehicle principal payment of $200 to total $705 beginning monthly in February (cash disbursements, short-term liabilities payments) while interest is tracked in its own account (cash disbursements, interest). Notice also that the owner proposes a buy-out in the exit options.

Eclectic Interiors
by Monica
Honolulu, Hawaii

Business Plan

Confidential Information

Prepared for:
Ms. Wilma S. Stillwell
Business Loan Officer
Bank of Hawaii
851 Bishop Street
Honolulu, Hawaii 96813-2202

Prepared by:
Monica Davis
(800) 555-4321

November 17, 20XX

Contents

Executive Summary

Company Description

Industry Analysis

Market and Competition

Strategies and Goals

Products

Marketing and Sales

Management and Organization

Operations

Financial Pro Formas

Loan Request

Business Plan Exhibits

Executive Summary Eclectic Interiors by Monica

Business Concept
Progress Status
Keys to Success
Financial Overview

Company Description Eclectic Interiors by Monica

Name and Business Concept
Ownership and Legal
Leadership and Location
Geographic Sales Area
Current Status and Milestones

Current Milestones Eclectic Interiors by Monica

Milestone	Projected Date	Projected Budget	Actual Date	Actual Costs	Variance
Pre-opening advertising	30 Oct.	$1,200	30 Oct.	$1,200	$ 0
Purchase van	1 Nov.	3,500	30 Oct.	4,200	700
Purchase auto	3 Nov.	16,000	3 Nov.	14,000	(2,000)
Utility deposits	30 Nov.	200	30 Nov.	260	60
Business plan complete	30 Nov.	N/A	30 Nov.	N/A	N/A
Deposit and rent	1 Dec.	3,800	1 Dec.	$3,808	8
SBA loan submittal	1 Dec.	N/A	1 Dec.	N/A	N/A
Receives ES container	3 Dec.	20,000		On credit	
Licenses	10 Dec.	50			
Receive Johnson line	10 Dec.	7,650		On credit	
Press release	15 Dec.	N/A		N/A	N/A
Yellow Pages ad	15 Dec.	250			
Leasehold improvements	23 Dec.	2,500			
Sign	21 Dec.	2,000			
Fixtures	26 Dec.	4,000			
Radio ad	26 Dec.	140			
Direct mail	27 Dec.	320			
Buy supplies	28 Dec.	400			
Open for business	1 Jan.	N/A		N/A	N/A
SBA loan approval	2 Mar.	N/A		N/A	N/A
Sales breakeven	15 Apr.	N/A		N/A	N/A

Industry Analysis

Eclectic Interiors by Monica

Industry Analysis Summary

Industry Description

Industry Size and Maturation

Industry Trends and Impact Factors

Industry Standards

Industry Obstacles

Industry Opportunities

Market and Competition

Eclectic Interiors by Monica

Market and Competition Summary

Market Description – Segments and Target Markets

Market Size and Trends

Competition Identification

Main Competitors

Competitor Analysis

Market Share

Customer Needs

Market Obstacles

Market Opportunities

Strategies and Goals

Eclectic Interiors by Monica

Strategies and Goals Summary

Long-range Goals and Strategies

Strategy Implementation

Products
Eclectic Interiors by Monica

Products Summary

Products Description

Products Positioning

Comparison with the Competition

Technology and Intellectual Protection

Future Products

Marketing and Sales
Eclectic Interiors by Monica

Marketing and Sales Summary

Marketing Strategy

Marketing Plan

Marketing Budget

Month	Graphic Design	Printed Materials	Advertising Plan	Direct Mail
January	(Preopening expenses)		$ 140	$ 320
February			433	320
March			436	320
April			390	320
May			423	320
June			185	320
July			188	320
August			637	320
September			516	320
October			580	320
November			1,302	320
December			1,727	320
Subtotals	$	$	$6,957	$3,840

Total: $10,797

Marketing and Sales (continued)   Eclectic Interiors by Monica

Advertising Plan

Month	Local Television[1]	Local Radio[2]	Consumer Magazines	News-Papers[3]	Yellow Page	Special Events
January	$	$ 140	$	$	$	$
February		108		76	249	
March		108	100	153		75
April		137	100	153		
May		170	100	153		
June		109		76		
July		112		76		
August	453	108		76		
September		218	100	153		45
October		218	100	153		109
November	720	218	100	264		
December	720	436	100	264		207
Subtotals	$1,893	$2,082	$700	$1,597	$249	$436

Total: $6,957

---

[1] Day-time cable network
[2] Guaranteed designated spots
[3] Week-end shopper inserts

Sales Force and Forecast

Sales Forecast

Eclectic Interiors by Monica

	Month												Year
	Jan.	Feb.	March	April	May	June	July	Aug.	Sept.	Oct.	Nov.	Dec.	1
Total Sales - $													
Product Line 1	920	1,506	1,512	1,419	1,486	1,011	1,015	1,914	1,672	1,799	3,244	4,093	21,591
Product Line 2	920	1,506	1,512	1,419	1,486	1,011	1,015	1,914	1,672	1,799	3,244	4,093	21,591
Product Line 3	1,150	1,882	1,890	1,774	1,858	1,264	1,269	2,392	2,090	2,249	4,055	5,117	26,989
Product Line 4	1,150	1,882	1,890	1,774	1,858	1,264	1,269	2,392	2,090	2,249	4,055	5,117	26,989
Product Line 5	1,150	1,882	1,890	1,774	1,858	1,264	1,269	2,392	2,090	2,249	4,055	5,117	26,989
Product Line 6	690	1,129	1,134	1,064	1,115	758	761	1,435	1,254	1,349	2,433	3,070	16,194
Product Line 7	690	1,129	1,134	1,064	1,115	758	761	1,435	1,254	1,349	2,433	3,070	16,194
Product Line 8	920	1,506	1,512	1,419	1,486	1,011	1,015	1,914	1,672	1,799	3,244	4,093	21,591
Product Line 9	690	1,129	1,134	1,064	1,115	758	761	1,435	1,254	1,349	2,433	3,070	16,194
Product Line 10	920	1,506	1,512	1,419	1,486	1,011	1,015	1,914	1,672	1,799	3,244	4,093	21,591
Product Line 11	1,150	1,882	1,890	1,774	1,858	1,264	1,269	2,392	2,090	2,249	4,055	5,117	26,989
Product Line 12	1,150	1,882	1,890	1,774	1,858	1,264	1,269	2,392	2,090	2,249	4,055	5,117	26,989
Total Sales	11,502	18,819	18,900	17,739	18,576	12,636	12,690	23,922	20,898	22,491	40,554	51,165	269,892
Cost of Goods Sold													
Product Line 1	460	753	756	710	743	505	508	957	836	900	1,622	2,047	10,796
Product Line 2	460	753	756	710	743	505	508	957	836	900	1,622	2,047	10,796
Product Line 3	575	941	945	887	929	632	635	1,196	1,045	1,125	2,028	2,558	13,495
Product Line 4	575	941	945	887	929	632	635	1,196	1,045	1,125	2,028	2,558	13,495
Product Line 5	575	941	945	887	929	632	635	1,196	1,045	1,125	2,028	2,558	13,495
Product Line 6	345	565	567	532	557	379	381	718	627	675	1,217	1,535	8,097
Product Line 7	345	565	567	532	557	379	381	718	627	675	1,217	1,535	8,097
Product Line 8	460	753	756	710	743	505	508	957	836	900	1,622	2,047	10,796
Product Line 9	345	565	567	532	557	379	381	718	627	675	1,217	1,535	8,097
Product Line 10	460	753	756	710	743	505	508	957	836	900	1,622	2,047	10,796
Product Line 11	575	941	945	887	929	632	635	1,196	1,045	1,125	2,028	2,558	13,495
Product Line 12	575	941	945	887	929	632	635	1,196	1,045	1,125	2,028	2,558	13,495
Total Cost of Goods Sold	5,751	9,410	9,450	8,870	9,288	6,318	6,345	11,961	10,449	11,246	20,277	25,583	134,946
Total Gross Profit	5,751	9,410	9,450	8,870	9,288	6,318	6,345	11,961	10,449	11,246	20,277	25,583	134,946

Management and Organization
Eclectic Interiors by Monica

Management and Organization Summary

Management Team

Key Personnel Responsibilities and Duties

Management Philosophy

Key Personnel Incentives

Organizational Structure

Personnel Plan

Job Title	Name	Jan.	Feb.	March	April	May	June	July
Marketing and Sales								
Salesperson #1	Tracey Buggs	$450	$450	$450	$450	$450	$450	$450
Salesperson #2	Shea Johnson	450	450	450	450	450	450	450
General and Administration								
President	Monica Davis	Draw	Draw	Draw	Draw	Draw	Draw	Draw
Office Manager		0	0	0	0	0	0	0
Bookkeeper		0	0	0	0	0	0	0
Total Payroll		$900	$900	$900	$900	$900	$900	$900
Payroll Burdon		$144	$144	$144	$144	$144	$144	$144
Total Personnel (owner and two part-time)		3	3	3	3	3	3	3

Job Title	Name	August	Sept.	Oct.	Nov.	Dec.	1st Year
Marketing and Sales							
Salesperson #1	Tracey Buggs	$450	$450	$450	$450	$450	$ 5,400
Salesperson #2	Shea Johnson	450	450	450	450	450	$ 5,400
General and Administration							
President	Monica Davis	Draw	Draw	Draw	Draw	Draw	Draws
Office Manager		0	0	0	0	0	0
Bookkeeper		0	0	0	0	0	0
Total Payroll		$900	$900	$900	$900	$900	$10,800
Payroll Burdon		$144	$144	$144	$144	$144	$1,728
Total Personnel (owner and two part-time)		3	3	3	3	3	3

Operations
Eclectic Interiors by Monica

Operations Summary

Operations Description

Human Resources

Facility

Production

Equipment Schedule

Equipment Description	Manufacturer Name	Model	Serial Number	Date of Purchase	Purchase Price	Monthly Payment	Depreciation Schedule	Useful Life	Maintenance Required
Automobile 1	Toyota	98 Camry		12/01/XX	$14,000	$274	$389	3	
Delivery Van	Ford	91 Aero		12/01/XX	4,200	0	117	3	
Computer	IBM	Aptiva		12/16/XX	1,100	0	18	5	
Printer	HP	820cxi		12/16/XX	325	0	5	5	
Cash Register	Univers	M320		12/16/XX	395	0	7	5	
Fax/Copier	Canon	B640		12/16/XX	380	0	6	5	
Lateral file, steel	Hon	400		12/16/XX	180	0	3	5	
Desk	Hon	Sgl Ped		12/16/XX	250	0	4	5	
Chair	Of. Max	Secr.		12/16/XX	125	0	2	5	
Fixtures				12/16/XX	4,000	0	67	5	
Other furnature				12/16/XX	400	0	7	5	
Sign				12/22/XX	2,200	0	37	5	
Equipment Totals					$27,555	$274	$661		
Leasehold Improvements					2,400		40	5 year lease	
			Total Depreciable Assets		$29,955		$701	Total Depreciation	

Supply and Distribution

Fulfillment

Customer Service Policy

Inventory Control

Efficiency Control

Cash Flow Control

Financial Pro Formas — Eclectic Interiors by Monica

Financial Summary

Using our sales forecast with a market share of 15 percent, total sales for the first year are projected to be $269,892.

When we developed our cash flow pro formas, we learned that our opening cash position of $19,475 would actually be just enough working capital if our first three months of inventory were paid for. Since this is not the case, it is the cost of the merchandise that dictates the amount of outside funds we need to raise. Consequently, our pro formas have been adjusted for a $40,000 loan (see long-term loan proceeds) in January.

Cost of goods sold are projected to be $134,946 — 50 percent of sales after freight adjustments, which is a gross profit margin of 50 percent and the industry standard markup of 50 percent. All other expenses total $83,826. Our total sales to break even during the first year are $167,654 with an operating profit of $51,120 and a net profit of $26,422. This is after paying the owner's income taxes and all other required Federal and state payroll burdens.

For our five-year pro formas, we have planned 10 percent increases in sales commensurate with our industry and our market for well managed start-up companies and 4 percent increases in operating costs, which is consistent with the gross domestic product. With these adjustments, the picture of our net profit margin shows a classic five-year growth sequence for retail businesses: 9.8 percent, 11.3 percent, 12.4 percent, 15.0 percent, and 15.8 percent.

With the merchandise loan, our quick ratio does not exceed 1 until the second year; however, our current ratio is above 2 at the end of the first year and rapidly climbing every year thereafter. With the merchandise loan in place and fully amortized, both our return on assets and return on equity are much above average; and our working capital grows every year and is $60,695 for year five, even after the loan is paid off. Running the business in succeeding years without a loan should prove enough working capital surplus to open another store.

Financial Pro Formas (continued)   Eclectic Interiors by Monica

Important Assumptions   Eclectic Interiors by Monica

	Year 1	Year 2	Year 3	Year 4	Year 5
Market share	15%	Increases 10% annually every year			
Average monthly sales	$22,491	$24,740	$27,214	$29,936	$32,929
Cash sales	100%	100%	100%	100%	100%
Sales on credit	0%	0%	0%	0%	0%
Cost of goods sold	50%	50%	50%	50%	50%
Average monthly costs of goods sold[1]	$11,246	$12,370	$13,607	$14,968	$16,465
Merchandise on-hand	90 days	90 days	90 days	90 days	90 days
Costs of goods sold accounts payable	90%	90%	90%	90%	90%
Costs of goods sold payment days	30 days	30 days	30 days	30 days	30 days
General accounts payable	100%	100%	100%	100%	100%
General payment days	30 days	30 days	30 days	30 days	30 days
Interest rate (long-term)	10.75%	10.75%	10.75%	10.75%	10.75%
Payroll taxes and benefits	16%	16%	16%	16%	16%
Income tax rate and FICA	43%	43%	43%	43%	43%
Hawaii sales tax	4.167%	4.167%	4.167%	4.167%	4.167%
Bank credit card charges[2]	2%	2%	2%	2%	2%
Auto loan – principal portion	$233	$233	$233	0	0
SBA loan – principal portion	$667	$667	$667	$667	$667

---

[1] Freight is included in cost of goods sold.
[2] Actual charge is 3%, 1/3 of sales are by personal checks, travelers' checks, and cash.

These assumptions show that we plan for all cash sales, 90-day merchandise on hand, purchasing mostly on established 30-day credit with 3 percent bank charges for approximately two-thirds of our sales. All freight has been included in our costs of goods sold and our markup and sales are net after returns and allowances. The $50 equipment lease amount in the pro forma income statement is for our credit card terminal. From the bank, we have learned that the current interest rate for our five-year SBA loan is 10.75 percent.

(continued)

Financial Pro Formas (continued)

Eclectic Interiors by Monica

Opening Balance Sheet

Eclectic Interiors by Monica

Assets   November 17, 20XX

Current Assets:		
	Cash in register	$ 175
	Cash in bank	19,300
	Marketable securities	40,000
	Accounts receivable	0
	Other current assets	5,663
Total current assets		65,138
Long-term Assets		
	Depreciable assets	29,955
	Accumulated depreciation	0
	Net depreciable assets	29,955
	Non-depreciable assets	0
Total Long-term Assets		29,955
Total Assets		$95,093

Liabilities and Equity		
Current Liabilities:		
	Cost of goods sold accounts payable	$40,000
	Non-cost of goods sold accounts payable	0
	Taxes payable	0
	Short-term notes payable	0
Total current liabilities		40,000
Long-term Liabilities		8,400
Total Liabilities		48,400
Equity		
	Retained earnings	46,693
Total Equity		46,693
Total Liabilities and Equity		$95,093

First-year Pro Forma Income Statement

Eclectic Interiors by Monica

	Month												Year
	Jan.	Feb.	March	April	May	June	July	Aug.	Sept.	Oct.	Nov.	Dec.	1
Sales	11,502	18,819	18,900	17,739	18,576	12,636	12,690	23,922	20,898	22,491	40,554	51,165	269,892
Costs													
Costs of Goods Sold (1)	5,751	9,410	9,450	8,870	9,288	6,318	6,345	11,961	10,449	11,246	20,277	25,583	134,946
Gross profit	5,751	9,410	9,450	8,870	9,288	6,318	6,345	11,961	10,449	11,246	20,277	25,583	134,946
Marketing and Sales													
Advertising	320	320	320	320	320	320	320	320	320	320	320	320	3,840
Other marketing	140	433	436	390	423	185	188	637	516	580	1,302	1,727	6,956
Total Marketing and Sales (2)	460	753	756	710	743	505	508	957	836	900	1,622	2,047	10,796
General and Administrative Expense													
Sales tax	479	784	788	739	774	527	529	997	871	937	1,690	2,132	11,246
Bank charges	230	376	378	355	372	253	254	478	418	450	811	1,023	5,398
Equipment lease	50	50	50	50	50	50	50	50	50	50	50	50	600
Rent and tripple net expense	1,904	1,904	1,904	1,904	1,904	1,904	1,904	1,904	1,904	1,904	1,904	1,904	22,848
Utilities and telephone	150	150	150	150	150	150	150	150	150	150	150	150	1,800
Auto	274	274	274	274	274	274	274	274	274	274	274	274	3,288
Depreciation	701	701	701	701	701	701	701	701	701	701	701	701	8,412
Payroll	900	900	900	900	900	900	900	900	900	900	900	900	10,800
Payroll taxes and benefits	144	144	144	144	144	144	144	144	144	144	144	144	1,728
Insurance	60	60	60	60	60	60	60	60	60	60	60	60	720
Supplies and postage	150	175	175	170	175	160	160	180	180	180	220	220	2,145
Travel	0	0	300	0	0	300	0	0	300	0	0	300	1,200
Entertainment	50	50	50	50	50	50	50	50	50	50	50	50	600
Legal and accounting	0	0	50	0	0	50	0	0	50	0	0	550	700
Non-income taxes and fees	0	0	0	0	0	0	0	0	0	0	0	45	45
Other operating expenses	125	125	125	125	125	125	125	125	125	125	125	125	1,500
Total G & A Expense (3)	5,217	5,694	6,049	5,622	5,679	5,647	5,301	6,013	6,177	5,925	7,079	8,628	73,030
Total Operating Costs (total rows 1 + 2 + 3)	11,428	15,856	16,255	15,201	15,710	12,471	12,153	18,931	17,462	18,070	28,978	36,257	218,772
Operating Profit	74	2,963	2,645	2,538	2,866	165	537	4,991	3,436	4,421	11,576	14,908	51,120
Interest Expense	432	425	419	413	407	400	394	388	382	375	369	362	4,766
Profit Before Income Taxes	(358)	2,538	2,226	2,125	2,459	(235)	143	4,603	3,054	4,046	11,207	14,546	46,354
Income Taxes and Owners FICA	(154)	1,091	957	914	1,058	(101)	61	1,979	1,313	1,740	4,819	6,255	19,932
Net Profit	(204)	1,447	1,269	1,211	1,402	(134)	81	2,624	1,741	2,306	6,388	8,291	26,422

Financial Pro Formas (continued) — Eclectic Interiors by Monica

Five-year Pro Forma Income Statement — Eclectic Interiors by Monica

	Year 1	2	3	4	5
Sales	269,892	296,881	326,569	359,226	395,149
Costs					
Costs of Goods Sold (1)	134,946	148,441	163,285	179,613	197,574
Gross profit	134,946	148,441	163,285	179,613	197,574
Marketing and Sales					
Advertising	3,840	3,994	4,153	4,319	4,492
Other marketing	6,956	7,235	7,525	7,826	8,139
Total Marketing and Sales (2)	10,796	11,229	11,678	12,145	12,631
General and Administrative Expense					
Sales tax	11,246	12,371	13,608	14,969	16,466
Bank charges	5,398	5,938	6,531	7,185	7,903
Equipment lease	600	600	600	600	600
Rent and tripple net expense	22,848	22,848	22,848	22,848	22,848
Utilities and telephone	1,800	1,872	1,947	2,025	2,106
Auto	3,288	3,288	3,288	0	0
Depreciation	8,412	8,412	8,412	2,009	2,009
Payroll	10,800	11,232	11,681	12,149	12,634
Payroll taxes and benefits	1,728	1,797	1,869	1,944	2,022
Insurance	720	720	720	720	720
Supplies and postage	2,145	2,231	2,320	2,413	2,509
Travel	1,200	1,248	1,298	1,350	1,404
Entertainment	600	624	649	675	702
Legal and accounting	700	728	757	787	819
Non-income taxes and fees	45	45	45	45	45
Other operating expenses	1,500	1,560	1,622	1,687	1,755
Total G & A Expense (3)	73,030	75,514	78,196	71,405	74,541
Total Operating Costs (total rows 1 + 2 + 3)	218,772	235,183	253,159	263,163	284,747
Operating Profit	51,120	61,698	73,411	96,063	110,402
Interest Expense	4,766	3,493	2,638	1,782	927
Profit Before Income Taxes	46,476	58,205	70,773	94,281	109,475
Income Taxes and Owners FICA	19,985	25,028	30,432	40,541	47,074
Net Profit	26,491	33,177	40,340	53,740	62,401

Break-even Analysis — Eclectic Interiors by Monica

	Year 1	2	3	4	5
Total Sales	269,892	296,881	326,569	359,226	395,149
Break-even Sales	167,654	173,486	179,746	167,102	174,344

Appendix B – Business Plan Differences for Retail and Wholesale Businesses 277

First-year Pro Forma Statement of Cash Flow

Eclectic Interiors by Monica

Month	Jan.	Feb.	March	April	May	June	July	Aug.	Sept.	Oct.	Nov.	Dec.
Starting Cash Position	19,475	25,955	33,738	37,303	34,080	33,884	26,807	29,002	34,912	17,122	20,296	28,323
Cash Receipts (sources of cash)												
Cash sales	11,502	18,819	18,900	17,739	18,576	12,636	12,690	23,922	20,898	22,491	40,554	51,165
Sales on credit	0	0	0	0	0	0	0	0	0	0	0	0
Short-term loan proceeds	0	0	0	0	0	0	0	0	0	0	0	0
Long-term loan proceeds	40,000	0	0	0	0	0	0	0	0	0	0	0
Equity capital proceeds	0	0	0	0	0	0	0	0	0	0	0	0
Total Cash Receipts	51,502	18,819	18,900	17,739	18,576	12,636	12,690	23,922	20,898	22,491	40,554	51,165
Cash Disbursements (uses of cash)												
Merchandise	40,000	339	4,009	9,326	7,471	9,488	383	6,332	26,519	6,685	17,010	46,783
Payroll	900	900	900	900	900	900	900	900	900	900	900	900
Payroll taxes and benefits	144	144	144	144	144	144	144	144	144	144	144	144
Non-payroll expenses	0	3,932	4,701	5,060	4,587	4,677	4,408	4,064	5,225	5,268	5,080	6,956
Depreciable asset purchases	0	0	0	0	0	0	0	0	0	0	0	0
Non-depreciable asset purchases	0	0	0	0	0	0	0	0	0	0	0	0
Interest	432	425	419	413	407	400	394	388	382	375	369	362
Owner's draw	3,500	3,500	3,500	3,500	3,500	3,500	3,500	3,500	3,500	3,500	3,500	3,500
Short-term liabilities payments	0	0	0	0	0	0	0	0	0	0	0	0
Long-term liabilities payments	200	705	705	705	705	705	705	705	705	705	705	705
Total Cash Disbursements	45,176	9,945	14,378	20,048	17,714	19,814	10,434	16,033	37,375	17,577	27,708	59,350
Income taxes	(154)	1,091	957	914	1,058	(101)	61	1,979	1,313	1,740	4,819	6,255
Total Cash Disbursements After Taxes	45,022	11,036	15,335	20,962	18,772	19,713	10,495	18,012	38,688	19,317	32,527	65,605
Net Change In Cash	6,480	7,783	3,565	(3,223)	(196)	(7,077)	2,195	5,910	(17,790)	3,174	8,027	(14,440)
Ending Cash Position	25,955	33,738	37,303	34,080	33,884	26,807	29,002	34,912	17,122	20,296	28,323	13,883

First-year and Five-year Pro Forma Balance Sheets

Eclectic Interiors by Monica

	Quarter 1	Quarter 2	Quarter 3	Year 1	Year 2	Year 3	Year 4	Year 5
Assets								
Current Assets								
Cash - on hand	175	175	175	175	175	175	175	175
Cash - in banks	37,128	26,633	16,948	13,709	12,303	11,972	14,897	26,494
Merchandise	28,350	21,546	31,347	76,749	37,110	40,821	44,903	49,394
Other current assets	5,663	5,663	5,663	5,663	5,663	5,663	5,663	5,663
Total Current Assets	71,316	54,017	54,133	96,296	55,251	58,631	65,638	81,726
Long-term Assets								
Depreciable assets	29,955	29,955	29,955	29,955	29,955	29,955	29,955	29,955
Accumulated depreciation	2,103	4,206	6,309	8,412	16,824	25,236	27,245	29,254
Net depreciable assets	27,852	25,749	23,646	21,543	13,131	4,719	2,710	701
Non-depreciable assets	0	0	0	0	0	0	0	0
Total Long-term Assets	27,852	25,749	23,646	21,543	13,131	4,719	2,710	701
Total Assets	99,168	79,766	77,779	117,839	68,382	63,350	68,348	82,427
Liabilities and Equity								
Current Liabilities								
Cost of goods sold accounts payable	8,613	0	5,322	37,351	8,150	12,525	13,777	15,155
Non-cost of goods sold accounts payable	5,060	4,408	5,268	8,930	5,442	5,659	5,621	5,876
Taxes payable	0	0	0	0	0	0	0	0
Short-term notes payable	0	0	0	0	0	0	0	0
Total Current Liabilities	13,673	4,408	10,590	46,281	13,602	18,184	19,398	21,031
Long-term Liabilities	46,790	44,675	42,560	40,445	32,490	24,535	16,580	8,625
Total Liabilities	60,463	49,083	53,150	86,726	46,092	42,719	35,978	29,656
Equity								
Retained earnings	38,705	30,683	24,629	31,113	22,290	20,631	32,370	52,771
Total Equity	38,705	30,683	24,629	31,113	22,290	20,631	32,370	52,771
Total Liabilities and Equity	99,168	79,766	77,779	117,839	68,382	63,350	68,348	82,427

Financial Pro Formas – Business Ratios — Eclectic Interiors by Monica

Key Business Ratios	Year 1	Year 2	Year 3	Year 4	Year 5
Quick ratio	0.42	1.33	0.98	1.07	1.54
Current ratio	2.08	4.06	3.22	3.38	3.89
Debt to assets	0.74	0.67	0.67	0.53	0.36
Debt to equity	2.79	2.07	2.07	1.11	0.56
Sales to assets	2.29	4.34	5.16	5.26	4.79
Working capital	$50,016	$41,649	$40,447	$46,241	$60,695
Gross profit margin	50%	50%	50%	50%	50%
Net profit margin	9.8%	11.3%	12.4%	15.0%	15.8%
Return on assets	22%	49%	64%	79%	76%
Return on equity	85%	149%	196%	166%	118%

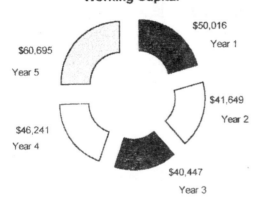

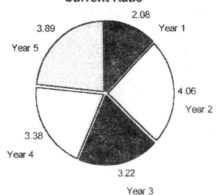

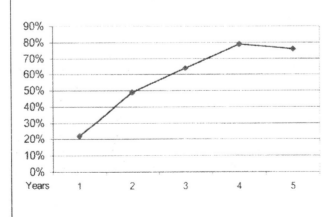

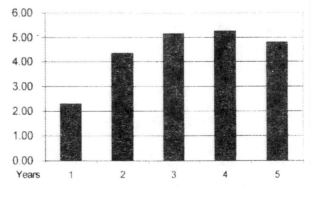

Loan Request
Eclectic Interiors by Monica

Loan Request Summary

Our total start-up costs are $95,093. To date, we have raised $55,093 in owner's funds including $8,400 from an auto loan and $46,693 in cash of which we still have $19,475 on hand for working capital. The difference between the start-up costs and the capital raised is $40,000 — which is the cost of our unpaid merchandise for a three-month inventory.

To cover this, we are seeking an SBA loan for a minority start-up company for the full amount of the merchandise, $40,000 for five years, to be fully amortized at the quoted rate of 10.75 percent (3 percent over current prime rate). While the merchandise represents hard collateral at one-half its retail value, we fully expect the bank to secure the business assets with a blanket security interest for the life of the loan.

We will need the funds by the end of January to pay off our merchandise.

Our pro forma financial statements in the last section show that we can begin making payments of $864.72 ($507 principal) in February. As a backup plan, the owner's personal financial statement shows marketable securities worth $120,000 which Dr. and Mrs. Davis are willing to pledge $40,000 of these to repay the debt should the SBA loan default.

Start-up Costs

Description	Total Estimated	Actual Paid	Date Paid	Balance to Pay	Date Needed
Initial lease/purchase	$ 1,904	$ 1,904	12/01/XX	$	Existing loan
Lease deposit	1,904	1,904	12/01/XX		
Utilities deposit	260	260	11/30/XX		
Licenses and fees	45	45	12/10/XX		
Leasehold improvements	2,400	2,400	12/23/XX		
Insurance	0	0			
Vehicle 1	14,000	5,600	11/28/XX	8,400	Existing loan
Vehicle 2	4,200	4,200	12/15/XX		
Fixtures	4,000	4,000	12/26/XX		
Other Equipment	3,155	3,155	12/27/XX		
Merchandise	40,000			40,000	1/15/XX
Supplies	350	350	12/29/XX		
Signage	2,200	2,200	12/21/XX		
Pre-opening Advertising	1,200	1,200	12/15/XX		
Working capital	19,475	19,475	in bank		
Totals	$95,093	$46,693		$48,400	

The major expenses of the start-up costs are inventory, $40,000; working capital, $19,475; vehicles, $18,200; leasehold improvements, fixtures, and office equipment, $9,555; prepaid rent and deposit, $3,808; and our sign, $2,200.

Loan Request (continued) — Eclectic Interiors by Monica

Funds Raised and Funds Needed

To date, the owner has raised $55,903 in capital consisting of $8,400 in the form of an auto loan against the company's Toyota Camry and $46,693 in cash which has been used either in prepaid pre-opening expenses, $27,218, or reserved in cash for operating capital, $19,475 ($19,300 in the bank and $175 on hand). The difference between the funds raised and the total start-up costs, $95,093, represents the funds needed, $40,000, which is the cost of our merchandise for inventory.

Loan Request Proposal — Eclectic Interiors

Hard Costs

Facility/site	Leased
Leasehold improvements	$ 2,400.00
Vehicle #1	14,000.00
Vehicle #2	4,200.00
Fixtures	4,000.00
Equipment	3,155.00
Merchandise	40,000.00
Signage	2,200.00
Total Hard Costs	**$69,955.00**

Soft Costs

Deposits and prepaid rent	$ 4,068.00
Licenses and fees	45.00
Supplies	350.00
Pre-opening advertising	1,200.00
Working capital	19,475.00
Total Soft Costs	**$25,138.00**

Total Start-up Funds	**$95,093.00**
Less our cash investment	55,093.00
Loan Amount Needed	**$40,000.00**

Loan Requested: SBA-guaranteed loan for minority start-up business owner for $40,000 net to borrower, at 10.75 percent interest rate (3 percent over prime rate) fully amortized over 5 years with loan fee of 2 points based on 80 percent of loan.

Remarks: We request net proceeds of $40,000.00 to be disbursed in January with first payment due in February; and further, we request a waiver of any pre-payment penalty for early loan payoff.

Collateral: For collateral we anticipate and pre-approve the bank to secure this loan with 100 percent of the business assets.

(continued)

Loan Request (continued) — Eclectic Interiors by Monica

Potential Risks

For every business, there are associated risks. Our major risks are:

- Natural disaster, especially hurricanes and tsunamis in our location. Although we have insurance to cover these for loss and damage, either disaster could interrupt our day-to-day business and cause us to fall short of our sales forecast for the month of the occurrence.
- Economic downturn, especially for a business selling mostly luxury items to upper-middle class buyers. Although our Industry Analysis shows the economy is in an upswing in Hawaii and should remain so over the next five years, we will prepare to weather a downturn by upgrading to higher end-users who are not as easily affected by market fluctuations.
- Start-up company uncertainties while developing our market, managing our inventory, managing cash flow, and generating our sales presence pose numerous risks. We believe these can be mitigated with a carefully designed and professionally executed business plan. For its execution, we are fortunate to have the experience and proven-track record of Monica Davis, as shown in the Management and Organization segment. Her wealth of experience and success in the antique and interior design industries, salesmanship, and accounting and financial business management provide a solid foundation for this business.
- Missing our sales projection. With a sales break-even of 62 percent of total sales, this is a higher protection than most businesses have and is due in part to the strong profit margin ratio of 50 percent.
- Illness of the main operator. Two strategies have been designed for this event. While Monica's health is excellent, if she were to become ill and unable to work a few days, her husband, Dr. Davis, is prepared to fill in. As joint owner, Dr. Davis has been involved in every aspect of the business and has been responsible for setting up all credit accounts with suppliers. If Monica is ill for a lengthy period, an independent interior designer, Marlene Lathrop, has agreed to fill in for the owner's draw as compensation, see résumés in the exhibits.

Exit Options

Our long-range exit option includes the growth plan as detailed in Strategies and Goals. After we have opened and successfully operated ten stores, it is a strong possibility that one of the larger furniture chains on the mainland will be interested in buying us out to have additional stores in Hawaii. When that time comes, we will actively market our stores with the same energy as we market our products.

Business Plan Exhibits — Eclectic Interiors by Monica

Industry Research

Personal financial statements

SBA Application

List of Supplier Agreements

List of Letters of Intent of Presales

Résumé of Marlene Lathrop

Appendix C

Business Plan Differences for Service Businesses

This abbreviated plan is for Room Service, Ltd. It is a small service business that contracts with various popular restaurants to take orders for carry-out meals, pick them up, and deliver them by dispatching company drivers in company vans. Dispatched drivers have routes and, if both the restaurant and the customer are within the same route, the meals are delivered directly from the source to the customer. In cases where the restaurants and the customers are not in the same route, meals picked up are first taken to Room Service, Ltd. headquarters for redistribution. There they may be held briefly for a second dispatch and delivery by the driver of the appropriate route to the waiting customer.

The first significant difference in developing a business plan for this type of middle-man service appears in section eight, the sales forecast. Notice direct costs (the term for costs of sale for service businesses) are set at zero. Because mileage and driver time for each order is too cumbersome to track and assign to each sale, all vehicle and driver expenses are tracked as general and administrative expenses. You can see this best in the financial pro formas.

In Section 10, Financial Pro Formas, the important five-year assumptions explain the company's anticipated sales comprising 50 percent cash (upon delivery) and 50 percent credit. However, credit sales, like room service charges, are signed for and paid later (in this case, within 30 days by check). Note cash sales are 50 percent, sales on credit are 50 percent, and collection days are 30. Again, direct costs are zero.

In the financial statements, the opening balance sheet shows a large depreciable assets account because of the high number of company vehicles. The account for non-direct costs accounts payable is equal to the start-up costs stated in the opening financial summary. The first- and five-year pro forma income statements and the pro forma cash flow are set up as typical for service companies, where *direct costs* replaces *cost of sales*. In this case, all the entries in the row are zero. This results in gross profit equaling sales on the pro forma income statement. All expenses are either categorized as marketing or general and administrative.

The pro forma cash flow shows that the company has correctly planned for the loan they seek, as can be seen by the account "home-equity loan proceeds" where $35,000 is to be disbursed in January, with offsetting monthly principal payments of $200 starting in February. The long-term liability payments are principal payments toward the company's initial equipment loan for vehicles.

While the five-year pro forma income statement shows a rapid growth in sales, this appears consistent with the assumptions of adding delivery vans and delivery personnel, and clearly shows the advantageous results expected on the pro forma balance sheets. All business ratios are strong and if the working capital turns out as liquid as Room Service, Ltd. forecasts, this company would be wise to learn more about increasing capital investments.

Room Service, Ltd.
Honolulu, Hawaii

Business Plan

Confidential Information

Prepared for:
Mr. Mark S. Yates
Home Mortgage Loans
Bank of Hawaii
815 Bishop Street
Honolulu, Hawaii 96813-2202

Prepared by:
John Clark
(800) 555-9991
e-mail: RoomService@aol.com

November 17, 20XX

Contents

1. Executive Summary
2. Company Description
3. Industry Analysis
4. Market and Competition
5. Strategies and Goals
6. Services
7. Marketing and Sales
8. Management and Organization
9. Operations
10. Financial Pro Formas
11. Loan Request
12. Exhibits

1. Executive Summary   Room Service, Ltd.

- Business Concept
- Progress Status
- Keys to Success
- Financial Overview

2. Company Description   Room Service, Ltd.

- Name and Business Concept
- Ownership and Legal
- Leadership and Location
- Geographic Sales Area
- Current Status and Milestones

3. Industry Analysis   Room Service, Ltd.

- Industry Analysis Summary
- Industry Description
- Industry Size and Maturation
- Industry Trends and Impact Factors
- Industry Standards
- Industry Obstacles
- Industry Opportunities

4. Market and Competition
Room Service, Ltd.

Market and Competition Summary

Market Description – Segments and Target Markets

Market Size and Trends

Competition Identification

Main Competitors

Competitor Analysis

Market Share

Customer Needs

Market Obstacles

Market Opportunities

5. Strategies and Goals
Room Service, Ltd.

Strategies and Goals Summary

Long-range Goals and Strategies

Strategy Implementation

6. Services
Room Service, Ltd.

Services Summary

Services Description

Services Positioning

Comparison with the Competition

Technology and Intellectual Protection

Future Services

7. Marketing and Sales

Room Service, Ltd.

    Marketing and Sales Summary

    Marketing Strategy

    Marketing Plan

    Marketing Budget

    Sales Force and Forecast

Sales Forecast

Net Sales	January	February	March	April	May	June
Delivery Units	1,619	3,239	4,800	5,200	6,500	8,500
Total Net Sales $	40,482	80,964	120,000	130,000	162,500	212,500
Direct Costs						
Total Direct Costs	0	0	0	0	0	0
Total Gross Profit $	40,482	80,964	120,000	130,000	162,500	212,500

Net Sales	July	August	September	October	November	December
Delivery Units	6,500	6,500	8,535	16,320	18,456	21,783
Total Net Sales $	162,500	162,500	213,375	408,000	461,400	544,575
Direct Costs						
Total Direct Costs	0	0	0	0	0	0
Total Gross Profit $	162,500	162,500	213,375	408,000	461,400	544,575

Year-end Totals   Units Delivered: $107,652   Net Sales: $2,698,796   Gross Profit: $2,698,796

8. Management and Organization

Room Service, Ltd.

    Management and Organization Summary

    Management Team

    Key Personnel Responsibilities and Duties

    Management Philosophy

    Key Personnel Incentives

    Organizational Structure

    Personnel Plan

9. Operations
Room Service, Ltd.

Operations Summary

Operations Description

Human Resources

Facility

Production

Supply and Distribution

Fulfillment

Customer Service Policy

Inventory Control

Efficiency Control

Cash Flow Control

10. Financial Pro Formas
Room Service, Ltd.

Financial Summary

Using our sales forecast with a market share of 23 percent, total sales for the first year are projected to be $2,698,796.

Although we still owe $57,705 of our start-up costs, from developing our cash flow pro formas we learned that our opening cash position of $24,385 together with our first months' sales would only fall short $32,000 for our company to have enough working capital to launch our business. Therefore, we are seeking a loan for $35,000 and have adjusted our pro formas to show the net proceeds as home-equity loan proceeds which will cover our working capital shortfall and the financing costs of the loan.

Direct costs for our service company are negligible and unrealistic to assign, so every expense is shown as either a marketing expense or a general and administrative expense. Our total operating expenses are $1,611,373, which in this case with zero direct costs, are our sales to break even during the first year. Our first-year operating profit is projected at $1,087,423 and our net profit (after taxes) at $694,150. For our five-year pro formas, we have planned 7 percent sales increases which is conservatively appropriate from our market analysis for a well-managed start-up company in this industry. For increases in costs, our lease has a built-in term of 6 percent increases and other operating costs have been adjusted with 4 percent increases, consistent with the gross domestic product. With these adjustments, the picture of our net profit margin shows a textbook five-year growth pattern for service businesses: 25.7 percent, 26.6 percent, 27.3 percent, 27.8 percent, and 29.4 percent.

10. Financial Pro Formas (continued)   Room Service, Ltd.

Although our president's personal home-equity loan is being requested for fifteen years, the funds are being used for the business with the intention of being paid back within one year. Because of this our accountant is treating the loan as a short-term loan in our pro formas. After the home-equity loan is paid off in December, all ratios look strong, especially the quick and current ratios. Return on assets and return on equity come together at 24 percent by the end of year five. At that time our working capital would be a whopping $4,396,527 if we continue with a conservative approach to growth shown by these pro formas.

Important Assumptions

These assumptions show that we plan for 50 percent cash sales because we will offer accounts receivable for regular customers, approximately 50 percent on credit. While we have no assigned direct costs, all expenses will be on 30-day credit which we have established. Cash sales will be either cash or check as is customary with food delivery, so there are no credit card charges. With the annual increases in sales we have added more trucks and employees to compensate for the additional deliveries.

Important Assumptions for Financial Pro Formas   Room Service, Ltd.

	Years				
	First	Second	Third	Fourth	Fifth
Market share	22.72%	Increases 7% annually every year			
Average monthly sales	$244,900	$240,643	$257,488	$275,512	$294,798
Cash sales	50%	50%	50%	50%	50%
Sales on credit	50%	50%	50%	50%	50%
Collection days	30	30	30	30	30
Direct costs	0%	0%	0%	0%	0%
General accounts payable	100%	100%	100%	100%	100%
General payment days	30	30	30	30	30
Interest rate (equity home loan)	9%	9%	9%	9%	9%
Interest (long term)	11%	11%	11%	11%	11%
Income tax rate	35%	35%	35%	35%	35%
Rent	$72,000	Increases 6% annually every year			
Delivery people	17	18	19	21	22
Delivery vans	17	18	19	21	22

(continued)

10. Financial Pro Formas (continued)   Room Service, Ltd.

Opening Balance Sheet   Room Service, Ltd.

Assets	November 17, 2000
Current Assets:	
Cash	$24,385
Marketable securities	0
Accounts receivable	0
Other current assets	21,330
Total current assets	45,715
Long-term Assets	
Depreciable assets	211,875
Accumulated depreciation	0
Net depreciable assets	211,875
Non-depreciable assets	0
Total Long-term Assets	211,875
Total Assets	**$257,590**

Liabilities and Equity	
Current Liabilities:	
Direct costs accounts payable	$ 0
Non-direct costs accounts payable	57,705
Taxes payable	0
Short-term notes payable	0
Total current liabilities	0
Long-term Liabilities	175,500
Ford Ranger (3 years) $16,000	
Taxes payable $26,400	
Total Liabilities	**233,205**
Equity	
Shareholders equity	0
Retained earnings	24,385
Total Equity	24,385
Total Liabilities and Equity	**$257,590**

First-year Pro Forma Income Statement

Room Service, Ltd.

	Month Jan.	Feb.	March	April	May	June	July	Aug.	Sept.	Oct.	Nov.	Dec.	Year 1
Sales	40,482	80,964	120,000	130,000	162,500	212,500	162,500	162,500	213,375	408,000	461,400	544,575	2,698,796
Costs													
Direct Costs (1)	0	0	0	0	0	0	0	0	0	0	0	0	0
Gross profit	40,482	80,964	120,000	130,000	162,500	212,500	162,500	162,500	213,375	408,000	461,400	544,575	2,698,796
Marketing and Sales													
Mailings	1,214	2,429	3,600	3,900	4,875	6,375	4,875	4,875	6,401	12,240	13,842	16,337	80,964
Advertising	4,858	9,716	14,400	15,600	19,500	25,500	19,500	19,500	25,605	48,960	55,368	65,349	323,855
Other marketing	2,024	4,048	6,000	6,500	8,125	10,625	8,125	8,125	10,669	20,400	23,070	27,229	134,940
Total Marketing and Sales (2)	8,096	16,193	24,000	26,000	32,500	42,500	32,500	32,500	42,675	81,600	92,280	108,915	539,759
General and Administrative Expense													
Rent	6,000	6,000	6,000	6,000	6,000	6,000	6,000	6,000	6,000	6,000	6,000	6,000	72,000
Utilities and telephone	3,000	3,000	3,000	3,000	3,000	3,000	3,000	3,000	3,000	3,000	3,000	3,000	36,000
Payroll	40,145	40,145	40,145	40,145	40,145	40,145	40,145	40,145	40,145	40,145	40,145	40,145	481,740
Payroll taxes and benefits	6,423	6,423	6,423	6,423	6,423	6,423	6,423	6,423	6,423	6,423	6,423	6,423	77,078
Auto payments	4,407	4,407	4,407	4,407	4,407	4,407	4,407	4,407	4,407	4,407	4,407	4,407	52,884
Auto expenses	6,000	6,000	6,000	6,000	6,000	6,000	6,000	6,000	6,000	6,000	6,000	6,000	72,000
Depreciation	5,698	5,698	5,698	5,698	5,698	5,698	5,698	5,698	5,698	5,698	5,698	5,698	68,376
Maintenance and repairs	2,000	2,000	2,000	2,000	2,000	2,000	2,000	2,000	2,000	2,000	2,000	2,000	24,000
Insurance	4,500	4,500	4,500	4,500	4,500	4,500	4,500	4,500	4,500	4,500	4,500	4,500	54,000
Supplies and postage	7,683	7,683	7,683	7,683	7,683	7,683	7,683	7,683	7,683	7,683	7,683	7,683	92,196
Travel and entertainment	0	0	0	0	0	0	0	0	0	0	0	0	0
Legal and accounting	1,400	1,400	1,400	1,400	1,400	1,400	1,400	1,400	1,400	1,400	1,400	1,400	16,800
Other outside services	500	500	500	500	500	500	500	500	500	500	500	500	6,000
Non-income taxes and fees	545	545	545	545	545	545	545	545	545	545	545	545	6,540
Other operating expenses	1,000	1,000	1,000	1,000	1,000	1,000	1,000	1,000	1,000	1,000	1,000	1,000	12,000
Total G & A Expense (3)	89,301	89,301	89,301	89,301	89,301	89,301	89,301	89,301	89,301	89,301	89,301	89,301	1,071,614
Total Operating Costs (total rows 1 + 2 + 3)	97,397	105,494	113,301	115,301	121,801	131,801	121,801	121,801	131,976	170,901	181,581	198,216	1,611,373
Operating Profit	(56,915)	(24,530)	6,699	14,699	40,699	80,699	40,699	40,699	81,399	237,099	279,819	346,359	1,087,423
Interest Expense	1,838	1,803	1,768	1,733	1,698	1,663	1,628	1,593	1,558	1,523	1,488	1,207	19,500
Profit Before Income Taxes	(58,753)	(26,333)	4,931	12,966	39,001	79,036	39,071	39,106	79,841	235,576	278,331	345,152	1,067,923
Income Taxes and Owners FICA	(20,564)	(9,217)	1,726	4,538	13,650	27,663	13,675	13,687	27,944	82,452	97,416	120,803	373,773
Net Profit	(38,190)	(17,117)	3,205	8,428	25,351	51,373	25,396	25,419	51,897	153,124	180,915	224,349	694,150

10. Financial Pro Formas (continued)　　　　　　　　　　　　　　Room Service, Ltd.

Five-year Pro Forma Income Statement　　　　　　　　　　　　　　Room Service, Ltd.

	Year 1	Year 2	Year 3	Year 4	Year 5
Sales	2,698,796	2,887,712	3,089,852	3,306,141	3,537,571
Costs					
Direct Costs (1)	0	0	0	0	0
Gross profit	2,698,796	2,887,712	3,089,852	3,306,141	3,537,571
Marketing and Sales					
Mailings	80,964	86,631	92,696	99,184	106,127
Advertising	323,855	346,525	370,782	396,737	424,508
Other marketing	134,940	144,386	154,493	165,307	176,879
Total Marketing and Sales (2)	539,759	577,542	617,970	661,228	707,514
General and Administrative Expense					
Rent	72,000	76,320	80,899	85,753	90,898
Utilities and telephone	36,000	37,440	38,938	40,495	42,115
Payroll	481,740	502,885	524,950	550,004	574,033
Payroll taxes and benefits	77,078	80,462	83,992	88,001	91,845
Auto payments	52,884	52,884	52,884	52,884	0
Auto expenses	72,000	74,880	77,875	80,990	84,230
Depreciation	68,376	75,048	81,720	95,064	101,736
Maintenance and repairs	24,000	24,960	25,958	26,997	28,077
Insurance	54,000	56,160	58,406	60,743	63,172
Supplies and postage	92,196	95,884	99,719	103,708	107,856
Travel and entertainment	0	0	0	0	0
Legal and accounting	16,800	17,472	18,171	18,898	19,654
Other outside services	6,000	6,240	6,490	6,749	7,019
Non-income taxes and fees	6,540	6,802	7,074	7,357	7,651
Other operating expenses	12,000	12,480	12,979	13,498	14,038
Total G & A Expense (3)	1,071,614	1,119,916	1,170,055	1,231,140	1,232,325
Total Operating Costs (total rows 1 + 2 + 3)	1,611,373	1,697,458	1,788,025	1,892,368	1,939,839
Operating Profit	1,087,423	1,190,254	1,301,826	1,413,773	1,597,732
Interest Expense	19,500	9,653	4,827	0	0
Profit Before Income Taxes	1,067,923	1,180,601	1,296,999	1,413,773	1,597,732
Income Taxes and Owners FICA	373,773	413,210	453,950	494,820	559,206
Net Profit	694,150	767,390	843,049	918,952	1,038,526

Break-even Analysis　　　　　　　　　　　　　　　　　　　　　　　Room Service, Ltd.

	Year 1	Year 2	Year 3	Year 4	Year 5
Total Sales	2,698,796	2,887,712	3,089,852	3,306,141	3,537,571
Break-even Sales	1,611,371	1,697,459	1,788,026	1,892,369	1,939,837

First-year Pro Forma Statement of Cash Flow

Room Service, Ltd.

Month	Jan.	Feb.	March	April	May	June	July	Aug.	Sept.	Oct.	Nov.	Dec.
Starting Cash Position	24,385	10,664	3,486	16,340	28,610	62,303	125,518	142,756	170,017	233,931	427,822	621,259
Cash Receipts (sources of cash)												
Cash sales	40,482	80,964	120,000	130,000	162,500	212,500	162,500	162,500	213,375	408,000	461,400	544,575
Sales on credit	0	0	0	0	0	0	0	0	0	0	0	0
Home-equity loan proceeds	35,000	0	0	0	0	0	0	0	0	0	0	0
Long-term loan proceeds	0	0	0	0	0	0	0	0	0	0	0	0
Equity capital proceeds	0	0	0	0	0	0	0	0	0	0	0	0
Total Cash Receipts	75,482	80,964	120,000	130,000	162,500	212,500	162,500	162,500	213,375	408,000	461,400	544,575
Cash Disbursements (uses of cash)												
Direct costs	0	0	0	0	0	0	0	0	0	0	0	0
Payroll	40,145	40,145	40,145	40,145	40,145	40,145	40,145	40,145	40,145	40,145	40,145	40,145
Payroll taxes and benefits	6,423	6,423	6,423	6,423	6,423	6,423	6,423	6,423	6,423	6,423	6,423	6,423
Non-payroll expenses	57,705	45,131	53,228	61,035	63,035	69,535	79,535	69,535	69,535	79,710	118,635	129,315
Depreciable asset purchases	0	0	0	0	0	0	0	0	0	0	0	0
Non-depreciable asset purchases	0	0	0	0	0	0	0	0	0	0	0	0
Interest	1,838	1,803	1,768	1,733	1,698	1,663	1,628	1,593	1,558	1,523	1,488	1,207
Owner's draw	0	0	0	0	0	0	0	0	0	0	0	0
Home-equity loan payments	0	200	200	200	200	200	200	200	200	200	200	33,000
Long-term liabilites payments	3,656	3,656	3,656	3,656	3,656	3,656	3,656	3,656	3,656	3,656	3,656	3,656
Total Cash Disbursements	109,767	97,358	105,420	113,192	115,157	121,622	131,587	121,552	121,517	131,657	170,547	213,746
Income taxes	(20,564)	(9,216)	1,726	4,538	13,650	27,663	13,675	13,687	27,944	82,452	97,416	120,803
Total Cash Disbursements After Taxes	89,203	88,142	107,146	117,730	128,807	149,285	145,262	135,239	149,461	214,109	267,963	334,549
Net Change In Cash	(13,721)	(7,178)	12,854	12,270	33,693	63,215	17,238	27,261	63,914	193,891	193,437	210,026
Ending Cash Position	10,664	3,486	16,340	28,610	62,303	125,518	142,756	170,017	233,931	427,822	621,259	831,285

First-year and Five-year Pro Forma Balance Sheets

Room Service Ltd.

	Quarter 1	Quarter 2	Quarter 3	Year 1	Year 2	Year 3	Year 4	Year 5
Assets								
Current Assets								
Cash	16,341	125,520	233,934	831,389	1,550,494	2,416,249	3,351,543	4,472,882
Marketable securities	0	0	0	0	0	0	0	0
Accounts receivable	0	0	0	0	0	0	0	0
Other current assets	21,330	21,330	21,330	21,330	21,330	21,330	21,330	21,330
Total Current Assets	37,671	146,850	255,264	852,719	1,571,824	2,437,579	3,372,873	4,494,212
Long-term Assets								
Depreciable assets	211,875	211,875	211,875	211,875	231,875	251,875	291,875	311,875
Accumulated depreciation	17,094	34,188	51,282	68,376	143,424	225,144	320,208	421,944
Net depreciable assets	194,781	177,687	160,593	143,499	88,451	26,731	(28,333)	(110,069)
Non-depreciable assets	0	0	0	0	0	0	0	0
Total Long-term Assets	194,781	177,687	160,593	143,499	88,451	26,731	(28,333)	(110,069)
	232,452	324,537	415,857	996,218	1,660,275	2,464,310	3,344,540	4,384,143
Liabilities and Equity								
Current Liabilities								
Direct costs accounts payable	0	0	0	0	0	0	0	0
Non-direct costs accounts payable	61,035	79,535	79,710	145,950	86,589	91,447	96,608	97,685
Taxes payable	0	0	0	0	0	0	0	0
Home-equity loan liability (11 mo.)	34,600	34,000	33,400	0	0	0	0	0
Total Current Liabilities	95,635	113,535	113,110	145,950	86,589	91,447	96,608	97,685
Long-term Liabilities	40,849	39,298	37,747	36,196	30,860	25,524	24,648	23,772
Total Liabilities	136,484	152,833	150,857	182,146	117,449	116,971	121,256	121,457
Equity								
Stock & paid-in capital	24,385	24,385	24,385	24,385	24,385	24,385	24,385	24,385
Retained earnings	(52,100)	33,053	135,766	694,155	1,461,545	2,304,594	3,223,546	4,262,073
Total Equity	95,968	171,704	265,000	814,072	1,542,826	2,347,339	3,223,284	4,262,686
Total Liabilities and Equity	232,452	324,537	415,857	996,218	1,660,275	2,464,310	3,344,540	4,384,143

10. Financial Pro Formas – Business Ratios   Room Service, Ltd.

	Year				
Key Business Ratios	1	2	3	4	5
Quick ratio	5.84	18.15	26.66	34.91	46.01
Current ratio	5.84	18.15	26.66	34.91	46.01
Debt to assets	0.28	0.11	0.05	0.03	0.02
Debt to equity	0.39	0.12	0.06	0.03	0.02
Sales to assets	2.71	1.74	1.25	0.99	0.81
Working capital	$706,669	$1,485,235	$2,346,132	$3,276,264	$4,396,527
Gross profit margin	100%	100%	100%	100%	100%
Net profit margin	25.7%	26.6%	27.3%	27.8%	29.4%
Return on assets	51%	48%	41%	36%	31%
Return on equity	97%	52%	36%	28%	24%

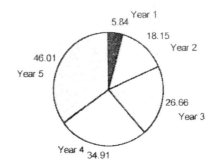

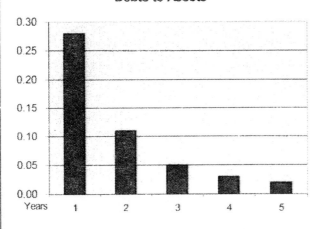

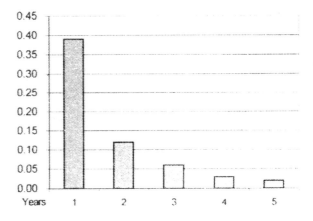

11. Loan Request   Room Service, Ltd.

Loan Request Summary

Start-up Costs

Funds Raised and Funds Needed

Loan Request Proposal

Potential Risks

Exit Options

---

12. Exhibits   Room Service, Ltd.

A. Industry Research

B. Personal Financial Statements

C. Home Sales/Purchase Agreement

D. List of Restaurants

E. List of Regular Customers by Routes

Appendix D

Business Plan Differences for Restaurant and Combination Businesses

In this illustration, the Coffee Museum and Visitor Center is a combination retailer. The business sells retail products, in this case packaged coffee; it has a full coffee bar restaurant that sells food service and beverage; and it operates a museum that rents leased space to a few other vendors.

To properly prepare a business plan for this type of business, all three businesses — packaged coffee, the coffee bar and food service, and the rental space — should be separately researched. All three should be tracked separately as three unique entities for each segment in these sections — Industry Analysis, Market and Competition, Strategies and Goals, Products and Services, and Marketing and Sales — and presented as three subdivisions (separate businesses) in each segment. However, in the sections, Executive Summary, Company Description, Management and Organization, Operations, Financial Pro Forma, Financial Request, and Exhibits, you can combine all three businesses and present them as a whole in each segment. This can make for a fairly lengthy business plan, but justifiably so since there are actually three businesses in one. The itemization below presents the requirements for each section.

1. Executive Summary — use all standard segments.
2. Company Description — use all standard segments. Either a review or a preview format summarizing the business overall with key elements of each of the three businesses pointed out, but basically summarizing the overall or total effects of the three businesses as a whole.

3. Industry Analysis — use all standard segments. No specific separation of the three businesses other than describing the basics.
4. Market and Competition — use all standard segments. In each segment, separately summarize the three businesses as three divisions of that segment.
5. Strategies and Goals — use all standard segments. In each segment, separately summarize the three businesses as three divisions of that segment.
6. Products or Services — use all standard segments. In each segment, separately summarize the three businesses as three divisions of that segment.
7. Marketing and Sales — use all standard segments. In each segment, separately summarize the three businesses as three divisions of that segment.
8. Management and Organization — use all standard segments. In each segment, separately summarize the three businesses as three divisions of that segment.
9. Operations — use all standard segments. No specific separation of the three businesses are needed other than describing the basics.
10. Financial Pro Formas — use all standard segments. No specific separation of the three businesses are needed other than describing the basics.
11. Financial Request — use all standard segments. No specific separation of the three businesses are needed other than describing the basics.
12. Exhibits. No specific separation of the three businesses are needed other than presenting the basics.

Following, is the first-year pro forma income statement for Coffee Museum and Visitor Center. It has been designed as both an example of a restaurant pro forma income statement and a combination business pro forma income statement to show how similar it can be to a one-business pro forma income statement.

No other real differences exist. The pro forma statement of cash flow and pro forma balance sheet are no different than for any other business.

First-year Pro Forma Income Statement

Coffee Museum and Visitor Center

	Month Jan.	Feb.	March	April	May	June	July	Aug.	Sept.	Oct.	Nov.	Dec.	Year 1
Sales													
Packaged Coffee	129,417	89,751	39,821	39,452	39,505	39,821	59,731	69,812	79,641	109,632	129,542	169,294	995,419
Coffee Bar and Foodservice	57,193	39,595	17,597	17,468	17,504	17,597	26,397	30,796	35,196	48,394	57,193	74,790	439,720
Other Income	16,630	11,513	5,117	5,117	5,117	5,117	7,675	8,954	10,234	14,070	16,630	21,746	127,920
Total Sales	203,240	140,859	62,535	62,037	62,126	62,535	93,803	109,562	125,071	172,096	203,365	265,830	1,563,059
Cost of Sales													
Packaged coffee	51,508	35,721	15,849	15,702	15,723	15,849	23,773	27,785	31,697	43,634	51,558	67,379	396,178
Coffee bar and foodservice	18,016	12,472	5,543	5,502	5,514	5,543	8,315	9,701	11,087	15,244	18,016	23,559	138,512
Other income expenses	4,159	2,874	1,279	1,287	1,286	1,279	1,919	2,235	2,559	3,514	4,154	5,436	31,981
Total Cost of Sales (1)	73,683	51,067	22,671	22,491	22,523	22,671	34,007	39,721	45,343	62,392	73,728	96,374	566,671
Gross profit	129,557	89,792	39,864	39,546	39,603	39,864	59,796	69,841	79,728	109,704	129,637	169,456	996,388
Marketing and Sales													
Advertising	1,353	1,083	1,243	383	655	658	655	383	655	1,138	1,353	973	10,532
Other marketing	17,388	470	570	468	570	150	888	150	570	788	570	470	23,052
Total Marketing and Sales (2)	18,741	1,553	1,813	851	1,225	808	1,543	533	1,225	1,926	1,923	1,443	33,584
General and Administrative Expense													
(Payroll credit in package costs)	(2,847)	(1,975)	(876)	(868)	(869)	(876)	(1,314)	(1,536)	(1,752)	(2,412)	(2,850)	(3,724)	(21,899)
(Payroll credit in bar)	(6,692)	(4,633)	(2,059)	(2,044)	(2,048)	(2,059)	(3,088)	(3,603)	(4,118)	(5,662)	(6,692)	(8,750)	(52,966)
Payroll	17,217	17,217	17,217	17,217	17,217	17,217	17,217	17,217	17,217	17,217	17,217	17,217	206,604
Net payroll	7,678	10,609	14,282	14,305	14,300	14,282	12,815	12,078	11,347	9,143	7,675	4,743	133,257
Payroll taxes, benefits	1,228	1,698	2,285	2,289	2,288	2,285	2,050	1,933	1,816	1,463	1,228	759	21,321
Pro rata facility, principal	6,563	6,563	6,563	6,563	6,563	6,563	6,563	6,563	6,563	6,563	6,563	6,563	78,756
Utilities	6,000	6,000	6,000	6,000	6,000	6,000	6,000	6,000	6,000	6,000	6,000	6,000	72,000
Telephone	250	250	250	250	250	250	250	250	250	250	250	250	3,000
Equipment lease	300	300	300	300	300	300	300	300	300	300	300	300	3,600
Depreciation	893	893	893	893	893	893	893	893	893	893	893	893	10,716
Maintenance and repair	200	200	200	200	200	200	200	200	200	200	200	200	2,400
Insurance	1,500	1,500	1,500	1,500	1,500	1,500	1,500	1,500	1,500	1,500	1,500	1,500	18,000
Supplies and postage	50	50	50	50	50	50	50	50	50	50	50	50	600
Auto and expenses	725	725	725	725	725	725	725	725	725	725	725	725	8,700
Legal and accounting	160	160	160	160	160	160	160	160	160	160	160	160	1,920
Other outside services	1,500	1,500	1,500	1,500	1,500	1,500	1,500	1,500	1,500	1,500	1,500	1,500	18,000
Non-income taxes & fees	300	300	300	300	300	300	300	300	300	300	300	300	3,600
Other G & A expenses	200	200	200	200	200	200	200	200	200	200	200	200	2,400
Total G & A Expense (3)	27,547	30,948	35,208	35,235	35,229	35,208	33,506	32,652	31,803	29,247	27,544	24,142	378,269
Total Operating Costs (rows 1 + 2 + 3)	119,971	83,568	59,692	58,577	58,977	58,687	69,056	72,906	78,371	93,565	103,195	121,959	978,524
Operating Profit	83,269	57,291	2,843	3,460	3,149	3,848	24,747	36,656	46,700	78,531	100,170	143,871	584,535
Interest Expense	17,670	17,620	17,571	17,522	17,473	17,423	17,374	17,325	17,276	17,227	17,177	17,128	208,786
Profit Before Income Taxes	65,599	39,671	(14,728)	(14,062)	(14,324)	(13,575)	7,373	19,331	29,424	61,304	82,993	126,743	375,749
Income Taxes	22,960	13,885	(5,155)	(4,922)	(5,013)	(4,751)	2,580	6,766	10,298	21,456	29,048	44,360	131,512
Net Profit	42,639	25,786	(9,573)	(9,140)	(9,311)	(8,824)	4,792	12,565	19,125	39,848	53,945	82,383	244,237

Appendix E

Business Plan Differences for Nonprofit Organizations

A nonprofit organization can be set up as a manufacturing, resale, wholesale, or service business. While there are many differences in setting up the business as a nonprofit organization from setting up a profit making business, the principals of writing a business plan for a nonprofit organization vary little from a plan for a business for profit.

The key differences lie in three documents in Section 10, Financial Pro Formas. The typical opening balance sheet and pro forma balance sheets for a nonprofit organization are usually termed opening consolidated statement of financial position and pro forma consolidated statements of financial position. However the structure and format of these two documents are exactly the same as for their business-for-profit counterparts. Only one other term is changed within the documents themselves: the term *equity* for a nonprofit organization on both of these forms is changed to *net assets*. Therefore, the three lines in the form that are usually termed Liabilities and Equity, Equity, and Total Liabilities and Equity are simply changed to Liabilities and Net Assets, Net Assets, and Total Liabilities and Net Assets, respectively. There are no other changes within these forms. The layout and calculations are the same for consolidated statements of financial position for nonprofit organizations as the balance sheets for businesses for profit.

The primary difference lies in the third document, the traditional pro forma income statement for a business for profit. First, for a nonprofit activities. Because there are several other differences in this form, the one-page example in this appendix for Newmark Association details a pro forma consolidated statement of activities with the changes that are usually incorporated into it.

Notice the first line shows "changes in net assets." Under this heading are other changes in classification. Where revenues and gains are itemized, Sales is changed to Revenues and Gains and Total Sales is changed to Total Revenues and Gains. Where revenues and gains are not itemized, the one-line entry Sales is simply called Revenues and Gains.

In a typical nonprofit organization, Expenses is changed to Expenses and Losses. Expenses are then broken down into Variable Expenses and General and Administrative Expenses. After these are totaled (Total Expenses and Losses) the line of entries is subtracted from the line Total Revenues and Gains, and the results (usually called Operating Profit in a business for profit) are called Change in Net Assets.

Since a nonprofit organization pays no income taxes, interest expense is tracked as a regular general and administrative expense above, instead of below, the change in net assets, and the line for interest is omitted. And of course, nonprofit organizations do not have profit before income taxes, income taxes, or net profit, so these traditional lines are also deleted.

Below the changes in net assets, however, there are two additional lines of entries recorded for a nonprofit organization:

- Net Assets, Beginning of the Month
- Net Assets, End of the Month

They pick up the net assets that may have existed before this document was initiated — in the case of a start-up nonprofit organization, the number is zero. These beginning of the month entries are then added to the monthly change in net assets for a set of running totals tracking net assets across the bottom line of the document. That's it. Important assumptions, the pro forma statement of cash flow, the break-even analysis, and business ratios all have the same formats as the Kona Gold Coffees examples.

Likewise, requests for both equity and debt financing can be handled in the same manner; usually however, donations or assessments are sought. Those types of financing and the tax benefits available to benefactors are beyond the scope of this text.

You can find more information on nonprofit organizations in Ted Nichols' book, *The Complete Guide to Nonprofit Corporations: Step-By-Step Guidelines, Procedures and Forms to Maintain a Nonprofit Corporation*, published by **Dearborn Trade.**

First-year Pro Forma Income Statement

Newmark Association

	Month Jan.	Feb.	March	April	May	June	July	Aug.	Sep.	Oct.	Nov.	Dec.	Year 1
Changes In Net Assets													
Revenues and Gains													
Dues	100,070	100,070	100,070	100,070	100,070	100,070	100,070	100,070	100,070	100,070	100,070	100,070	1,200,840
Publications	15,450	15,450	15,450	15,450	15,450	15,450	15,450	15,450	15,450	15,450	15,450	15,450	185,400
Education	11,500	11,500	11,500	11,500	11,500	11,500	11,500	11,500	11,500	11,500	11,500	11,500	138,000
Sponsorships	208	208	208	208	208	208	208	208	208	208	208	208	2,500
Contributions	8,333	8,333	8,333	8,333	8,333	8,333	8,333	8,333	8,333	8,333	8,333	8,333	100,000
Other revenues	3,042	3,042	3,042	3,042	3,042	3,042	3,042	3,042	3,042	3,042	3,042	3,042	36,500
Total Revenues and Gains	138,603	138,603	138,603	138,603	138,603	138,603	138,603	138,603	138,603	138,603	138,603	138,603	1,663,240
Expenses and Losses													
Variable Expenses													
Salaries	46,100	46,100	46,100	46,100	46,100	46,100	46,100	46,100	46,100	46,100	46,100	46,100	553,200
Travel and meetings	6,261	6,261	6,261	6,261	6,261	6,261	6,261	6,261	6,261	6,261	6,261	6,261	75,136
Meeting rooms	3,019	3,019	3,019	3,019	3,019	3,019	3,019	3,019	3,019	3,019	3,019	3,019	36,224
Consulting	10,450	10,450	10,450	10,450	10,450	10,450	10,450	10,450	10,450	10,450	10,450	10,450	125,400
Special supplies	2,863	2,863	2,863	2,863	2,863	2,863	2,863	2,863	2,863	2,863	2,863	2,863	34,356
Special telephone	3,242	3,242	3,242	3,242	3,242	3,242	3,242	3,242	3,242	3,242	3,242	3,242	38,900
Education	291	291	291	291	291	291	291	291	291	291	291	291	3,488
Printing and artwork	13,500	13,500	13,500	13,500	13,500	13,500	13,500	13,500	13,500	13,500	13,500	13,500	162,000
Mailing and handling	3,563	3,563	3,563	3,563	3,563	3,563	3,563	3,563	3,563	3,563	3,563	3,563	42,750
Promotions	633	633	633	633	633	633	633	633	633	633	633	633	7,600
Other variable expenses	2,000	2,000	2,000	2,000	2,000	2,000	2,000	2,000	2,000	2,000	2,000	2,000	24,000
Total Variable Expenses (1)	91,921	91,921	91,921	91,921	91,921	91,921	91,921	91,921	91,921	91,921	91,921	91,921	1,103,054
General and Administrative Expense													
Administrative salaries	7,954	7,954	7,954	7,954	7,954	7,954	7,954	7,954	7,954	7,954	7,954	7,954	95,450
Loss or disposal of FFE*	1,000	1,000	1,000	1,000	1,000	1,000	1,000	1,000	1,000	1,000	1,000	1,000	12,000
Rent	7,750	7,750	7,750	7,750	7,750	7,750	7,750	7,750	7,750	7,750	7,750	7,750	93,000
Utilities	4,333	4,333	4,333	4,333	4,333	4,333	4,333	4,333	4,333	4,333	4,333	4,333	52,000
Telephone	252	252	252	252	252	252	252	252	252	252	252	252	3,020
Equipment	0	0	0	1,000	0	0	0	0	0	0	400	0	1,400
Depreciation	2,367	2,367	2,367	2,367	2,367	2,367	2,367	2,367	2,367	2,367	2,367	2,367	28,400
Maintenance and repairs	450	450	450	450	450	450	450	450	450	450	450	450	5,400
Insurance	5,000	695	695	695	695	695	695	695	695	695	695	695	12,646
Supplies and postage	2,192	2,192	2,192	2,192	2,192	2,192	2,192	2,192	2,192	2,192	2,192	2,192	26,300
Auto, travel, and entertainment	1,038	1,038	1,038	1,038	1,038	1,038	1,038	1,038	1,038	1,038	1,038	1,038	12,450
Legal and accounting	2,000	7,000	2,000	2,000	2,000	2,000	2,000	2,000	2,000	2,000	2,000	2,000	29,000
Other outside services	2,500	2,500	2,500	2,500	2,500	2,500	2,500	2,500	2,500	2,500	2,500	2,500	30,000
Taxes and fees	4,050	4,050	4,050	4,050	4,050	4,050	4,050	4,050	4,050	4,050	4,050	4,050	48,600
Interest expense	934	934	934	934	934	934	934	934	934	934	934	934	11,213
Other G & A expenses	1,800	1,800	1,800	1,800	1,800	1,800	1,800	1,800	1,800	1,800	1,800	1,800	21,600
Total G & A Expense (2)	43,619	44,315	39,315	40,314	39,314	39,314	39,314	39,314	39,314	39,314	39,714	39,314	482,479
Total Expenses and Losses (rows 1 + 2)	135,541	136,236	131,236	132,236	131,236	131,236	131,236	131,236	131,236	131,236	131,636	131,236	1,585,533
Change In Net Assets	3,063	2,367	7,367	6,368	7,368	7,368	7,368	7,368	7,368	7,368	6,968	7,368	77,707
Net Assets, Beginning of Month	0	3,063	5,430	12,797	19,165	26,533	33,901	41,268	48,636	56,004	63,372	70,339	77,707
Net Assets, End of Month	3,063	5,430	12,797	19,165	26,533	33,901	41,268	48,636	56,004	63,372	70,339	77,707	155,414

*FFE, Fixtures, Furniture, and Equipment

Appendix F

In-Depth Business Plan Calculations

The calculations throughout the text are sufficient to generate the basic numbers in most business plans. For those that require more detail, the following in-depth calculations are provided to address inventory cash flow, additional business ratios, and various scenarios of return on investment.

Inventory

Inventory calculations are for those businesses — retail, wholesale, and manufacturing and assembly companies — that maintain an ongoing inventory and need to closely monitor cash flow for the cost of sales – inventory account in their Pro Forma Statement of Cash Flow.

Begin by locating the cost of sales payment days in your Assumptions, Chapter 10. This is the average number of days you take to pay for cost of sales items. For service businesses, this is mostly labor costs; for retailers and wholesalers, this is the cost of your merchandise; and for manufacturing and assembly companies, this is direct costs of goods sold.

Example 1. Using Cost of Sales Payment Days of 30

For this example, assume that it takes you an average of one month (30 days) to pay cash for purchases on credit — your cost of sales payment days is 30. Assume also that the current month is March. In March, you will pay for 100 percent of the cost of sales items that you purchased on credit 30 days before during the month of February.

Pro Forma Cash Flow, Cost of sales, inventory for March (payment days of 30) =
    Cost of sales purchased during February [unknown, see A below]
    × Percent of Cost of sales accounts payable [from your Assumptions]

    [A] Cost of sales purchased during February =
        Cost of sales items on hand at the end of February [unknown, see B below]
        − Cost of sales items on hand at the beginning of February [unknown, see C below]
        + Cost of sales items sold in February [from your Pro Forma Income Statement]

    [B] Cost of sales items on hand at the end of February =
        Cost of sales in February [from your Pro Forma Income Statement]
        × Number of days of inventory on-hand [from your Assumptions]
        Divide the results by 30

    [C] Cost of sales items on hand at the beginning of January =
        Cost of sales in January [from your Pro Forma Income Statement]
        × Number of days of inventory on-hand [from your Assumptions]
        Divide the results by 30

Example 2. Using Cost of Sales Payment Days of 60

For this example, assume that your cost of sales payment days is 60 and the current month is March. In March, you will pay 100 percent of the cost of sales items you purchased on credit during the month of January.

Pro Forma Cash Flow, Cost of sales, inventory for March (payment days of 60) =
    Cost of sales purchased during January [unknown, see A below]
    × Percent of Cost of sales accounts payable [from your Assumptions]

    [A] Cost of sales purchased during January =
        Cost of sales items on hand at the end of January [unknown, see B below]
        − Cost of sales items on hand at the beginning of January [unknown, see C below]
        + Cost of sales items sold in January [from your Pro Forma Income Statement]

    [B] Cost of sales items on hand at the end of January =
        Cost of sales in January [from your Pro Forma Income Statement]
        × Number of days of inventory on-hand [from your Assumptions]
        Divide the results by 30

    [C] Cost of sales items on hand at the beginning of December =
        Cost of sales in December [from your Pro Forma Income Statement]
        × Number of Days of Inventory on-hand [from your Assumptions]
        Divide the results by 30

Example 3. Using Cost of Sales Payment Days of 45

Assume for this example that your cost of sales payment days is 45 and that the current month is March. For March, you will pay 100 percent of the cost of sales items you purchased on credit during the 30-day period that includes the first half (15 days) of February and the last half (15 days) of January.

Pro Forma Cash Flow, Cost of sales, inventory for March (payment days of 45) =

Cost of sales purchased during first 15 days of February and last 15 days of January [unknown, see A below]

× Percent of Cost of sales accounts payable [from your Assumptions]

[A] Cost of sales purchased during first 15 days of February and last 15 days of January =

Cost of sales items on hand at the middle of February [unknown, see B below]

− Cost of sales items on hand at the middle of January [unknown, see C below]

+ Cost of sales items sold in the first half (15 days) of February and in the last half (15 days) of January [from your Pro Forma Income Statement]

[B] Cost of Sales items on hand at the middle of February =

1/2 Cost of sales in January plus 1/2 Cost of sales in February [from your Pro Forma Income Statement]

× Number of days of inventory on-hand [from your Assumptions]

Divide the results by 30

[C] Cost of Sales items on hand at the beginning of December =

1/2 Cost of Sales in December plus 1/2 Cost of Sales in January [from your Pro Forma Income Statement]

× Number of Days of Inventory on-hand [from your Assumptions]

Divide the results by 30

By following the steps in these examples, you can find the cost of sales figures for all the months you must enter in your Pro Forma Statement of Cash Flow. See Chapter 10 for further information.

If you sell all of your inventory every month, not keeping any on hand, your cost of sales for any one month will be the same as your cost of sales purchases for that month, even though you pay for them later when purchasing them on credit. You might want to seek your accountant's assistance in calculating your cost of sales – inventory for your Pro Forma Statement of Cash Flow if your cost of sales payment days differs from these examples.

Business Ratios

Hundreds of accounting ratios exist, but only the more popular ones are covered here. In these ratios, debt is equal to total liabilities; short-term debt is current liabilities; and quick cash equals cash plus marketable securities and accounts receivable. The ratios are grouped in several categories.

Solvency Ratios

Solvency ratios provide a measure of your company's overall financial ability to pay its debts. Liquidity ratios examine your company's overall financial position and its ability to pay short-term debt. They also evaluate the quality and sufficiency of current assets to cover current liabilities. Safety ratios evaluate your investment in the company in comparison to funds used from outside sources. These ratios also indicate perceived risks, such as your company's ability to weather a downturn in sales or profits.

This information is very important to lenders and investors in their assessment of the perceived risk of loan applications. Simple calculations of numbers from your company's balance sheet can show whether or not your business has the ability to pay its obligations without problems.

Liquidity Ratios (from the balance sheet)

$$\text{Current ratio} = \frac{\text{Current assets}}{\text{Current liabilities}}$$

$$\text{Quick ratio} = \frac{\text{Cash + Accounts receivable = Quick assets}}{\text{Current liabilities}}$$

$$\text{Debt to assets} = \frac{\text{Total liabilities}}{\text{Total assets}}$$

$$\text{Short-term debt to assets} = \frac{\text{Current liabilities}}{\text{Total assets}}$$

$$\text{Long-term debt to assets} = \frac{\text{Total liabilities} - \text{Current liabilities}}{\text{Total assets}}$$

$$\text{Working capital} = \text{Current assets} - \text{Current liabilities}$$

Safety Ratios (from the balance sheet)

$$\text{Short-term debt to equity} = \frac{\text{Current liabilities}}{\text{Total equity}}$$

$$\text{Short-term debt to total debt} = \frac{\text{Current liabilities}}{\text{Total liabilities}}$$

$$\text{Debt to equity} = \frac{\text{Total liabilities}}{\text{Total equity}}$$

$$\text{Current to total assets} = \frac{\text{Current assets}}{\text{Total assets}}$$

$$\text{Fixed to worth} = \frac{\text{Long term assets}}{\text{Total equity}}$$

$$\text{Net quick assets} = \text{Quick assets} - \text{Current liabilities}$$

Safety Ratios (from the income statement)

$$\frac{\text{EBIT}}{\text{Interest}} = \frac{\text{Net profit}}{\text{Interest expense}}$$

$$\text{EBIT to interest} = \frac{\left(\frac{\text{Gross profit}}{\text{Sales}}\right) - \text{Operating expenses}}{\text{Interest expense}}$$

Efficiency Ratios

These ratios provide the information necessary to compare your company's operating performance with that of other companies and with the average for your industry. Levels of acceptability vary among different industries, but, generally, retail stores should have higher turnover ratios.

Activity Ratios (from the income statement and the balance sheet)

$$\text{Collection days} = \frac{\text{Accounts receivable}}{\text{Sales}} \times 365$$

$$\text{Sales to receivables} = \frac{\text{Sales}}{\text{Accounts receivable}}$$

Operating Ratios (from the income statement and the balance sheet)

$$\text{Accounts payable to sales} = \frac{\text{Accounts payable}}{\text{Sales}}$$

$$\text{Accounts receivable turnover} = \frac{\text{Sales}}{\text{Accounts receivable}}$$

$$\text{Accounts payable turnover} = \frac{\text{Cost of sales}}{\text{Accounts payable}}$$

$$\text{Receivables to payables} = \frac{\text{Accounts receivable}}{\text{Accounts payable}}$$

$$\text{Cost of sales to payables} = \frac{\text{Cost of sales}}{\text{Accounts payable}}$$

$$\text{Sales to assets} = \frac{\text{Sales}}{\text{Total assets}}$$

$$\text{Sales to net working capital} = \frac{\text{Sales}}{\text{Current assets} - \text{Current liabilities}}$$

$$\text{Inventory turnover} = \frac{\text{Cost of sales}}{\text{Inventory}}$$

In the discussion of business ratios in Chapter 10, several of these efficiency ratios are discussed more fully to help you better understand their uses and calculations. Be sure to take the time to get a clear understanding of how they work. Also, your accountant can assist you in this process.

Profitability Ratios

These ratios can be used to examine the profit level made by your company and to determine if your company yields profits comparable to alternative investments. Also, they can be used to assess your business' value as an investment and to compare your business' success with the rest of the industry in terms of profit in such areas as gross margin, net profit margin, and return on assets.

The return on assets ratio and the return on equity ratio were explained in more detail in Chapter 10. Those discussions can help you visualize how these ratios use numbers from the income statement and balance sheet to provide valuable management information.

(from the income statement)

$$\text{Return on sales or Pretax profit margin} = \frac{\text{Net profit}}{\text{Sales}}$$

$$\text{Gross profit margin} = \frac{\text{Gross profit}}{\text{Sales}}$$

$$\text{Sales break-even} = \frac{\text{Total operating costs} - (\text{Costs of sales} + \text{Commissions} + \text{Freight})}{1 - (\text{Cost of sales \%} + \text{Commission \%} + \text{Freight \%})}$$

(from the income statement and the balance sheet)

$$\text{Return on assets} = \frac{\text{Net profit}}{\text{Total assets}}$$

$$\text{Return on equity} = \frac{\text{Net profit}}{\text{Total equity}}$$

$$\text{Sales to equity} = \frac{\text{Sales}}{\text{Total equity}}$$

Return on Investment

If you use your business plan as an offering proposal for obtaining equity financing, it is important to show your investors what they can expect as return on their investment. After you present the basics, there are several methods they can use to evaluate how strong their investment would be in their portfolio. This can be best described by providing an example.

Suppose in the model of Kona Gold Coffees, that the owners find they cannot get the commercial line of credit they are applying for in their loan request. As an alternative, they might try to obtain investor capital by offering to sell 15 percent of the ownership for a $100,000 investment. In their investment offering, they might set five years as the point at which they will buy out the investor for the original amount of the investment. The company's Pro Forma Income Statement would show the investor receiving 15 percent dividends each year based on the profit before income taxes.

Kona Gold Coffees	Year 1	2	3	4	5
Profit Before Income Taxes	$306,256	$357,002	$406,007	$473,006	$531,441
15% to Investor	$ 45,938	$ 53,550	$ 60,901	$ 70,950	$ 79,716

At the end of the fifth year, the investor will have received $311,055 plus his or her buy-out of the original $100,000, a total of $411,055. At that point the investor will receive a 411 percent return over 5 years, or an average annual return of 82.2 percent. For most investment scenarios, this is all you need to show, because nearly every investor has his or her own favorite way of evaluating the return and quality of an investment. But if you want to illustrate further, there are other ways you can show return on investment.

One common method is to compare the return of the investment opportunity with the return of a strong, low-risk investment commonly used by investors, such a the purchase of a U.S. Treasury bill (T-bill). If an investor put the same principal amount of $100,000 into a T-bill for five years, at an interest rate of 10 percent, the total return would be $161,051.

Yearly compounding of 10% interest for 5 years = principal $\times (1 + 10\%)^{5 \text{ (years)}}$

Basis:	$100,000
Year 1	10,000
Year 2	11,000
Year 3	12,100
Year 4	13,310
Year 5	14,641
Total	$161,051

In order to have an assurance of greater safety, the $100,000 invested in a T-bill would have a return of only $161,051, while the investment of

$100,000 in Kona Gold Coffees could have a return of $411,055 if the investor is willing to weather the risks of a start-up company. By making this comparison, you can illustrate potential value to an investor.

If you think it might be helpful, you could provide the investor with an assurance that, in the event they don't get back at least an equivalent of the current interest of a T-bill through their dividends over five years, you will guarantee to buy them out at the end of the period at the prearranged equivalent of what the total return on a T-bill would be.

There are also several methods of using comparisons with the present value of money. The weakness of this or any other approach that must assume a future increase in percentage of return is its subjectivity. The most popular comparison is with the current interest rate of a U.S. Treasury bill for a comparable time period. The present value is calculated using a formula that is, by the way, programmed into financial calculators. Here, the PV is for five years using a 10 percent rate of return.

$$PV \text{ (in 5 years)} = \frac{(\text{principal}) \times 1.10}{(1 + 10\%)^{5 \text{ (years)}}}$$

A novel way to assess this investment is to look at the present value of each of the projected dividends plus the final payout and compare the results with the original amount invested in T-bills at 10 percent. The Kona Gold Coffee and T-bill present value returns would be:

	Actual Dividends	Present Value
End of Year One	$ 45,938	$ 41,762
End of Year Two	53,550	44,256
End of Year Three	60,901	45,756
End of Year Four	70,950	48,460
End of Year Five (plus return of $100,000 basis)	179,716	111,589
Total Payout	$411,055	$291,823

This comparison shows that the investor would have to put $291,823 into 10 percent T-bills, today, to earn the same $411,055 over five years as a $100,000 investment, today, in Kona Gold Coffees will earn in the same time period. Converting this present value to a percentage, it is a 291 percent over-all return or an annualized return of 58.4 percent on the original investment.

Appendix G

Financing Sources

AdVenture Capital Register
www.adventurecapital.com

A Miami company that serves businesses, investors, and entrepreneurs in finding venture capital.

America's Business Funding Directory
www.businessfinance.com

A free online service designed to help those in need of capital.

America's Small Business Financial Center
www.netearnings.com

A one-stop shop for small business insurance, loans, credit cards, payroll services, quotes, and online applications.

American Bankers Association
www.aba.com

A good site for information on financial publications, sources, and advice.

Capital Alliance Ventures, Inc.
www.cavi.com

A Canadian labor sponsored investment fund providing venture capital to high-tech biz.

Datamerge, Inc.
www.datamerge.com/news/archives/sbiconly/

A listing source for over 300 SBICs, many of which are sources of equity financing.

Ernst & Young Entrepreneurs Services
www.ey.com

A source for tips on financing, operating strategies, acquisitions, and expansion.

Money Online
www.money.com

Based on *Money* magazine, this site features a list of financial sites for new startups.

National Association of Small Business Institute Companies (SBICs)
www.nasbic.org

Central contact agency to find the SBIC nearest you and what these offices can do for your new business.

National Venture Capital Association (NVCA)
www.nvca.org

Designed to help you find sources of venture capital.

North Ranch Financial
www.northranchfinancial.com

Links institutional venture capital sources with entrepreneurs.

Quicken
www.cashfinder.com

This free service lets you shop online for biz loans, credit cards, lines of credit, and leases.

Small Business Development Centers (SBDCs)
www.sbaonline.sba.gov/SBDC

A major listing of the 57 lead SBDCs that provide financial assistance for small businesses.

SSB Commercial Banking
www.ssbonline.com

A banking source for revolving lines of credit and working capital loans.

Technology Funding
www.techfunding.com

A Silicon Valley venture capital firm and member of NASD/SIPC provides venture capital funding for high-tech biz.

Vanguard Venture Partners
www.vanguardadventures.com

A venture capital firm that has financed over 90 start-up companies.

Venture Associates
www.Venturea.com

A Denver financial consulting firm that offers information on finding angels, venture capital, investment bankers, management consultants, and more.

Venture Capital Center
www.uscap.com

A major listing site of venture capital firms.

Venture Capital Finance Online
www.vcaonline.com

A global directory for linking entrepreneurs and investors.

Venture Capital Market Place, The
www.v-capital.com

Provides a current list of direct investment opportunities for private companies seeking venture capital.

Venture Capital Online
www.vcapital.com

Information and networking opportunities for entrepreneurs and venture capitalists.

Venture Capital Search
www.venture-capital-search.com

A Newport Beach, California company that links new companies with venture capital firms.

VentureList.com
www.venturelist.com

A directory of venture capital firms, venture capital consultants, equipment leasing, factoring accounts receivable, and venture capital clubs and associations.

Venture-Preneurs Network
www.venturepreneurs.com

Offers services to startups, including locating venture capital.

Index

the 4 Ps, 109–111
the 5 Fs, 110–111

A

ABC (inventory management), 159
accountant
  as consultant, 2
  fees, 181
  on management team, 127, 131, *226*
accountant assistance, recommendations for
  business plan check, 9, 165, 213, 223–224
  cost of sales calculations for cash flow, 188
  important assumptions, 168, 171, 172
  income taxes, 160, 189
  sales on credit determination, 187
  site selection, 38
  utilities, cost forecast, 180
  vesting decision, 35
  wage rate determination, 139
accounting methods
  accrual method, 166–167
  cash method, 166–167
accounts payable
  balance sheet, 174, 176
  business ratios, 199–200
  cash flow, statement of, 188
  important assumptions, 168–172
  payment system, 163
  turnover, 199, *309*
accounts receivable
  balance sheet, 173–175
  business ratios, 196–197, 199
  collection system, 163
  turnover, 196, 199, *226, 256, 309*
accumulated depreciation, 174–175, *251, 274, 292*
acquisition, 217–218, *231*
advertising
  agencies, 112, 118
  gifts, 113
  plan, 7, 23, 30, 58, 108, 112–114, 118–121, 179, *241–242, 267–268*
  vehicles, 113, 116, 118–119
after-sale policies, 158
American Association of Advertising Agencies, 112
American Statistics Index, 48
angels, 204, *314*
annual business plan, 162, *248*
annual planning, 162
appraisal, 78, 221–222
articles of corporation, 42, 221
ASI Abstracts, 48

assets
- balance sheet, 166, 173–176, 194
- business ratios, 196–200
- control, 159
- depreciable, 180, 189
- family, 37
- start-up costs, 203
- starting cash position, 187

assumptions, see important assumptions

attorney
- as consultant, 2
- fees, 181
- on management team, 127, 131, 133

attorney assistance, recommendations for
- business plan check, 213
- lease negotiation, 39
- LLC creation, 37
- risk identification, 215
- vesting decision, 35, 205

auctions, 116–117
auto, travel, and entertainment, 181
average monthly cost of sales, 169–171
average monthly sales, 169–171, *250, 273, 291*

B

bad checks, 163
bad debt, 163
balance sheet, explained step by step, 175–176, see also pro forma balance sheet and opening balance sheet
bankers, 2, *313–314*
Berra, Yogi, 89
billboards and signs, 113, 116
binder, three-ring, 8
binding, 8, *246, 248*
- strips, 8

Board of Directors, 40, 132, 204
bookkeeping system, 166–167
Bottom Line Basics, 159
break-even
- analysis, 3, 7, 167, 182, 184, *303*
- point, 167, 196
- sales, 25, 31, 182, 184

Bridge between NAICS and SIC, 46
broadcast media, 113–114, 120
brochures, 101, 113, 116, 221, *233*
Bureau of the Census Catalog and Guide, 48
business
- concept
  - company description, 19, 33–34
  - executive summary, 6, 26–28
  - points to remember, 44
  - ready for biz, 2
- consultants, 2, 127, 131
- objectives, 3–4, 27
- references, 7, 222
- résumé, personal, 127–128
- specialty, 19, 26–27, 34, 223

Business Owner's Guide to Accounting and Bookkeeping, 200
Business Periodicals Index, 47
business plan
- current use, x
- exhibits
  - in outline, 4, 7
  - photos, 9
  - purpose of, x
  - sales materials, 101
  - suggested documentation, 221–222
  - table of contents, 219–220
- length, x
- organization, 3–5
- outline for startups, 5–8
- outlines, 3–7, 19
- purpose of, x
- structure of, 1, 4, 190
- support documents

business ratios, 196–201, *256, 279, 297*
- equations, 197–200, *307–310*
- graphs, 201, *256, 279, 297*

buyout, 217, *260*

C

capacity (production), 149–151
cash
- disbursements, 187–189, *226, 262*
- method, see accounting
- on hand and in banks, 175
- receipts, 187–189, *226, 262*
- sales, 168–171, 187, *250, 273, 283, 291*

cash and carry businesses, 184, 186
cash flow
- control
  - business plan segment, 162–163
  - operations, 24, 144
  - in outline, 7
- statement of, explained step-by-step, 187–189
- statement of, see also pro forma statement of cash flow

cash only sales, 169, 171
CENDATA, 48
certificate of incorporation, 221
certificate of need, 221
Chamber of Commerce, 38, 72, *232*
charity assistance, 117
charts, 9, 72
chat rooms, 116
chief
- executive officer, 40, 127–130, 132
- financial officer, 127, 130–131
- operations officer, 127

Cialdini, Robert, 124
clipart, 14
collateral, 212–213, *259, 262, 280–281*
collection
- calls, *249*

days
  business ratios, 199
  important assumptions, 169–171
  sales on credit, 187
  limit, 163
color, 8–9, *248*
commercial business analysis, 69
commercial finance companies, 204
commercial lenders, 204
commercial strength, 80–81, 84
commissions
  break-even analysis, 182
  important assumptions, 169–170, 172
  income statement, 177, 179
  industry standards, 60
  sales force, 121
company description
  business plan section, 33–44
  executive summary, 5, 19–20
  in outline, 6
competition, see also market and competition
  identification, 7, 65–66, 78, *235, 266, 288*
  survey, 81
competitor analysis, 3, 7, 21, 66, 78–82, 84, 103, *235, 266, 288*
components, twelve basic, 5
confidentiality, 12–13
Congressional Information Service, 48
consumer
  credit, 28, 204, *230, 232, 257*
  demographic analysis, 68–70, 74
  demographics, 69–70, 74, 114, 119, *241*
  geographic analysis, 68, 72, 75
  needs, 70
  profile, 21, 23, 29–30, 66–68, 72, 75, 77, 108, 111, 119, *240*
  psychographic analysis, 68, 70–71, 75
contents, table of, 15, *228, 246, 286*
contests, 117
convertible debt, 205
cooperative advertising, 118
copyediting, 9
copyright, 20
copywriters, 118
corporation, 20, 35–37, 43, 59, 176, 221, *303*
cost of
  food and beverages, 169, 171, 177, 179
  goods sold, 169, 171, 177, 179, *262, 272–274, 305*
  labor, 60–61, 171, 179
  materials, 60–61
  money, 185
  overhead, 60
  revenue earned, 177
cost of sales
  accounts payable, 169–171, 174, 176, *251, 306–307, 309*
  break-even analysis, 182
  business ratios, 199
  cash flow, statement of, 188
  executive summary, 25, 31
  financial summary, 168
  important assumptions, 169–171
  income statement, 177, 179
  industry standards, 60–61
  payment days, 169–171, *305–307*
cost of sales – inventory, 188, *305, 307*
County Business Patterns, 48, 72, 78, 83–84, *232*
coupons, 117, 119
cover letter, 10–11, 16
covers, 8–9
creativity driven (strategy), 91
credit
  days, 171
  sales, 167–168, *283*
cross-training, 149–150
cultural events, 23, 30, 108, 119
current assets, 166, 174–175, 187, 197–198, *251, 274, 292, 308–309*
Current Industrial Reports, 48
current liabilities, 166, 174, 176, 197–198, *251, 274, 292, 307–309*
current ratio, 196–198, *256, 272, 279, 297, 308*
current status and milestones, 6, 20, 33, 41–43, 159, *232, 265, 287*
customer
  analysis, 66–70
  demographic analysis, 68–70, 74, 115
  feedback, 149, 152–153, 158
  geographic analysis, 68, 72, 75
  loyalty, 53–54, 79–81
  needs
    business plan segment, 85
    executive summary, 21
    five Fs of, 110
    monitoring, 107
    in outline, 7
  opinion, 158
  profile, 52, 66–67, 70, 72, 87, 113–115
  psychographic analysis, 68, 70–71, 75
  service policy, 7, 24, 144, 158, *226, 248, 271, 290*
customer-focus driven, 93
customer-service driven, 28, *236*
CyberExpoSearch, 118

D

data retrieval systems, 163
Datapro Office Automation Reports, 151
days, cost of sale, 171
days, credit, 61, 122, 168, 171, 187, *249, 306*
days, general accounts payable, 168, 172, *250, 273*
days of inventory, 168, *306–307*
days of sale, 171
debt financing, 12, 190, 204, 211, 217–218, *303*

debt to equity, 196, 198, *256, 279, 297, 308*
delinquent accounts, 163
demographic analysis, 68–70, 74
depreciable
    asset purchases, 189
    assets, 174–175, 180, 189, *251, 274, 284, 292*
depreciation
    accumulated, 175
    cash flow, statement of, 188
    equipment, 151
    important assumptions, 172
    income statement, 180
desktop publishing, 8, 128
direct
    costs 169, 171, 177, 179–180
    labor, 171, 179
    mail, 112–113, 115
director(s), 4, 40, 127, 132, 204
    of operations, 127, 131
    of sales and marketing, 127
disclaimer, 5, 12
discounts, 109, 117, 163, 179
display cases, 117
distribution and supply, 57–58
distributors or wholesalers, 113
dividends, 36, 189–190, 207, 214, *311–312*
Dow-Jones News Retrieval (website), 49
draw (for owners), *245, 282*
driven, see market-driven strategies
Dun & Bradstreet, 46, 50, 60, 112, 197, 199

E

EBIT-to-interest, 198
economic census, 46
Economic Censuses and Related Statistics, 48
economic downturns, 216, *282*
economic sectors, 47, 50
education, 74–75, 126, 129
efficiency
    control, 7, 24, 144, 161–162, *226, 248*
    driven (strategy), 94
    employee reviews, 146–148
Encyclopedia of Business Information Sources, 47
ending cash, 186–187, 189–190, 194
end-user (consumer), 67–68
EOQ (inventory management), 159
equipment
    business plan segment, 151
    depreciation, 175, 189
    income statement, 180
    leases, 204
    operations, 145
    production, 149
    safety, 162
    schedule, 153
    start-up costs, 166
    waiver, 39

equity
    balance sheet, 175–176, 194
    business ratios, 196, 198, 200
    cash flow, statement of, 188
    financing, 204–205
    investor offering, 206–207
    start-up costs, 166
    stock shares, 136
equity capital proceeds, 188, 190, 193, 207
equity financing, 12, 190, 204–205, 211, 217, *311, 313*
escrow, 127, 221
    closing statement, 221
    instructions, 221
exclusive offerings, 117
executive summary
    business plan section, 17–32
    preview format, 26
    review format, 19
exit options, 7, 25, 203, 206, 213, 217–218, *260, 262, 282, 298*
exit plan, 217–218
exit strategy, 25, 217
expense control, 161
expense, general and administrative, 127, 168, 171, 177, 179, 181, 188
experience, 23, 126–129
ExpoGuide (website), 118

F

facility, 2, 7, 20, 24, 38–39
family limited liability company, 37
fast-response orders, 155
Ferguson, Michel J. T., 99
fictitious business name (dba), 33, 37, 221
fictitious business name statements, 221
FIFO (inventory valuation), 160
financial
    overview, 6, 26, 31, *230, 265, 287*
    pro formas
        in appendices, (A) *226, 228, 231, 239, 241, 248–251, 253, 256*; (B) *261, 272–274, 276, 279*; (C) *283, 286, 290–292, 294, 297*; (D) *299–301*; (E) *302–304*
    balance sheet, 194–195
    business plan section, 164–202
    cash flow, statement of, 184–194
    executive summary, 19, 25
    income statement, 177–182
    in outline, 4, 6–7
    request, 135, 203, 213, *299–300*
    requirement, 3, 6–8, 25, 31, 42, 166, 168, 181, 203–218
    requirement summary, 7, 25, 31, 203, 205, 218
    sources, 203–204
    summary, 7, 25, 167–168, 202, *249, 272, 284, 290*
financing sources, Appendix G, 204, *313–314*
fixed expenses, 171, 182

floor plan, 221
fonts, 8
Ford, Henry, 45
Ford, Henry II, 203
format
    business plan, 3, 8
    executive summary, 18, 32
    résumé, 128–130
The Franchise Redbook, 2, 79
franchising, 2, 113, 217
Franklin, Benjamin, ix
free
    estimates, 117
    freight, 148, 156–157, 166, 169–170, 172, 179, 182
    products or services, 117
    trials, 117
frequent buyer cards, 117
Frigstad, David B., 65
fulfillment, 7, 24, 144, 152, 156–157
Fulfillment Systems International, 157
Fuller, Thomas, 165
funds raised and funds needed, 7, 203, 210–211, 213, *258, 281, 298*
future products or services, 7, 22, 99–100, 105

G

The Gale Directory of Publications and Broadcasting Media, 47
GBC® presentation bindings, 8
general
    accounts payable, 169–170, 172, 188, *249–250, 273, 291*
    and administrative expenses, 127, 168, 171, 177, 179, 181, 188, *241, 283, 303*
    partnership, 20, 35–36, 221
    payment days, 169–170, 172, 188, *250, 273, 291*
geographic
    analysis, 68, 72, 75
    sales area, 6, 20–21, 33, 41, 76, 93, *265, 287*
    segments, 67
    trends, 57
gifts, 24, 30, 85, 111, 113, 117, 139
goals (see strategies)
Good Standing, 221
government agencies, 216
government fees, 162
grand opening, 43, 117, 166, 210
graphic artists, 118
Greenewalt, Crawford H., 33
gross domestic product (GDP), 49–51, 55–57
gross national product (GNP), 49
gross profit, 49, 52, 61, 179
gross profit margin, 21, 25, 31, 168, 196, 198
gross state product (GSP), 49–51, 55–56
growth projections, 77
growth rate projections, 66
guarantees, 18, 20, 36, 207, 213, *240, 312*

H

handing down (exit option), 216
hard costs, 204, 212–214, *259, 281*
Harvard Business School, 94
health permit, 221
highest-standard driven (strategy), 91
hiring procedure, 146
home
    based business, 137, 146, 148, *232, 240*
    equity loans, 204
    office business, 125
human resources
    business plan segment, 146–148
    management, 131
    operations, 144
    organization, 137
    in outline, 7

I

ibico binding, 8
impact factors, 6, 21, 45, 57–59, *234, 266, 287*
important assumptions, 7, 166–173, 180–182, 187–188, 202, *249, 273, 291, 303*
    explained step by step, 171–172
incentives
    human resources, 146
    key-personnel, 125, 136, 147
    payroll, 180
    promotional, 110, 117
income
    and expense statement, 177
    statement, explained step by step, 179–181, see also pro forma income statement
    tax rate, 169–170, 172, 181, *250, 273, 291*
    taxes
        cash flow, statement of, 189
        due and payable, 176
        important assumptions, 172
        income statement, 181
industry
    analysis
        business plan section, 45–64
        executive summary, 21
        in outline, 4, 6
    description, 6, 21, 45, 51–54
    group, 47, 52–54, 70
    maturation, 51
    obstacles, 7, 21, 45, 52, 62
    opportunities, 7, 21, 45, 51, 62–63
    research, 46
    size and maturation, 45, 54, 56–57, 83
    standards, 6, 21, 45, 52, 60–61
    summary, 21, 51–52, 64
    trends, 6, 45, 57–59
industry-driven strategies, 92
industry-leader driven (strategy), 92
Influence: The New Psychology of Modern Persuasion, 124

Information, USA, 47
initial public offering (IPO), 217
innovator driven, 92
institutions, 68–69, 115
insurance
    collateral, 212
    companies, 204
    coverage, 7, 216, 222
    employee, 147
    income statement, 180
    lease, 39
    list of coverages, 222
    in outline, 7
    owner, 139
    start-up costs, 166
    unassigned task, 162
intellectual property, 20, 37, 100, 104
intellectual protection, 7, 99, 104–105, *267, 288*
interest
    expense, 181, 189, 198, *246, 303, 309*
    rate (long-term debt), 172
    rate (short-term debt), 172
Internet, 45–46, 48–50, 58, 113, 116, 151, 157
    web sites, 108, 113, 153, 240
inventory, 156–157, 165, 169, 174–175
    calculating (Appendix F) 188, 200, *305–307, 309, 311*
    control, 7, 24
    insurance, 222
    management, 159–160, 186
    MIS, 159–160
    on-hand, 61, 169–170, 172, *306–307*
    tax, 176
    turnover, 60, 62, 196, 199, *309*
    turnover days, 196, 199
investment
    clubs, 204
    offering, 8, 193, 202–203, 205–207, 212–214, 216, *311*
    offering proposal, 8, 203, 213
    offering summary, 193, 205–207, 213
investor proposal, 4
investor requirement, 214
investors, 12, 25, 35–36, 173, 204–206, 210, 212–213

J, K

keys to success, 3, 6, 26, 29–30, 79, *230, 265, 287*
Know Your Market, 65
Kyne, Peter B., 125

L

La Fontaine, Jean de, 219
leadership and location, 6, 20, 33, 40, *225, 232, 265, 287*
lease negotiation, 2, 39, 148
legal and accounting, 181
legal documents, 7, 221

Lewis, Sinclair, 107
liabilities and equity, 173–176, 194, *251, 274, 292, 302*
library, 45, 47–48, 147, 151
licenses, 37, 135, 162, 181, 210, 212, 214, 221, 244, *257, 259, 265, 280–281*
licensing, 93, 104–105, 113, 181, 217
life insurance, 139, 147, 204, 213, 222
LIFO (inventory valuation), 160
limited liability
    company (LLC), 20, 35, 37, 221
    family company, 37
    partnership (LLP), 37
limited low-priced offers, 117
limited partnership, 20, 35–36, 221
limiteds (Ltd.), 36
liquidity ratio, 197–198
loan request
    business plan segment, 211
    cash flow, statement of, 192
    executive summary, 26
    funds raised and funds needed, 210
    proposal, 7, 203, 212, *259, 281, 298*
    in outline, 7
    start-up costs, 208
    summary, 205–206, *257, 280, 298*
loans, home equity, 204
location
    company description, 33, 40–41
    effects of, 58
    executive summary, 20, 29
    facility (see facility)
    in outline, 6
    ready for biz, 2
    rent, 180
    selecting, 38
    signs for, 116
Location, Location, Location, 2
long-term
    assets, 166, 174–176, *251, 274, 292*
    debt, 172, 176, 204, *308*
    liabilities payments, 188–190
    liability, 189, *284*
    loan proceeds, 188, *262, 272*
long-range goals, 90
Low, Robert J., 159
Lowy, Walter H., 65

M

magazine advertising, 108, 113–115, 121
main competitors, 78
maintenance and repairs, 180
management, 44, 53, 94, 135, 159–160, 187, 196, 216
    philosophy, 7, 23, 125, 135–136
    summary, 7, 125–127, 141, *270*
    team, 127, 133
Management Advisory Services, 182

management and organization
    business plan section, 125–142
    executive summary, 19, 24, 27, 29
    exhibits of résumés, 219
    in outline, 4, 7
management driven (strategy), 94
manager responsibilities, 125, 133
managerial talent, 30
manufacturing and assembly company, x, 3, 169
market
    analysis, 3–4, 21, 42, 57, 67, 72, 114, 216, *290*
    niche, 27, 85–86, 93, 102, 106
    obstacles, 7, 21, 66, 85–86, *235*
    opportunities, 7, 21, 29, 66, 86–87
    segmentation, 21, 67–68, 72
    segments, 52, 66–68, 73
    size and trends, 7, 21, 65–66, 76–77, 83, *235, 266, 288*
market and competition
    business plan section, 65–88
    in executive summary, 19, 21
    in outline, 4, 7
    summary, 7, 65–66, 87, *235*
market share
    analysis, 82–84
    business plan segment, 82–84
    distribution, 83–84
    executive summary, 21, 27
    important assumptions, 169–171
    market and competition summary, 66
    in outline, 7
marketable securities, 174–175, 197
market-driven strategies, 22, 27, 86, 92–93
market-leader driven (strategy), 28, 92
marketing
    consultants, 109, 113, 118
    promotions, 97, 111, 117–119
    strategy, 7, 23, 78, 93, 109–111
marketing budget and advertising plan, 108
    examples of, 120–121, *241, 267*
    executive summary, 23, 30
    income statement, 179
    in outline, 7
marketing plan
    business plan segment, 112–113
    examples of, 119, *240*
    executive summary, 23, 30
    in industry, 58
    in outline, 4, 7
marketing and sales
    business plan section, 107–124
    executive summary, 19, 23
    expenses in income statement, 179
    in outline, 4, 7
    summary, 7, 23, 107–108, *240*
media interviews, 117
merging, 217
milestones, 20, 28, 33, 42–44

milestones table, 43–44, 95
minimum level, 159–160
minimum orders, 154–155
MIS (inventory management), 159–160
mission statement, 3, 27–28, 86
Moss Adams LLP, 182
most professional, 63, 94, 102, *236*
most-personalized driven (strategy), 92

N

NAICS, 46–47, 50, 52, 70, 177
NAICS and SIC, 46
National Fulfillment Services, 157
National Trade and Professional Associations of the United States, 47
net change in cash, 186, 189
net depreciable assets, 174–175, *251, 274, 292*
net fixed assets, 175
net profit, 25, 31, 49, 177, 181, 200
new customer offers, 117
new employee orientation, 134, 146–147
new-market driven (strategy), 93
newspapers, 113–117, 119
NEXIS EXPRESS, 49
niche-market driven, 93, *236*
No Money Down Financing for Franchising, 2
no-minimum orders, 154–155
non-cost of sales
    accounts payable, 174, 176, *251*
    expenses, 177, 182, 184
non-depreciable
    asset purchases, 189
    assets, 174–175, 189, *251, 274, 292*
non-disclosure, 12
non-payroll expenses, 188
nonprofit organization (business), x, 3, 5, *302–304*
North American Industry Classification System, 46, 197

O

offering proposal, 8, 203, 213–214, *311*
one-function-excellence driven (strategy), 94
one-trend-market driven (strategy), 93
opening balance sheet
    business plan segment, 173
    examples of, 174, *251, 274, 292*
    financial pro formas, 167
    in outline, 7
operating
    expenses, 25, 31, 166, 168, 182, *290, 309*
    profit, 25, 31, 168, 181, *231, 249, 272, 290, 303*
operations
    business plan section, 143–164
    description, 7, 144–146, *226, 246, 290*
    executive summary, 19, 24
    manual, 143–146
    in outline, 4, 7
    risks, 214

strategies, 94
summary, 7, 144–145, 164, *245, 290*
operations-driven strategies, 94
organizational
  chart, 138
  structure, 7, 125, 137
outlines, 3–5, 8
overdue letters, 163
Ovid Technologies, 49
owner's draw, 189, *236, 245, 282*
ownership and legal, 6, 20, 33, 35, 40, *231*

P

page layout, 8
Pasca., Blaise, 17
patent, 20
payroll
  cash flow, statement of, 188, 191–193
  income statement, 178, 180, 183
  industry analysis, 54–57
  industry standards, 61
  personnel plan, 139
payroll taxes and benefits, 139, 169–172, 179–180, 188, *245, 273*
permits, 154, 162, 181, *238–239, 244*
personal business résumé, 127–128
personnel plan
  business plan segment, 139
  examples of, 140, *270*
  executive summary, 23
  important assumptions, 169
  income statement, 180
  in outline, 7
  management and organization summary, 125–126
photographs, 222
place, as an element of the 4 Ps, 109
planning department, 76
point-of-purchase displays, 117, 119
Polybius, 1
positioning (products or services), 7, 22, 89–90, 99–100, 102
power words, 116, 124
preliminary title report, 221
Prentice Hall Direct, 50
press conferences, 117
press packets, 117, 119
press releases, 23, 30, 108, 117, 119, *241, 265*
preview executive summary, 6, 18, 26–32
price, as an element of the 4 Ps, 109
price driven (strategy), 91
price-leaders, 117
print media, 113
printers, ink-jet and laser, 9
printing, 8–9, 49, *233, 241, 246, 248, 258*
private placement offering, 204
pro formas, financial
  balance sheet, first- and five-year, 194

  examples of, 195, *255, 278, 296*
  explained step-by-step, 175–176
  balance sheet, opening, 173–174
    examples of, 174, *251, 274, 292*
  business plan section, 165–202
  cash flow, statement of, 184
    examples of, 191–193, *254, 277, 295*
    explained step-by-step, 187–189
  income statement, 177
    examples of, 178, 183, *252–253, 275–276, 293–294, 301, 304*
    explained step-by-step, 179–181
product reviews, 117
product or service line, 19, 34, 58, 91, 101, 103, 105–106
product- or service-driven strategies, 91
production, 24, 52, 94, 144, 149–153
production and technology, 151
production manager, 126–127, 131, 137, 162
production-line method, 149–150, 152
productivity (production), 149–150
products or services
  business plan section, 99–106
  company description, 34
  competitor analysis, 81
  description, 7, 99–100
  element of the 4 Ps, 109
  executive summary, 19, 22, 27
  in outline, 4, 7
  positioning, 7, 99, 102, 110
  strategies, 89, 91
  summary, 7, 22, 99–100, 106
professional associations, 47, 68–69
profit and loss, 167, 177
profit before income taxes, 181, 184–185, 207, 214, *303, 311*
Profit Mentor™, 132, 182
progress status, 6, 26, 28–29, 31, *229, 265, 287*
proliferation driven, 91
promotion, 109–111, 117–118, 122, 216, *240*
proofreading, 9
property taxes, 39, 139, 181
psychographic analysis, 68, 70–71, 75
public relations, 117–119, *246*
public speaking, 117
publicity, 108, 113, 117, 119, *237, 241*
purchasing patterns, 121

Q

qualifications summary, 129–130, *244*
quality control, 134, 145, 149, 151–153, *247–248*
quality driven, 91
quick ratio, 196–197, *256, 272, 279, 297, 308*

R

rebates, 117
receiving, 148, 155
refunds, 158

regulatory
	changes, 57–58
	impacts, 216
relationship driven (strategy), 93
rent, 39, 166, 180, 221
repair, 39, 97, 158, 180
repayment, 185–186
research and development, 91–92, 105–106, 137
research findings, 221
résumé
	full, personal business, 127–128
	summary, 128–129, 131, 219
retained earnings, 174, 176, *251, 274, 292*
return on assets, 196, 200, *256, 272, 279, 291, 297, 310*
return on equity, 25, 31, 168, 196, 200, *231, 249, 256, 272, 279, 291, 297, 310*
return on investment, 207, 213, *305, 311*
	calculating (Appendix F), *311–312*
review executive summary, 6, 19, 32
reviews, employee, 146–148
risks, 7, 203, 214–215
Robert Morris Associates, 46, 50, 60, 112, 197
Rush Order, Inc., 157
rush orders, 156–157

S

S corporation, 20, 35–36
safety, 134, 137, 147, 162
safety margin, 186, 190, 210, 212
safety ratio, 198
salaries and benefits, 146–147
sale and leaseback, 204
sales
	on credit, 168–171, 175, 187, *250, 273, 283, 291*
	force, 7, 23, 94, 108, 113, 121, *268, 289*
	methods, 79, 113–114, 124
	tax, 176, *273*
sales driven (strategy), 23, 93
sales forecast
	business plan segment, 121–122
	examples of, 123, *243, 269, 289*
	executive summary, 23
	important assumptions, 169
	income statement, 179
	marketing and sales summary, 108
sales to assets, 196, 199, *256, 279, 297, 309*
Salvaneschi, Luigi, 2
SBA-backed lenders, 204
Scott, Sir Walter, xi
seasonal effects, 58
seasonal impact, 112
sector, 2, 21, 47, 49–57, 63, 70, *230, 244*
sector maturation, 50
service business, 151, *225–226, 283, 302*
service mark, 20, 37, 104
shareholder interests, 205
shareholders, 20, 36–37, 174, 176, *251, 292*

shareholder's equity, 174, 176
shop method, 149–150
shortfall, 86, 185–186, 209, *290*
short-term
	liabilities payments, 188–190, 193, *262*
	loan proceeds, 168, 188, 190, 193, *226, 249*
	notes payable, 174, 176, *251, 274, 292*
SIC, 46, 52–53, 61, 112, 197
	Main Page, 46
sideheads, 8–9
site layout, 221
site selection, 2, 38
skimming, 163
Small Business Administration (SBA), 204, *262, 265, 273, 280, 282, 314*
Small Business Investment Companies (SBICs), 204, *313–314*
soft costs, 204, 212–214, *259, 281*
software, 159–160, 163, 167, 182, 196
sole proprietorship, 20, 35–36, 176, *229, 231, 245–246, 249*
solutions driven (strategy), 92
specialization driven (strategy), 91
Standard Industry Classification (SIC), see also SIC, 46
starting cash, 186–187, 189–190
start-up costs
	business plan segment, 209–210
	examples of, 210, *257, 280*
	executive summary, 25–26, 28–29
	list to verify, 166
	marketing send-off, 120
	in outline, 7
start-up costs schedule, 210
start-up inventory, 221
stock, 35, 37, 136, 159–160, 176, 204–205, 207, 217
straight-line depreciation, 175, *246*
strategic alliances, 41, 108, 113, 118
strategies
	income statement, 177
	products and services, 102
strategies and goals
	business plan section, 89–98
	executive summary, 19, 22, 27–28
	implementation, 90, 96–97, *225, 237, 266, 288*
	in outline, 4, 7
strategies and goals summary, 7, 90
subchapter S corporation, 20, 35–36
subcontractors, 144, 149–150
subsector, 47, 50, 52–53, 70
summary résumé, 128, 131, 219
supplies and postage, 181
supply and distribution, 7, 20, 24, 29, 40, 52, 62, 80, 144, 146, 154–156, *226, 271, 290*
sweepstakes, 117

T

table of contents, 6, 9–10, 15, 127–128, 219–220
tabs, 9, 219

target market, 7, 21, 26, 34, 65, 67–68, 74–76, 107
tax consequences, 35
tax rates, 168
taxes payable, 174, 176, *251, 274, 292*
Teagle, Walter C., 143
technological advancements, 57–58, 92
technologically driven, 92
telemarketing, 113
telephone
    expense, 178, 180, 183
    marketing and sales, 117, 121
    system, 151
television and radio, 113–114
Thomas Register (website), 151, 154
Thomas Register of American Manufactures, 151
title page, 6, 8, 10, 12, 14–15
trade
    associations, 38, 47, 71, 145
    name, 20, 37, 104
    publications, 47–48, 97, 105–106, 113, 115, 117, 119, *237, 246*
    shows, 105, 108, 117
Trade Shows and Exhibitions (website), 118
trademark, 20, 37, 104, 105
training
    customer service, 92, 158
    employees, 134, 147
    sales, 121
    start-up costs, 166

U

undercapitalized, 189–190
U.S. Bureau of the Census, 46–48
U.S. Bureau of the Census, twelve regional offices, 48

U.S. Bureau of Economic Analysis, 49
U.S. Bureau of Labor Statistics, 48
U.S. Government Printing Office, 49
U.S. Industry & Trade Outlook, 47, 49
utilities
    cost of sales, 171
    expense, 180
    owner's budget, 139
    start-up costs, 210

V

variable expenses, 171, 182, *303*
variable labor, 134, 149–150, 153, 180
Velobinder®, 8
venture capital, 204, *313–314*
vesting, 3, 20, 28, 35, 37, 70, 205, 213, 223
video tapes, 117
volume orders, 150, 154

W

warranty, 85, 158
Wire Bind™, 8
work force, 134, 150
working capital
    business ratios, 196, 198
    investment offering, 213
    loan request, 211
    margin of safety, 209
    rule-of-thumb, 186
    start-up costs, 166, 209
working capital requirement, 166, 202, 209, 211

X, Y, Z

Yellow Pages, 78, 113, 115–116, *233, 240, 265*